BASICS
WITH BABISH

BASICS
WITH BABISH
ANDREW REA

Recipes for Screwing Up, Trying Again,
and Hitting It Out of the Park

WITH SUSAN CHOUNG AND KENDALL BEACH
Photography by Evan Sung

SIMON
ELEMENT

An Imprint of Simon & Schuster, Inc.
1230 Avenue of the Americas
New York, NY 10020

First Simon Element hardcover edition October 2023

SIMON ELEMENT is a trademark of Simon & Schuster, Inc.

For information about special discounts for bulk purchases, please contact
Simon & Schuster Special Sales at 1-866-506-1949 or business@simonandschuster.com.

The Simon & Schuster Speakers Bureau can bring authors to your live event.
For more information or to book an event, contact the Simon & Schuster Speakers Bureau
at 1-866-248-3049 or visit our website at www.simonspeakers.com.

Interior production management by Stonesong

Manufactured in China

10 9 8 7 6 5 4 3 2 1

Library of Congress Cataloging-in-Publication Data has been applied for.

ISBN 978-1-9821-6753-0
ISBN 978-1-9821-6754-7 (ebook)

Prop Styling by Dayna Seman
Food Styling by Spencer W. Richards
Kitchen Production by Kendall Beach
Kitchen Production by Nicolas Borbolla

TO MY DAD. YOU TAUGHT ME HOW TO SEE THE WORLD DIFFERENTLY, TELL STORIES COMPASSIONATELY, AND CAPTURE MOMENTS HUMBLY—WITH OR WITHOUT A CAMERA.

CONTENTS

Foreword by Roy Choi 10

Introduction 12

Let's Get Down to Basics 16

CHAPTER 1
BREAD 40

Rosemary Focaccia 44

Southern-Style Cornbread 48

Pan Cubano 51

Sandwich Loaf 56

Roti 58

Brioche Dough 62

Hamburger Buns 64

Herb-Garlic Monkey Bread 65

Marble Rye 66

Bagels 72

English Muffins 75

Babka 78

Chocolate Babka Filling 84

Cinnamon Sugar Babka Filling 84

Everything Babka Filling 84

Streusel 85

Simple Syrup 85

Baguettes 86

CHAPTER 2
PIZZA 92

Pan Pizza 96

New York–Style Pizza 99

Chicago-Style Pizza 102

Neapolitan-Style Pizza 106

CHAPTER 3
PASTA 112

Fresh Pasta Dough 116

Trenette al Pesto 120

Pesto Formula 123

Tarragon Shrimp Scampi 126

Blender Mac and Cheese 130

Baked Mac and Cheese 132

Cacio e Pepe 133

Carbonara 136

Butternut Squash Ravioli in Brown Butter 140

Sausage Tortelloni with Broccoli Rabe Pesto.... 146

Crispy Gnocchi with Gorgonzola Dolce 148

Sweet Corn Caramelle with Beurre Blanc
and Basil Oil 154

Tortellini en Brodo 158

Pappardelle Bolognese 161

CHAPTER 4

EGGS 164

French Scrambled Eggs with Roasted
Mushrooms on Toast.................... **168**

Eggnog French Toast **172**

Ajitsuke Tamago **175**

Spicy Honey Shakshuka.................. **176**

Pastrami Hash with Baked Eggs........... **179**

Spring Vegetable Quiche
(with Lots of Bacon and Cheese)......... **182**

Eggs Spenedict........................ **186**

Deviled Eggs **189**
    Pickled Red Onion.................. **190**

Jammy Scotch Eggs **191**

CHAPTER 5

VEGETABLES/ SIDE DISHES 194

Charred Winter Vegetables with
Roasted Garlic Vinaigrette **198**

Browned Butternut Squash Soup **200**

Bacon-Roasted Brussels Sprouts....... **203**

Latkes **205**

Panzanella **208**

Real Deal Caesar Salad **211**

Grilled Artichokes with Lemon Faux-Aioli.......... **213**

Le Grand Aioli **216**

Falafel with Lemon Tahini **218**

Pastaroni Salad **222**

Caponata **224**

Vegetable Fried Rice................. **226**

CHAPTER 6

SEAFOOD 230

Fried Haddock with Chips **234**
    Chips **237**
    Tartar Sauce **237**

Shrimp and Grits..................... **238**
    Cheese Grits **239**

Poke Bowls.......................... **240**
    Sushi Rice **242**
    Tenkasu **243**
    Spicy Mayo Sauce **243**

Flounder en Papillote with Tarragon Butter...... **244**

Seared Ahi Tuna Tostadas **246**

Lemon-Butter Tilapia with Fried Capers **248**

Tteokbokki........................... **251**

Pan-Fried Tteokbokki **253**
    Korean Anchovy Broth (Dashima)....... **253**

Lobster Rolls........................ **254**

Cold Lobster Rolls **256**

Hot Lobster Rolls **257**

Red Snapper Ceviche with Mango
and Jalapeño **258**

Whole Branzino with Grilled Lemons...... **260**

CHAPTER 7

POULTRY 264

Chicken Stock...**268**

Chicken Piccata...**270**

Chicken Quesadillas......................................**272**

"Airline" Chicken Breasts with
Herb Pan Sauce..**275**

Chicken Parmesan...**278**
    Simple Tomato Sauce...........................**281**

One-Pan Crispy Braised Chicken Thighs
and Fennel Pasta..**282**

Whole Spatchcocked Chicken with
Compound Butter...**285**
    Compound Butter.................................**287**

Chicken Noodle Soup....................................**288**

Cornish Hens with Fig-Port Sauce..............**290**
    Parsnip Puree..**293**
    Garlic Confit...**293**

Nashville Hot Chicken with
Bread and Butter Pickles...............................**294**
    Quick Bread and Butter Pickles..........**297**

Fried Wings with Buffalo Gochujang............**298**
    Gochujang Buffalo Sauce....................**300**

Really Orangey Orange Chicken.................**301**
    Orange Sauce.......................................**302**
    Oleo-Saccharum....................................**303**

CHAPTER 8

PORK 304

Homemade Bacon...**308**
    Classic Seasoning.................................**311**
    Pastrami Seasoning..............................**311**
    Guanciale Seasoning............................**311**

B.L.E.C.T...**312**
    Homemade Mayonnaise........................**312**

Candied Bacon...**313**

Roasted Pork Tenderloin with
Bourbon-Mustard Pan Sauce.......................**314**

North (East) Carolina–Style Pulled Pork.........**317**

Potstickers...**320**

Tonkotsu Ramen...**326**

Gas Grill–Smoked Ribs.................................**330**

Sausage and Béchamel Lasagna.................**334**

Tamales...**337**

CHAPTER 9

BEEF   342

Demi-Glace.........................346
     Bone Broth...................347

Meatloaf...........................348

Oxtail Birria Tacos.............352

Dad's Pot Roast.................358

Cheesesteak Pinwheels.....361

Braised Short Ribs with Potatoes Aligot...........366
     Potatoes Aligot..............369

Shepherd's Pie..................370
     Cheesy Mashed Potatoes....373

Steakhouse Burgers..........374
     Caramelized Onions........376

Pimento Smash Burgers.....377
     Pimento Cheese Topping...379

Beer-Braised Corned Beef with Herby Horseradish Cream.........380

Steak Tartare with Tarragon Vinaigrette and Quail Egg.........384

World Famous Chili (con Carne)...............387

Rib Roast with Yorkshire Pudding...........390
     Beef Jus......................393
     Yorkshire Pudding..........393

Reverse-Seared (and Forward-Seared) Porterhouse with Compound Butter.........394

Butter-Basted Ribeye.........398

Beef Tenderloin with Sauces....400
     Chimichurri..................401

CHAPTER 10

DESSERTS   402

Master Cookie Dough.........406

Classic Cookie Dough........408

Chocolate Cookie Dough....409

Tres Leches Cake..............410

Bourbon Apple Pie............414
     Pie Dough....................417

Cannoli............................418

Cheesecake.....................420

Brownies..........................423

Cakey Brownies................425
     Chocolate Frosting.........425

Fudgy Brownies................426

Melty Brownies.................427

Churros...........................428

Pain au Chocolat..............432

Doughnuts.......................440
     Pastry Cream................443
     Chocolate Glaze............443

Cinnamon Rolls................444

Ice Cream Base (Crème Anglaise)....450

Ice Cream Sandwiches.......452

Acknowledgments.............455

Index..............................457

FOREWORD

Ok, I'm going to be brutally honest, and it may piss off some of you die-hard Babish fans. When I first met Babish in the early days of *The Chef Show*, I had absolutely no idea who the hell he was.

Shoot, I didn't even know his name was Andrew till recently. I remember Jon Favreau telling me about this guy that has a YouTube channel and re-creates recipes found in films, and all I could think of was, man, this can't be good. But Jon is the man, and I always trust his instincts, so I opened my mind. (There are two reasons for my ignorance that have nothing to do with Andrew. First, I don't pay that much attention to YouTube. Second, the whole world of overnight Internet chefs is something I thought was an illusion. A mirage. And when I pinched/punched myself and realized it was real, I accepted it with love and grace, but kept one eye open like a half-sleeping watchdog watching over a craft that takes a lifetime to learn.)

And I am so glad I stayed open-minded and didn't fall into my old, guarded, protective, curmudgeon ways, because the world of Babish sparked a movement that has now brought so many new faces and inquisitive souls into the food world through vlogging, pop-ups, #asmr cooking, content creation, *mukbanging*, and you—the *Binging with Babish* faithful. It cracked open an insular world and made cooking more diverse than it's ever been.

Thank you, Andrew. It's all because of Babish.

But beyond the cultural impact and the chain of events that followed, all of this would have been flawed from the get-go if the cooking was never any good or if it was all just a con for the fame. Which leads me back to the first day I met Andrew; cameras in our faces, getting ready to make French Onion Soup and Chocolate Lava Cake. This wasn't a farce. I immediately noticed how nervous he was, how precise he was, and how much he cared. These are the Three Musketeers of doing anything great, and especially cooking great: be nervous, be detailed, and care with all your heart.

We made some delicious food that day. Although it looked like I was teaching, I was actually the one learning from him. Since then, I've been following along on his journey and am now at a point where I truly believe he might be a better cook than I. Maybe I'll read this book and learn the basics again, and just maybe I, too, can become an Internet chef sensation when I grow up!

Congrats, Andrew. I jest and bust your balls because that's what friends do, but I am so proud of you and am honored to be your friend for life and a part of this wonderful Babish universe.

—Roy Choi

INTRODUCTION

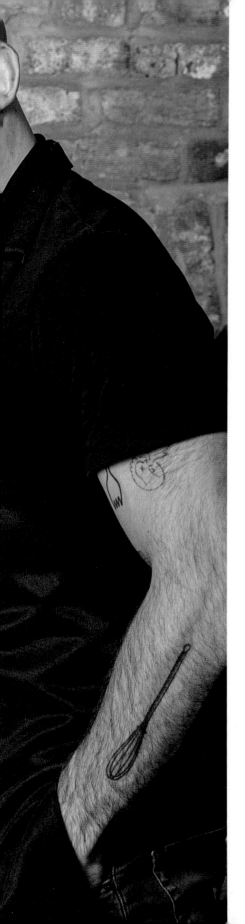

MISTAKES PERMEATE EVERYTHING I DO.

That might sound like self-deprecation to some, but over the past seven years of making cooking videos, I've been saying it with a growing degree of pride.

When making my first cooking show, *Binging with Babish*, I started showing my mistakes early on. My debut blunder is in the second-ever episode, wherein I try to peel garlic using an old trick I had heard of: placing the cloves in a lidded container, shaking it violently, and watching them emerge naked, freed from their papery prisons. Upon opening my container, however, I was disappointed to discover that just like me, they were still covered in skin. So I shrugged my shoulders, poured myself a whiskey, and began peeling the garlic manually. When the time came to edit the episode, instead of being annoyed with my ineptitude, I was charmed. I thought viewers might get a snort out of my experience, so I threw it in as a joke—and unbeknownst to me, the heart of the show had begun to beat.

Mistakes had always been pivotal in my managing to learn anything, and now I realized that the audience could learn along with me as I failed, perhaps even saving themselves from future failures along the way. Some episodes, like recreating the dalgona from *Squid Game*, became almost entirely about my mistakes, becoming a supercut of my half dozen attempts and the lessons learned from each. After many years, I even learned that my garlic peeling trick didn't work because of the rigidity of my container, which should ideally be metal. See, you're learning from my mistakes already!

incredulously surveyed my tiny kitchen: It was hardly suited for cooking, much less producing a cooking show. Despite our already rocky relationship and immediately apparent lack of chemistry, I shook off my jitters and got down to business, starting with my strong suit: steak. I reverse seared a mammoth bone-in ribeye, cooking it to a(n almost) perfect medium-rare, slicing it into steakhouse slabs, and presenting it with fried rosemary and garlic. I offered it up to the crew, which they sort of politely declined, so I ate damn near the whole thing myself on camera. It wasn't until they hurriedly ordered lunch that I saw the newest crack in our already fractured menagerie: most of them were vegan, and the director in particular was militantly so. Over a bowl of stir-fried seitan, he outlined his moral outrage at the consumption of all animal products, the smell of seared beef still heavy in the air, and me picking ribeye out of my teeth. When they finished lunch and I started getting ready to film the next episode (a whole roast chicken with its spine violently ripped out), the cramped kitchen grew hotter and hotter, as our tiny air conditioner's little heart had given out. Between the ARRI lights the crew had furnished and my crappy oven pissing heat into the air, the place must've gotten up to 95°F before we wrapped for the day. I crawled into bed, had myself a little cry, and tried to find comfort in having to do it only four more days before giving up forever. When Friday finally came and went, I joyously texted my girlfriend at the time, who responded immediately by saying, "Great job, proud of you—we need to talk." You see, she had been waiting until after I had completed this torturous marathon to break up with me. Which was considerate of her.

Basics with Babish itself was almost a mistake that never saw the light of day. My first steps venturing outside the comfort of pop-culture-cookery were taken warily, as I wasn't sure if I had anything original to add to YouTube's pantheon of culinary instruction. I also had grander aspirations: higher production value, multiple camera angles, a stylized introduction with a theme song. Not knowing where else to turn, I haphazardly hired a production company through a friend of a friend, and plopped down $5,000 for a (deeply-discounted) week's worth of shooting. A four-person crew arrived at my Harlem apartment on a rainy Monday morning, and right away, I knew we were screwed. After dragging mountains of Pelican cases up four flights of stairs in the pouring rain, they

So, needless to say, I had to start from scratch. Within a month, I had hooked up with my management outfit in Nashville, who sent a crew to help *Basics* be realized. They would end up becoming some of my closest friends, one of whom is now my full-time employee, and we made a show together we could be proud of; but I was still terrified to release it. I was certain that I was a novelty, something people could background watch while ironing their clothes or browsing Reddit, good for the occasional sharp nose exhale elicited from a clumsily executed dad joke. By putting out purely instructional videos, not only was I eschewing the pop culture reference crutch, I was purporting to be a learned person in my field. A teacher. An authority figure. Someone who, when the urge strikes you to finally invest in a stand mixer and try your hand at homemade pasta, you entrust with your time and effort to steer you in the right direction. All things that, I'll be the first to loudly admit, I am not. I am not a trained chef, I have never attended culinary school, and the one time I worked in an honest-to-god restaurant, I cut my finger so badly on my first day that I was promptly bandaged up and fired. The first few episodes of *Basics* are primarily about knife skills. Do you have buyer's remorse yet?

Well, don't print out your return label or bust out that gift receipt just yet. I started writing this book, indeed this very introduction, when I saw a collocation of *Basics* thumbnails on YouTube. It was the *Pizza* episode, published all the way back in 2018, juxtaposed against a more recent *Pizza Dough* episode. The former **(FIG. 1)** was a misshapen, pallid, triangular flatbread of orangey sauce and browned cheese, somehow simultaneously both over- and under-cooked, and dotted with wrinkled bits of burnt basil. The latter **(FIG. 2)** was the picture of pizza perfection: a wafer-thin, chewy-crisp disk, delicately scattered with buffalo mozzarella and San Marzano tomatoes, crowned with an aureole of uniform, airy crust dappled with char marks. I saw tangible, tastable evidence of what I had learned from dozens and dozens of missteps: be they burnt bottoms or crackerlike crumbs, every public and private stumble had paid off. Even plunging a knife into my finger during the lunch rush back in 2009 eventually yielded fruit—you can bet your ass that I now practice good finger discipline when chopping onions—and now, I feel ready to pass that mistake-derived skillset on to you. I'm not a terribly confident person; I'm fast to admit when I've messed up and shy away from anyone singing my praises. But I will look you in the eye, hold both your hands in mine, and whisper to you unflinchingly as our noses nearly touch: I know how to make really, really fucking good pizza. And I can show you how. Follow me.

Okay, that got intense. Like I said, I get very uncomfortable accepting the fact that I might be good at something, so the least I can do is make you uncomfortable, too. Now that we've got that out of the way, we can get cooking—or learning to cook. Whether it's your first day or your last (yeesh), it is about making mistakes, not being afraid of making mistakes, and learning from those mistakes. So let's start screwing up together—you can let go of my hands now. Okay, you can keep one.

FIG. 1   FIG. 2

LET'S GET DOWN TO BASICS

Wow, you're reading all the supplemental material instead of just the recipes? You got moxie, kid, I'll give you that. Let's talk a little bit about how best to use this book—that's right, this book, basically an instruction manual, comes with its own instruction manual!

Basics with Babish was originally intended to be a linear, serialized cookery course, best watched beginning to end. We quickly realized, however, that we were making content for YouTube, where people want a la carte answers to very specific questions, and *never* watch anything in order. We quickly pivoted to start making episodes about singular dishes, intended to be a resource for anyone looking to make something specific. This book, however, seeks to capture the original spirit of the series by presenting recipes in a specific order: not necessarily easiest to hardest, but there's a good chance a recipe on page 300 will draw from knowledge dropped on page 15. I haven't done the page counts yet, but you know what I mean.

One of my favorite reviews of the *Binging with Babish* cookbook described it as one of the few, if any, cookbooks that tells you in the headnote if a particular recipe is any good or not. I admit, I've never seen it anywhere before. I'm an innovator, okay? So, too, with this cookbook, shall I create something wholly unique (if not a little odd). Every recipe is accompanied by three things: first, a charming and pithy headnote describing my experience making the particular dish. Second, a list of ways in which I have personally screwed up said dish myself, so you can avoid my pitfalls. Third, every recipe will be accompanied with troubleshooting, a listing of the problems you could potentially have with the recipe

and recommended solutions. Not gonna lie, I was pretty proud of myself when I thought of this one—I mean how many times do you wish you could ask the recipe's author why your thing didn't turn out right? Now you can! Sort of.

Do's and Don'ts

Taking on cooking as a hobby or vocation can be a daunting thing: endless, seemingly trivial measurements and directions, very sharp things, very hot things, and the long life stories of bloggers that accompany almost every recipe. Your friends' or family's very nourishment became dependent on you the moment you volunteered to try making dinner tonight, and their grimacing smiles through half-chewed bites (or an emergency pizza order) await you if you fail. Instructions quickly become a triage scenario, deciding which steps can be skipped as sauces congeal, salads wilt, and this steak just won't seem to cook through—wait is something burning?

If the above sentences gave you agita, don't worry: just like any skill worth having, cooking is a matter of practicing with—and slowly gaining knowledge of—your food and how it behaves. There are many (many) pitfalls I wish I had avoided when I was just getting started in the kitchen, so a fitting way to kick off this book felt like a list of Do's and Don'ts. I couldn't think of a B-word to name it. Babish's Bullet Points? Blunders with Babish? Maybe the first "Don't" should be "Don't make a cooking show that requires letter-specific alliteration." Anyway.

These Do's and Don'ts are primarily aimed at newcomers to the kitchen, but even if you know your way around the galley, I think there's information to be gleaned here. If you're super-advanced, I'm not sure why you bought my book, but thank you—hopefully these will at least give you a chuckle.

DON'T bite off more than you can chew, so to speak. Lots of us want to wow our friends, family, or significant other with a technically-impressive dish—it's both a show of skill and a demonstration of how much we value their trusting us with making a meal. For my very first-ever dinner party, I tried to make a ten-course tasting menu for a dozen coworkers. As pans piled up on the stove and my sweat soaked through my shirt, ten courses quickly turned into fiveish, most of which were eaten more out of politeness than anything else. If, instead, I had furnished them with a properly-cooked roast, an imaginative side dish, and a bright/peppery salad, they would've left much more impressed (not to mention full). Clearly I've been thinking about this for years. Leonardo da Vinci once said, "simplicity is the ultimate sophistication"—and that guy knew his way around good food—he was Italian, after all.

DO practice mise en place. Mise en place is the fancy-sounding phrase to describe the simple-sounding act of getting your shit in order before you start doing anything. Chopping onions, measuring spices, weighing flour, and bringing eggs to room temperature—these steps not only make your life easier, they exponentially increase your odds of success in the kitchen. How do you know what to prep? The answer lies in the recipe ingredients: they'll typically be listed as something like "1 large onion, finely minced." "1 tablespoon freshly ground pepper." "16 hot dogs, puréed until smooth." Anything that needs to be broken down, measured, divided, or mixed: do all of it before you even look at the recipe directions. Your everything will thank you for it.

DON'T be afraid to make mistakes. This one is a doozy: beyond being one of the core tenants of my show, it's maybe the most important life lesson I've learned, and it's something I'm still learning every day. I don't know about you, but I get pretty down on myself when I mess up. Especially in cooking, when you have measurable evidence of your failure laid out in front of you; the sum total of hours or even days of your life, seemingly squandered and irretrievable. With time (especially as you get older), however, you can start recognizing mistakes as the learning experiences they are—but only if you actively work to learn something from them. If your first collapsed soufflé made you give up cooking forever, then sure, that soufflé will haunt you for the rest of your days. If, however, you do a little poking around: realize that soufflés are *supposed* to collapse a bit, maybe make sure your egg whites are stiff but not over-whipped, next time you could end up with a jiggling tower of

eggy perfection. Suddenly, you might look back on that "failure" as an important, formative experience. It's taken me years to become even halfway decent in the kitchen, and I have only my mistakes to thank for it. Maybe them and J. Kenji Lopez-Alt.

DO try new things in the kitchen. I always recommend that newcomers work to master their favorite dishes first, but the only way you're going to grow as a cook (and indeed as a person) is to push yourself out of your comfort zone. Are you scared of baking bread? Time to bake some bread then, numbnuts. Oh, your first loaf came out pale on the outside and gummy on the inside? Tough shit, try again. Okay, sorry too harsh. My point is that you're never going to get halfway decent at something without at least trying and failing first. None of us want to waste time, effort, or ingredients, so I understand your trepidation. But just read and reread the recipe, watch a video about it (maybe one of mine?), learn what you can about what you're trying to do—it might mean the difference between ending up with something in the trash bin vs. something at least edible.

DON'T cut hot peppers without gloves. I know you think you can handle spicy food, but after going to the bathroom, you will discover that your genitals cannot.

DO invest in high-quality essential tools (if you're able). Knives, cutting boards, a 12-inch skillet, a Dutch oven: a kitchen could be handsomely furnished for a few hundred dollars and be capable of making the vast majority of dishes in this book. You'll save time, you'll be more relaxed, you'll cook more often, you'll get better faster, your spouse will fall back in love with you, you'll get a higher-paying/more fulfilling job, and (depending on your preference) your facial hair will grow thicker or finally disappear altogether. Maybe not all of those, but at least the first few. It might seem like a lot now, but if you've got the scratch, spend it on tools that you love (and will love you back).

DO follow recipes to the letter (if you're just starting out). We've all seen them in recipe reviews: "This turned out awful! I didn't have any eggs or flour, so I used applesauce and sorghum flakes, and my oven wasn't working, so I baked it by placing it in my car on a hot day. Didn't look anything like the photos—0 stars, don't waste your time!!" I once read a negative review of one of my recipes: the fellow in question didn't have any red wine for a beef braise, so they used red wine *vinegar*—if you are familiar with these two ingredients, you may be aware that they are decidedly not interchangeable. Generally speaking, all the ingredients and instructions in a given recipe are there for a reason, and omitting, skipping, or replacing any of them could potentially ruin the dish. A good rule of thumb is: if you don't know what something is or why it's in the dish, don't omit or substitute it. Once you learn its function, however . . .

DON'T follow recipes to the letter (once you've mastered the Basics™®©). I realize that this directly contradicts the above, but after years of cooking, you're going to start to notice stuff in recipes you don't like, and you're going to know what you can do differently without destroying the resultant dish. For example, let's say you come across a pancake recipe and the ingredients all sound tasty, but when the time comes to put them together, the recipe calls for you to beat the batter thoroughly with a hand mixer until completely smooth. You may suddenly feel a twinge of nostalgia, recalling those rainy Sundays when pops would whip up a steaming stack of flapjacks, and he'd insist that a lumpy batter is more than just okay, it's desirable. Then maybe you'll remember any given pancake episode of mine, when I repeatedly and proudly exclaim that your father was right! Over-mixing pancake batter can result in gluten development, which makes pancakes turn out thin and tough. Just like anyone you might admire, famous chefs are human beings trying to figure shit out, same as you. Even veritable demigods like Gordon Ramsay can put out the occasional epic misfire (just search for his ultimate grilled cheese; and Josh Scherer's impassioned breakdown of everything wrong with it). With practice and knowledge, you'll start "seeing the matrix" in terms of how and why food behaves the way it does, and only with that familiarity comes the ability to play jazz with recipes. Hell, that's kind of the main point of this whole book!

DO know when to use a scale. I know this seems like an unnecessarily fussy pain in the ass, but especially when baking, using a scale can be essential to getting consistent and replicable results. Anyone that's ever advocated for scale usage will be quick to tell you a halting fact: a cup of flour can vary in accuracy by as much as 20 percent in either direction, which in something as sensitive as bread or cake, could be disastrous. But that being said, there is a time and a place for these qualifiers of quantity. First off, unless you have a remarkably accurate scale, I tend to avoid measuring salt or other small-amount ingredients by weight. Kitchen scales tend to be relatively accurate, but not precise—that is, many won't accurately register the difference between 5 and 10 grams of salt. Try adding salt to a bowl in 1-gram increments and you'll see what I'm talking about. Oh, you've got way better things to do with your time? I understand. Anyway, how do you know when to use a scale? At least in this book, if an ingredient is specified first by weight, well, there's your answer! Out there in the rest of the world? A good rule of thumb is to ask yourself: "Can I accurately add the same amount of [ingredient] as the recipe specifies, and does it matter if I do?" For example, a stew might call for thickening its sauce with 3 tablespoons of flour. Unless you really pile as much as is physically possible on each tablespoon, the potential variance isn't going to ruin your end product, and you can measure by volume. On the other hand, if you're making a bread dough with a specific hydration percentage, and a strange man brandishing a deadly weapon is threatening you with grievous bodily harm should your focaccia not turn out light and airy enough—well, a scale might just save your life.

Kitchen Glossary

The following is a sort of glossary of cooking terms, items, and ideas. The intention is to define, break down, and hopefully clarify a host of concepts that tend to confuse kitchen newcomers. Like with the majority of this book, if you're more advanced, there's still, hopefully, information to be gleaned here. Hell, if I get just one of you to try using kosher salt, I've done my job.

BOILING POINTS: As you may have read in the news or the bible, water reaches an excitable state around 212°F or 100°C, at which point it begins to dance wildly and vomit steam into the air as though the drugs just kicked in. This state of matter, transitioning from a liquid to gas, is referred to as a "boil." In practice, however, boiling is slightly less scientific, and a wealth of subtleties emerge that yield varied results in cooking. *Poaching*, for example, typically refers to the ghostly state of water around 180°F (82°C), when it meanders spookily about the pot without yet producing any bubbles. A *Bare Simmer* refers to a slightly more lively cooking environment, tiny bubbles beginning to form on the bottom of the pot and, if they be so bold, occasionally breaking the surface, between 180 to 190°F (82 to 88°C). A *Simmer* is, for all intents and purposes, a particularly gentle boil, wherein the water is being agitated visibly and of its own volition, approaching but not exceeding 205°F. A *Boil*, or perhaps more accurate, a *Rolling Boil*, is achieved at 212°F, where the water is just so excited to get out in the open air, it can no longer be contained by your pasta pot's lid, and your stove's flames sputter and flare as it foams over and makes a very-difficult-to-clean mess of your cooktop. Especially when the subtleties lie in mere single digits of degrees, it can seem trivial or unnecessary to heed the specific type of boil outlined in a recipe, but failing to do so can very quickly (or slowly) ruin a dish. Short ribs, for example, become meltingly tender when braised gently at a *Bare Simmer*, but when subjected to something more like a *Rolling Boil*, will more quickly contract muscle fibers, squeezing out all the delicious fat and connective tissue, rendering your dinner more useful as a dog's chew toy.

COOKWARE (CARBON-STEEL): You might be most familiar with it in its wok form, but carbon steel is an indispensable tool in restaurants and home kitchens alike. Think of it as Cast Iron Lite: it's quite literally lighter and it can't retain or distribute heat as well, but it also relies on a well-maintained seasoning to stay nonstick, and is excellent for high-heat applications. Because most of us are unfamiliar with it/intimidated by it, it remains in relative home chef obscurity, but deserves a spot on your pot rack. Seeing an egg skate around on a rink of blue steel you've lovingly seasoned yourself is not unlike seeing your child take their first steps. I imagine.

COOKWARE (CAST-IRON): This one's a doozy for most newcomers. To the uninitiated, buying cast iron reads like adopting a new pet: you need to care for it, love it, maintain it, give it frequent rubdowns with oil, house-train it, give it daily heartworm medication. But in reality, apart from having to occasionally reseason it, about the most inconvenient thing about cast iron is that you can't run it through the dishwasher. If you use it frequently, use high heat, give it a coat of oil once in a while, and don't let food or water sit in it, you'll be made in the shade. Go ahead and wash it with soap, give it a mighty scrub—it might need a little oil and heat afterward to bolster its seasoning, but it's not going to self-destruct or anything. "Seasoning" is the highly-prized jet-black polymerized cooking fats built up from years of high-temperature cooking and the very act of "seasoning" itself: the most popular method is to give the whole pan a rubdown with neutral oil (vegetable, canola, grapeseed), and place it in a 450°F oven for 1 to 2 hours, until blackened. This, however, can lead to smoke alarms and frantic pizza peel fanning, so I prefer to leave it roasting on a hot grill for an hour or so, where I can push the heat farther and bake on a thicker, harder seasoning. Store dry and unstacked, reseason it once in a while, and read it *The Cricket in Times Square* by George Selden—that's its favorite. The advantages to cast iron are many: It retains and distributes heat evenly, which is important when you're doing something like searing a steak. It practically has nonstick qualities when properly seasoned, and nothing looks quite so lovely as sunny-side-up eggs in a cast-iron pan. Over a roaring campfire. A horse by your side. Your only companion in this undiscovered wilderness. That's the secret to owning and using cast-iron cookware: act like someone who does.

COOKWARE (NONSTICK): While its use is widespread and its utility undeniable, nonstick cookware is a controversial tool. It's known to release toxic fumes when overheated, and is sometimes manufactured with a potentially cancer-causing chemical compound, PFOA. Will nonstick kill or even harm you? The answer is no, probably not . . . but maybe. Probably not though. For most people, that's good enough—but it's understandable to have reservations. After all, an overheated pan emits a toxin that can give you flu-like symptoms—to me, that's scary, even if I certainly won't die from it. So while when it comes to eggs, nonstick cookware is nothing short of an angel sent to earth in cookware form, there are drawbacks worth avoiding. Some best practices include never heating the pan past its manufacturer's recommended temperature, and most important, never using sharp or metallic tools on its surface. A scratched-up nonstick pan is literally leaching chemical scraps into your food—it might not kill you, but I mean come on, that can't be *good* for you.

COOKWARE (STAINLESS STEEL): This is the mainstay of most kitchens, and probably the most versatile medium for the making of food. It's definitely intimidating to start, primarily from the associated fear of food becoming glued to its gleaming industrial-chic surface. What's usually happening here is the pores of the metal, contracting as they get hotter, gripping your food like a hundred million terrifying little metal mouths, indicating that your pan was not hot enough when added. The secret to working with "sticky" cookware is the same secret behind why restaurant food tastes so good: fat and heat. Generally speaking, a little extra oil or butter

and a slightly hotter flame is the magic combo that will demystify stainless steel cookware for you. Conversely, sometimes you want things to stick. No matter how much you lube up the pan, your steak will likely glue itself to the bottom when you drop it in. But as it develops an even, golden-brown crust, it will lift off the bottom of the pan like a beefy miracle, and flavorful fond will be left behind in the jaws of the little monster below. On the other hand, unless they're positively swimming in fat, eggs tend to be troublemakers in this arena.

EMULSION: This might be the most important and, at least in my experience, most unsung hero in the kitchen. Much in the same way *Fermentation* is the unsung hero behind many of the oldest and greatest flavors known to man, so too is emulsion for its textures. The first place you're going to hear about it is its vital role in sauces: the process of *Emulsifying* together things like butter and pasta cooking water, oil and vinegar, duck fat and stock. What you're really doing is suspending one substance in the other, so that instead of a layer of fat floating on a layer of water, you're creating billions of little droplets of fat suspended in water (or vice-versa). Milk, dressings, sauces, meringues, cake batter, cheese, butter, gravy, ice cream—they're all emulsions, and they all owe their texture to this microscopic process. Substances that aid in the permanency of these emulsions are called *Emulsifiers*—the most common you'll see on packaged foods is *Lecithin*. But you're using lecithin yourself whenever you make hollandaise—egg yolks are packed with it, making them natural emulsifiers and ubiquitous in rich sauces. It's a very sciency subject, making it one of my weak suits—but the more I understand it, the better I am at creating rewarding textures and complex flavors.

FAT: Fat refers to, well, fat. Any substance with a high (or pure) fat content, put to use in the cooking or enrichment of food. That means basically all the things in life that are as delicious as they are essentially poisonous for you: butter, olive oil, vegetable oil, duck fat, bacon fat, straight-up lard. But fat isn't just for flavor; it's also an essential lubricant to prevent foods from sticking during the act of cooking, and other double entendres. It also plays an essential role in the browning of food (aka the Maillard Reaction, more to come on this), facilitating the flavorful caramelization of the food's exterior. Everything in life comes down to balance, and in some recipes (like pasta sauce), adding butter is just as bad for you as it is entirely optional. But it's good.

FROZEN FOODS: Many foods suffer from freezing, but some are offered distinct advantages by being introduced to this very very chilly process. Frozen produce is widely considered more nutritious, as it was frozen closer to having been picked, preserving it at the peak of its freshness. Frozen peas are typically even better-tasting than fresh ones, as fresh peas deteriorate quickly on their way to the grocery store. Frozen shrimp, in most grocery store contexts, are a much better option than the stuff packed in snow next to the fresh salmon. Most grocery store "fresh" shrimp were shipped frozen and thawed before being put on display! So unless you live on the bayou and are grabbing shrimp by the handful straight out of the nets, you're likely getting a better product from the freezer aisle. On the other hand, many other foods don't take so kindly to the freezing process: most aged cheeses, for example, will not survive a stint in the icebox. A cooked steak, while not made inedible, will be a sorry sight after having been brought back to room temperature—conversely, a raw steak takes to the freezer quite well, so long as it's defrosted gently and properly!

GRILLS: This is not a book about grilling, but grills are used when available. I've tried to keep this book within the confines of the home kitchen, but let's face it, if you have the space and ability to grill, you really ought to. Gas and charcoal grills operate entirely differently when it comes to the most important part of cooking: heat control. Charcoal grills, like any fire, thrive off oxygen—so opening the vents and cracking the lid will feed the coals and help to generate white-hot conditions for searing and charring. Gas grills, whose heat output is constant no matter the position of the lid, actually gets hotter when fully closed down,

behaving more like a gas oven than a grill. Charcoal is undoubtedly the best for flavor, imbuing the subjects of its radiant glow with smoke and wood-fired naturalism. Gas, while not flavorful in and of itself, both creates a flavorful cooking environment and offers unparalleled control and convenience. More convenient still, and inexpensive though they may be, electric grills are not grills at all, but ridged surfaces that get hot, not unlike a ridged frying pan. Useful as they can occasionally be, it isn't the shape of grill marks that give grilled food its pleasurable flavor, it's the radiant heat and smoke generated by suspending your food directly over a heat source, fat being allowed to drip down onto it, and little whispers of smoke dancing back up in retort. Some of that smoky flavor ends up on your food, and bing bang boom, stuff cooked outside tastes better than cooked inside.

HEAT (CONVECTION): Sometimes mistakenly referred to as an "air fryer," a convection oven is an oven whose insides are windy. In other words, a fan circulates the hot air so that some foods can enjoy a more even, slightly more intense cooking environment. As such, recipes are typically adapted by reducing oven temperatures by 25°F when using convection heat, as the circulating air can cause things to brown (and potentially burn) more quickly. Some foods fail fantastically in convection ovens—cakes, for example—whose rise is inhibited when its crust forms more quickly in the circulated heat. Conversely, browning the skin on a turkey has never been more easily or beautifully accomplished than that emerging from a convection oven, the whooshing air both drying out and crisping every inch of exposed bird. So if you have the luxury of a fan built into your hotbox, think about what your food is trying to accomplish during its time in the oven, and if convection might be the right choice for its goals.

HEAT (INDIRECT): Most applicable to grilling, indirect heat is the act of using heat, however indirectly. Sorry that was stupid, but it really is as simple as it sounds: Blast the heat on one side of your grill by pushing coals or maxing out burners, place the food on the "cool" side of the grill, and cook it with ambient heat not unlike a common home oven. When grilling foods to a desired temperature, this indirect zone becomes especially important, acting as a buffer zone where foods can escape the violence of direct heat and gently approach their desired doneness. You might've already utilized indirect heat without even knowing it: Ever finished the hot dogs before the burgers, but you want to keep them warm till their flat beefy counterparts are done? You turn off (or turn down) the burners on half the grill, keep the dogs toasty, and continue flaming the poor burgers till they're well-done enough for your in-laws to feel safe consuming.

HEAT (STOVETOP): Be it medium or medium-high, here is where many dishes go awry. An example instruction might say, "Cook over medium heat for 2 to 5 minutes, until soft," which contains a glaring potential issue: your stovetop. No, there's nothing wrong with your stovetop, I'm sorry for even inferring that; the problem lies in the wildly inconsistent power of stoves the world over. Your author may have test-driven this recipe on a two-burner electric coil hotplate or on a La Cornue Château French Top,

and either way, their timing and temperatures won't translate very well to your stove. Like *Time* (entry follows), this is a direction that relies heavily on your intuition and paying attention to the way your food's behaving: Are the onions barely making any noise, and do they move sluggishly around the pan? Well then crank the heat up to medium-high, those onions need more firepower! Are they sizzling loudly and darkening rapidly? Well then cool your literal jets, you're annihilating your aromatics! Moral of the story? This is a term you should take with a grain of salt (heh), and rely on your eyes/ears/nose to guide your hand as you spin the knobs of fire.

HERBS (DRIED VS. FRESH): There are very few examples of dried herbs that function any better, or even nearly as well, as their freshly-harvested brethren. Most herbs take on an off-flavor when they've been dried or freeze-dried, and if your finished dish is a chorus of beautiful voices, it's the one singing slightly off-key. Not saying that will ruin it, but in the vast majority of circumstances, fresh herbs simply taste better than dried. Especially dried basil, have you ever smelled dried basil? It smells like fish food. There are, of course, several notable exceptions: dried bay leaves perform just as beautifully as their fresh counterparts. Dried oregano, especially on pizza, can even taste a great deal better than the fresh stuff. Sometimes, dried herbs can be more easily incorporated into a recipe (e.g.: ground rosemary in a barbecue spice rub). I know fresh herbs are an annoying proposition: they're far more expensive, have a very limited shelf life, and you generally end up having to buy an entire bouquet of the stuff for the 1 tablespoon in your recipe. But if you can spare the extra scratch, they could end up making a demonstrable difference in your dinner.

MAILLARD REACTION: This, for the most part, is the chemical process that occurs when you use heat to brown food. It's amino acids being rearranged or whatever, I won't bore you with the chemistry. No guys, seriously, I understand the chemistry, I do, I'm just worried you won't, and that's the only reason

I'm not writing about it right now. All you need to know is that it's responsible for some of the most delicious words in the English language, including but not limited to: brown, sear, crust, toast, crisp, fry, sauté, crunch, roast, caramel, caramelize, and so many more. It's also one of the reasons that the food in restaurants tastes so good: between the mammoth burners, weathered pans, and robust ventilation systems, restaurant kitchens are unafraid to apply heat liberally to maximize flavor and texture. Make every effort to embrace this chemical reaction whenever possible and appropriate.

OILS: If you're anything like me, when you're starting out cooking, you subconsciously categorize extra-virgin olive oil as "better" than any other oil, for either cooking or consuming (most likely because it's expensive). Just like salt, however, there's a time and a place for every style of oil, one that's mostly determined by its smoke point, or the point at which the oil begins to, well, smoke. While searing things in EVOO might sound more gourmet, even bringing it close to its smoke point can turn things acrid and bitter. High smoke-point oils, like peanut or grapeseed, are ideal for those high-heat applications, as their flavors will not deteriorate until they hit much higher temperatures. Save the extra-virgin stuff for finishing and dipping, and for the higher heat applications, stick to the light olive oil. Olive oil carries with it another little-known bugaboo: it quickly spoils. Your average consumer olive oil takes on putrid smells and rancid flavors that you don't want to end up in your pasta and should be removed from duty within a year of purchase. I know that ten-gallon bucket of olive oil at Costco is tempting from a value standpoint, but unless you really think you're going to go through it by New Year's, maybe stick to one bottle at a time. Rancidity can be slowed by keeping your oil in a dark-colored bottle, away from sunlight, heat, and bad influences at school.

PASTA (DRIED VS FRESH): Far too many people, consciously or otherwise, think that fresh pasta is universally "better" than dried, when in fact they both play very different roles. Fresh cooks extremely quickly (usually 90 seconds or less), has a rougher texture for grabbing on to sauces, and not to mention a richer, eggier flavor. For extraordinarily thick sauces, mac and cheese, baked casseroles, or recipes where the pasta is beaten and pressed within an inch of its life, dried is often the far-better solution. Be sure to look for dried pasta cut with bronze dies—not only does it sound fancier, it results in a rougher texture on the pasta's exterior, releasing more starch into the cooking water and creating a surface ideal for saucin'. Take great care not to overcook fresh pasta, and when making it (see recipe on page 116), don't be afraid to positively drown it in semolina or flour to prevent sticking.

PEPPER (FRESHLY GROUND): Jim Gaffigan has a great, characteristically incredulous bit about fresh-ground pepper where he confronts a hypothetical waiter as a pepper snob: "Hey, wait a minute! This isn't fresh pepper—I grew up on a pepper farm." But just like most freshly ground spices, peppercorns have a brighter, spicier, more floral quality to them when they've been freshly ground. Do me a favor—pour some pre-ground pepper into a bowl, then crack some fresh into another bowl. Give each a big ol' sniff, and once you've finished panic-sneezing, try and tell me that the freshly ground stuff didn't smell better. That bigger, brighter smell and flavor are going to translate directly into your dish. It might seem like a small thing, but paying attention to all the little details of a recipe has a cumulative effect, often producing a noticeably better outcome.

REDUCTION: This is exactly what it sounds like; bringing a liquid of some kind to a boil, allowing some of it to evaporate, and *reducing* its physical volume, the space that it takes up in . . . space. Hell, if you boil water and half of it disappears, you technically made a reduction. Despite that, reduction once found itself at the very epicenter of food snobbery, sometimes even used to parody chefs as they explained the seventh course of their tasting menu tableside to uninterested diners. Luckily, with the advent of foams and molecular gastronomy, reduction has returned to the shelf of old reliables where it belongs—it just comes down to what you're reducing, and for whom you're reducing it. Balsamic reductions, while they might funk up your kitchen for an hour, make for a finishing glaze that looks as striking as it tastes. Red wine reductions, while they might sound sexy, produce a bitter potion capable of burning a hole through a steak like thermite.

ROUX: A method for the beautiful and selfless act of thickening, a roux is little more than a cooked paste of flour and butter. Notoriously easy to make grainy or lumpy, it must be whisked constantly while slowly adding splashes of the liquid to be thickened, allowing it to incorporate fully into the paste before adding more. When this procedure is executed with whole milk, what you end up with is a *Bechamel*, one of the five French "mother sauces." Far and away the easiest of the quintet, it's also the fastest way to make friends by using it to replace ricotta in a lasagna (see page 336), where it becomes a river of richness woven throughout the sauce and cheese. I'm getting off topic; there are four categorizations of roux, referring to its color—white, blonde, brown, and dark brown. The latter offers an almost insane savory flavor, maybe most famously in gumbo, while the former hardly makes its presence known, save for a thick, buttery texture.

SALT: The most omnipresent of all ingredients (probably?), it's also a source of a great deal of confusion. There are a great number of salts, from pink Himalayan to black lava, but there are really only three you need to know about: table, kosher, and finishing. You need to know the difference because not only do they all serve different purposes, they are not directly interchangeable—and that's not me just being a snooty chef—you'll see what I mean. Table (iodized) salt is what you generally see pouring from the metal spout of a cylindrical cardboard container: the ultra-fine grained salt with nearly the same consistency as sugar. This salt is usually for inconspicuously sprinkling on under-seasoned dishes at the dinner table, but it's also ideal for baking, as it's typically the salt being used (unless otherwise specified) when baking recipes are being written. Kosher salt is a larger-grained, somewhat flaky, pinchable salt, one that's gained God status on my show. It's the salt choice of most cooks for a few reasons: first, it's less salty. Not because it contains less salt flavor, but because it's made of large and irregular crystals, which don't allow you to pack as much salt into the same space. In other words, a teaspoon of table salt contains more actual salt than a teaspoon of kosher salt. As such, it's more forgiving—its pinchable form factor also allows you to season your food by hand, which gives you a much better sense of how much you're adding. As you learn how food behaves and how much salt makes sense for a given amount of food, this felt connection becomes increasingly important. Finishing salt is a very large, flaky, thin and crunchy salt, used almost exclusively in an effort to live up to its name: finishing stuff. It's the last thing to go on a dish to add visual flair, crunch, and, well, saltiness. It's also much more expensive than regular or kosher salt, so I can't think of any earthly reason why you'd use it for anything else.

SAUTÉ PAN: This is usually referring to the higher-walled variety of wide, shallow pans—and if that's the case, then we're talking about my very favorite kind of pan. Specifically a 12-inch, high-walled, stainless

steel sauté pan (sometimes mistakenly called a Dutch oven, or without a handle, a brazier). This pan offers the very widest array of utility in the kitchen, perhaps my most oft-used tool outside of a knife. An ideal environment for boiling, braising, deep-frying, even cooking spaghetti, there's a great deal more to do in a sauté pan than simply sauté.

SOUS VIDE: This term, being French, both sounds and is actually fancy. Translating literally to "under vacuum," it refers to the vacuum-sealing and cooking of food in a precision-controlled water bath. Once a prohibitively expensive piece of equipment confined to Michelin-starred kitchens and Zagat-rated laboratories, immersion circulators are now affordably priced to make a fine Christmas present for a cousin or coworker you're pretty close with. It's a bit of a fussy process, but it allows for the easification and ensurance (both words used incorrectly) of consistent and quality results in food, particularly proteins. For example, a steak can be placed in a 130°F water bath and held there for anywhere from 30 minutes to 4 hours, cooked to a perfect medium rare and never exceeded. Once it emerges from the vac bag like an alien placenta, it can be patted dry and seared up crisp on the outside, perfect edge-to-edge medium-rare on the inside. Foods normally braised, like short ribs or pork belly, can achieve otherworldly textures both tender and toothsome. Some stuff can even be pasteurized, like eggs, to keep them functionally raw but entirely safe to eat. There are those that will try and convince you that it's the next microwave, but its many components and time-consuming, planning-oriented methodology keep it primarily in the wheelhouse of enthusiasts and hobbyists. But hey, that's you—I mean, you're reading the glossary of a cookbook. Nerd.

SPICES: Some spices tend to have a pretty universal quality to them—buying organic cumin generally won't net you a better end result—but grinding it yourself most certainly will. Much like how pepper tastes, smells, and dare I say looks better when you grind it yourself, so, too, will the vast majority of spices. When ground and bottled, spices quickly lose their complexity and potency, so by the time

you shake that chili powder into your . . . chili, its flavor has been whittled down to a stale, single-dimensional shadow of its former self. Freshly ground (and for bonus points, toasted) spices generally just have a bigger, brighter, more floral and more pleasing flavor—and you can have them today for little more than the cost of your time and a cheap coffee grinder dedicated to spice grinding—don't use it for coffee, unless you want your morning brew to taste like tikka masala.

STOCK/BROTH: More of a pain-in-the-ass than most cooks would like to admit, a homemade stock also has the greatest potential to take a dish from good to great. How can I convince you to spend 4 to 24 hours making boiled meat juice? Well, I've got a dare for you: take a big ol' swig of store-bought chicken stock. Too gross? Bring some to a boil and take a big whiff. There are few things so objectively disgusting and yet so widely used as boxed stock, and when you consider what an elemental role it plays in most dishes, it starts to make sense why the foodies in your life swear fealty to the homemade stuff. Yes, it is time consuming, but it can also be meditative. Do you enjoy reading, watching TV, or playing the odd video game? These are all perfect pastimes during which a bubbling cauldron of stock can become a background task, made in large batches that can be frozen for up to six months. You can even concentrate the stock, boiling it down to half or quarter of its original volume, ready to be diluted and put to glorious work in your favorite soup or stew at a moment's notice.

STOVETOPS TYPES: Gas is, far and away, the preferred cooktop for exactly 100 percent of all recipes from all of time and space. A strong case can be made for induction, but nothing quite beats the "feel" of gas—it's like listening to your favorite album on vinyl. It's got personality. Unfortunately, we can't all be so lucky, and many of us are stuck with electric ranges. Don't worry, you can still make great food with electric burners, but the rules are decidedly different. The most important factor to account for is the slow speed at which your burner heats up and cools off. If a recipe calls for sautéing something for five minutes and then removing from the heat, that's exactly what you gotta do: you can't just turn off the burner, because that coily bastard stays plenty hot long after you've cut off the juice. Likewise, let's say you're sautéing something, and things are getting a little too lively: your onions are browning very quickly, oil is smoking, things are sputtering. If you turn down the heat on a gas or induction range, that adjustment is very quickly translated into the metal of the pan. An electric range changes gears very slowly, however, so your food will continue receiving too much heat for many minutes after the knob's been turned. It becomes a sort of delicate dance, moving pots on and off of burners to compensate for slowly heating or cooling coils, but it's very doable with a little practice and a lot of understanding of food/cookware behavior.

TIME: Is just, like, a construct, man. One that's very problematic to cook by. Very few recipes might require exact cook times, but thanks to about 45 fucktillion potential variables, relying on cooking times is a "recipe for disaster." Sorry, I had to, and you know it. Especially for meat, you might as well throw cook times out the window altogether—take a beef roast for example. The size and shape of the meat, its core temperature when first put in the oven, your oven's (actual) temperature, whether Mercury is in retrograde; these are just some of the potential pitfalls of following a suggested roast time. We authors do our best and give a range of time ("cook for 2 to 5 minutes," "sun-dry for 3 to 15 weeks"), and usually offer a sensory indication of a step's completion ("bake until set but slightly jiggly," "stab lobster repeatedly until no longer alive"). The latter are the ones you really want to pay attention to: they're the best and most reliable instructions for how to tell if any given step is complete. Cook times can definitely still be good guidelines—I always start checking a food for doneness/readiness just shy of the suggested cook time, and stay as observant as possible after that.

WINDOWPANE TEST: This test, clearly named in the 1950s (who says "windowpane"?), is the gold standard by which you can measure your dough's readiness to become bread. Here's how you do it: grab a golf ball–size piece of dough, and flatten it out between your palms. Then, gently coax the dough in the center of the disc as thin as you can possibly get it before it breaks. Generally speaking, if you can make it translucent when held up to the light, you are officially a baker and can legally practice bakery in most states. Moreover, it means that you've developed enough gluten in the dough so that it can stretch fantastically thin, which means your resultant loaf will have the strong network to support cavernous crumbs under crackling crusts.

Your Spice Rack and You

One of the most requested episodes of *Basics* has been a spice rack breakdown—what are the essential spices, what herbs taste better fresh, what spices should be used for which dishes? Like most aspects of the cooking arena, there are general rules of thumb, and room for experimentation. The following is an attempt to break down what you can expect from your spices, and more important, what they can expect from you. It's mostly just about being present, ya know?

You'll have to forgive some of my descriptors, because let's face it, it's hard to describe what elemental flavors taste like. For example, describe to me what a cherry tastes like. It tastes bright? Fruity? Tart? I dunno dude, it tastes like a cherry. The best way to find out what it tastes like is to taste it! Lick your finger and dip it into the mysterious powder, carefully whiff at its curious aromas, imagine the weathered hands of the spice farmer that harvested it. One way I like to really experience and isolate what flavor a particular spice is going to bring to a dish: take a bite of something unseasoned and very flavor neutral, like cooked oatmeal or plain yogurt, then add a sprinkle of the spice or herb in question and take another bite. Is this pleasant, tasty, or even that fun? No, not really—but if you're curious about just what the hell paprika is actually doing when you add it to your paella, it's a way to shush the rest of the orchestra so you can hear what the flutes sound like on their own.

Generally speaking, almost all herbs are better fresh, almost all whole dried chiles are better than chili powder, and almost all spices are better ground from whole seeds or pods. One of the notable exceptions to the rule is a sort of "nostalgia factor." Were you raised on packets of dried ranch, like me? Dried dill is probably going to create a more familiar, enjoyable sense memory for you in certain dishes. Has your local pizza shop always kept shakers of dried oregano and granulated garlic next to the napkin dispenser and the half-scale Italian chef stereotype statue? Then you're probably going to derive more pleasure from them than you would the bracing, overpowering flavor of freshly chopped garlic and oregano. It's kind of like knowing when to use "their, they're, or there"— yes there are established rules (recipes) that outline when to use each, but after you've written (cooked) long enough, one just feels (tastes) right when you see (eat) it. See what I did there?

ALLSPICE: Despite its deceiving name, allspice doesn't work in everything. I know, that's what I thought when I first saw it, too. It shows up in apple pie spice along with nutmeg, cinnamon, cloves, and ginger, because it shares many of their characteristics: peppery, warm, earthy, and pungent. Its unique flavor (going to have a hard time not using that phrase repeatedly in this section) also dominates Caribbean, European, and Middle Eastern stews, cures, and sausages. Grind it yourself whenever possible.

BASIL: Dried basil is one of those dried herbs I can confidently say unanimously sucks. It smells, tastes, and looks worse than its fresh brethren—about the only time you want to use it is when it needs to be dry, like in a spice rub. Other than that, always stick to the fresh stuff when you can.

BAY LEAVES: Fresh bay leaves are cool when you can find them, but dried bay leaves perform just fine in your favorite slow 'n' low. Their slightly minty, almost bitter flavor supposedly lightens up otherwise heavy soups and stews. I can't personally attest to that, but have a very hard time finding any slowly-cooked, savory dish that doesn't benefit from its presence.

CAYENNE: This spice is a reliable source for pure heat and a dash of color. It's one of the few spice rack mainstays that's actually high in capsaicin, the chemical compound that makes you sweat profusely and start coughing uncontrollably on a first date when you order a vindaloo to split. It does bring a subtle flavor, can be used in virtually anything, and a

tiny pinch of it can augment and enhance the existing flavors, particularly in fat-rich dishes like mac and cheese or hollandaise.

CHILI POWDER: Here's where we get into tricky territory. Chili powder is an undeniably essential spice, but the garden variety ones you find at the supermarket are going to be pretty bland and flat. Is it perfect for taco seasoning? Absolutely. Are you going to win any blue ribbons in the chili cook-off with it? Absolutely not. If the flavor of your dish relies heavily on chili powder (see *Chili*, page duh), you're way better off grinding or pureeing your own dried chiles. A mix of fruity/bright (Aleppo, cascabel, habanero), smoky/earthy (pasilla, ancho, chipotle), and sweet (mulato, guajillo, ají) chiles will kick the ever-loving shit out of any dried chili powder, and that's a Babish Guarantee™.

CINNAMON: There are a few types of widely available cinnamons: cassia and Ceylon are the most prevalent. Ceylon is generally considered the "real" cinnamon, and is known for its sweeter and more subtle properties compared to the strong, spicy cassia variety. Fresh-ground can be nice, but it's more difficult to grind than most spices and still just fine preground. Cinnamon sticks are best for either decoration or stews/brines, so they can impart their delicate flavor and be easily fished out later on.

CLOVES: One of the most deceptively powerful spices in your spice rack, cloves have a flowery, medicinal, pungent flavor that can overpower your entire dish if not used responsibly. The vast majority of recipes call for "one whole clove" or "1/16 teaspoon ground cloves, to taste" for a reason—my dad once accidentally mistook cloves for chili powder in his favorite pot roast, and the result was so awful that here I am writing about it in my cookbook more than two decades later. Tread lightly.

CUMIN: Reminiscent of pepper, flowers, and just a whiff of BO, many of your favorite recipes would not be possible without cumin: Mexican, Middle-Eastern, BBQ, Indian, and more lean heavily on this seed's unique and ubiquitous flavor. It's also one of the spices that most greatly benefits from being toasted and freshly ground, so be sure to pick it up whole and process it yourself after tossing it around in a dry, hot pan for a quick minute!

CURRY POWDER: The apple pie spice of the savory world (what?), curry powder is generally a blend of coriander, fenugreek, turmeric, pepper, bay leaf, clove, nutmeg, ginger, cayenne, ginger, cumin, and sometimes more. Would I use it to make an authentic chicken tikka masala? No—but for a quick jolt of flavor to an otherwise-boring chicken salad or roasted sweet potatoes, it's hard to do much better.

DILLWEED: I'm not sure why dried dill is referred to as "dillweed" and fresh dill is just "dill," and it seemed unimportant enough not to research before writing this. Ah, what the hell I'll google it—hang on—ah, okay they're synonyms. Their flavors, however, are not synonymous—like most dried herbs, dried dill (weed) is muted, flat, and a bit stale. I'm also something of a dill fiend, especially when it comes to chicken noodle soup, so you'll rarely find me reaching for a jar of the dry stuff.

GROUND GINGER: Here's a great example of a spice that is demonstrably worse than its fresh counterpart but still offers great utility. Dried ginger can be easily added to most baked goods, and unlike the fresh stuff, doesn't diminish in flavor when cooked. Should you use it in cocktails, soups, or stir-fry? Most assuredly not. Should you use it in apple pie, gingersnaps, barbecue rubs, and dips? Giddyup!

NUTMEG: Preground nutmeg cannot be compared to its origin: a playful, zesty little seed, the fractal pattern of its interior shivering into a thousand nutty snowflakes as it's whittled through a rasp, the air newly perfumed with its secrets, a ticker tape parade of flavor delicately falling and forming the snow caps on mountains of whipped cream or mashed potatoes. Yes, I have a passion for freshly grated nutmeg, and once you give it a try, so, too, shall you.

MACE: Annoyingly more difficult to find here in the States, mace is a sister plant to *nutmeg* (which by now you know I'm obsessed with), and it can stand in as a subtler, gentler, and frankly tastier alternative to cloves. You know what? Never mind—cloves are an alternative to mace, if anything.

ONION POWDER: This is an effective way to sneak onion flavor into dishes without having actual chunks of onion in the damn thing. Particularly useful in marinades and spice blends, it's even useful in dishes already featuring fresh onion if you want to amp it up a bit. Also available: minced dried onion, which I'd only really recommend using in everything-bagel seasoning.

OREGANO: My chief example when demonstrating the rare instances in which dried herbs outperform fresh, dried oregano has an almost entirely different flavor from the currently alive variety. While the latter is bracing and grassy, dried oregano is subtle and peppery. If you put the fresh stuff on pizza, it's all you'd taste—if you put the dried stuff on pizza, that's amore.

PAPRIKA: Here in the States, paprika is about as bland, universal, and inoffensive a spice as ever there was, often being added for its striking color more than anything else. Spanish, Hungarian, hot, and smoked paprikas are some of the many varieties that will bring their own unique flavor to a dish—smoked paprika in particular being an effective way to bring barbecue flavors indoors.

PARSLEY: About as useful as a second appendix, dried parsley is devoid of any scent, flavor, texture, or purpose for being. As cynical a scam as ever was perpetuated on an unwitting populace, dried parsley still finds its way into nearly every one of our pantries. There's no use fighting it; that bottle of flavorless flakes is an omnipresence, and we are powerless against its ubiquity. Sprinkle some into your pasta once, look at it incredulously after your first bite, and let it turn to dust in your cabinet for the rest of time. From the earth we came, and to the earth we shall return.

PEPPERCORNS: There are subtle differences between the many different colors of peppercorn, but generally speaking, you can't go wrong with the good ol' fashioned black peppercorn (piper nigrum). Freshly ground, it's head and shoulders above anything you ever got out of a shaker, and when served with something simple (like eggs), can mean the difference between goodness and greatness.

RED PEPPER FLAKES: Like cayenne but a bit bigger—both in physical size and personality—red pepper flakes bring a lighter, fruitier heat to virtually any recipe. Their flavor is especially pronounced when roasted or fried, which is why they're often added to the pan along with garlic, so they can catch a glimpse of that desirable dry heat before they're quenched by a glug of wine or a swig of stock.

ROSEMARY: Yet another example of an herb whose most desirable traits are staled and oddified in the drying process. With a flatter, more cardboard-y taste than the bright, piney bushels from whence it came, you are almost always better off using fresh rosemary. You might grind up the dry stuff to coat a prime rib of beef, but there is the "nostalgia factor," particularly via the prime rib served at the Friday night fancy restaurant in your hometown.

SAFFRON: Okay this one's a bit tricky—a lovely spice to be sure, but extremely expensive and oft counterfeited. If you're trying to whip up an authentic paella, make sure to look for threads that slightly bulge at one end, are mostly a deep red, and turn tepid water a rich golden-yellow after 30 minutes to 1 hour. It should also be upsettingly expensive.

SAGE: While another example of a weaker, flatter version of its former self, dried sage's flavor doesn't suffer *too* too badly from the drying process. Good for using in a pinch or a spice rub, or in a pinch of spice rub.

STAR ANISE: An absolute must-have for a variety of savory braises, unique confections, and cozying cocktails, this seed pod imparts a sweet, soft, almost licoricelike flavor. And this is coming from a guy that straight-up hates licorice.

TARRAGON: Same deal hotshot, go for the bright green bundle in the produce section over the grayish-green stuff in the bottle. Dried tarragon has a more artificial, medicinal flavor than its grassy-looking fresh origins, which furnishes a sweet, almost star anise–like flavor.

THYME: For like the umpteenth time, here's an herb you generally want to use fresh. The dried stuff tastes stale, the fresh stuff works in damn near anything, it probably lasts longer than any fresh herb in the fridge, and its low moisture content means you can process it into a relatively fine powder straight off the twig. It's a botanical miracle.

VANILLA: I know vanilla isn't a spice, but it is frequently both sold and stored next to the spices, so here it is. About the only thing to avoid here is imitation vanilla—sure, it costs $0.50 less, but you'll end up paying dividends . . . in flavor. Did that make sense? Pure vanilla extract delivers a strong, natural vanilla flavor; vanilla paste yields a subtler, sweeter flavor; and whole pods furnish both those delightful little specks and a far more subtle, complex flavor. Try to add vanilla off-heat whenever possible, as too much heat can diminish its potency, just like alcohol or a computer.

CHAPTER ONE

BREAD

Bread is everything you've heard—a mighty challenge, a rewarding experience, a cornerstone of civilization—and when you're a hobbyist, a tremendous amount of work, sometimes, with questionable payoff. It's every bit as difficult to master as you've imagined, and every prick like me that says, "Naw, dawg, it's easy!" has only figured that out after, you guessed it, baking hundreds of loaves of bread. But that's why you're here, right? To learn from someone who knows their shit? Well, someone who knows their shit well enough, so they're going to try and clearly, but breezily, explain what to do without drowning you in bread history and bread theory? Sound good? Here we go, into the no-stupid-questions zone!

WHAT IS BREAD? Seriously? It's bread. You've seen bread. Sorry, I said no stupid questions—bread is, in its most basic form, a combination of flour and water, most often leavened by yeast and baked until set. This makes the nutrients in flour digestible, which is what makes it such an important part of our history as human beings: It represents our ability to use tools, most notably heat, to sustain ourselves. Kinda romantic, when you think about it.

WHY IS BREAD? I'm not entirely sure what you mean by that, but I suppose the "why" of bread is to make something nutritious and edible out of things that aren't. Michael Pollan famously popularized the fun fact I recite at every dinner party I've ever been to: If you tried to survive off flour, water, and yeast separately, you wouldn't last a month. Combine them together and heat them, however, and you could survive indefinitely. Yes, that is a fun fact, that's why I say it. There is indeed something elemental about taking these raw ingredients and transforming them into something nutritious, even delicious.

WHO IS BREAD? Okay now you're just being silly.

WHAT BREAD SHOULD I START WITH? Back on track. I think the best place to start with bread is enriched bread, which refers to the addition of sugar, dairy, and/or fat to the dough (or all three). These breads are generally characterized by thin, yielding crusts and soft, pillowy interiors: sandwich bread, challah, dinner rolls, brioche, burger buns, even croissants are technically enriched. At first, this may seem counterintuitive: Doesn't more ingredients mean more complexity? In fact, the added complexity is what makes enriched bread more forgiving: the dough is easier to manage and shape, the proofing is more forgiving, the baking easier to interpret.

SOURDOUGH? That's not really a question but I know what you're getting at—sourdough is the "original" bread, made from naturally-occurring yeast present on the flour, on your hands, in the air, everywhere. This yeast is allowed to grow, or "culture," by adding water to flour and making a paste where these tasty li'l fungi can thrive. It has a distinct and slightly tangy taste (hence the name), yields a sandy-colored dough, and bakes up with a delightfully soft/chewy interior and deeply browned, sometimes even charred exterior. People get uncomfortably invested in sourdough for a reason: every starter has a story. There are starters in San Francisco that are over one hundred years old, passed down and tended to by generations. I cultivated my first starter when I locked myself in a cabin in Vermont, trying to shake off all the sadness and booze left in the wake of a bad breakup. Too much information? I told you, people get intense about sourdough.

HOW DO I KNOW IF I'VE KNEADED MY BREAD ENOUGH? It is very, very, *very* difficult to over-knead bread, especially when you're just starting out. I've been baking it for years and still break a mighty sweat trying to get my dough to pass the windowpane test. You could potentially over-knead using a stand mixer, but again, you'd have to really overdo it. So my advice to newcomers, generally, is to just go apeshit on your bread when you're kneading it. Unless you've been doing forearm workouts religiously for the past few years, I guarantee you're not done kneading until you feel like you're going to die from failure of the *flexor digitorum profundus*. That's your forearm.

WHAT'S THE WINDOWPANE TEST? This is in the Kitchen Glossary (page 23), which I fully understand you not having read, being a glossary and all; so here it is in a nutshell. The windowpane test is a rule-of-thumb for most breads to determine whether or not you've developed enough gluten, the complex network of proteins formed in bread that gives it its structure and texture. Grab a piece of your dough, and trying to coax it into a sort of square, stretch it as thin as you can. If your gluten is properly developed, you should be able to stretch it into a paper-thin membrane that light clearly passes through. If it starts to tear before you can get it to that point, I know it's frustrating, but keep kneading!

I MADE A TERRIBLE LOAF OF BREAD. SURELY I DON'T HAVE THE GENETIC MARKERS NECESSARY TO BE A BAKER, AND I SHOULD SKIP RIGHT TO THE PASTAS BECAUSE THAT SOUNDS EASIER? Woah, you're chatty all of the sudden. Look I'm not going to lie to you—chances are, your first loaf is gonna suck. It's going to be sunken, tight, pallid, crumbly, dry, or doughy, or somehow all these at once—and you're going to be discouraged. Now you're going to expect me to quote Aaliyah ("dust yourself off and try again"), but I'm not. By all means, feel your feelings—allow yourself to be upset about trying something and failing—we all feel this way from time to time, and it's not something to be ashamed of or push away from. Life is a series of ever-evolving, steadily increasing challenges that vary and intensify in difficulty and complexity, and like dying for the first time in *Dark Souls*, you discover that there's actually joy to be found in the dogged pursuit. As burnished bubbles begin to blister and pillowy, chewy interiors open wide with yawning chasms of crumb, synapses fire and reward centers are activated; and that first slice, slathered with salty butter, crackling between your teeth as it offers up its yeasty prize, is your reward. It's a reward worth pursuing.

ROSEMARY FOCACCIA

Focaccia: the one you always make sure you get a piece of when the server comes around with the bread basket. The one you don't mean to fill up on before the appetizers even arrive—but you do. Light and crisp on the outside, sometimes speckled with fresh herbs and salt flakes, with a moist, chewy crumb stretched out inside. This is the bread that needs no butter, needs no jam, needs no oil—partially because the bottom is half-soaked and crunchy from having been lightly fried in olive oil. Clearly, I have a thing for focaccia, but it's also an excellent beginner bread. It's super-high hydration, so it can be a bit unwieldy and sticky, but it also illustrates how dough can be extremely wet but workable. Despite being one of the wettest doughs, it should be shiny, bouncy, and feel sort of . . . alive. That is, until you bake it dead.

How I've Screwed This Up

You're going to find that most of my follies and foibles in bread—and in life—revolve around impatience and inconsistency. Does it *really* need to prove that long? Do I *really* need to measure by weight instead of cups? Should it *really* be this wet? Do I *really* need to knead it this long? "It's probably been long enough," "cups are close enough," "I should add some flour"—these are the death rattles of loaves the world over, and I've killed my fair share.

Troubleshooting

MY DOUGH DIDN'T RISE DURING PROOFING. Your kitchen may be cold (less than 75°F), or your yeast may be dead. Double your proofing time, and if it still ain't puffing, you might be dealing with dead bugs. Add a teaspoon of your yeast to a cup of tepid (about 110°F) water and see if it gets all foamy—if not, toss it and get some new yeast!

MY FOCACCIA DIDN'T RISE IN THE OVEN. Sounds like a cold oven to me—get a cheap oven thermometer and make sure it's reaching the target temp.

MY CRUST CAME OUT FLAT/DIDN'T BROWN WELL. Once again, sounds like your oven is running cold. The combination of the sprayed water and hot Dutch oven should produce a positively crackling crust. Lack of bubbles/color could point to the loaf not cold-fermenting long enough.

MY CRUMB IS TIGHT/TENDER. This is a sign of either under-developed gluten or under-hydrated bread. Try giving it a couple more rounds of lift/folds, and make sure you're hitting the precise hydration ratio outlined in the recipe—the dough should be soft and slack.

MY FOCACCIA STUCK TO THE PAN. Not enough oil.

MY FOCACCIA IS OILY. Too much oil.

MAKES ONE 18-BY-13-INCH FOCACCIA

850 grams bread flour

680 milliliters water, at room temperature

2¼ teaspoons active dry yeast

2 tablespoons kosher salt

Light olive oil, for greasing

2 fresh rosemary sprigs, leaves removed

Flaky sea salt, as needed

In a stand mixer fitted with the dough hook attachment, combine the flour, water, yeast, and kosher salt. Mix on medium speed until the dough is fully combined, about 5 minutes.

Generously oil a large bowl with olive oil, add your dough, cover, and let sit for about 2 hours at room temperature.

Using a rubber spatula, scrape the dough stuck to the bowl and fold in toward the center.

Generously coat an 18-by-13-inch rimmed baking sheet with olive oil.

Coat the bottom of the dough with olive oil and transfer the dough to the prepared baking sheet. Using your hands, fold the dough onto itself a few times then spread the dough to the edges of the baking sheet. If the dough keeps springing back to the center, add more olive oil to the dough, cover with plastic wrap, and let it rest for 15 minutes. You may have to do it a few times, but the dough will eventually spread across the entire baking sheet.

Once the baking sheet is filled out, drizzle the dough with more olive oil, and then cover it with plastic wrap and let ferment overnight in the fridge, about 12 hours. If any bubbles form, just poke them with a knife, and using oiled fingers, pull the dough just off the edges of the baking sheet.

Coat the top of the dough with more olive oil, cover it with plastic wrap, and let sit at room temperature for about 1 hour. Uncover and dimple the dough with your fingers. Press the dough into the corners of the baking sheet then cover with plastic wrap and rest if necessary.

Meanwhile, preheat the oven to 450°F.

Drizzle the dough one last time with olive oil and sprinkle with the rosemary leaves and flaky sea salt. Bake until the focaccia is crisp at the edges and golden brown all over, about 30 minutes.

Transfer the focaccia to a wire rack for to cool, about 1½ hours.

Store any leftover focaccia in an airtight container at room temperature for up to 3 days, or in the refrigerator for up to 7 days.

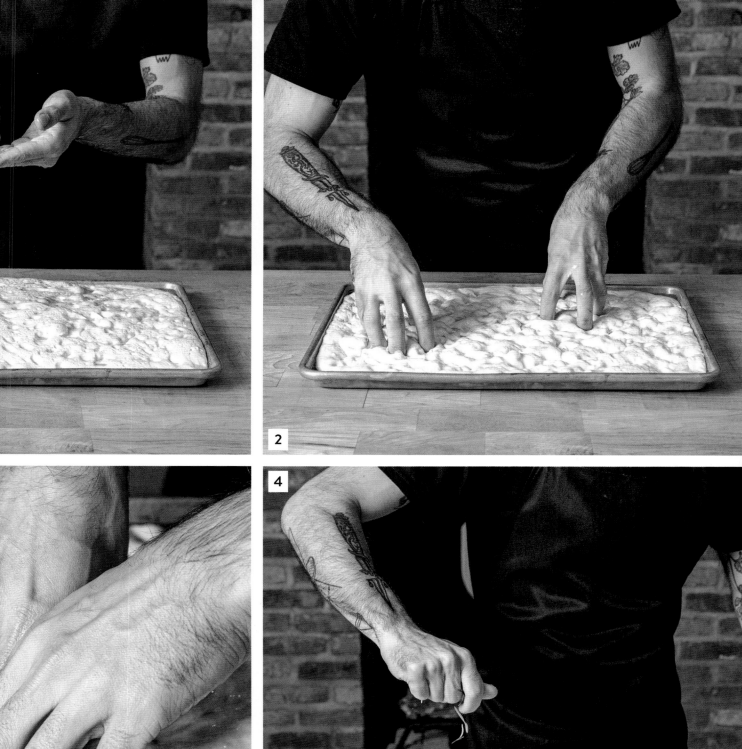

SOUTHERN-STYLE CORNBREAD

I'm gonna go ahead and potentially get myself in a whole mess of trouble and say that this is a genuine Southern-style cornbread. It gets all of its rise from eggs and the combination of baking soda and buttermilk, it contains zero flour, and it gets fried up in the shimmering fat of your choice before baking in the oven. One of the stronger cases to be made for owning a 10-inch cast-iron skillet, this batter gets precariously piled into a pool of sizzling bacon fat/lard/oil/whatever fat you've got lying around the house, and fry-baked into a tender, sweet, moist, crispy corn cake, perfect for smearing with salted butter or using to sop up the last of your chili. Cheddar cheese, canned corn, floury mix out of a box? Why don't you head back up to West Virginia, Yankee. We're gluten-free 'round these parts.

How I've Screwed This Up

Apart from deviating from tradition, this one's pretty hard to screw up. You can't really overmix the batter (since there's no gluten), and so long as your batter has the right consistency and you get your fat ripping hot, you should end up with some pretty solid cornbread. My biggest problem has come from using too coarse a grind of cornmeal, which can end up having a raw/crunchy texture that gets rather unpleasantly lodged in one's teeth.

Troubleshooting

MY CORNBREAD CAME OUT PALE/SOFT. Your oven and fat aren't hot enough. Make sure your oven's up to temp, and make sure to preheat the skillet per the directions!

MY CORNBREAD DIDN'T RISE. Baking powder has a surprisingly short shelf life, and can begin to lose its potency in as little as six months. You also need buttermilk for more than just flavor—it makes the rising reaction possible!

MY CORNBREAD ISN'T VERY FLAVORFUL. Being Southern-style, this cornbread well and truly relies on its corn content. You need high-quality cornmeal to bring the flavor, and even with the best in the business, it's still going to be pretty bland on its own. That's why you use it as a vehicle for butter, gravy, chili, or other fats in liquid form.

MAKES ONE 10-INCH-ROUND CORNBREAD

275 grams coarsely ground cornmeal, plus more as needed

1 teaspoon kosher salt

½ teaspoon baking powder

½ teaspoon baking soda

2 large eggs

360 grams buttermilk

100 grams lard

Preheat the oven to 425°F.

In a medium bowl, whisk together the cornmeal, salt, baking powder, and baking soda.

In a large bowl, whisk the eggs and buttermilk together. Whisk in the cornmeal mixture. You're looking for something that's thicker than pancake batter. To adjust for texture and consistency, gradually add more cornmeal if needed, and mix with a rubber spatula.

In a 10-inch cast-iron skillet, melt the lard over medium heat. Once melted, but not too hot, add about half of it to your cornbread batter and whisk to combine.

Place the skillet with the remaining lard over medium-high heat until shimmering and very hot. (This will create a super crisp crust on the bottom of your cornbread.) Carefully pour the batter into the skillet, where it should begin to sizzle. Smooth out the top of the batter.

Bake for 20 to 25 minutes, until set, light brown in the center, and deep golden brown around the edges. Carefully remove the cornbread from the skillet and let cool on a wire rack for 10 to 15 minutes before slicing and serving.

PAN CUBANO

Beyond being an absolute necessity for authentic Cubano sandwiches, pan Cubano can sing in several sandwich situations. Its soft and fluffy crumb, enriched with lard instead of butter, revels in being pressed and toasted, making it ideal for everything from burgers to garlic bread. Its crust bakes up paler than you might expect, so a smear of butter on both sides before getting crushed in the jaws of a panini press yields a grilled cheese with a crunchy, rich exterior. Best of all, it's dastardly difficult to find pan Cubano in your average grocery store, so more than most breads in this book, it's especially worth whipping up!

How I've Screwed This Up

I actually tried to make pan Cubano for the Cubano sandwich episode of *Binging*, but this was in the early days of my baking bread, so naturally it was a failure. I only made enough dough for one loaf, I ended up overbaking it, and didn't have enough time to try again—so it was off to the closest Cuban bakery in Harlem. Other than its pale crust, this loaf is pretty forgiving, so just keep an eye on it and try to rely on temperature!

Troubleshooting

MY PAN CUBANO IS COMING OUT DRY. It's very easy to overbake, so make sure to pull it from the oven when its thickest point registers 195° to 205°F!

MY PAN CUBANO IS EXPLODING. Stop trying to make pan Cubano in your meth lab's oven. Kidding, I assume you mean the seam is blowing out? Make sure you pinch it shut thoroughly when you're shaping the dough, don't be shy about it, and position each loaf seam-side down when it goes into the oven.

MY PAN CUBANO IS BAKING UP UNEVENLY. This guy likes to brown his own way, and might need some effort to even out the heat. If your oven has a convection function, crank it on during the last 10 minutes of baking. If not, be sure to rotate the loaf halfway through baking, and again as necessary if browning unevenly!

MAKES ONE 21-INCH LOAF

480 grams bread flour, plus more for dusting

7 grams instant dry yeast

2 teaspoons sugar

55 grams melted lard

300 milliliters water, at room temperature

12 grams kosher salt

Neutral oil (such as canola, vegetable, or grapeseed) or nonstick cooking spray, for greasing

Cornmeal, for dusting

In the bowl of a stand mixer, whisk together the flour, yeast, and sugar.

With the mixer fitted with the dough hook attachment and running at medium-low speed, gradually add the lard along with the water to the dry ingredients and mix until the dough forms a ball, 4 to 6 minutes. Add the salt and knead on medium speed until a firm but supple dough forms, 10 to 12 minutes.

Meanwhile, grease a large bowl with neutral oil or nonstick spray.

Pull the dough off the dough hook and form it into a ball. Transfer to the prepared bowl, cover the bowl tightly with plastic wrap, and let the dough rise at room temperature until doubled in size, about 1½ hours.

Dust a rimmed baking sheet with cornmeal and set aside. (This will help prevent the pan Cubano from sticking and add a nice crunchy bottom to your final loaf.)

Transfer the dough to a lightly floured work surface and pat it out to an 8-by-12-inch rectangle.

Starting with one of the longer sides, roll up the rectangle, pinching and pressing to make sure there are no bubbles. Pinch the seam underneath the loaf until you end up with a torpedo shape. Transfer the loaf to the prepared baking sheet. Cover with generously greased plastic wrap and let it proof at room temperature until doubled in size, about 1 hour.

Toward the end of the proofing time, preheat the oven to 400°F.

Score the dough lengthwise across the top and bake for 20 to 25 minutes, until lightly browned and the internal temperature at the thickest point registers about 200°F. Let cool completely, about 3 hours.

1

3

SANDWICH LOAF

Wonder® bread changed bread forever by blah blah blah I'm not going to vomit Wikipedia all over you. All's I can tell you is that sandwiches made with homemade sandwich bread are a *cut* above. Sorry, you left that one wide open for me. Every slice identical, as though pressed by a cookie cutter, with a hearty, squishy, soft, lightly sweet crumb ensconced in a buttery crown of tender crust? Toasted to an even, nutty brown, serving as the crunchy pulpit from which other ingredients can finally speak?! Homemade's forgiving nature and sheer superiority over store-bought make it a great loaf for beginners, while the incrementally superior results yielded from subtle, practiced improvements make it a loaf worth rehearsing. Can you rehearse bread?

How I've Screwed This Up

Many rookie mistakes—using the wrong loaf pan, shaping the dough incorrectly, measuring by volume vs. weight, over-proofing, under-proofing—have haunted my early loaves. Just like most any bread, attention to detail at every step is crucial and translates directly into a better end product.

Troubleshooting

MY LOAF IS SHORT 'N' STOUT. Lots of potential reasons why a loaf doesn't rise to the occasion: water's too cold, water's too hot, too much salt, too much flour, over-proofed, bad yeast, the geopolitical climate at the time of baking—about the best advice I have for you is to try again, paying extra-close attention to the detail of each step outlined in the recipe. Sorry, I know that's a disappointing answer.

MY LOAF SPILLED OVER THE EDGES OF THE PAN. If the loaf ripped slightly on the side, it was probably under-proofed, so the yeast freaked out in the oven and made the loaf kind of explode. If it just sagged over the sides, you're probably using too small a loaf pan.

MY LOAF HAS A TIGHT, CRUMBLY CRUMB. Sounds like your gluten was underdeveloped. Try adding 3 to 5 more minutes of kneading time to your next loaf, and make sure that the dough passes the sacred windowpane test (see page 32) before bulk fermenting (undergoing its first rise)!

MAKES ONE 8½-INCH LOAF

400 grams all-purpose flour

2 teaspoons instant dry yeast

25 grams sugar

1½ teaspoons kosher salt

50 grams melted unsalted butter, plus more for brushing

125 grams whole milk, warmed (75 to 80°F)

125 milliliters water, warmed (75 to 80°F)

Neutral oil (such as canola, vegetable, or grapeseed) or nonstick cooking spray, for greasing

In the bowl of a stand mixer, whisk together the flour, yeast, sugar, and salt.

In a medium bowl, whisk together the butter, milk, and water. Pour into the dry ingredients. With the mixer fitted with the dough hook attachment, mix on medium-low speed until a shaggy dough forms, 3 to 5 minutes. Scrape the sides and bottom of the bowl, if necessary, and pull the dough off the dough hook to make sure all of the ingredients are incorporated. Continue mixing the dough on medium speed until smooth and homogeneous, 6 to 8 minutes. The dough should pass the windowpane test (see page 32); if it doesn't, knead until it passes the test.

Transfer the dough to a well-oiled bowl. Cover with plastic wrap and let rise at room temperature until doubled in size, 1 to 2 hours.

Meanwhile, lightly coat a 9-by-5-inch loaf pan with oil or nonstick spray.

Punch down the risen dough and transfer it to a work surface. Shape the dough by gently pulling/pushing it into a rough rectangle, then folding each side into the center to form a seam. Roll the dough lengthwise until the seam is well sealed and about the length of the loaf pan.

Place the dough into the prepared loaf pan and loosely cover it with greased plastic wrap.

Let the dough proof at room temperature until risen above the sides of the loaf pan, 1 to 2 hours.

Toward the end of the proofing time, preheat the oven to 350°F.

Brush the proofed dough with more melted butter. Bake the loaf for 20 to 35 minutes, until golden brown and the internal temperature reaches 200°F.

Remove the loaf from the oven and immediately brush with more melted butter.

Let the bread cool completely before slicing. Store any leftover bread in an airtight container for up to 3 days, or in the refrigerator for up to 1 week.

ROTI

One of our earliest and most essential foods as human beings is unleavened flatbread. It contains the fewest ingredients of anything in this cookbook (just flour and water, salt if you're feeling spunky), but it is far from the most simple. A practiced hand knows the sweet spot where the gluten has developed enough to provide a nice chew, but not so much that it won't be able to be rolled paper-thin. Dough that's hydrated enough to just *barely* stick to the table, but dry enough to not need extra bench flour. A skillet hot enough to brown the outside without burning, but not so cold that the bread is dried out by the time it's cooked through. Like all bread, even this super-simple iteration only succeeds through a delicate balance of understanding how bread works. The good news is that it's about as cheap a food item as is feasible to make, so while practice makes perfect, at least it won't cost you this time!

How I've Screwed This Up

I was taught to make roti by the incomparable Floyd Cardoz, who sadly passed away in 2020. He was a strong, quiet, patient, and knowledgeable man, all qualities that reward bread in particular. So, when he came to my apartment and effortlessly cranked out four styles of Indian bread in a matter of hours, I was understandably discouraged by my own inability (or lack thereof). So now, when I inevitably get frustrated with dough, I try to channel Floyd: I take a deep breath, chill the F out, and remember that it's just bread.

Troubleshooting

MY ROTI ARE COMING OUT WEIRD. As with pancakes, virtually every batch of roti starts with a few funky ones. Misshapen, dry, burnt, whatever—by the third or fourth roti, you'll figure out how to roll them rounder and flatter, hit them with just the right temperature, and yank them off the flame before they burn. These guys go stale faster than modern clocks can calculate, so wrap them in a towel immediately after cooking so they can stay soft from residual heat and trapped steam.

MY ROTI WON'T ROLL OUT. You may have over-kneaded, toughening the gluten to the point where it doesn't want to stretch out. Try letting it rest for half an hour wrapped in plastic and try again. If the dough won't roll out because it's too dry, best to scrap and start over—it's very easy to add flour to a sticky dough, but very difficult if not impossible to add water to a dry dough.

MY ROTI IS DRY. If your roti has very light brown spots, your griddle likely isn't hot enough—really blast that thing with heat, it should be lightly smoking. If it starts off flexible and dries out, it's because you're not wrapping it in a towel to keep it soft!

MY ROTI TASTES STRANGE/OFF. Whole wheat flour has a much shorter shelf life than white flour, as short as one to three months. Give it a sniff—does it smell musty or sour? Toss it and start over!

MAKES ABOUT 8 ROTI

360 grams whole wheat flour, plus more for dusting if needed

9 grams kosher salt

275 to 300 grams hot water (about 160°F)

15 grams neutral oil (such as canola, vegetable, or grapeseed)

Bread flour, for dusting

Melted ghee, for serving

Minced garlic, for serving

In a stand mixer fitted with the dough hook attachment, mix together the whole wheat flour and salt until well combined. Add 275 grams of the hot water and the oil, and mix on medium speed until a slightly tacky dough mound forms, about 1 minute. If the dough is too dry, add more hot water as necessary.

Transfer the dough to a lightly floured work surface and knead the dough by hand until elastic, 12 to 15 minutes. The dough will not pass the windowpane test (see page 32) at this point.

Heat a large cast-iron skillet over medium-high heat to a surface temperature of 475°F.

Meanwhile, shape the dough into 8 golf ball–size balls, then roll out each one to a round, 10 to 12 inches in diameter and as thin as you can roll it without tearing.

Add one roti at a time to the preheated skillet and cook over medium-high heat until the roti is dry, 20 to 30 seconds on each side.

Move the skillet off the heat and, using tongs, carefully transfer the roti to the open flame, and cook until puffed, just a few seconds on each side.

Transfer the cooked roti to a plate, and cover with a clean dish towel to keep them warm.

Brush with melted ghee, sprinkle with minced garlic, and serve hot.

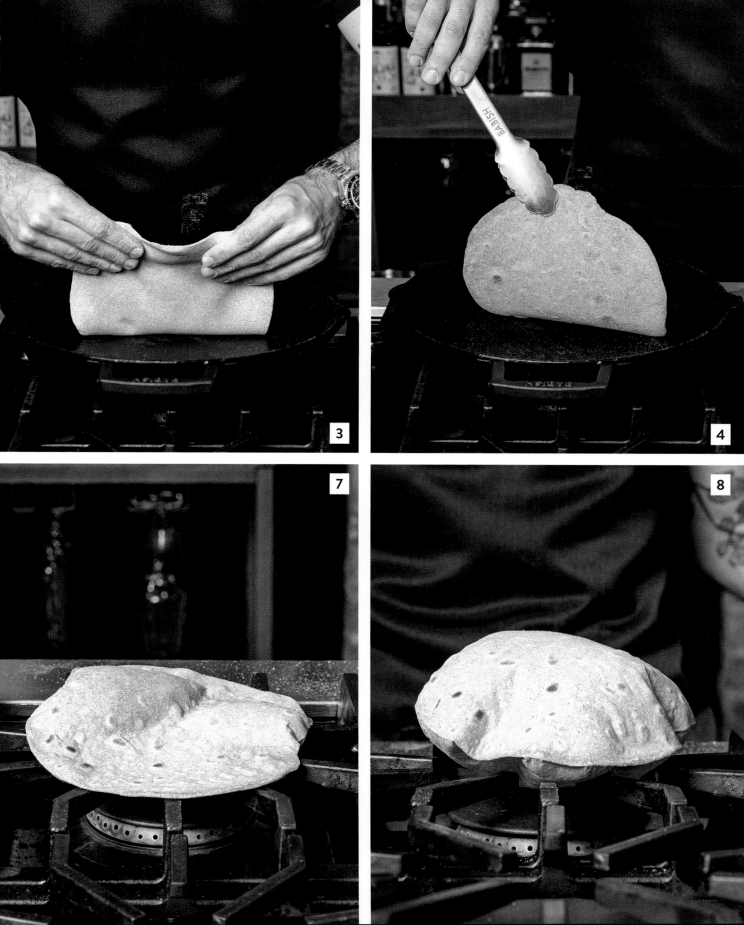

BRIOCHE DOUGH

Proper brioche is a rich, ethereal, luxurious experience. Crappy brioche is usually what you get the first time you make brioche (I sure did), so don't get discouraged if that's what you end up with. In addition to the proper gluten development, rising, shaping, and proofing that most great bread requires, this guy needs high-quality butter gently and patiently emulsified into its silky, sumptuous dough. Luckily, gluten development and emulsification go hand in hand, as the butter needs to be added one small piece at a time, until fully/visibly incorporated. This solidly three-minute-long process, plus the additional 5 to 7 minutes recommended kneading time, virtually guarantee that your brioche dough will pass the windowpane test (see page 32) with its buttery eyes closed. That sounded better in my head.

How I've Screwed This Up

My first time making brioche was in the "Rum French Toast from *Mad Men*" episode of *Binging*, and you can only charitably call it brioche. Lacking both a stand mixer and upper arm/core strength, I valiantly (not really) tried to knead together this notoriously tricky dough by hand, and ended up with outrageously underdeveloped gluten. In addition to an accidental over-proofing, I was doomed to a tight, crumbly crumb and a pallid, crackerlike exterior.

Troubleshooting

MY BRIOCHE IS SHORT AND CRUMBLY. Definitely underdeveloped gluten. Make sure to knead the dough for a solid 5-plus minutes after incorporating the butter, which should ensure that it passes the windowpane test (see page 32).

MY BRIOCHE HAS BIG AIR POCKETS IN IT. This could've come from any number of things, but my first suspect is the shaping process. Make sure that before shaping, you punch down the dough to lose any large air bubbles.

MY BRIOCHE STILL HAS BIG AIR POCKETS IN IT. Okay, then you might've used too much flour in the shaping process, which could cause gaps in the middle of the loaf that expand in the oven. Sticky dough could be over-hydrated or underworked, so try and nail your dough's texture first.

MY BRIOCHE STILL HAS BIG AIR POCKETS IN IT. Okay, then your kitchen might be too warm and causing the loaf to "over-spring," suddenly activating dormant yeast when it hits the oven. The ideal room temperature proof is around 75°F.

MY BRIOCHE STILL HAS BIG AIR POCKETS IN IT. Okay, then maybe you used too much yeast? Too much yeast can do that.

MY BRIOCHE STILL HAS BIG AIR POCKETS IN IT. Welcome to the world of bread.

Hamburger Buns

MAKES 6 BUNS

Brioche Dough

500 grams bread flour

7 grams instant dry yeast

25 grams granulated sugar

100 grams whole milk, warmed to about 85°F

200 milliliters water, warmed to about 85°F

10 grams kosher salt

85 grams unsalted butter, cubed and very soft (75 to 80°F)

Light olive oil, for greasing

Nonstick cooking spray, for greasing

Egg Wash and Finishing

1 large egg

1 large egg yolk

Pinch of kosher salt

White sesame seeds

FOR THE BRIOCHE DOUGH: In the bowl of a stand mixer, combine the flour, yeast, and sugar using a whisk or fork. Add the milk, water, and salt. With the mixer fitted with the dough hook attachment, mix the dough on medium-low speed until almost homogeneous. With the mixer running on medium speed, add the softened butter 1 cube at a time and mix until incorporated after each addition. Increase the speed to medium-high and mix until the dough is smooth, elastic, and clears the sides of the bowl, 6 to 8 minutes.

Transfer the dough to a large greased bowl and cover it with a clean dish towel or plate.

Let the dough rise until about doubled in size, 1 to 2 hours depending on the warmth of the room.

Line a baking sheet with parchment paper.

Remove the dough from the bowl and place it on a lightly oiled work surface. Divide the dough into 6 equal pieces and shape each into a bun by cupping your hands around the dough ball, moving in a circular motion, pressing the edges of the dough to pull the top smooth and taut. Transfer to the prepared sheet.

Loosely cover the buns and let the dough proof until puffed, 45 minutes to 1 hour.

Meanwhile, preheat the oven to 350°F.

FOR THE EGG WASH: In a small bowl, whisk together the egg, egg yolk, and salt until well combined. Brush onto the proofed buns and sprinkle with sesame seeds.

Bake for 30 to 35 minutes, turning halfway through, until the dough is cooked through (reaches an internal temperature of 200° to 205°F) and golden brown on top. Let the buns cool completely before slicing.

Herb-Garlic Monkey Bread

MAKES 1 LARGE TUBE OR BUNDT PAN, OR A LOAF PAN, OR 6 JUMBO MUFFINS

Brioche Dough

500 grams bread flour

7 grams instant dry yeast

50 grams sugar

100 grams whole milk, warmed (about 85°F)

200 milliliters water, warmed (about 85°F)

10 grams kosher salt

85 grams unsalted butter, cubed and very soft (75 to 80°F)

Light olive oil, for greasing

Nonstick cooking spray, for greasing

Flaky sea salt, for sprinkling

Herb-Garlic Butter

½ cup melted and cooled unsalted butter

¼ cup your choice of chopped fresh herbs, such as parsley leaves, chives, and/or dill fronds

3 to 4 garlic cloves, minced

Kosher salt and freshly ground black pepper

FOR THE BRIOCHE DOUGH: In the bowl of a stand mixer, evenly combine the flour, yeast, and sugar using a whisk or fork. Add the milk, water, and kosher salt. With the mixer fitted with the dough hook attachment, mix the dough on medium-low speed until almost homogeneous. With the mixer running on medium speed, add the softened butter 1 cube at a time and mix until incorporated after each addition. Increase the speed to medium-high and mix until the dough is smooth, elastic, and clears the sides of the bowl, 6 to 8 minutes.

Meanwhile, grease a large bowl with olive oil or nonstick cooking spray.

Remove the dough from the mixer and roll it into a taut ball on a lightly oiled work surface. Transfer the dough to the prepared bowl and cover with plastic wrap.

Let the dough rise until about doubled in size, 1 to 2 hours depending on the warmth of the room.

Meanwhile, generously spray 1 large tube or Bundt pan (or a loaf pan or a 6-cup jumbo muffin tin) with nonstick spray.

Transfer the dough to a lightly oiled work surface. Roll into a log, then divide and shape the dough into even golf ball–size portions. (If using a muffin tin, make portions half the size.)

FOR THE HERB-GARLIC BUTTER: In a medium bowl, combine the melted butter, herbs, and garlic. Season with salt and pepper and whisk together.

Roll each dough ball in the herb-garlic butter then place evenly in the prepared pan. Reserve the remaining butter for brushing the baked monkey bread.

Lightly coat a sheet of plastic wrap with nonstick spray and loosely cover the pan. Let the dough proof until puffed, 45 minutes to 1 hour.

Meanwhile, preheat the oven to 350°F.

Once the dough has proofed, remove the plastic wrap from the pan. Bake the monkey bread for 30 to 35 minutes, turning halfway through, until the dough is cooked through (reaches an internal temperature of 200 to 205°F) and golden brown on top.

Let the bread cool for 10 minutes, then flip onto a serving platter. Brush the dough with any remaining herb-garlic butter and sprinkle with flaky sea salt. Serve warm.

MARBLE RYE

Marble rye, apart from its *Seinfeld*-ian fame, is a study in sandwich success. Dark and light rye are very similar in flavor, so the swirl mainly stands to give visual flair to an otherwise bland-looking lunch, and the starkness betwixt the two is exaggerated with a hint of cocoa powder. It's also, according to my personal trainer friend, the very most nutritious of breads—at least the varieties that aren't half bird feed. It's high in fiber, high in flavor, and clearly I'm trying to pad this because I'm running out of things to say about rye bread. Just make it, it's good.

How I've Screwed This Up

As evidenced by my second *Seinfeld* special, I was not always proficient at making marble rye. My loaf came out tight, pale, and stalwartly antidentite—but since then, I've learned the virtues of proper proofing, not to mention a thorough egg-washing.

Troubleshooting

See Sandwich Loaf (page 56)

MY MARBLE RYE HAS BIG GAPS IN IT. You might've had too much flour on the individual doughs prior to rolling together, which can cause gaps between the two different colors.

MY MARBLE RYE WAS STOLEN BY A YOUNG MAN. Well you shouldn't have bought the last one when George is trying to fish for rye.

MAKES 1 LOAF

360 grams all-purpose flour, plus more for dusting

185 grams plus 1 tablespoon dark rye flour

45 grams potato flour

28 grams dried milk

1½ teaspoons onion powder

1 tablespoon caraway seeds

2¼ teaspoons kosher salt

2 tablespoons sugar

2 teaspoons instant dry yeast

400 milliliters water, at room temperature

35 grams vegetable oil, plus more for greasing

1 tablespoon unsweetened cocoa powder

1 large egg

1 tablespoon water

In the bowl of a stand mixer, whisk together the all-purpose flour, the 185 grams rye flour, the potato flour, dried milk, onion powder, caraway seeds, salt, sugar, and yeast. Add the room temperature water and the oil. Attach a dough hook to the stand mixer and knead on medium-low speed, until the mixture has come together into one cohesive dough, 5 to 8 minutes. Stop and scrape down the hook as it kneads if the dough starts to climb it.

Turn the dough out onto a lightly floured work surface and knead by hand for about 1 minute and form into a taut ball before dropping into a well-oiled large bowl. Cover with plastic wrap and let rise at room temperature until doubled in size, about 90 minutes.

Turn the dough out onto an unfloured work surface and divide in half. Wrap one half in plastic wrap and set aside.

In a small bowl, whisk the cocoa powder with the remaining 1 tablespoon rye flour. Combine it with the other half of the dough in the bowl of the stand mixer. Knead with the dough hook on medium-low speed, scraping down the dough hook, until everything is evenly mixed, about 3 minutes.

On a generously floured work surface, roll out the plain dough into a rectangle 12½-by-10 inches. Repeat with the cocoa dough.

Lay the cocoa dough on top of the plain dough, making sure there are no gaps between the two doughs, and roll into a tight loaf. Place seam side down in a well-oiled 13½-by-4½-inch loaf pan. Let proof under a loosely tented sheet of oiled plastic wrap until doubled in size, about 90 minutes.

Toward the end of the proofing time, preheat the oven to 400°F.

In a small bowl, beat the egg with the water. Brush onto the entire surface of the loaf. Using a bread lame or sharp knife, score the top of the loaf with 3 deep cuts.

Loosely tent the pan with aluminum foil and bake for 15 minutes then lower the oven temperature to 350°F and bake for 20 minutes. Uncover and bake for a final 5 minutes or until the internal temperature reaches 195 to 205°F.

Remove the bread from the loaf pan and let cool on a wire rack for 3 hours before slicing.

STEP-BY-STEP IMAGES, PAGE 70-71

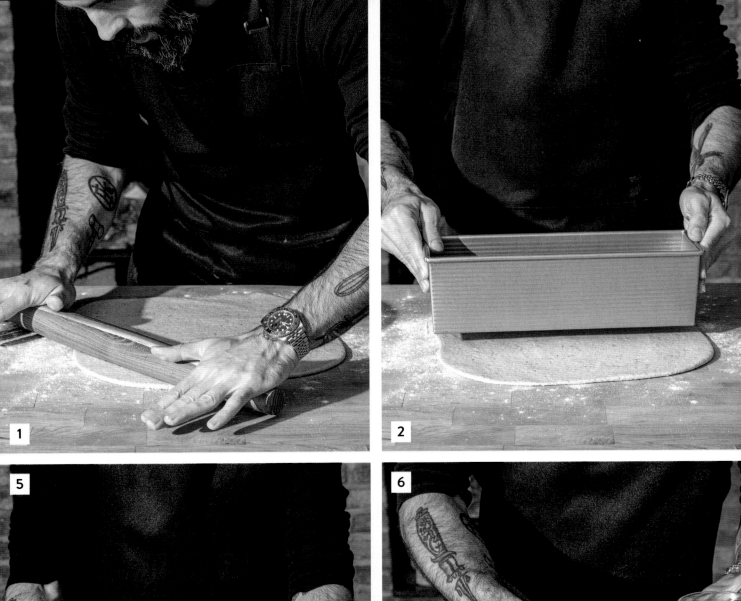

BAGELS

Being a New Yorker (technically, having lived here for the requisite minimum ten years), I prefer a dense, crunchy, chewy bagel, and I think we've developed a truly special recipe here. The days-long cold ferment not only lends flavor and texture to the dough, it yields a truly beautiful crust, dotted with a leopard print of bubbles and blisters. Whether it's stuffed with breakfast sandwich trappings or an uncomfortable amount of cream cheese, it's the ultimate expression of everything I ever hoped a bagel could be. What do you mean, "Babish, you're overselling this"? What do you mean, "Why did you repeat that?" What do you mean, "Why are you reciting my own full sentences back to me word-for-word? Are you going to repeat this one? Only one way to find out I guess"?

How I've Screwed This Up

Bagels are more forgiving than you'd imagine, but there are still many pitfalls: twisting in particular has given me agida, but I've also had issues with uneven baking and rising. I far prefer the two-fingers-through-the-center-and-twist-it-around-them-like-a-doughnut method of shaping, but the true New York way is to master the notoriously problematic twist-a-long-piece-of-dough-around-your-hand-and-join-the-seam-under-your-palm method.

Troubleshooting

MY BAGELS ARE BORING-LOOKING/-TASTING. The three-day cold ferment might seem like tedious overkill, but it's essential to this recipe. The long, chilly rise not only develops the flavor and gluten of the final bagel, it allows hundreds of bubbles to form under the "skin" on the bagel, creating that mesmerizing pattern on its surface.

MY BAGELS KEEP SPLITTING. Purists will scoff, but try forming the bagels by rolling it around two fingers. The old-fashioned bagel shoppe way of twisting a length of dough around your palm and pressing it together is wrought with issues, most notably uneven size and splitting seams!

MY BAGELS ARE BROWNING UNEVENLY. This is why I like to crank on the convection, if you've got it, during the final ten minutes of baking—don't do it while the bagels are still rising in the oven, as this will limit their oven spring. If you don't have convection, try and giving the bagels one to two extra rotations during their bake time, shuffling around the baking sheet if you have to in an effort to even out the heat.

I HATE NEW YORK BAGELS. I got nothin' to say to you.

MAKES 8 BAGELS

700 grams bread flour

1 teaspoon instant dry yeast

350 milliliters water, at room temperature

25 grams plus 1 tablespoon barley malt syrup

10 grams kosher salt

Vegetable oil, for greasing

1 teaspoon baking soda

MAKE THE STARTER: In the bowl of a stand mixer, combine 250 grams of the bread flour with the yeast and water. Mix into a paste using a rubber spatula, cover, and let sit at room temperature for at least 4 hours, or up to overnight.

Add the 25 grams barley malt syrup, the remaining 450 grams bread flour, and the kosher salt to the starter. With the mixer fitted with the dough hook attachment, mix at medium-high speed for 10 full minutes. Form into a taut ball and place back into the bowl. Cover with a damp kitchen towel and let proof at room temperature for 1 hour.

Line a rimmed baking sheet with parchment paper. Portion out the dough into 8 equal pieces, weighing 130 grams each, then roll each piece into a ball. Place on the prepared baking sheet, cover with a damp towel, and let sit at room temperature for 30 minutes.

Working with 1 piece of dough at a time, gently punch a hole through the middle using a thumb and widen it into a bagel shape using two spinning fingers.

Generously oil some plastic wrap and cover the bagels. Refrigerate for at least 24 hours, ideally up to 72 hours.

Preheat the oven to 425°F.

In a stock pot, combine 1 gallon water with the remaining 1 tablespoon barley malt syrup and the baking soda. Mix together and bring to a boil. Add the bagels straight from the fridge and boil for 20 seconds on each side.

Place on a lightly greased wire rack on a rimmed baking sheet and bake until you see spotty browning on the bagels, about 15 minutes. Flip the bagels and continue baking for an additional 10 to 15 minutes.

ENGLISH MUFFINS

Did you know that English muffins are simply referred to as "muffins" across the pond? It's true, I just looked it up. Anyway, so long as they're split with a fork, toasted, and drowned in butter, even store-bought English muffins are a thing of breakfastian beauty. A red squiggly line didn't suddenly appear under "breakfastian" when I typed it, so I'm going to assume it's legit from this day forth! Anyway, as great as store-bought can be, homemade is lightyears ahead. I actually just tweeted about the word "breakfastian," and Twitter seems to think it's misspelled—look up the tweet if you want to see exactly what day and time I wrote this headnote! Anyway, watching your homemade English muffins slowly rise in the heatwaves of a ripping-hot piece of cast-iron, while tricky, is a process as rewarding as it is delicious.

How I've Screwed This Up

The first time I made English muffins, it was in an ill-fated attempt to prepare eggs benedict from scratch for my then-girlfriend in her then-apartment, an Upper East Side broom closet with what could only charitably be called a kitchenette. If the scrambled hollandaise and ghostly poached eggs weren't bad enough, the muffins were wrong in quite literally every possible way. Underworked, over-proved, raw on the inside, burnt on the outside, with just a hint of rancidity from the years-old bottle of olive oil I used in the dough for some reason. (Yes, olive oil expires, see page 28).

Troubleshooting

MY ENGLISH MUFFINS ARE WOEFULLY LOW ON NOOKS AND CRANNIES. First off, you have my sympathy. Second, this is likely from underworked dough and/or underhydrated dough, two attributes that help give cavernous bubbles to a bread's interior.

MY ENGLISH MUFFINS ARE BURNT ON THE OUTSIDE, RAW ON THE INSIDE. Skillet's too hot!

MY ENGLISH MUFFINS ARE FLAT AND PALE. Skillet's too cold! You're shooting for about 300° to 350°F.

MY ENGLISH MUFFINS LACK AN ACCENT. Try this: Énglish muffins.

THAT WAS DUMB. Yeah it was.

MAKES 12 ENGLISH MUFFINS

625 grams bread flour, plus more for dusting

40 grams unsalted butter, softened

2 teaspoons instant dry yeast

1½ tablespoons sugar

1 tablespoon kosher salt

300 grams whole milk

135 milliliters water

Neutral oil (such as canola, vegetable, or grapeseed) or nonstick cooking spray, for greasing

Semolina flour, for the baking sheets

In a stand mixer fitted with the paddle attachment, combine the flour, butter, yeast, sugar, and salt. Mix on low speed until the butter is well distributed, 1 to 2 minutes. Add the milk and water. Switch the attachment to the dough hook. Mix on medium-high speed until the dough is relatively smooth and clears the sides of the bowl, 6 to 8 minutes. Transfer to a well-oiled large bowl and cover with a plate or damp towel. Let the dough rise in the fridge overnight.

(Alternatively, combine the dry ingredients in a large bowl. Then, add the wet ingredients and mix the dough by hand until homogeneous. Transfer the dough to a well-oiled large bowl, lift and fold the dough every 15 minutes for 1 hour. Then, cover the bowl and refrigerate overnight.)

Generously coat 2 large rimmed baking sheets with semolina flour.

Gently transfer the dough to a well-floured work surface. Divide into 12 (90-gram) pieces. Roll each piece into a round and transfer to the prepared sheets, leaving 1 to 2 inches of space between each round. Roll each round in the semolina flour to coat the top and bottom, then flatten with your hand to about ½ inch thickness.

Loosely cover the rounds with a greased sheet of plastic wrap or a lightly damp dish towel. Let proof until puffed, 1 to 2 hours at room temperature.

Preheat a large griddle or well-seasoned cast-iron skillet over medium heat to 300° to 350°F, 3 to 5 minutes. Decrease the heat to low.

Working in batches if necessary, carefully transfer the muffins, using a fish spatula, to the prepared cooking surface. Cook on the first side until golden brown and crisp, 5 to 7 minutes. Flip and gently flatten the muffin. Cook on the second side until golden brown and cooked through (internal temperature registers 200°F), 7 to 8 minutes. If the muffins are browning unevenly or too quickly, rotate the muffins 180° and/or turn down the heat.

Transfer the cooked English muffins to a wire rack to cool completely. Optionally, cover with a clean, dry dish towel and let them sit overnight. This firms them up a bit and allows for easier splitting and a better crumb.

Store the English muffins at room temperature for 3 to 4 days in an airtight bag or container and/or freeze the muffins in an airtight container for up to 3 months.

BABKA

Probably made most famous by *Seinfeld* (and included in my last book as such), this twisty labyrinth of chocolate (or cinnamon) is a decadent New York City staple. Channels of filling weave their way through a soft, enriched dough—and if you're lucky, it's ensconced in a crunchy, sweet streusel. As a brunchtime staple, it holds its own with little more than a cup of coffee, maybe a single strawberry for your health. It keeps nicely at room temperature, almost gaining character as it stales, eventually becoming the basis for a positively sinful French toast. No sugar needed for this breakfast bomb: all that chocolate (or cinnamon) will fry up beautifully with little more than an egg and milk slurry.

How I've Screwed this Up

The first few times I made this, I was certain the cutting/twisting/shaping would be my downfall, but it ends up being surprisingly forgiving. The real challenge here lies in nailing the bake time and temperature—there are few things more disappointing in life than a bone-dry or doughy-raw babka. This is a loaf you'll want to temp using an instant-read thermometer, not pulling it out of the sauna until it hits 185°F.

Troubleshooting

MY BABKA IS DRY.
You overbaked it.

MY BABKA IS RAW.
You underbaked it.

MY BOBKA DOESN'T LOOK QUITE RIGHT. You spelled it wrong that time.

MY BABKA ISN'T CHOCOLATEY/ CINNAMONY ENOUGH. Don't be afraid to really pile on that filling, your babka can handle it!

MY BABKA GETS MESSY WHEN CUT AND SHAPED. Make sure you chill your dough thoroughly so that the filling is no longer soft and the layers can be sliced cleanly. How you twist and shape your dough is up to you and the size/shape of your loaf pan, and it just takes some practice to get it right, but this might be the most forgiving part of the process.

MAKES TWO 9-BY-5-INCH BABKAS

550 grams (4½ cups) all-purpose flour, plus more for dusting

2½ teaspoons instant dry yeast

2 large eggs, at room temperature

160 grams (⅔ cup) whole milk, warmed (80 to 90°F)

55 grams (¼ cup) granulated sugar

2 teaspoons kosher salt

1 teaspoon vanilla paste (optional)

140 grams (10 tablespoons) unsalted butter, softened, plus more for greasing

Neutral oil (such as canola, vegetable, or grapeseed)

Chocolate Babka Filling, Cinnamon Sugar Babka Filling, or Everything Babka Filling (recipes follow)

Muscovado or turbinado sugar, for dusting (optional)

Streusel Topping (recipe follows; optional)

Egg Wash (page 64), for the Everything Babka

Simple Syrup (recipe follows), for the Chocolate Babka

In the bowl of a stand mixer, whisk together the flour and yeast.

In a medium bowl, whisk together the eggs, milk, granulated sugar, salt, and vanilla paste (if using). Pour into the dry ingredients and add the butter.

With the dough hook attached to the stand mixer, mix at medium speed until completely homogenous and a smooth, elastic dough forms, 6 to 8 minutes.

Turn the dough out onto an oiled work surface and gently shape into a rough rectangle. Wrap tightly in plastic wrap and refrigerate overnight.

Unwrap the dough and transfer to a lightly floured work surface. Divide into two equal pieces. Roll one piece into a 10-by-18-inch rectangle about ⅛ inch thick. Spread evenly with your filling of choice (see Note). Roll into a log, starting from one short side, and transfer to a parchment paper–lined baking sheet. Repeat with the other piece of dough. Freeze for 15 to 20 minutes, until the dough is firm.

Grease two 9-by-5-inch loaf pans with butter and line each with parchment paper. Optionally, apply more butter to the parchment paper and coat in muscovado or turbinado sugar (skip this step if making the Everything Babka).

Using a long knife, slice each log in half lengthwise. With the cut-side facing up, twist the two halves around each other.

Transfer the shaped babkas onto the prepared loaf pans. Cover with a damp towel and allow to proof until it about doubles in size, 1 to 2 hours.

Toward the end of proofing, preheat the oven to 350°F.

If using the streusel topping, sprinkle it all over the proofed babkas now (skip this step if making the Everything Babka). If making the Everything Babka, brush the top of the babka with egg wash now. Bake for 45 to 55 minutes, until the internal temperature reaches at least 195° to 200°F.

Remove from the oven and allow to cool for 10 minutes. Carefully remove the babkas from the pans and allow to cool completely before slicing. If making the chocolate babka, brush with the simple syrup before it cools.

Note: *Each of the filling recipes makes enough for two babkas. Feel free to make both babkas the same flavor or mix and match.*

STEP-BY-STEP IMAGES, PAGE 82-83

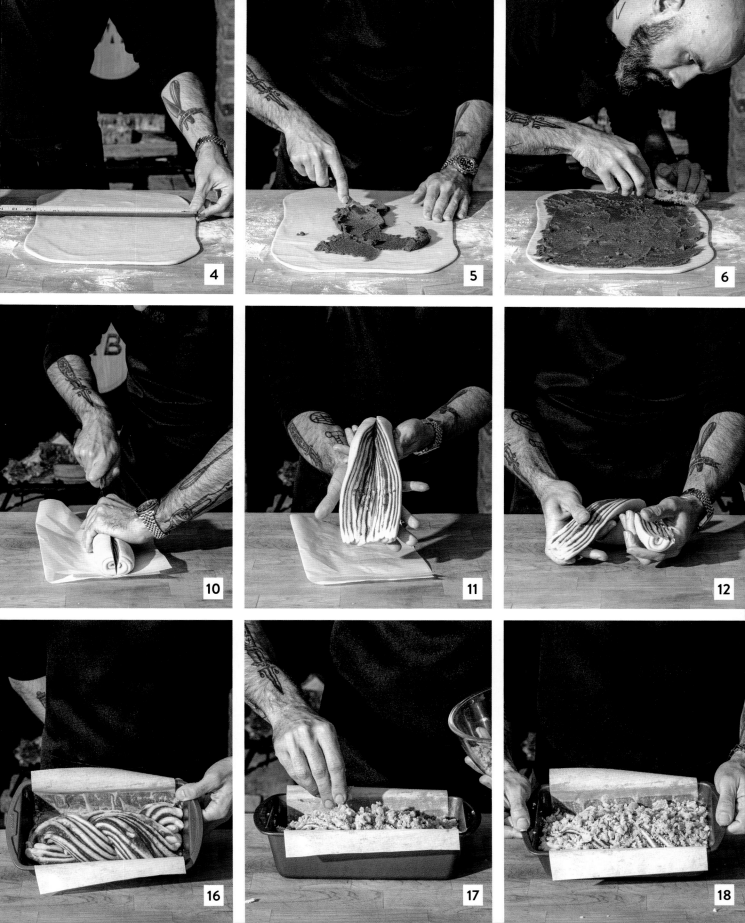

CHOCOLATE BABKA FILLING

115 grams (8 tablespoons) unsalted butter, cubed

190 grams dark chocolate, chopped

35 grams unsweetened cocoa powder

80 grams powdered sugar

½ teaspoon ground cinnamon

120 to 150 grams bittersweet chocolate chips

Melt the butter and chocolate over a double boiler.

Stir in the cocoa powder, sugar, and cinnamon.

Allow the mixture to cool and slightly thicken.

Set aside until ready to use, up to 4 hours.

Once spread onto the dough, finish with a sprinkling of the chocolate chips.

CINNAMON SUGAR BABKA FILLING

250 grams dark brown sugar

30 grams all-purpose flour

2 tablespoons ground cinnamon

½ teaspoon kosher salt

45 grams unsalted butter, melted

1 large egg white

Combine the sugar, flour, cinnamon, and salt in a small bowl. Stir to combine.

In a small ramekin, whisk together the melted butter and egg white. Pour into the cinnamon sugar mixture and fold to combine. Set aside at room temperature until ready to use.

EVERYTHING BABKA FILLING

2 teaspoons white sesame seeds

2 teaspoons black sesame seeds

1 teaspoon poppy seeds

1 teaspoon onion flakes

1 teaspoon garlic flakes

¾ teaspoon flaky sea salt

225 grams (one 8-ounce package) cream cheese, softened

60 grams unsalted butter, softened

In a small bowl, whisk together the sesame seeds, poppy seeds, onion flakes, garlic flakes, and salt.

In a medium bowl, fold together the cream cheese and butter. Add the everything seasoning and fold to combine.

Set aside at room temperature until ready to use, up to 4 hours.

STREUSEL

85 grams light brown sugar

60 grams all-purpose flour

½ teaspoon kosher salt

40 to 50 grams unsalted butter, melted

In a medium bowl, combine the sugar, flour, salt, and 40 grams butter and fold together, adding more butter as needed, until the mixture resembles sand.

Squeeze the mixture in the palm of your hand to create clumps of streusel. Set aside until ready to use, up to 4 hours.

SIMPLE SYRUP

¾ cup granulated sugar

¾ cup water

Combine the sugar and water in a small saucepan. Bring to a simmer over medium-high heat, then cover with a lid and cook for 1 to 2 minutes. This will help prevent crystallization.

Uncover and cook until the syrup reaches 225°F.

Allow the syrup to cool to room temperature before using. Can be refrigerated for up to 1 month.

BAGUETTES

These sleek, carby torpedoes are more than just the props proudly protruding from every grocery bag ever seen on film; when used for something other than their intended purpose, they can make an excellent comedic prop for a stereotypical French character. They're the last meal of choice for chefs the world over, and with good reason: when made well, with little more than a smear of salty butter, they're things of incontrovertible beauty. The very apex of this art form, in my opinion, is bookended with a pair of pointed, charred, practically sharp *le quignon* (the pointed ends of the baguette), characteristic of *baguette de tradition* or *baguette ancienne*. Is it just me or is this the sexiest paragraph of the book?

How I've Screwed This Up

Shaping and scoring are the name of the game with baguettes, and they're two things I'm decidedly bad at. These are skills born of patience and repetition, and while I've rolled my fair share of the finicky tubular bastards, they've come out very far from perfect. Popped seams, pale bottoms, ineffectual slashes, varying thicknesses like a bready earthworm: I've seen 'em all, and honestly, I've yet to whip up a perfect batch. Yes, I know this is strange to hear from the person whose recipe you're currently reading, but rest assured, the technique in this book is sound. Kendall, my Kitchen Producer, was a contributing author, after all!

Troubleshooting

MY LOAF LOOKS PALE AND BORING. Make sure you're allowing the dough to bulk ferment (undergo its first rise) at room temperature for at least 12 hours, ideally 18! Baguettes also love two things when they bake: lots of heat and moisture. It helps with oven spring (the amount by which the bread is able to grow in the oven before a crust sets), gives an open, airy crumb, and a positively crackling crust.

MY CRUMB IS TIGHT/TENDER. Sounds like your gluten is under-developed. Make sure the dough passes the windowpane test (see page 32) before giving it its half-day bulk ferment, which further helps develop your gluten network.

MY BAGUETTE IS MISSHAPEN. Here's where only practice can make perfect. Shaping and scoring baguettes is a process where the smallest subtleties can make a tremendous difference. Watch some videos, keep trying, and get yourself a bread lame for precise scoring!

MY BAGUETTE IS TOO SMALL. Happens to lots of guys. Luckily for you, it's not the size of the baguette that matters—what you just made is a demi baguette!

MAKES 2 DEMI BAGUETTES

Overnight Poolish

130 grams bread flour

⅛ teaspoon instant dry yeast

130 milliliters water, at room temperature

Baguettes

450 grams bread flour, plus more for dusting if using a couche for baking

2 teaspoons instant dry yeast

18 grams malt syrup

1 tablespoon kosher salt

285 milliliters water, at room temperature

Neutral oil (such as canola, vegetable, or grapeseed), for greasing

MAKE THE OVERNIGHT POOLISH: In a medium bowl, whisk together the flour and yeast. Add the water and whisk until no dry lumps remain. Cover and let sit at room temperature for at least 12 hours, up to 18 hours.

FOR THE BAGUETTES: In a large bowl, combine the flour and yeast. Quickly whisk together, add the malt syrup, salt, water, and the overnight poolish. Using a rubber spatula, mix together until just combined. Knead by hand in the bowl until a shaggy dough forms. (Alternatively, add the dough ingredients to a stand mixer fitted with the dough hook attachment.) Knead the dough on medium speed until the dough is smooth, elastic, and passes the windowpane test (see page 32), 6 to 8 minutes.

DUMP THE DOUGH ONTO AN UNFLOURED WORK SURFACE AND CONTINUE TO KNEAD VIA THE SLAP AND FOLD METHOD: Pick the dough up, slap it down on the work surface, and fold it onto itself. Repeat until the dough passes the windowpane test (see page 32), 8 to 15 minutes.

Shape the dough into a ball and place in a large bowl, cover with plastic wrap, and let rise for 2 hours at room temperature. Halfway through the rise, lift one edge of the dough and fold it into the center, rotating the bowl as you repeat this 5 times with another edge of the dough. (Optionally, refrigerate the risen dough for 1 to 3 days to cold ferment before proceeding with the next step).

After the rising time has passed, place the dough on a well-floured work surface and divide into quarters; pat each quarter into a rectangle, with one of the longer sides facing you. Working with 1 rectangle at a time, fold the side closest to you toward the center and repeat with the other side, then press down vigorously to seal the seam.

Repeat the process of folding over each long side of the rectangle toward the center, making sure to pat down to seal. Then using your hands, roll out from the center of each rectangle to form a log about 14 to 15 inches long, pressing harder at the ends to taper the dough.

To bake in a baguette loaf pan, place each baguette in the loaf pan then inside a proofing bag. Inflate the bag, tie it closed (or fold the excess underneath the pan), and let the dough proof for 45 minutes.

To proof in a couche, heavily flour a large linen cloth then fold to create trenches. Place each baguette in a trench, cover with a damp towel, and let proof for 45 minutes.

Toward the end of the proofing time, preheat the oven to 450°F with a pizza stone (see Note), if using, for 45 minutes.

When the proofing time is up, score three long diagonal slashes on top of each baguette using a razor blade, knife, or bread lame.

IF USING A PIZZA STONE: Place the baguettes directly on the pizza stone, spray them with water, and bake for 17 to 20 minutes, until the crust is a deep golden brown.

IF USING A BAGUETTE PAN: Place the baguettes in the oven, spray them with water, and bake for 22 to 25 minutes, until the internal temperature reaches 195° to 205°F and the crust is deep brown.

Let the baguettes cool for at least 20 minutes before slicing.

Note: *If you don't have a baguette pan or pizza stone, you can use a heavy baking sheet in place of the pizza stone.*

1

4

CHAPTER 2

PIZZA

They say there's no such thing as bad sex or bad pizza. I posit that whoever coined this phrase has *only* ever had bad sex and bad pizza, because that is some bullshit: granted, the floor on how bad something even resembling bread with cheese on it is incredibly high, but it's certainly not a floor I'd want to have sex on, if you get my meaning. You don't? Yeah, that metaphor didn't land. But seriously, doesn't "No such thing as bad sex or bad pizza" sound like some shitty dude came up with it? The same kind of lecherous mid-90s dotcom bubble-brat that says he likes his coffee how he likes his *[fill in the blank]*, and has decals on his jet ski?

I digress. Pizza, despite being an occasional source of contention (particularly over toppings), is primarily a unifier. When Valentine's Day candy has come and gone, love can be expressed with a different kind of flat, stout box full of delicious goodies. However loud partygoers greet an incoming guest is, at best, a quarter as loud as the cheer heard when the pizza finally arrives. "Detective Torres, warm up a pot of coffee and order us a pizza; this case isn't going to solve itself. If his latest riddle is to be believed, we've only got 12 hours until the flip-flop strangler strikes again." Its very form factor—divided into uniform, grabbable slices with a handy sauceless grip—suggests that which is shared communally by friends or family. Or at least so you don't have to roll it up into a pizza-burrito when you're eating one all by yourself. It's okay, we've all been there.

WHAT IS PIZZA? Ah, okay, we're doing this again—pizza, as we know it, was developed in Naples in the eighteenth or nineteenth century. Here, raw tomatoes were processed into a sauce, spread onto a wafer-thin sheet of a lean, high-hydration dough, topped with cheese, and cooked at an unreasonably high temperature until it produced one of those charred, bubbly food frisbees we now know so well.

WHY IS PIZZA—? Okay, we're not doing this again.

WHAT KINDS OF PIZZA ARE THERE? Thank you. While their base ingredients might only vary slightly, they produce more kinds of pizza than you can shake a proverbial stick at, most of which stem from regionality. The best variety, inarguably, is Lunchables when you're ten years old. Sure they might taste like melted tomato ice cream spread onto an oversized communion wafer, but when you're the only kid in the cafeteria holding, it's the closest most of us will ever get to experiencing real power.

MY PIZZA NEVER COMES OUT RIGHT—WHAT DO I DO? Pizza, being a kind of bread, is a fickle little bastard. It is indeed very difficult to make acceptable, much less top-notch pizza at home—different doughs require different treatment, home ovens are haplessly underpowered and hopelessly inaccurate, and Big Dairy has convinced us that it's okay to use pre-shredded cheese.

I CAN'T USE PRE-SHREDDED CHEESE ON MY PIZZA?
Absolutely not. This isn't me being a snob; do you ever make pizza (or anything baked with cheese on top), and the cheese comes out as a sort of dried-out blob, many of the shreds still having retained their shape? That's 'cause you went and used pre-shredded cheese, which is covered in anticaking agents like potato starch, preventing them from morphing into the gooey, stretchy cheese of our mind's eye.

WAIT, PIZZA IS BREAD? WHY ISN'T THIS PART OF THE BREAD CHAPTER? Because . . . I don't know. It feels like its own thing, doesn't it?

DOES PINEAPPLE BELONG ON PIZZA? When it comes to pizza toppings, I am a strict libertarian: Anything you do in the privacy of your own home, so long as it doesn't harm yourself or others, and so long as you do not indoctrinate or force your life decisions upon me, is your right and indeed your privilege. I will defend this right with my life—just don't ask me to try any.

IS A HOT DOG A SANDWICH? I think you have the wrong chapter but I see what we're doing here. I'll answer your question with another question: Is fire alive? It consumes energy and oxygen, it multiplies, it moves through its environment, it adapts to suit its environment, it has a finite life cycle. Despite having many of the characteristics of life, however, it is not alive, but for the seemingly pedantic requirement of life to have a cellular structure. So, on an entirely unrelated note, hot dogs are not sandwiches. Because they're hot dogs. If you ordered a sandwich at a restaurant and I handed you a hot dog without further explanation, depending upon your local laws regulations, you would be well within your right to place me under citizen's arrest.

IS A PIZZA A SANDWICH? No . . . are you okay?

PAN PIZZA

This is not only my favorite pizza recipe to make, but honestly, my favorite pizza full stop. It's got a thick, focaccialike crust, lightly fried in olive oil on the bottom and tender-chewy underneath all the sauce and cheese. It's an especially good platform for hundreds of greasy little roni-cups, cut from a whole stick of natural-casing pepperoni, barely adhered to the cheese so some inevitably end up on your plate for later snacking. It's a very high-hydration dough, so you might think it's too wet and slack, but this ensures that cavernous air bubbles form in its chewy crumb. Got leftovers? Heat it up in a covered pan, giving the pan a spritz of water occasionally to prevent burning and assist in remelting the cheese. If we're talking the morning after, fry up a runny egg for over top, and you've got yourself a heart-healthy breakfast.*

How I've Screwed This Up

Most of my pan pizzas have come out great, as it's a very forgiving recipe; but there have certainly been exceptions. Dry, pale crusts from too little oil in the pan have been the most frequent culprit, but I've also been too shy with my cheese, denying me the lacy, crunchy edges normally enjoyed on a pan pizza's crust. Make sure that cheese is all the way up to and over the edges of the dough for dominion over Domino's!

Troubleshooting

MY CRUST IS PALE AND BORING. You might want to try an aluminum pan or baking sheet—if your pizza stone isn't sufficiently preheated (or if your oven isn't pulling its weight), the crust won't get the blast of heat it needs, and you'll end up with Wonder bread on the bottom.

MY PIZZA IS SHORT WITH A TIGHT CRUMB. It sounds like the dough was underhydrated—this should be an extremely wet, sticky dough. Make sure you don't add extra flour because you think it seems too wet!

MY PIZZA IS STICKING TO THE PAN. No way are you using enough fat—this pizza should be swimming in olive oil, ensuring both a crunchy and effectively nonstick crust.

MY PIZZA WON'T STRETCH TO THE EDGES OF THE PAN. Cover it with plastic wrap for 15 minutes to let the gluten relax and try again—you want this spread as evenly and thinly as possible, because, brother, it's gonna puff!

HONESTLY, I'VE NEVER BEEN A FAN OF CHEESE, SAUCE, AND BREAD TOGETHER. I mean that's your preference, but maybe this just isn't your chapter of the book!

*This statement is not evaluated by the FDA, Surgeon General, or any other body of authority or knowledge.

MAKES ONE 10-INCH PAN PIZZA

240 grams bread flour

2 teaspoons instant dry yeast

170 milliliters water

1 tablespoon light olive oil, plus ¼ cup for the skillet

4 grams kosher salt, plus more for the tomatoes

1 (14-ounce) can whole San Marzano tomatoes

8 to 12 ounces low-moisture mozzarella cheese, shredded or torn

4 to 6 ounces pepperoni, thickly sliced

½ to 1 ounce Parmesan cheese, freshly grated

In a large bowl, whisk together the bread flour and yeast. Add the water for a dough with a hydration of 70%. Next, add the 1 tablespoon olive oil to add flavor and shorten the gluten strands. Mix with your hands to combine. Then, add the salt and continue mixing until no dry spots remain. Lift one edge of the dough and fold it into the center, rotating the bowl as you repeat this 5 times with another edge of the dough. Let the dough rest in an oiled container, covered, in the refrigerator for at least 8 hours, up to 24 hours.

Generously grease a 10-inch cast-iron skillet with the ¼ cup olive oil. Carefully place the chilled ball of dough in the skillet. Flip the dough once to coat it with oil and gently press it out to fill the bottom of the skillet. Depending on how cold your dough is, you may experience some resistance. If so, cover with plastic wrap and let it rest for 15 minutes before trying again. Once shaped, it should be out of the refrigerator for about 1½ hours before topping and baking.

To begin, preheat a pizza stone in the oven at 550°F for at least 1 hour, ensuring that the bottom of the pizza gets blasted with enough heat to make it crisp.

In a food processor, roughly purée the tomatoes and add a generous pinch of kosher salt.

Once the dough has proofed, use your fingers to gently deflate the dough. Then top with a generous layer of the tomato purée and a thick layer of mozzarella, making sure to sprinkle it all the way out to the edges for a cheesy crunch on the outside. Add some slices of pepperoni and top everything off with some freshly grated Parmesan.

Transfer the skillet to the pizza stone and bake anywhere from 10 to 15 minutes, rotating once halfway through.

Let the pizza rest for at least 10 minutes to absorb the oil. If the bottom of the crust is not crunchy enough, cook it in the cast-iron skillet on the stovetop over medium heat until the bottom is crisp, 2 to 3 minutes. Slice and serve as desired.

NEW YORK–STYLE PIZZA

Ah, New York. The city I'm legally allowed to say I'm from (having lived here for at least ten years, as is the custom. Did I make this joke in an earlier headnote? I think I did). The land of a million yellow taxis (ten years ago), clanging subway tokens (twenty years ago), and the raging floods from multiple annual hurricanes (ten years from now). Where "I'm walkin' here!" can be legally used as a defense in court. The land of the giant, thin-crusted, lightly sauced, heavily cheesed, two-oily-paper-plate slice dusted with dried oregano and chili flakes. Whereas Neapolitan pizza is a high-hydration, lean dough cooked at an unspeakably high temperature (950°F), New York–style incorporates a bit of enrichment in the form of sugar and oil, spending a little more time in a comparatively balmy 600° to 700°F oven. The method here, while adapted for the home oven, would still feel right at home in those car-size pizzeria metal monstrosities.

How I've Screwed This Up

Well, jeez, where to start? How about with my "New York–Style Pizza" episode of *Binging*? Between the dough not having been stretched out thin enough and my oven being too cold, it ended up thick and pale, mocked incessantly (and correctly) for its chodelike appearance. The fact is, to get a slice even resembling New York–style pizza out of your home oven, you're going to have to get serious about it. You need either a high-quality stone or, preferably, a pizza steel. You need to max out your oven for a solid hour to ensure that your pie gets absolutely blasted with heat from below. You need a big ol' goddamn peel, and need to have a dough with strong enough gluten to stretch out paper-thin upon it. You need to practice gently shuffling the dough onto the stone, with just enough flour or semolina so that it doesn't stick or become misshapen, but not so much that a pile of it is left charring in your oven. Like most breads, it's an uphill battle: a delicate balance of heat, confidence, and (seemingly) unnecessarily fussy technique that yields diminishing returns. It's like rock scrambling: I see someone trying to run as fast as they can, *uphill*, over a labyrinth of alternately steep and jagged rock faces, and I think "Why does this person hate themselves so much?" Meanwhile, they'll pull out their waterproof rock-watching binoculars or whatever, and look down at me gingerly arranging foil-wrapped fire bricks in the commercial oven I've (inadvisably/illegally) tweaked to cough up an extra hundred sweltering degrees, singeing my knuckle hair off in exchange for one pale, doughy failure after another. And they'll think the same thing.

Troubleshooting

MY PIZZA IS SQUAT AND PUFFY. You need to get this dough just about as thin as you can manage—this will both deflate the larger bubbles and give you a giant, thin-crust pizza. Make sure your gluten is very well-developed!

MY PIZZA IS BURNT. Good job! But is the crust browned or blackened? Some black char marks are desirable, especially on the bottom—browning, however, actually makes me think your oven is too cold, because the pizza didn't look "done" enough and you left it in there too long at too low a temperature.

MY PIZZA IS TOO FLAT. Pizza's supposed to be flat, but if you mean that your crust is also flat, then okay we have a problem. About the only reason I can think that your crust didn't rise is dead yeast or seriously overproofing.

MY PIZZA IS EXTREMELY EXPENSIVE, CROWDED, PUNISHINGLY HOT IN THE SUMMER, CRIPPLED BY SNOW IN THE WINTER, IT SAYS IT'S IN AN "OPEN MARRIAGE" AND WE CAN ALL TELL IT'S DOING COKE IN THE BATHROOM. That's New York, baby!

MAKES TWO 14- TO 16-INCH PIZZAS

500 grams bread flour, plus more for dusting

25 grams sugar

10 grams kosher salt

2 teaspoons instant dry yeast

300 milliliters ice water

1 tablespoon light olive oil, plus more for greasing

2 to 3 cups Pizza Sauce (depending on sauce-to-cheese ratio preference; recipe follows), cooked

16 ounces low-moisture mozzarella cheese (shredded or torn)

In a food processor, combine the flour, sugar, salt, and yeast.

In a large liquid measuring cup, combine the ice water and oil.

Pulse the flour mixture together a few times just to combine everything. With the machine running, stream the water and oil mixture through the feed tube and process until a ball of dough forms. This should give you a dough with a hydration of about 60%.

Lightly oil a container, a work surface, and your hands. Knead the dough until it cohesively comes together in a very soft and smooth mass. Form it into a taut ball then transfer to the oiled container and cover with a lid or inverted baking sheet. Let rise in the fridge overnight to improve the dough's texture and flavor.

Divide the chilled dough in half and stretch it into two taut balls. Transfer to a lig htly floured rimmed baking sheet or proofing box, cover, and let proof for about 2 hours at room temperature or until it is light and easy to work with.

IF USING A PIZZA OVEN: Preheat the oven to 700°F an hour into the proofing time. If using a home oven, see opposite page.

Flour both your work surface and the dough itself; generously flour a pizza peel and set aside. Pat one of the dough balls out into a round as wide as possible with your fingers. Leave a very small rim around the edge that will eventually become the crust.

Begin gently and slowly stretching the round by passing it knuckle over knuckle until it is as thin as you can get it, which in this case, is 14 to 16 inches in diameter. Place the stretched out round on the prepared pizza peel.

Top the round with half of the pizza sauce in a thin even layer, leaving a border around the edge, followed by half of the mozzarella.

Shuffle the pizza from the peel into the oven and bake until the exterior is deeply browned and the cheese is melted and golden brown, 5 to 7 minutes. Rotate the pizza often and make sure to pop any air bubbles before taking it out of the oven once the exterior is deeply browned and the cheese is melted and golden brown.

Let the pizza rest for 5 minutes before slicing and serving.

IF USING A HOME OVEN: Preheat the oven to 550°F with a pizza stone or steel on the very top rack for at least 1 hour an hour into the proofing time.

Shuffle the pizza from the peel onto the stone and bake until the exterior is deeply browned and the cheese is melted and golden brown, 7 to 10 minutes. Rotate the pizza halfway through baking to ensure even browning.

Let the pizza rest for 5 minutes before slicing and serving.

Repeat shaping, topping, and baking with the second round of dough, or wrap and refrigerate for up to 5 days. Bring to room temperature before shaping.

PIZZA SAUCE

Makes 3 cups

1 (28-ounce) can whole San Marzano tomatoes

2 to 3 tablespoons light olive oil

½ white onion, finely chopped

Few garlic cloves, minced or crushed in a garlic press

Pinch of crushed red pepper flakes

Shake of dried oregano

Shake of dried basil

2 to 3 tablespoons tomato paste

1 tablespoon sugar

In a large bowl, using your hands, crush the tomatoes with their juices until the pieces are bite-size. Set aside.

In a high-walled sauté pan, heat the olive oil over medium heat until shimmering. Add the onion and cook, stirring, until translucent around the edges, 2 to 3 minutes. Add the garlic and cook, stirring, until fragrant, about 1 minute. Add the red pepper flakes, oregano, basil, and tomato paste. Cook, stirring, until fragrant, 1 minute. Add the tomatoes with their juices and the sugar. Simmer over medium heat, stirring regularly to prevent scorching, until the raw tomato flavor is cooked off and the sauce is thick, 20 to 30 minutes. You know it's thick enough when you drag a spoon through the sauce and it parts.

CHICAGO-STYLE PIZZA

The debate as to whether or not Chicago-style pizza is, indeed, pizza at all rages on to this day. But I'm here to settle it: just because you don't like something doesn't mean it isn't a thing. I'm ready to say publicly (and in the comfortable obscurity of a recipe headnote) that, even as a New Yorker, I love Chicago-style pizza. What's not to love?! Its crust lacks the chew of my native pie, but it's so positively loaded with toppings that it needs a thick, biscuitlike crust just to contain it all. It holds more cheese in its bready vault than in all of Switzerland, a single slice can sustain a hobbit for an entire day, and even when delivered through the brutal winters of Chicago, it somehow arrives hotter than when it left. Jon Stewart famously quipped "Some people say there's no such thing as bad sex or bad pizza—[Chicago-style pizza] is like sex with a corpse made of sandpaper." I might not be as good of a writer (or person) as Mr. Stewart, but damn it, I'll defend *this* pizza-bread bowl with my life.

How I've Screwed This Up

It's honestly pretty tough to screw up Chicago-style pizza! The crust is very forgiving, and the rest of it is just melted cheese and toppings—so as long as the thing is cooked through and the cheese is melted, it's certainly not going to be bad. In fact, I'd say it has the most success stories of anything I've ever been tagged in on Instagram. That being said, I have thoroughly destroyed a pie by using too coarse a grind of cornmeal, giving it both a gritty texture and distinctly corny taste.

Troubleshooting

MY PIZZA IS RAW ON THE BOTTOM/BURNT ON TOP.
Unlike most other pizzas, Chicago-style is best prepared slow 'n' low, giving plenty of time for the crust to cook through and the cheese to melt.

MY PIZZA FLOWED LIKE A MOLTEN LAVA CAKE. You gotta give this guy a few minutes to set up after baking—it'll still be plenty hot 'n' good after the requisite 15-minute cooling off period!

I DON'T LIKE CHICAGO-STYLE PIZZA. Then what . . .? Why . . .? Just go make another pizza.

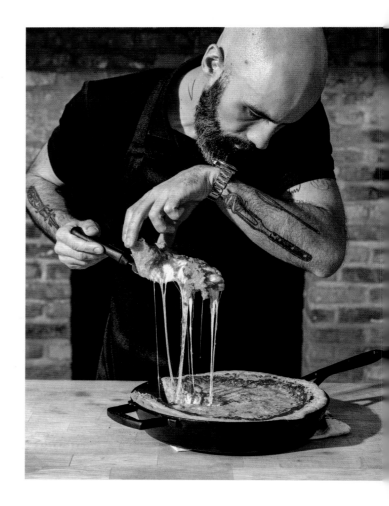

MAKES ONE 12-INCH DEEP-DISH PIZZA

240 milliliters water, at room temperature

7 grams active dry yeast

1 teaspoon sugar

354 grams all-purpose flour, plus more for dusting if necessary

70 grams medium-grind cornmeal

1½ teaspoons kosher salt

⅛ teaspoon cream of tartar

⅓ cup plus 2 tablespoons vegetable oil, plus more for greasing

Pizza Sauce (page 101)

1 pound sweet Italian sausage, uncooked, casing removed (optional)

8 slices deli-style Provolone cheese

16 slices deli-style low-moisture mozzarella cheese

Pre-grated Parmesan, for sprinkling

Light olive oil, for drizzling

In the bowl of a stand mixer, combine the water, yeast, and sugar. Let bloom until foamy, about 10 minutes.

In a large bowl, whisk to combine the flour, cornmeal, salt, and cream of tartar. Pour into the yeast mixture, then add the vegetable oil. Fit the mixer with the dough hook attachment and mix on low speed until the dough clears the side of the bowl, 1 to 2 minutes. Then knead at medium speed until smooth and elastic, 7 to 8 minutes. If the dough is too hydrated (aka sticky), lightly flour a work surface and knead by hand until the dough is soft and tacky, but not sticky, 1 to 2 minutes.

Stretch the dough into a ball and transfer to a lightly oiled bowl, tossing to make sure it's fully covered in oil. Cover the bowl with plastic wrap and let sit at room temperature until the dough is doubled in size, 60 to 90 minutes.

Grease a 12-inch cast-iron skillet with vegetable oil. Grease your hands and coax the dough out of the bowl and into the skillet. Push into the shape of a pizza by stretching and pushing the dough up to the sides. Cover with plastic wrap and let rest for 20 to 30 minutes to let the gluten relax.

While the dough rests, you can start your pizza sauce and preheat the oven to 425°F with a pizza stone or steel on the bottom rack.

Press the dough to the sides of the skillet, and it should easily hold its shape. **OPTIONAL:** crumble the sausage into a nice even layer on the dough before adding the cheese. Layer on the Provolone, shingling the slices around the skillet, followed by the mozzarella. More cheese = more cheese stretch!

Generously top the cheese with the pizza sauce until the cheese is hidden. Then, sprinkle the Parmesan over the sauce and drizzle the olive oil on both the sauce and around the edge of the crust.

Transfer the skillet to the preheated stone and bake, rotating once halfway through, until cooked through, 25 to 35 minutes. Run a thin spatula around the outside edge to make sure that there's no sticking. Slide the pizza out of the skillet and wait at least 15 minutes before cutting and serving. Enjoy!

NEAPOLITAN-STYLE PIZZA

The original, most Italian, and therefore fussiest of all pizza recipes, Neapolitan-style is a notoriously difficult pie to master. It's an unenriched dough, so it's by far the least forgiving, and requires the perfect balance of gluten development and cold-fermentation to achieve the right flavor and texture. You thought the windowpane test (see page 32) was hard? Now try stretching out an entire ball's worth of pizza dough to the same barely-there membrane of dough. Oh, you want to make this in your home oven? *Mi fai schifo!* You need an oven handed down through generations, hand-built with bricks from Calacatta and fired with violin wood from the dwindling forests of Paneveggio! Okay, but seriously, you do need an oven that can get mighty hot; Neapolitan-style pizza's moisture content and lack of sugar/fat turn it into a pale cracker in ovens shy of 800°F. Luckily, real-deal pizza ovens are becoming more and more affordable, so this is becoming an accessible option for home cooks. That being said, if you want to use the ol' range at 450°F, you might want to stick to Pan Pizza for now.

How I've Screwed This Up

My god, how *haven't* I screwed this up? As I mentioned in the book's introduction, I made a feeble attempt to churn Neapolitan-style pizza out of my home oven in the first "Pizza" episode of *Basics*, and it shows. Pale, flat crust with burnt cheese is perhaps the most infuriating combo as a home pizza chef. But even years later, I still manage to output inferior pies now and again: even a week ago at the time of this writing, I didn't age my dough long enough and didn't roll it out thin enough, and ended up with a thick, doughy disc. So keep at it!

Troubleshooting

MY PIZZA IS THICK AND DOUGHY. You ain't stretched it out thin enough. Before applying any toppings, the dough should be so thin that you're certain it's going to tear, but it just barely doesn't.

I DON'T LIKE RAW TOMATOES. Well there's very little of it, and it's going in such a hot oven, it'll be fully cooked by the time it comes out! That being said, use the sauce of your choice, but be prepared for Italians to sneeze at/on you.

MY PIZZA IS BURNT. Good job! But is the crust browned or blackened? Some black char marks are desirable, especially on the bottom—browning, however, actually makes me think your oven is too cold, because the pizza didn't look "done" enough and you left it in there too long at too low a temperature.

MY PIZZA HAS A POOL OF LIQUID IN THE CENTER. This, believe it or not, is actually a "desirable" trait in some circles, as it's indicative of super-fresh mozzarella— that being said, I get it, you don't want wet pizza. Make sure to drain every drop of excess liquid from your tomatoes before blending, and feel free to cook the tomatoes for 30-some-odd minutes to thicken the sauce. If that still doesn't work, use a lower-moisture mozzarella.

MY PIZZA IS THIN IN THE CENTER, BUT HAS A HUGE/ BUBBLY CRUST. You need to get the entire pie super-thin—your crust can be ever so slightly thicker, but even if it's uniformly thin, it will still puff up nicely when not weighed down with toppings. Make sure the entire ring is as thin as you can physically get it.

LA MIA PIZZA NON HA IL SAPORE CHE FACEVA MIA MAMMA. *Allora, vai a chiamare tua mamma!*

WHY DOES ITALIAN LOOK BETTER IN ITALICS? I think you just answered your own question.

MAKES SIX 12-INCH PIZZAS
(if making fewer, you can store or cold ferment the leftover dough in the fridge for up to five days)

850 grams bread flour, plus more for dusting

12 grams instant dry yeast

550 milliliters water

17 grams kosher salt

Light olive oil, for greasing

1 (28-ounce) can whole San Marzano tomatoes, drained

24 to 36 ounces fresh mozzarella cheese, shredded or torn

Fresh basil leaves, for topping

In a large bowl or the bowl of a stand mixer, whisk together the flour and yeast. Add the water and combine with your hands or dough hook attachment, if using a stand mixer. Next, add the salt then knead the dough by hand for 15 to 20 minutes, or in a stand mixer fitted with the dough hook attachment until the dough is smooth, elastic, and passes the windowpane test (see page 32), 8 to 10 minutes.

Place the dough into a large oiled bowl and cover with plastic wrap. Let the dough rest at room temperature for 2 hours. Or, for a cold ferment, let the dough rest in the refrigerator for 3 to 5 days.

Divide the dough into 6 equal pieces by weight to ensure accuracy. Shape each piece into a ball by rolling the dough between your hands and pinching the edges down underneath the dough itself until each piece is as round and taut as possible. Transfer to a lightly floured rimmed baking sheet or a proofing container. Cover and let proof at room temperature until the dough spreads out but doesn't quite double in size, about 1 hour if you made the dough the same day or 1½ to 2 hours if the dough is refrigerator cold.

Toward the end of the proofing time, preheat your pizza oven to 932°F.

Flour both your work surface and the dough itself; generously flour a pizza peel and set aside. Pat one of the dough balls out into a round as wide as possible with your fingers. Leave a very small rim around the edge that will eventually become the crust.

Begin gently and slowly stretching the round by passing it knuckle over knuckle until it is as thin as you can get it, which in this case, is about 12 inches wide. Place the stretched out round on the prepared pizza peel.

Using an immersion blender, purée the drained tomatoes in a large high-sided container or bowl. (Alternatively, puree the tomatoes in a blender.) Add a generous pinch of kosher salt.

Top the round with the pureed tomatoes and mozzarella as desired.

Shuffle the pizza from the peel into the pizza oven and bake until the dough is puffed, set and a deep speckled brown and the cheese is melted and just beginning to brown in a few places, only about 1 minute. Rotate the pizza often and make sure to pop any air bubbles before taking it out of the oven. Once it emerges from the oven, top it off with some freshly torn basil leaves. Slice and serve as desired.

CHAPTER 3

PASTA

While this chapter may be primarily pertaining to pasta, what I really want to talk about are starches. "Starches" is the most boring term imaginable used to describe maybe the most delicious stuff in this book. Pasta? Check. Rice? Check. French fries? Fuckin', *check*. If it's chewy, crispy, fluffy, creamy, and/or instinctually satisfying, there's a high likelihood starches are involved. We're primordially programmed to seek out and enjoy starches, because like most of the great pleasures in life, they're bad for us. The building blocks of carbohydrates and sugars, they're dense sources of energy, ending up as fat deposits in our ever-expanding bodies. But whatever, this stuff tastes so good that even when it's bad, it's still pretty good. The vast majority of recipes in this chapter revolve around pasta because not only is it one of the few things I can confidently, competently, consistently make well, but because you can, too. Pasta is one of the great comfort foods, indulgent and satisfying but light enough so that, after dinner, you can still get busy . . . doing the dishes. Dishes, of course, being a coy euphemism for furious lovemaking. So roll up your sleeves and get ready for that uncomfortable sensation when flour gets stuck in your actual fingerprints. Let's make some pasta!

WHAT IS PASTA? Pasta is a cooked dough made out of basically any imaginable iteration of two elemental ingredients: starch and liquid.

WHAT IS STARCH? You might as well ask me why it's so delicious: it's carbohydrates! The gluten-free gluten (as I like to incorrectly call them), these pasty polysaccharides aren't just responsible for the very foundation of the food pyramid: they're a building block of sugar, the makers of things like dessert and alcohol, the creators of creaminess in your favorite risotto or mashed potatoes, the powdery spray that makes your shirts stiff. They're everything right and wrong with unchecked capitalism, the bedrock of both basic need and wanton excess, the alpha and the omega, the omnipresent I Am.

IS STARCH GLUTEN? No—foods like russet potatoes, even though they're high in starch, are entirely gluten-free. Starch can sometimes behave like gluten, forming networks and chemical bonds when subjected to kneading, but isn't the same and cannot act alone as a substitute for gluten.

IS STARCH A SUGAR? Honestly I'm Googling this shit as I write it, you should probably refer to someone who knows what they're talking about.

IS THAT BECAUSE YOU'RE RUNNING OUT OF QUESTIONS TO ANSWER ABOUT STARCH? Wow, especially considering your questions in the first two chapters, you are surprisingly perceptive. Yeah, I know I talked a big talk about starches up front, but I blew most of my material on the introduction. Passionate though I may be, it's more from a conceptual standpoint than an intellectual one.

GOOD, THAT WAS GETTING DRY, I'LL CHANGE THE SUBJECT. SHOULD I GET A DOG? Now there's a question I can answer! If you have the space, financial security, time, and inclination to give a good home to a dog, then hell yes you should get a dog. I'd get one myself but my stairs are super slippery and I'm worried about a clumsy pupper taking a tumble on them. Plus we have three cats, so.

SHOULD I GET A CAT? That's honestly a more subjective question—dogs tend to love enthusiastically and unconditionally, while cats are much more reserved in sharing their affection. Personally, I like the gunslinger relationship you often have with a cat, but it's probably because I identify with them: I, too, am a solitary creature that likes to retreat and recharge from socializing, so I respect a cat's need for independence.

SHOULD I HAVE KIDS? Alright I appreciate that this chapter heading is going off the rails, but now I feel like you're messing with me.

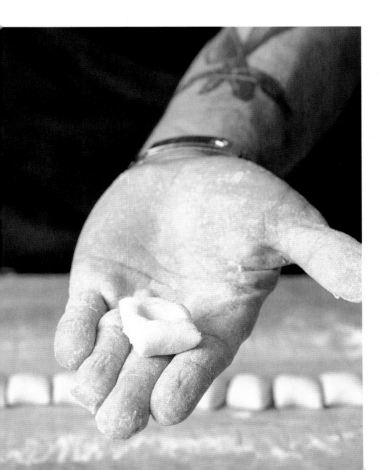

NO SERIOUSLY—I HAVE A GREAT JOB (IT'S NOT MY DREAM JOB OR ANYTHING, BUT IT PAYS WELL AND THE HOURS ARE FLEXIBLE), I LIVE IN A QUIET NEIGHBORHOOD WITH GOOD SCHOOLS, AND I'M NOT GETTING ANY YOUNGER . . . Well first off I think we're veering back into "Andy shouldn't be answering this question" territory, because I'm not sure if I'll ever be ready to have kids. It makes me feel selfish sometimes, but the fact is that I can barely take care of myself, much less someone who is wholly dependent on me. But that being said, I understand why people have kids—beyond it being our biological imperative, some people just have more love in their hearts than they can give to any one person. I feel like when obligation enters into the mix, that's when you could face issues with resentment, which no one wants to be on the receiving end of. So forget school systems and jobs—*why* do you really want to have a kid?

I DON'T KNOW HOW ELSE TO EXPLAIN IT, I JUST FEEL KIND OF . . . READY. I WANT TO BRING SOME SMALL AMOUNT OF BEAUTY INTO THE WORLD. I'M JUST SCARED THAT I WON'T BE A VERY GOOD PARENT. Let me stop you right there—I think that kind of fear alone indicates that you're going to be a good parent. *Everyone* thinks that they're going to be a bad parent, but so long as you're even a modicum of improvement over the generation that raised you, then you've done it right. No one is a perfect parent, everyone screws up, and we all have various traumas from our childhood, these things are unavoidable. Being aware of your capacity to make mistakes, however, helps make you aware of their potential as learning experiences. Only you can tell if you're ready—but for what it's worth, I think you'd make a great parent.

HEY, THANKS. THAT ACTUALLY MEANS A LOT. Now, you ready to make some pasta?

FRESH PASTA DOUGH

When I was a youth, I labored under the delusion that so often plagues newcomers to the kitchen: "Fresh pasta is better than dried." Not so! Both have their strong suits, weaknesses, and myriad applications. As you've no doubt already read and reread in the Kitchen Glossary (page 23), many dried pastas offer flavors, textures, and shapes that aren't achievable with the fresh variety. Likewise, fresh pasta stands out (and is often downright essential) in other recipes. The real difference lies in homemade vs. store-bought—homemade pasta offers greater control and, once made semicompetently, runs circles around the stale and flavorless vacuum sleeves of machine-excreted pasta. Okay, that's too harsh—the store bought stuff isn't bad at all, but a dough conjured into being by your own hand has a specialness to it. An occasionality. A joie de vivre.

Making pasta by hand is a practice only achieved through one thing: practice. You need to know what good pasta looks, feels, and eventually tastes like. You need to see a smooth, matted glow in your marigold-yellow dome of freshly kneaded dough. You need to feel a bounciness as the tacky-but-not-sticky dough grows ever-thinner. You need to feel a toothsome bite in the cooked pasta's flesh, not quite hard but again not quite soft. Don't plan on your first batch coming out perfectly, and that's okay! It might cost you time and effort, but it won't cost you too much money; a bag of flour and a dozen eggs will furnish a full day's practice and enough pasta to feed an army. Any surplus will freeze handsomely and standby ready to be cooked from frozen at a moment's notice.

How I've Screwed This Up

Every imaginable way. Pasta that's chewy, pasta that's soft, pasta that's gluey, and pasta that's tossed. Pasta that's pale, pasta that's flabby, pasta that's frail, and pasta that's shabby. Pasta not even a mother could love, pasta that's stony and cold—pasta that couldn't pass for a glove, pasta that's covered in mold.

Troubleshooting

MY PASTA IS TOO SOFT. Underdevelopment of gluten—pasta dough needs to be kneaded until smooth and bouncy. Roll your dough into a ball and press your finger into it—does the divot stay put or spring back quickly? If the former, you knead to keep needing. Sorry—you need to keep needing. Sorry—you knead to keep kneading. Sorry—you need to keep kneading. I know that sounds repetitive, but it's the only way to achieve a cohesive and toothsome pasta.

MY PASTA IS GUMMY OR CHEWY. It could be undercooked, but more likely, it was overworked—this is especially common if you're making your pasta by machine. I also recommend laminating the pasta (rolling it out, folding it in thirds, and rolling it out again) to develop gluten in a less labor-intensive way, but this can result in chewy pasta if you overdo it.

MY PASTA IS STICKY. Too wet! Keep working flour into the dough generously until it feels like it *might* be verging on too dry. Flour needs time to hydrate, and the dough will soften as moisture is absorbed during the initial 30-minute resting period. It's also far easier to add flour than to add water: You can dust the dough with flour while laminating it in the roller until the perfect consistency is achieved.

MY PASTA IS CRUMBLY. Too dry! Not all moisture in pasta needs to come from eggs, you can try to add water after the fact, but it can be very difficult to incorporate too late in the game.

MY PASTA IS TEARING WHEN I RUN IT THROUGH THE MACHINE. This occurs when there's either too little gluten development or you're rolling it out too thin too quickly—or both! Laminate two to four times, dust with flour if it feels gummy, and see if it rolls out better.

MY PASTA DIDN'T COME OUT RIGHT THE FIRST TIME. Yeah, no shit.

MAKES 12 OUNCES OF DOUGH

225 to 275 grams all-purpose flour, plus more for the pasta rolling machine

140 grams eggs

1 teaspoon kosher salt

In a food processor, combine 225 grams of flour, the eggs, and salt. Process until a dough forms, about 1 minute. If the dough is sticking to the sides of the machine, add the remaining flour as necessary and process until well incorporated.

Remove the dough and form it into a ball. Wrap tightly and let rest for at least 1 hour at room temperature or up to overnight in the fridge.

Using a pasta rolling machine, work in batches to roll out the dough, starting on the widest setting then decreasing the size by two settings with every roll. If the dough feels gummy, dust with flour. Roll until the dough reaches the second thinnest setting (or to your preference).

Cut, fill, and shape the dough as desired.

1

5

9

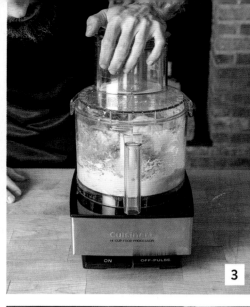

TRENETTE AL PESTO

Here's one of the classic Italian dishes prepared for *Binging* that we're borrowing for *Basics*, mostly because we covered it so expertly and flawlessly that it wouldn't warrant revisiting. I'm kidding, please don't throw a brick through my window. Trenette, a microscopically wider cousin to linguine, is an absolute requirement for the dish to come out correctly. I'm kidding again, you could really use any variety of pasta you like—in fact, this dish is a bit easier to eat with a shorter pasta like fusilli. Something you absolutely cannot do without, however, is Ligurian olive oil, without which your pasta won't even turn out edible, much less delicious. I should stop kidding, you're going to not know when to trust me. The buck stops here. Important things in this recipe are: fresh basil, high-quality ingredients, and an olive oil that's light and fruity, rather than intense and spicy. Less important things in this recipe are: the size/shape of your noodles, the use of a mortar and pestle, and cooking your pasta with or without the use of water. Sorry I had to get one more in there.

How I've Screwed This Up

Like I mentioned before, my first and only attempts at trenette al pesto were impeccable in every sense of the word. Or was it?! In fact, my first pesto broke in the mortar and pestle, as I had added the oil too quickly. Luckily, a quick spin in a food processor will make short work of a broken pesto!

Troubleshooting

MY PESTO HAS A DISTINCT CRUNCH TO IT. You gotta wash your basil better, bud. More than most any other herb at the supermarket, basil has a tendency to arrive with a sometimes imperceptible coating of sandy soil. Thoroughly rinse and pat it as dry as possible, making sure not to squeeze the basil too hard, which can bruise it.

I'M ALLERGIC TO PINE NUTS. The beauty of pesto is you can use pretty much any nut (or herb, for that matter) that suits your fancy! Try stuff like sunflower seeds, walnuts, pecans—go "nuts."

MY PESTO TURNED BROWN. That's a tale of oxidized basil if I've ever heard a tale of oxidized basil. Pesto quickly loses color after an enzyme it contains is exposed to oxygen, so you've got two options: Eat it within twenty-or-so minutes of making it, which shouldn't be a problem. Or if you want to make pesto to keep in the fridge for a spell, you can either pack it in oil or blanch the basil briefly before plunging it into ice water, which deactivates the enzyme and preserves the basil's bright green color after processing.

MY PESTO IS TOO THICK. You can thin it out with a bit more oil, but if your pesto is a greasy paste, you might've over-processed things. Ideally, pesto has a somewhat smooth but textural texture, with little bits of garlic, cheese, and nuts still intact.

MY PESTO IS BITTER. If you made it in a food processor, my first guess would be that it was over-processed, which can embitter high-quality olive oil. You also might be using too much garlic, or your garlic itself may be too strong. Try using fresh, young garlic—if your garlic has been hanging around a while, try removing the greenish germ that often sprouts through its center. Your nuts may also be rancid, give them a big ol' sniff before using them. Do they smell like crayons? Toss them and make something else. Same with the olive oil—does it smell like a wet basement? Throw it away, it will ruin anything it touches.

I HONESTLY CAN'T THINK OF ANYTHING ELSE. Don't you usually ask me a slightly absurd question at the end I can answer with my trademark dry wit?

UH . . . MY PESTO EXPLODED! Can you respect the process please?

SORRY. HOW ABOUT—MY PASTA HAS POTATOES IN IT FOR SOME REASON. WAS THAT INTENTIONAL? Yeah it was. Long story, don't ask.

BETTER? Better.

SERVES 4 TO 6

2 teaspoons kosher salt

10 ounces yellow skin potatoes

5 ounces green beans, trimmed

1 pound trenette pasta (see Note) or dried fettuccine

Pesto Formula (page 123)

Extra-virgin olive oil, for drizzling

4 to 6 fresh basil leaves, for garnish

Bring a large pot of water to a boil. Add the salt.

Meanwhile, peel and cut the potatoes into 1-inch cubes.

Cut the green beans into 1-inch pieces.

Once the water is boiling, add the potatoes and cook over medium-high heat for 4 minutes. Add the pasta and cook according to the package directions until the pasta is al dente. In the last 3 to 4 minutes of cooking, add the green beans. Reserve about 1 cup of the pasta cooking liquid.

Drain the pasta, potatoes, and beans once cooked and transfer to a large bowl. Add the pesto and about ¼ cup of the reserved pasta water. Toss to combine, adding more reserved pasta water as needed to emulsify the sauce.

Serve the pasta in bowls, drizzle with olive oil, and garnish with the basil leaves.

Note: *If using a quick-cooking dried trenette pasta, in step 4, add the potatoes to the boiling water and cook for 10 minutes, then add the green beans and cook for 2 minutes more. Then, add the pasta and cook for just 2 more minutes.*

PESTO FORMULA

You might be asking yourself, especially if you're taking the trouble to read this headnote, "Why did they name this recipe 'pesto formula' instead of just 'pesto'?" Well the answer may fascinate you—or more than likely it won't—while traditional pesto may be strictly relegated to basil, pine nuts, garlic, Parmesan, salt, and oil, pesto *as a concept* can be made from and its ingredients substituted with virtually whatever similar looking thing you have around the house. Don't have any basil? Grab almost any leafy herb or green and mash it up all the same. Are pine nuts too expensive? I am literally struggling to think of a nut that wouldn't work in any given pesto. Are you on a *Chopped*-style cooking show competition and you've been given a basket of stinging nettles, Gruyère, water chestnuts, linseed oil, and gummy worms? The gummy worms are a curveball substitution for garlic, but honestly, I still think a pesto is your best bet. It won't win you any new Italian friends, but experimenting with pesto is not only an excellent use of leftovers and oddities in the fridge, it's a solid exercise in the culinary application of emulsion (see page 24). Here, you are breaking down and emulsifying all the solid ingredients into the oil, endeavoring to suspend their tiny particles weightlessly in a billion uncountable bubbles, bringing playful and consistent flavors to anything they touch.

How I've Screwed This Up

I've used shelf-stable jarred pesto before, so, that's how.

Troubleshooting

MY PESTO IS BITTER. More likely than not, your pesto was over-processed. Olive oil's polyphenols, while touted for their health, can release some bitter compounds when mechanically agitated to an irresponsible extent.

MY PESTO IS OILY. Your pesto's texture tells you just how strong your emulsification game is: if you're left with a bowl of bruised, wilted greens sitting squat in a pool of oil, different ingredients were likely added too early, too quickly, or with too little agitation. If you're having difficulty using a mortar and pestle, give this recipe a shot in a blender or food processor.

MY PESTO IS TOO THICK. Splash of oil never hurt nobody!

TELL THAT TO THE OCEAN. Wow. Dark.

MAKES ABOUT 1 CUP

1 garlic clove

1 ounce nuts of choice

1 teaspoon kosher salt

2 ounces greens and/or herbs of choice

1½ ounces cheese of choice, grated, plus more as needed

2½ to 3½ ounces extra-virgin olive oil, plus more if storing pesto

MORTAR AND PESTLE DIRECTIONS: In a mortar, combine the garlic, nuts, and salt. Using the pestle, muddle the ingredients in a circular motion until a paste forms. Add the greens, and using the pestle, pound into the garlic paste until the greens are broken down. If the greens are taking a while to break down, add a splash of the olive oil. Add the cheese and combine using the pestle. Add a small amount of the remaining oil at a time, pounding in between additions to combine, until the pesto reaches your desired consistency. If your pesto begins to break, add another sprinkling of grated cheese and combine.

FOOD PROCESSOR DIRECTIONS: In a food processor, combine the garlic, nuts, and salt. Pulse until the ingredients are the consistency of sand. Add the greens and cheese and process until combined. With the machine running, slowly pour the olive oil down the feed spout. Continue processing until the pesto is thoroughly combined and homogenous.

Use the pesto immediately or transfer to an airtight container. Before closing the lid, top the pesto with a thin layer of olive oil to prevent discoloring. Store in the refrigerator for up to 1 week.

1

4

TARRAGON SHRIMP SCAMPI

Shrimp scampi isn't *necessarily* a pasta dish, but here in the States, it's what we usually associate it with. It produces a garlicky, lemony, shrimpy sauce that's irresistible to emulsify with butter and toss with eggy, fresh pasta. In the search for spectacular scampers, Kendall and I developed a combination of herbs and some clever techniques to make the best damned scamps my taste buds have had the pleasure to come across. It may come off as a bit involved for a simple pasta dish, but trust me: you don't want to skimp on this scampi. Did some *Seinfeld* fan fiction just write itself? *"George, you're telling me that she skimped on the scampi?" "She's a scampi skimper, Jerry! She's the skipper of the scampi-skimping schooner!" "You know you can't skip a scampi." "Can't skip a scampi?" Can't skip a scampi, George, no matter how much said scampi has been skimped upon" "[George's panicked breathing] . . . George is getting a scampi!"* More like a Seinfeld fever-dream.

How I've Screwed This Up

The first time I attempted shrimp scampi, I was in high school and had very little seafood freshness awareness. Luckily my would-be-future-but-now-ex-mother-in-law gave the critters a sniff before I threw them in the pan, an emergency Thai takeout order was placed, and I had learned a valuable lesson in food safety. Since then it's been pretty smooth sailing, but the dry, stringy texture of an overcooked shrimp still occasionally plagues my plate.

Troubleshooting

MY SCAMPI IS OILY. Sounds like your sauce needs a hefty splash of pasta cooking water and some spirited agitation! Like any of the emulsified sauces in this book, there's a reliance on a delicate balance of water, fat, and movement (kind of like me). If your sauce is all fat, it ironically needs water to become smooth and creamy.

MY SHRIMP ARE TOUGH. The brief dry brine with salt and baking soda both seasons and tenderizes the shrimp (also helps them to brown better), but no amount of chemical prevention can protect you from overcooked shrimp. The FDA recommends 145°F, which will kill off any dangerous bacteria, but leave you with a tight and rubbery little curly crescent of crustacean no longer worth consuming. It may slightly increase your chances of foodborne illness or whatever, but I don't let shrimp go above 120°F at their thickest point.

I'M HONESTLY HARD-PRESSED FOR ISSUES WITH THIS RECIPE! That's so nice to hear! We worked hard on this recipe to make the absolute best scampi we had ever tasted. Glad to hear you like it.

THAT BEING SAID . . . Uh-oh.

I'M DEATHLY ALLERGIC TO SHELLFISH. Shit, seriously? Somebody call somebody!

SERVES 2 TO 4

1 teaspoon baking soda

Kosher salt and freshly ground black pepper

1 pound fresh large shrimp (31/35 count), peeled, deveined, and shells reserved

1 cup dry white wine

1 bay leaf

½ teaspoon whole black peppercorns

8 tablespoons (1 stick) unsalted butter, divided

½ cup panko bread crumbs

3 tablespoons light olive oil

6 to 8 garlic cloves, thinly sliced

½ teaspoon red pepper flakes

1 large shallot, minced

½ pound fresh fettuccine

Juice of 2 lemons

2 teaspoons chopped fresh tarragon leaves

1 tablespoon chopped fresh marjoram leaves

3 tablespoons chopped fresh parsley leaves

Zest of 1 lemon

In a medium bowl, combine the baking soda with 1 teaspoon salt. Add the shrimp and toss to combine. Allow the shrimp to dry brine at room temperature 20 to 40 minutes.

In a small saucepan, add the wine, bay leaf, peppercorns, and reserved shrimp shells. Bring to a simmer and continue cooking over medium heat until the wine is reduced by half, 5 to 10 minutes. Strain and set aside until ready to use.

Fill a large pot two-thirds of the way full with water and add 1 tablespoon salt. Bring to a boil.

Meanwhile, melt 2 tablespoons of the butter in a medium skillet over medium heat. Add the panko. Cook, stirring occasionally, until toasted, 4 to 6 minutes. Set aside until ready to serve.

In a large skillet, heat the olive oil over medium-high heat until shimmering. Add the shrimp one at a time in a single layer and cook for 30 seconds on each side, then transfer to a plate. (The shrimp will continue to cook later.) Add the garlic, red pepper flakes, and shallots. Cook, stirring, for 1 minute. Add the reserved infused wine, lower the heat to medium, and continue cooking for 3 minutes more.

Meanwhile, add the pasta to the boiling water and cook according to the package directions until al dente.

Add the remaining 6 tablespoons butter to the sauce in the skillet and allow to melt fully, then add the lemon juice. Stir to combine. Add the shrimp back to the skillet to finish cooking. Taste the sauce, then add salt and freshly ground black pepper to taste.

Using tongs, transfer the cooked pasta to the skillet directly from the pot, reserving all of the pasta water. Using the tongs, stir the pasta into the sauce. Add ¼ cup of the reserved pasta water, then stir the pasta until the sauce becomes thick, glossy, and homogenous. If the sauce becomes too thick or separates, stir in another ¼ cup of the pasta water.

Finish the pasta with the toasted panko, fresh herbs, and lemon zest.

BLENDER MAC AND CHEESE

A mac and cheese recipe in a Basics cookbook, just what exactly the hell are we gonna do here? This is well-worn territory: America's Test Kitchen has a stovetop mac so easy, it's literally on the table faster than Kraft. Every imaginable iteration, twist, and mash-up has been done and redone, recreated and reviewed, wrapped up in bacon and deep-fried on a stick. What could we possibly add to the pantheon of knowledge that's been built, tested, and retweeted within an inch of its life? How about a blender?

That's right folks, "Blender Mac and Cheese" is more than just a clickbait title (does that work in a book?). After learning to "carbonara anything" on the show (and on page 136), it didn't take long for me to try it out with cheddar and milk. The result is something certainly fussier than anything out of a box or a tube, but certainly less so than a roux, producing an impossibly smooth sauce and porny cheese stretches.

THE CHEESE DIDN'T MELT. If you add the cheese too late in the process, there's the danger of things not melting according to plan. You can carefully return it to low heat, stirring constantly, microwave for a few 15-second bursts, or even add more cheese and bake it, pretending that was your plan all along.

MY SAUCE BROKE. Ain't no saving it—if it's chunky from cooling and sitting around, try reconstituting it with a splash of milk, but if it somehow broke during cooking, it's toast forever. Try again!

THERE ISN'T ENOUGH SAUCE. This is hard to imagine considering the amount of milk being put to work here, but depending on your pasta's size and shape, it may absorb more or less liquid as it cooks. Don't be afraid to add a bit more milk to the sauce if needed.

TOO MUCH SAUCE! It may look like a frightening amount of sauce at first, but especially if you're going on to bake your mac, it seldomly ends up being too much.

MY SAUCE IS THIN. When fresh 'n' hot out of the blender, this sauce may have the consistency of heavy cream, but as it cools and is supplemented with more shredded cheese, it thickens to the perfect consistency.

MY SAUCE COAGULATED. This happens! Splash of milk, a rigorous stir, and maybe even a little heat will bring things back to life.

STILL CLUMPY. While it's very hard to cook the egg yolks in this sauce, it is still possible, so try not to cook the sauce for too long after adding it to the pot.

I CALL IT "ELBOW PASTA." That's weird, and you know it's weird, because why else would you choose to tell me that? I was just fine not knowing that about you.

SERVES 4

3 large egg yolks, beaten

1 teaspoon Dijon mustard

¼ teaspoon cayenne pepper

8 ounces mild cheddar cheese, shredded

5 ounces Monterey Jack cheese, shredded

5 ounces Gruyère cheese, shredded and divided

4 cups whole milk, plus more if needed

Kosher salt and freshly ground pepper

16 ounces elbow macaroni

In a blender, combine the egg yolks, mustard, cayenne pepper, 6 ounces of the cheddar, 4 ounces of the Monterey Jack, and 4 ounces of the Gruyère.

In a large high-walled skillet or saucepan, bring the milk to a boil over medium-high heat. Stir in 2 teaspoons salt. Add the pasta, then reduce the heat to medium low and cook, stirring occasionally to avoid scorching the milk, until the pasta is al dente according to the package instructions.

Drain the pasta, reserving the pasta cooking milk. Pour the milk into a pitcher. Transfer the pasta back to the skillet.

With the blender running, gradually pour the reserved milk into the egg-cheese mixture and blend until the sauce is smooth, 30 to 45 seconds. Pour the cheese sauce over the cooked pasta and stir to combine.

Fold the remaining 2 ounces mild cheddar, 1 ounce Monterey Jack, and 1 ounce Gruyère into the mac and cheese. It will look as though there is too much sauce, but it will thicken as it cools.

Season with salt and pepper, then serve. If the sauce thickens too much, just add more milk until the desired consistency is achieved.

Baked Mac and Cheese

SERVES 4

3 ounces panko bread crumbs

¾ ounce Parmesan cheese, grated

3 tablespoons unsalted butter, melted

Kosher salt and freshly ground pepper

Blender Mac and Cheese (page 130), prepared in an oven-safe pan or transferred to a 9-inch square baking dish

Preheat the oven to 400°F.

In a medium bowl, combine the panko, Parmesan, and butter. Stir until the mixture resembles wet sand. Season with salt and pepper. Sprinkle over the mac and cheese.

Bake 15 to 20 minutes, until the sauce is bubbling and the panko is toasted.

Allow the mac and cheese to cool 5 to 10 minutes before serving.

CACIO E PEPE

I'm having a hard time thinking of a recipe as simple as cacio e pepe that's also as easy to irreparably screw up. Despite having only five ingredients in its most traditional state, it can turn out decidedly delicious or repetitively revolting. While the addition of fat (in the form of butter, oil, or cream) will earn you the ire of Italians, it not only makes the dish remarkably easier, it mellows out the harshness of the cheese and pepper and adds richness to the sauce. We've opted for both olive oil and butter, which not only brings a diversity of flavor, it increases your odds of success by about tenfold. For an even more foolproof sauce, take a page out of Luciano Monosilio's book (literally) and emulsify the cheese, butter, oil, and pasta cooking water together in a blender, then add it to some very al dente pasta in a sauté pan and finish cooking them together. His method makes the sauce virtually impossible to break!

How I've Screwed This Up

Oh, brother. How about most of the times I've made it? Its most traditional version requires that the cook nail a very narrow margin of temperature, one that heats and melts the cheese without breaking it. Being an extremely imprecise person, this has historically given me an astronomical failure rate. Once finally giving up and adding fat, however, I can count on one hand the number of times I've screwed this up—and when I have, alcohol was probably involved, and it still probably ended up getting eaten anyway.

Troubleshooting

MY CACIO E PEPE IS BROKEN. This is usually a death sentence for cacio e pepe, and while you're probably better off starting over, you might be able to save it by adding more pasta cooking water to the situation. This liquid gold's starch and general wateriness can repair a fat/water emulsion like the creamy sauce of cacio e pepe, but there's only so much it can do if you've got clumpy globs of half-melted pecorino.

MY CACIO E PEPE IS GREASY. This just means your sauce isn't fully emulsified—in this case, you can most likely save it with some pasta cooking water. You're going to end up using more than you think you need, so be sure not to discard it!

MY CACIO E PEPE IS TOO SPICY. Believe it or not, raw black pepper can be kinda spicy! Sautéing it in the butter can both pronounce its flavor and dial back its heat, so be sure to add it to the skillet before adding the pasta.

MY CACIO E PEPE GOT ME IN TROUBLE WITH AN ITALIAN FRIEND. You might as well tell me that you got bruises from cage-fighting: this is as expected as it is inevitable.

SERVES 4 TO 6

16 ounces tonnarelli (or spaghetti)

Kosher salt

1 tablespoon extra-virgin olive oil

1 tablespoon unsalted butter

2 teaspoons coarsely ground black pepper, plus more for garnish

4 ounces Parmigiano-Reggiano, finely grated

4 ounces Pecorino Romano, finely grated, plus more for garnish

Bring a 12-inch high-sided skillet of water to a boil. Add 1 tablespoon salt, then the pasta, and cook according to the package directions until ust shy of al dente.

Meanwhile, in another large skillet, heat the olive oil and butter together until the butter melts. Add the coarsely ground pepper and cook, stirring occasionally, for 30 seconds over medium-low heat. Using tongs, add the cooked pasta, reserving the pasta cooking water. Toss the pasta in the olive oil and butter until all the strands are well coated. Add about ¼ cup of the reserved pasta water, then reduce the heat to low. Add the cheeses and stir to combine. Season with salt.

Plate the cacio e pepe and sprinkle with a little more pepper and Pecorino Romano.

CARBONARA

Italian dishes are regularly bastardized here in America, and carbonara is far from an exception. Bacon, peas, mushrooms, garlic, even scallops have invaded this simple Roman staple, and you know what? Who cares. Put what you want in your carbonara, just don't serve it to a purist (or post it on the Internet) if you don't want to catch an earful. I will not debate, however, that far and away the best expression of carbonara is the properly executed genuine article. Eggs (or just egg yolks for added richness and color) are practically whipped into an emulsion with pork fat and Pecorino Romano, creating what is perhaps the richest sauce in the pasta lexicon. The sauce's rich, complex flavor is largely furnished by guanciale, a difficult to find cured pork jowl. Luckily, the much more widely-available pancetta is a fine substitute!

How I've Screwed This Up

I was brutally skewered by three esteemed Italian chefs on a YouTube channel called Italia Squisita, in a video which sports 3.1 million views at the time of this writing. So, unlike most parts of this book, you can go watch a breakdown of precisely "How I've Screwed This Up." My cardinal sin was the use of garlic, but they had plenty to say about virtually every other thing I did wrong. I eventually addressed the controversy, but only after I made damn sure I knew how to make authentic carbonara.

Troubleshooting

MY CARBONARA IS THIN OR RUNNY. This could be from a number of factors, but my initial guesses would be too little egg, not enough residual heat left in the pan to cook said eggs, and not enough pasta cooking water to emulsify said eggs. It's a delicate balance between the three, one that's not going to be cut-and-dry until you've tried making the dish a few times. Don't be discouraged—if you think your eggs are raw (your carbonara is soupy), place the pan over your stove's lowest-possible heat while stirring constantly and removing frequently, and you may be able to thicken the sauce.

MY CARBONARA BECOMES AN IMMOVABLE MASS TEN MINUTES AFTER COOKING. Unfortunately, like cacio e pepe, carbonara has an extremely limited shelf life. As soon as it drops below reasonably hot, cheese and egg begin to coagulate, and your pasta becomes irreversibly clumpy. My best advice is to eat faster (and serve in a bowl that's been kept warm with boiling water)!

MY CARBONARA IS GREASY. You definitely want some guanciale fat left in the pan after frying, but most likely not all of it. Make sure you're discarding all but about two tablespoons with which to thoroughly coat the pasta!

MY CARBONARA IS CHUNKY. Honestly I don't know how the word "chunky" became a desirable descriptor in the world of junk food, hearing it makes me want to hurl, especially in this context. Chunky carbonara means coagulated eggs, which means too much heat. Try taking the pan entirely off the burner before adding the egg slurry, even giving it a few seconds to cool down if it's sizzling loudly. Also make sure it's not too close to the pot of boiling water, as the heat radiating off the neighboring burner can coagulate a small portion of your egg, which can ruin the whole batch.

I LIKE MY CARBONARA CHUNKY. Stop, I'm gonna hurl.

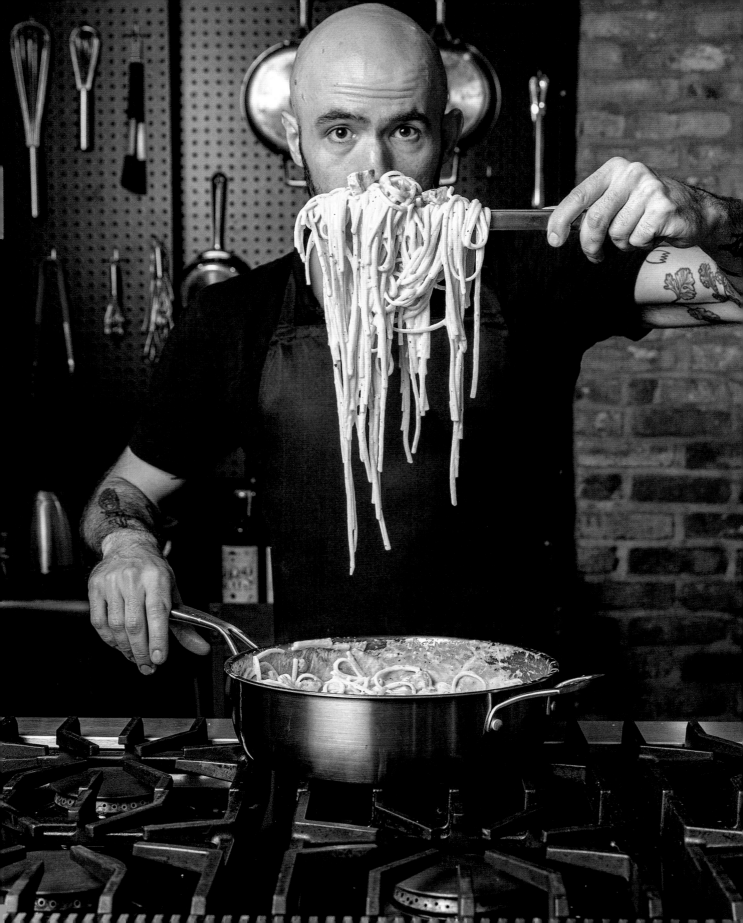

SERVES 4 TO 6

3 large eggs

1 large egg yolk

4 ounces of finely-grated Pecorino Romano or Parmigiano-Reggiano cheese (or 2 ounces of each!), plus more for serving

Kosher salt and freshly ground black pepper

½ pound guanciale or pancetta, diced

1 pound dried linguine

In a large, high-walled sauté pan, bring 2 quarts water to a boil, just enough in which to comfortably cook the pasta.

In a liquid measuring cup, combine the eggs, egg yolk, cheese, 1 teaspoon salt, and 2 teaspoons pepper. Whisk or beat with a fork until evenly combined. Set aside.

In another large sauté pan, combine the guanciale with ¼ cup water and cook over medium-high heat until simmering. Continue to cook until the water is evaporated and most of the fat from the guanciale has rendered out, anywhere from 5 to 10 minutes.

Meanwhile, add the pasta to the boiling water and cook for 1 minute less than the suggested cooking time on the package. Drain, reserving 1 cup of the pasta cooking water.

Discard all but 3 tablespoons of fat from the guanciale, lower the heat, and add the pasta along with ¼ cup of the reserved pasta cooking water. Cook, tossing, until the pasta is evenly coated in fat. Take the pan off the heat and allow to cool for 10 seconds if it's sizzling loudly. Add the egg and cheese mixture, immediately and vigorously stirring it into the pasta, taking care not to let any of the egg sit in one place for too long. Stir in more pasta cooking water, 2 tablespoons at a time, until the desired consistency is achieved. Season with more salt if necessary and serve with extra cheese grated over the top.

Note: *Try the (Michelin-starred chef and master of pasta) Luciano Monosiglio method—it's fun! Put the eggs and cheese in a blender and slowly stream in a half cup of pasta cooking water while the blender is running. Throw a hunk of guanciale in there if you really want some pervasive pork flavor, followed by 2 tablespoons of reserved fat from the pan. Blend until smooth and add back to the pasta in the hot pan, cooking over low heat until thick.*

BUTTERNUT SQUASH RAVIOLI IN BROWN BUTTER

One of the three pasta dishes in this book for our *Date Night Part I* episode of *Basics*, this is one of those pastas that makes you feel impressive when you announce to your dinner guest, loudly and without being prompted, that you made everything from scratch. Ravioli, unlike most filled pastas, isn't an exercise in repetition—it's an exercise in organization. Pasta dough must be cut into a proportional rectangle of even thinness, dollops of filling must be laid down with both consistent volume and spacing, egg gently brushed, and pasta folded, pressed, and decoratively cut so as to not leave any errant air bubbles, or holes through which filling can sneakily make its escape. But while challenging, like most filled pastas, practice makes perfect. Even better news: you can make your ravioli, test cook one to make sure it doesn't explode, place them on a baking sheet dusted with cornmeal, cover with plastic wrap and fridge for up to 24 hours. That way, when your date's in an Uber and you're trying to figure out how the hell to make a pisco sour, you're not also worrying about a process that demands both your complete attention and utmost respect.

How I've Screwed This Up

All the ways in which you might imagine one would screw up ravioli: burst seams, too delicate or too chewy pasta, not enough filling, too much filling, or forgot the filling altogether. Most ravioli dishes' difficulty is compounded by their accompanying sauce, but luckily, brown butter with sage is about as easy as it gets. I have, of course, burned my share of brown butter—so will you—but it only costs you about 5 minutes and $1.50 to try again!

Troubleshooting

MY RAVIOLI BURST. This could've been due to a large air pocket trapped in with the filling or a weak seam. Make sure to try and gently push all the air surrounding the squash out of the ravioli before sealing and cutting. Using an egg wash, pressing down the seams firmly with your finger, and cuts that complete through any seams should seal them up tight.

MY RAVIOLI HAVE CHEWY EDGES. The culprit in virtually any chewy homemade pasta situation is overdevelopment of gluten. If you've over-kneaded the dough (usually by machine) or over-laminated it during the rolling process, it can over-develop your gluten and cause your pasta to come out chewy. You might've undercooked your pasta, but given that it only takes 90-some-odd seconds to cook, it's unlikely.

MY SAGE TURNS SPOTTED WHEN I FRY IT. I honestly have no idea why this happens. I have never been able to prevent it, my Internet searches yield no results, I have not yet been offered any cryptic advice nor warning recited in Latin from a witch or wizard. I'm not really sure why I put it in the question-and-answer segment if I don't have an answer. I guess I want you to feel better about it.

MY BROWN BUTTER EXPLODED! That wasn't funny when you did it with the pesto.

NO, I'M BEING SERIOUS. Oh, my bad! Butter can, indeed, explode during the process of browning if it's not constantly kept in motion. If droplets of water separated from the butter get trapped underneath a layer of fat (you know how fat rises to the top of water?), it can superheat and cause a devastating explosion. I repeatedly show my butter exploding during a cookie livestream years ago as a funny example of this phenomenon, but in reality, it's a very dangerous situation. Butter can reach temperatures much hotter than boiling water during the browning process, and if your nose is hovering over the nutty aromas emanating from the pan when it happens, you're gonna have a real bad time. Keep the pan moving, keep the butter swirling, and lower the heat a bit!

SERVES 2 TO 4

8 tablespoons unsalted butter

1 tablespoon olive oil

Kosher salt and freshly ground black pepper

4 fresh sage leaves

2 garlic cloves, minced

½ pound Butternut Squash Ravioli (recipe follows)

½ cup freshly grated Parmesan cheese

In a large skillet, heat the butter and olive oil over medium heat and cook, swirling the pan constantly, until the milk solids have browned, 8 to 10 minutes. At this point, you can proceed with the next step, or transfer the brown butter to a heatproof bowl and keep covered at room temperature until ready to use (up to 2 days). Reheat the browned butter in a large skillet until frothy.

Bring a large pot of generously salted water to a boil.

Add the sage leaves and garlic to the brown butter. Cook, stirring, until the sage leaves are crispy, 3 to 5 minutes. Season with salt and pepper.

Add the ravioli to the boiling water and cook until the pasta is al dente, 1½ to 2 minutes. Using a slotted spoon, transfer the ravioli to the sauce and toss to combine, adding pasta cooking water as needed to help the sauce coat the pasta.

Top with Parmesan and serve immediately.

3

4

7

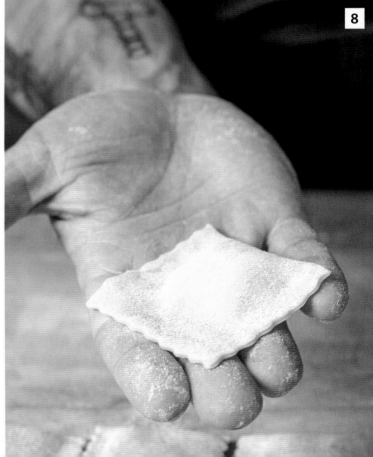

8

BUTTERNUT SQUASH RAVIOLI

Serves 2 to 4

2 cups pre-peeled and cubed butternut squash

1 small shallot, halved

3 large garlic cloves

2 fresh thyme sprigs, leaves picked and chopped

3 fresh sage leaves, chopped

1 tablespoon light olive oil

1 tablespoon pure maple syrup

Kosher salt and freshly ground black pepper

2 ounces mascarpone cheese

1 teaspoon white wine vinegar

Fresh Pasta Dough (page 116)

Preheat the oven to 400°F.

In a large bowl, combine the butternut squash, shallot, garlic, thyme, sage, olive oil, maple syrup, ½ teaspoon salt, and ½ teaspoon pepper, and toss to combine. Transfer to a small rimmed baking sheet and cover with aluminum foil. Cut holes in the foil to act as steam vents.

Roast 30 to 40 minutes, until the squash pierces easily with a paring knife. Remove from the oven and carefully remove the foil. Allow the squash to cool completely.

Transfer the roasted vegetables and herbs to a food processor and process until smooth. Transfer to a medium bowl and fold in the mascarpone cheese and vinegar. Cover and refrigerate until ready to use. Bring to room temperature before using.

Using a pasta rolling machine or a rolling pin, roll the dough out to about ⅛ inch thick. Trim the excess dough to form a rectangle about 12 inches long and about 4 inches wide. Arrange the rectangle with one long side facing you.

Using a piping bag or two small spoons, add the filling in dollops (about 2 teaspoons each) across the bottom half of the rectangle, spacing the dollops about 2 inches apart.

Dip your finger in clean water, then run it across the top of the rectangle and fold it over the fillings to form a pasta dough tube 12 inches long and 2 inches wide, pressing out any air bubbles before pressing down on the edges of the tube to seal them.

Using a ravioli cutter or pastry cutter, cut between the fillings to create 2-inch ravioli.

Repeat with any remaining dough and filling.

SAUSAGE TORTELLONI WITH BROCCOLI RABE PESTO

Troubleshooting

See Tortellini (page 158) or Pesto (page 120)

SERVES 2 TO 4

Kosher salt

About 8 stalks broccoli rabe, leaves removed and stems trimmed (about 4 ounces)

¼ cup walnut pieces, toasted and cooled

2 garlic cloves, roughly chopped

6 tablespoons light olive oil

½ cup grated Parmesan cheese, plus more for serving

½ pound Sausage Tortelloni (recipe follows), cooked, plus reserved pasta water

3 to 4 sundried tomatoes packed in olive oil, drained and roughly chopped

Fill a large pot halfway with water. Bring to a boil and add 1 tablespoon salt.

Meanwhile, prepare a large bowl of ice water.

Add the broccoli rabe to the boiling water and cook for 2 minutes. Using tongs or a slotted spoon, transfer to the prepared ice bath. Let sit for 10 minutes, then remove, and pat dry.

In a food processor, combine the broccoli rabe with the walnuts, garlic, olive oil, and 1 teaspoon salt. Process until well combined but not entirely smooth. Fold in the Parmesan. Transfer to a sealable container and refrigerate until ready to use or proceed with the next step.

Bring a large pot of generously salted water to a boil. Add the tortelloni and cook until the pasta is al dente, 2 to 2½ minutes.

Meanwhile, heat the pesto in a large skillet over medium-low heat, stirring occasionally, until loosened and heated through. Using a slotted spoon, add the cooked tortelloni and ¼ cup of the reserved pasta water, then toss to combine and emulsify the sauce. Add more pasta water as needed to adjust the thickness of the sauce.

Finish with the sundried tomatoes and more Parmesan and serve immediately.

SAUSAGE TORTELLONI

Serves 2 to 4

1 teaspoon light olive oil

8 ounces spicy Italian sausage, casings removed and discarded

5 ounces ricotta

1 ounce Parmesan cheese, grated

1 large egg, beaten

Fresh Pasta Dough (page 116)

Kosher salt

In a large skillet, heat the olive oil over medium-high heat until shimmering. Add the sausage and cook until browned on one side, 4 to 5 minutes. Break up the large chunks with a potato masher or wooden spatula. Continue cooking, stirring occasionally, until the sausage is fully cooked, 3 to 4 minutes. Transfer to a plate or small rimmed baking sheet lined with paper towels and let cool.

Meanwhile, in a medium bowl, combine the ricotta, Parmesan, and egg. Add the cooled sausage and fold to combine. Cover and refrigerate until ready to use.

Using a pasta rolling machine or a rolling pin, roll out the dough to about ⅛ inch thick.

Using a 3-inch round cutter, stamp out rounds from the pasta dough.

Add about 2 teaspoons of the filling to the center of each round, then run a damp pastry brush or finger around one half the circumference. Fold each round in half over the filling and press to seal the edge, forming a half-moon. Gently pull the two corners of each half-moon toward each other and press to seal them together.

CRISPY GNOCCHI WITH GORGONZOLA DOLCE

I'll tell you right up front: potato gnocchi are harder to make than ricotta gnocchi and offer a diminishing return on your extra time and effort. So why did you put potato gnocchi in the book there, Andypants? Because it is, indeed, harder—and if you can make this, you can 100 percent for-sure make ricotta gnocchi. Like an ancient Kung Fu master insisting that you continue punching the brick wall at full force even though your knuckles are raw and bleeding, so, too, shall I cryptically and mercilessly impart my knowledge, gently encouraging you to make the somewhat more difficult gnocchi first. Curse my name if you like, you will one day thank me.

How I've Screwed This Up

This is one of the earliest dishes I can remember attempting to cook when I first decided that I was a good chef. Bear in mind, I was not actually a good chef, but I had decided that I, in fact, was. So when half my gnocchi fell apart and my sauce came out gluey and cloying, I placed the blame where it rightfully belonged: on our crappy stove, *DAD*! I didn't revisit the recipe for nearly two decades, and was thrilled to find it not only a breeze to make, but a great playmate for my favorite spice: freshly grated nutmeg.

Troubleshooting

MY SAUCE IS GLUEY. Don't be afraid to thin this sauce out with more cream until you reach your desired consistency. It is very rich, so while you don't want it water-thin, you don't want it arranged in globby dollops all over your gnocchi either. (Globby Dollop sounds like he'd be a bad guy in Candyland™.)

MY GNOCCHI FELL APART. This is why most people fear making gnocchi. Only two things could've made this happen: not enough binder (egg, flour) in your dough, or not kneading your dough long enough.

MY GNOCCHI ARE TOUGH OR GUMMY. Ah, seems as though you took the above advice too far! Overworking the dough can develop too strong a gluten network, preventing your gnocchi from expanding and giving them a chewy texture.

MY GNOCCHI ARE SOGGY. Sounds like a case of waterlogging. Overcooking the potatoes can impregnate them with a ton of water, all of which ends up in your gnocchi. The only moisture you want going into your little dumplings is egg, so be sure to properly cook your potatoes and spread them out on a rimmed baking sheet the second they are fished out of the water. Hot potatoes release more steam, which means more moisture! That's also why leftover baked potatoes make for great gnocchi—the fridge is a very dry environment and it sucks even more moisture out of the potatoes.

MY GNOCCHI ARE LUMPY. These are likely lumps of undercooked potato—make sure your potatoes are extremely tender and use a ricer to ensure that any lumps have been obliterated.

MY GNOCCHI ARE SLUMPY. Sounds like a posture issue, remind your gnocchi to sit up straight and engage its core muscles when sitting.

SERVES 4 TO 6

2 pounds russet potatoes, unpeeled

Gorgonzola Dolce Sauce (recipe follows)

2 large egg yolks, beaten

Kosher salt

3½ to 5 ounces all-purpose flour, sifted, plus more for dusting

1 tablespoon vegetable oil

1 tablespoon chopped fresh parsley

Freshly grated nutmeg

Preheat the oven to 375°F.

Pierce the potatoes all over using a fork, then transfer the potatoes to a rimmed baking sheet. Bake for 1 hour or until the skins are crispy and the interior easily pierces with a knife.

Allow the potatoes to cool for 2 to 3 minutes, then using a clean kitchen towel, grab each potato, and remove the skin. (This will allow more steam to escape: Less steam = less moisture; less moisture = lighter, fluffier gnocchi!) Allow to cool to room temperature, then cover in plastic wrap and refrigerate for 1 to 2 hours.

While the potatoes are cooling, this is a good time to make the sauce.

Grate or rice the potatoes through the fine holes of a cheese grater or ricer. Transfer to a work surface and spread out evenly. Drizzle with the egg yolks and sprinkle evenly with 1 teaspoon salt and 3½ ounces of the flour, gently combining with a bench scraper and floured hands until a smooth dough forms. Knead by hand until a smooth dough forms, about 90 seconds. Add more flour as necessary to achieve a bouncy and cohesive but not too dense or firm dough.

Bring a large pot of generously salted water to a rolling boil. Divide the dough into 8 equal pieces. Work with one piece at a time and cover the remaining pieces with plastic wrap. Starting at the center of the piece, use your hands to roll out into a 1-inch-thick log on a floured work surface. Using a sharp knife or bench scraper, cut the log into 1-inch pieces. The gnocchi can then be cooked as is or shaped as desired. For the classic ridged shape, press each dough piece against the back of a fork, creating a longer piece the length of the tines, and rolling it up so the ridges face laterally around the outside of the pasta. Did that make ANY sense?! No? Well, then

it's your lucky day, because you can just roll the dough pieces into balls or poke them with your thumb! In fact, the poked gnocchi seem to work best for this recipe, as they have the most amount of flat surface area, making them better for panfrying. Gnocchi store wonderfully frozen and cook virtually identically out of the freezer as they do fresh, but they do not refrigerate terribly well—no longer than a day, covered (see Note).

Once the water is boiling, add the vegetable oil to a large nonstick or carbon steel skillet and heat over medium-high heat until shimmering, 1 to 2 minutes.

Meanwhile, gently place the gnocchi in the boiling water and cook until still firm but floating, about 90 seconds. Retrieve them with a spider or slotted spoon, shaking off as much excess water as possible then transfer to the skillet. Arrange the gnocchi in a single even layer and fry, undisturbed, until browned and crisp on the bottom, 2 to 3 minutes, then flip and repeat.

Transfer the gnocchi to a large serving bowl or individual bowls and drizzle with the Gorgonzola Dolce Sauce. Garnish with parsley and serve with a grating of fresh nutmeg.

STEP-BY-STEP IMAGES, PAGE 152-153

GORGONZOLA DOLCE SAUCE

Makes about 1½ cups

1½ cups heavy cream

5 ounces Gorgonzola dolce, rind removed and cheese cut into pieces

2 ounces Parmesan cheese, finely grated

¼ teaspoon freshly grated nutmeg

Kosher salt and freshly ground pepper

In a medium saucepan, bring the cream to a boil over medium-high heat. Reduce the heat to low and simmer until reduced by half, 15 to 20 minutes.

Add the Gorgonzola, Parmesan, and nutmeg; stir until all the cheese is melted. Season with salt and pepper. Cover and keep warm until ready to serve.

Note: *Once all of the dough has been cut and shaped into the desired gnocchi shape, place onto a rimmed baking sheet and cover with a dusting of flour. For non-immediate cooking, place in a freezer to solidify for 1 hour, then scrape off and place in a bag and back into the freezer.*

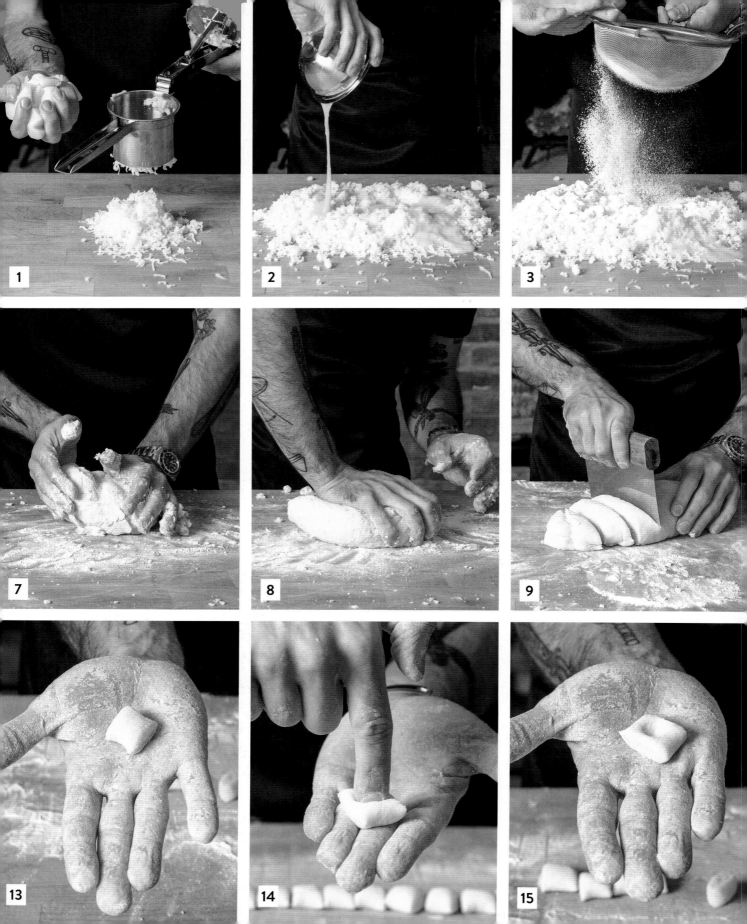

SWEET CORN CARAMELLE WITH BEURRE BLANC AND BASIL OIL

So after that whole tortelloni fiasco, I called my editor and begged him to let me do another filled pasta. I mean I really laid it all out there people, I voided any of my remaining dignity and self-respect, I left my soul in a pool of its own tears on the floor of that Zoom call. He said I could do one more filled pasta if I mow his lawn for a year, and while my first thought was "suckerrrrr," I then immediately remembered this late-summer hotness I once whipped up while trying to imitate a pasta I had eaten at a fine restaurant weeks prior. The result was my childhood in a bite. You see, I am very close with corn. I grew up (literally) surrounded by cornfields, which would waft their honeyed, earthy, silken smell across my backyard on hot August afternoons. My family lovingly sparred over whether the steaming-hot cobs, sunset-yellow and dripping with salted butter, should be consumed in a circular pattern or "typewriter style." I'm quite certain that corn cob holders outnumbered any other utensil four-to-one in our silverware drawers, and they were always breaking under constant and repeated use. This pasta has all the summertime joy of buttery corn on the cob, but it's elegant enough to make for a date; mostly because you don't need to wear a bib when you're eating it *and* floss immediately after.

How I've Screwed This Up

Having developed this recipe only a few brief months before writing this headnote and having only made it thrice, the only thing I've messed up is the timing. That is, starting to make it a mere 90 minutes before my guests' arrival. In other words, my guests became sous chefs. The filling can be made and the pasta can be filled, formed and refrigerated up to 24 hours before cooking, so remember that old childhood rhyme we all grew up hearing:

Many dinner guests are willing,
even ready, given the task,
to make your caramelle filling,
but don't expect the night to last.

Troubleshooting

See Ravioli (page 140)

MY BEURRE BLANC BROKE, YOU BASTARD! Beurre blanc requires pretty constant stirring to gently emulsify the butter and vinegar together—if it breaks, like most other sauces, it can be saved by whisking in a squirt of water.

MY CORN FILLING IS TOO THIN. The consistency of your filling is going to vary depending on how much moisture was in your corn, how thick your ricotta is, what mood the corn goddess is in, all that. Add some more corn if it's too thin—worst case, you're just adding more corn flavor.

SWEET CORN ISN'T IN SEASON. This is a seasonal dish for a reason: If you can't get ahold of high-quality, flavorful corn, it might not be the right time to make it! If you've got a hankering though, you can always go frozen—defrost and char the kernels in a cast-iron skillet and add a teaspoon of sugar to the filling to imitate the sweet corn . . . well, sweetness.

THIS DISH IS SOOO CORNY. You smartass. God I love you.

SERVES 4

2 ears sweet corn, shucked and silked

1 tablespoon vegetable oil

8 ounces fresh ricotta

2 ounces Parmigiano-Reggiano

1 large egg yolk

1½ teaspoons plus 1 tablespoon kosher salt, divided, plus more to taste

Fresh Pasta Dough (page 116)

1 large egg beaten with 1 tablespoon water

1 cup Beurre Blanc (recipe follows)

1 garlic clove confit (optional: see Confit Garlic, page 293)

1 teaspoon freshly ground black pepper

2 tablespoons Basil Oil (recipe follows)

Flaky sea salt (optional)

Preheat a grill to maximum heat.

Meanwhile, place the corn on a rimmed baking sheet, add the vegetable oil, and toss to evenly coat.

Grill the corn, turning frequently and keeping the lid closed as much as possible, until lightly charred and soft, 10 to 12 minutes. (Alternatively, wrap the corn in aluminum foil and bake in a preheated 425°F oven 20 to 30 minutes, until lightly charred and soft). Spread the corn out on the same baking sheet and let sit until cool enough to handle.

Using a sharp knife, cut the kernels off the corn cobs; discard the cobs.

In a blender, combine the ricotta, Parmigiano-Reggiano, egg yolk, 1½ teaspoons kosher salt with ¼ cup of the corn kernels (cover the remaining kernels and set aside). Process until smooth, 10 to 20 seconds, or until your desired texture is reached. Cover and set aside.

Divide the pasta dough into four equal pieces. Work with one piece at a time and cover the rest with plastic wrap. Using a pasta rolling machine or rolling pin if you're a real badass, roll out the piece into a rectangle 6 by 10 to 12 inches and ⅛ inch thick. Cut into thirds, yielding three 2-inch-wide strips.

Transfer the corn filling to a piping bag, cut a hole the size of a dime at the tip. Pipe 1-inch-long lengths of filling along the center of the pasta strip, leaving a 2-inch gap between each.

Just below the filling, brush the edge of the pasta lengthwise with the beaten egg. Fold the pasta over the filling, removing any air bubbles before pressing the dough tightly along the edge to seal. Trim off any excess dough to create a single long tube of pasta. Gently roll the sealed tube so that the seam side is down. Cut in between the filling to make individual pasta pieces. Then pinch and slightly twist the ends of each piece to resemble wrapped candy. Repeat with the remaining pasta strips and filling.

Cover and refrigerate until ready to cook, up to 24 hours.

Bring a large pot of water to a boil. Add the 1 tablespoon kosher salt.

Meanwhile, in a blender, combine the beurre blanc, remaining grilled corn (reserve a few kernels for garnish), and garlic confit (if using); blend until completely smooth, about 30 seconds. Pour into a wide sauté pan and heat over very low heat.

Add the caramelle to the boiling water and cook until all the pasta floats, about 90 seconds. Using a slotted spoon, transfer the caramelle to the beurre blanc sauce—don't bother shaking off too much water, as the pasta cooking water aids in the sauce's consistency. Add ¼ cup of the pasta cooking water and cook gently over low heat until the sauce is thickened and the pasta is well coated.

Serve the caramelle and a generous pool of sauce in wide, shallow bowls. Grind cracked pepper over the top, drizzle with the basil oil, and scatter with the reserved corn. Sprinkle with flaky salt (if using) and serve.

BEURRE BLANC

Makes about 2 cups

1 cup (2 sticks) unsalted butter, cut into small pieces

1 small shallot, finely minced

¼ cup dry white wine

¼ cup white wine vinegar

¼ cup heavy cream

½ teaspoon ground white pepper

1 teaspoon fresh lemon juice

In a large saucepan, melt about 1 tablespoon of the butter over medium heat until foaming. Once the foaming subsides, add the shallot and cook, stirring often, until beginning to soften, 1 to 2 minutes. Add the wine and vinegar, bring to a simmer, and cook until reduced to only a few tablespoons of liquid, 3 to 5 minutes. Add the cream, reduce the heat as low as possible, add the white pepper and lemon juice, and begin adding the remaining butter one piece at a time, whisking constantly to emulsify it into a sauce. If the butter is added too quickly or the sauce heated to a simmer, it will break. If that happens, whisk in a splash of water to re-emulsify the sauce.

Once all the butter is added, serve immediately—beurre blanc can be covered and kept warm briefly, but try to prepare it as close to serving time as possible.

BASIL OIL

Makes about 1 cup

Leaves from 1 bunch fresh basil

½ cup extra-virgin olive oil

½ teaspoon kosher salt

Bring a medium pot of water to a rolling boil and prepare a large bowl of ice water. Add the basil leaves to the boiling water for about 15 seconds then remove immediately and plunge into the ice bath. Drain the basil and pat as dry as possible with paper towels.

In a blender, combine the blanched basil, oil, and salt; blend until completely pureed, about 15 seconds. Allow the basil oil to rest until the foam dissipates, about 1 hour. Strain through a fine-mesh sieve, pressing on the basil with a spoon to extract as much oil as possible. Keep in an airtight container and refrigerate for up to 1 week.

TORTELLINI EN BRODO

Tortellini en brodo is a comforting, simple dish of cheese, pasta, and steaming hot broth. So why are there five thousand ingredients listed below and many hours of effort suggested for something so seemingly minimal? Because when any dish relies on so few things, every iota of care and attention can shine through in the final product. So we're going to conduct an experiment, like Bill Nye the Science Man! Below, you'll find two recipes for tortellini en brodo—neither is necessarily "better" than the other, but one is far simpler. It's an opportunity to see exactly how your time and effort are rewarded in the resultant dish: despite both ostensibly containing the same elements, one is an easy and quick weeknight meal, the other a decadent first course for a special occasion dinner.

How I've Screwed This Up

We're doing two versions of this dish, so I'll tell you how I've screwed up both! For the fancy: I've made tortellini with no structural integrity that's fallen apart upon hitting the water. So what we were left with for dinner was . . . broth. For the simple: I used dried tortellini, which are objectively awful, so what we were left for dinner was . . . broth.

Troubleshooting

See Tortelloni (page 146)

MY BROTH IS FLAVORLESS. Even if you go for the simpler version of this recipe, there is no way you aren't ending up with some flavorful broth. Try grabbing a spoonful, adding a tiny pinch of salt, and seeing if it just needed seasoning. If that doesn't help, let it simmer longer!

THERE'S A LAYER OF FAT ON MY SOUP. That's the idea! One of my favorite things to add to chicken soup is a good hit of schmaltz, creating tiny little droplets of rich fat in every spoonful. There shouldn't be too much though, so make sure if there's a 1-inch layer swimming up top that you're skimming most of it off before serving.

WHERE'S THE MEAT? You can totally use some meat tortellini if you like—deviations from the formula beyond that get you into "this is a different thing" territory, but if it tastes good, who cares!

WHY IS THERE A LITTLE HOLE IN THE MIDDLE OF MY TORTELLINI? This is a cute story! Tortellini is wrapped around the finger to emulate a ring, as it was invented by a legendary Italian jeweler, so the story goes. It was sixteenth-century Sardinia: he was madly in love with the son of a great chef who rejected his every advance, no matter how big or beautiful a piece of jewelry he could craft. He had all but given up hope, but as the jeweler watched him folding agnolotti in this forgotten Italian villa, he wrapped one of the delicate triangles around his love's finger and begged him to be his husband, to which he finally agreed.

YOU MADE THAT UP, DIDN'T YOU? I said it was a cute story, not a true story.

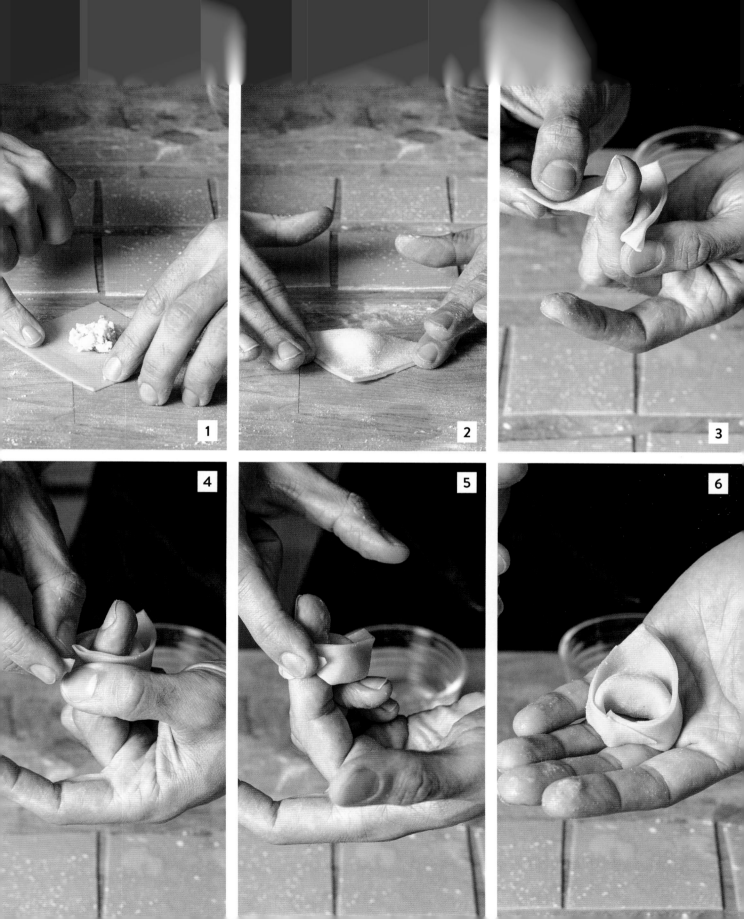

SERVES 4

Brodo

1 tablespoon schmaltz (chicken fat, see Kitchen Glossary, page 24), or fat of choice

1 small onion, quartered

2 celery stalks, roughly chopped

2 carrots, peeled and roughly chopped

5 fresh parsley sprigs

5 fresh thyme sprigs

1 tablespoon whole black peppercorns

1 head garlic, halved across the cloves

3 quarts homemade Chicken Stock (page 268) or Bone Broth (page 347)

½ pound Parmesan rinds

Tortellini

Semolina flour, for dusting

½ cup ricotta cheese

½ cup freshly grated Parmigiano-Reggiano

⅓ pound low-moisture mozzarella, shredded

1 large egg, lightly beaten

2 tablespoons minced fresh basil

Kosher salt, plus more for serving

Fresh Pasta Dough (page 116)

To Serve

4 tablespoons (½ stick) unsalted butter, cut into 1-tablespoon pieces

Freshly ground black pepper

¼ teaspoon freshly grated nutmeg

Parmigiano-Reggiano, for grating

MAKE THE BRODO: Melt the schmaltz over medium-high heat in a medium stockpot until shimmering. Add the onion cut-side down, lower the heat to medium, and sear until well-browned, about 2 minutes per side. Before any residue or fat burns on the bottom of the pot, add the celery, carrots, parsley, thyme, peppercorns, and garlic head. Cook, stirring occasionally, until every ingredient in the pot has been heated through, about 5 minutes. Add enough chicken broth to cover, bring to a boil, partially cover, then lower heat and bring to a simmer. Add the Parmesan rinds and cook at a bare simmer until the broth is deeply flavored with Parmesan, about 3 hours. Strain, discard the solids, and keep the brodo warm, covering the stockpot until ready to use.

MAKE THE TORTELLINI: Line a baking sheet with parchment paper and dust with semolina flour.

In a large bowl, combine the ricotta, Parmigiano, mozzarella, egg, basil and 1 teaspoon salt. Mix until homogenous then set aside.

Divide the pasta dough into four equal pieces. Work with one piece at a time and cover the rest with plastic wrap. Using a pasta rolling machine or rolling pin, roll out the piece to a sheet about 6 inches wide and ⅛ inch thick. Cut in half lengthwise, then into 3-inch squares. Place a small dollop (about 1 teaspoon) of the cheese filling in the center of each square. Brush water on two adjoining edges of a pasta square and fold in half diagonally, creating a triangle. Press the filling gently to the top of the triangle (the widest-angle corner). Pick up the triangle and wrap the two other corners around your pointer finger, pressing them together tightly between your thumb to seal. If necessary, wet the tips of the pasta with more water for a better seal.

Place the shaped tortellini on the prepared baking sheet, cover, and repeat with the remaining squares and filling. Refrigerate until ready to cook, up to 24 hours.

TO SERVE: Place 1 tablespoon of the butter in each serving bowl. Bring the brodo to a gentle simmer, add the tortellini and cook until they all begin to float, about 90 seconds. Ladle the tortellini and brodo into the bowls. Season with salt. Divide the pepper, nutmeg and Parmigiano among each bowl. Serve piping hot.

PAPPARDELLE BOLOGNESE

Bolognese is a sauce met with much confusion here in these United States, where on its worst day, it manifests as ground beef added to tomato sauce. Traditionally, Bolognese contains little-to-no tomato at all, earning its rich color from sheer meat and vegetable content. We opt for a happy middle ground, adding a healthy shot of tomato paste for that savory Italian aura, but relying on a multitude of animal products (beef, pork, lamb, chicken stock, milk, and cheese) to bolster and unite its many flavors and textures. Once again bucking the instincts of the average cook (aka, my instincts), it opts for white instead of red wine, the latter of which actually cooks down to a somewhat acrid syrup when reduced. While good ol' meatball mix is utilized in the savory blend, lamb can be opted for to achieve a more pronounced, slightly grassier flavor. Lastly, as with virtually any pasta sauce, finishing with butter, cheese, and tossing a bit of pasta cooking water emulsifies everything into a creamy, meaty masterpiece.

How I've Screwed This Up

In my younger years, I was certainly guilty of referring to a meaty marinara using the same name as the storied staple of Bologna. It's one of those things you slowly learn to forgive yourself for with time, realizing the ultimate futility of punishing yourself for errors of the past. After all, everything happens for a reason, doesn't it? Guys?

Troubleshooting

MY BOLOGNESE IS OILY. When you boil up a Bolognese in yer boombox (which is how I'm referring to ovens from now on), it's going to come out with a thick layer of oil on top. That's good! You might want to skim some of it off if there's excess, but you want a solid cup in there to emulsify into the sauce. Things like a splash of water and cream can act as emulsifiers, so adjust as necessary if things aren't coming together!

MY BOLOGNESE TASTES GAMEY. You might want to opt for veal instead of lamb—lamb brings distinct grassy and gamey notes, but even if you don't like lamb on its own, it can still be subtle enough to enjoy in this recipe.

MY BOLOGNESE IS TOO LIGHT, IT'S WEIRD-LOOKING. I feel like this is how our Bolognese ended up looking in the episode—it might've been some jacked color correction, but that sauce looks too light to me. During its long braise, the sauce should darken, but feel free to add a glug of stock (or ideally Demi-Glace, page 346), tomato paste, or even a little soy sauce to darken the color.

SERVES 8

2 tablespoons light olive oil

3 pounds mix of ground meat, such as beef, pork, veal, and/or lamb

1 large onion, finely chopped

2 medium carrots, peeled and finely chopped

3 celery stalks, finely chopped

4 garlic cloves, smashed and roughly chopped

¼ cup tomato paste

1 tablespoon anchovy paste

1 cup dry red wine

1 quart homemade Chicken Stock (page 268)

1 cup whole milk

3 bay leaves

1 fresh basil sprig

1 Parmigiano-Reggiano rind (optional), plus Parmigiano-Reggiano for serving

Fresh Pasta Dough (page 116)

Semolina flour, for dusting

¼ cup heavy cream

¼ cup unsalted butter

½ teaspoon freshly grated nutmeg

Kosher salt and freshly ground pepper

1 tablespoon extra-virgin olive oil, for finishing

Chopped fresh basil leaves, for serving

Preheat the oven to 300°F.

In a large Dutch oven, heat the olive oil over medium-high heat until shimmering, 2 to 3 minutes. Add the meat in batches if necessary to avoid overcrowding and cook, breaking up the meat into small pieces until browned, 3 to 5 minutes. Transfer to paper towels to drain, reserving 2 table-spoons of fat in the pot.

Return the Dutch oven to medium heat. Add the onion, carrots, and celery, and cook, stirring occasionally, until onion is translucent and vegetables begin to brown to lightly brown, 3 to 5 minutes. Add the garlic, tomato paste, and anchovy paste, and cook, stirring occasionally, until fragrant and the tomato paste begins to stick, about 1 minute. Add the wine, scraping up any fond on the bottom of the pot. Add the chicken stock, milk, bay leaves, basil, and the Parmigiano rind (if using). Bring to a simmer, cover partially with the lid, and transfer to the oven for 3 to 4 hours, until a thick layer of fat forms on top of the sauce.

MEANWHILE, MAKE THE PAPPARDELLE: Using a pasta rolling machine or rolling pin, roll out the pasta dough to 3 to 5 millimeters thick then cut into 1-inch-wide strips. Dust with semolina flour and twist into a nest. Cover with plastic wrap and refrigerate until ready to use.

Skim off about half the fat from the surface of the sauce, stirring in the rest. Remove the bay leaves and Parmigiano rind, and add the heavy cream, butter, and nutmeg. Season with salt and pepper. Serve immediately or refrigerate for up to 3 days (rewarm before using).

TO SERVE: Bring a large pot of heavily salted water to a boil. Cook the pasta until al dente, about 90 seconds. Reserve 1 cup of pasta cooking water then drain. Heat the same pot or a large high-walled skillet over medium-low heat. Add the cooked pasta, 2 to 3 cups of Bolognese sauce, the extra-virgin olive oil, and ¼ cup of the reserved pasta cooking water and cook gently, stirring, until the pasta is generously coated with the sauce. Serve with freshly grated Parmigiano and chopped basil.

CHAPTER 4

EGGS

Finally, let's get some protein in the mix! Albeit a weird one: Let's face facts, despite being one of the most familiar and essential foods, eggs are weird. A thin, candylike shell just barely encasing an ectoplasmic goo, itself subdivided into two distinct parts with entirely different consistencies, colors, uses, and nutritional content. When raw, we treat this mixture like radioactive waste, hurriedly washing our hands after exposure for fear of contracting transdermal salmonella. Once even barely qualifying as cooked, however, we'll gladly bathe our porous toast in its molten yellow core, eat its days-old gas-station-bought boiled innards like an apple, or slather its petrified breakfast-buffet remains in hot sauce and force it down with a glug of orange juice because, hey, free breakfast. Some French guy discovered that the cholesterol-laden nucleus of this alien offspring could be gently coaxed into a delicate custard, and another discovered that its whites could be whipped into spooky, airy pastries that crackle mysteriously and melt ethereally. Then some *really* crazy fuck was like "What if I use this unfertilized egg as a coating to fry its own mother in?," and so on and so forth. Like springs, rubber, or glass, eggs are as ubiquitous as they are surprisingly necessary behind the scenes, bringing levity to cakes, richness to sauces, and fatty proteins to nineteenth-century strongmen. Okay, on my fourth chapter heading, I'm just now realizing that I'm explaining food to you like you're an alien that's never heard of food before. On the off chance that's what you are, I'm gonna keep going. No one reads these things anyway.

WHAT ARE EGGS? Eggs, in a biological sense, are how the majority of the world's vertebrates reproduce. In a food sense, when combined with strong coffee and burnt toast, they are the only known way to get rid of this goddamned hangover.

WHAT KINDS OF EGGS ARE THERE? The most widely available eggs (here in the States at least) are chicken, duck, and quail eggs (which are surprisingly widely available . . . Who is cooking all these quail eggs?). In the sometimes-you-can-get-them-but-why-would-you-want-to category are ostrich, emu, goose, and turkey—and in the oh-snap-almost-forgot-about-that-category is caviar, of course! For this chapter, however, we're pretty much focusing on chicken eggs.

EGGS ARE GROSS. Not a question but I mean, I get it—they're alien when raw and still pretty alien when cooked, and unless you were force-fed them as a child, you're going to end up being weirded out by them for the rest of your life. Just remember that eggs are kind of like Brussels sprouts: if you've only ever had the boiled variety, you're likely going to hate them.

I HAVE AN EGG ALLERGY—WHAT'S MY OUTLOOK? For over-easy runny yolks? At the moment, you're SOL—but especially nowadays, there are myriad and ingenious egg substitutes functioning as both the ingredient and the main event. Apart from the commercially available vegetarian versions, some clever chemical combinations (like buttermilk and baking soda) can take eggs' place in your favorite pancakes, for example.

WHAT'S UP WITH REFRIGERATING EGGS? Ah yes, get this one all the time. Eggs in the US are rigorously, passionately washed before distribution and sale, stripping the egg shell of a natural protective sheen, making it susceptible to spoilage without refrigeration. Especially once refrigerated, it's imperative that eggs are kept refrigerated, as the condensation forming on the outside of an egg warming to room temperature can increase the risk of bacterial growth. But that's the grocery store eggs; did you get your eggs from the impeccably manicured front lawn of a sixth-generation Amish chicken farmer's family? Keep that shit out on the countertop next to the butter! Yes, I like to keep some butter at room temperature as well for easy toast spreading, and so should you.

MY EGGS EXPIRED YESTERDAY, SHOULD I THROW THEM OUT OR JUST BURN THEM? The world, the US in particular, suffers from a paralytic fear of food expiration dates. Not only are the dates printed on the packages merely rough guidelines cobbled together by a room full of suits that would gleefully cut your throat with a dull butter knife so that your job could be done by a robot, but especially when it comes to eggs, they're a bit pessimistic. I first learned this during the rapid consumption of a batch of brownies made by my ex's grandfather, shortly after which he proudly informed me he had utilized eggs that had been expired for several weeks. Once I induced vomiting and got my affairs in order, I realized that not only would I survive, I would thrive. That's because he had performed the float test: gently lowering the eggs in question into a bowl of room temperature water, and seeing what happens. A very fresh egg, little to no oxygen yet having permeated its microscopically porous shell, will sink and settle on the bottom. An older egg, while still viable, will stand on its end, the small bubble of air trapped inside making its broad end float like a buoy. A spoiled egg, enough air having built up inside the shell to allow bacteria to grow unencumbered, will playfully float on the water's surface like a child's bath toy. Fresher eggs are, on the whole, better options for almost every imaginable application, but especially for baking, older eggs have plenty of life left in 'em (not literally).

WHEN I CRACK EGGS, FULLY-GROWN DOVES KEEP FLYING OUT AND STARTLING ME. Yer a magician, Harry!

FRENCH SCRAMBLED EGGS WITH ROASTED MUSHROOMS ON TOAST

So you might see this, the only scrambled eggs in this purported "basics" cookbook, and be like "What the hell?" I understand your frustration—hell, I'm frustrated, too—but the damned publisher just simply will not allow me more than one scrambled egg recipe! Okay, fine, I made that up. The truth is that your scrambled eggs, not unlike a sexy set of abs, must be developed with time and repetition. Do you like them firm? Cook them more. Do you like them moist and custardy? Cook them over lower heat. Did your eggs come out overdone? Take them off the heat fifteen seconds earlier next time. These are the intrinsic microtransactions that take place every time you make scrambled eggs, and with the same energy that kung fu is taught in the movies, so too must you continue to fry, fry again, until you've found your sweet spot.

French scrambled eggs, unlike most other varieties, can be made reliably with as little as a few tries, and take your breakfast in a decidedly more luxurious direction. When eggs solidify from heat, the resulting shape and consistency is referred to as the "curd": in this case, throughout the cooking process, the eggs are beaten and agitated with great rigor in an effort to yield something of a curd continuum, one that has no distinct beginning nor end, no one that is distinguishable from the totality. In other words, instead of big bouncy fluffballs of fried egg, we're going for a creamy custard of coddled curd, folded with crème fraîche right at the end, and serving as a base for some rich, roasty mushrooms.

How I've Screwed This Up

Unless I give these eggs my undivided attention, it is all but a certainty that I will ruin them. As soon as you allow the eggs to rest for too long on the bottom of the pan, hard curds form, and your creamy dream toast turns into scrambled eggs on bread.

Troubleshooting

MY EGGS CAME OUT LUMPY.
Sounds like at one point or another, the eggs were exposed to too much heat, either by being left unmoving on the bottom of the pan or even over the flame for too long. If you start seeing the bottom of your pan quickly, make sure to remove the eggs from the heat entirely so that curds don't form and set.

MY EGGS CAME OUT RUNNY.
Definitely undercooked—there isn't a point at which your eggs will stop solidifying, so even if it feels like you've been at it for too long, keep applying the heat slowly and patiently. Before you know it, your custard will form like magic.

YOU KNOW GORDON RAMSAY—
YES, I KNOW, Gordon Ramsay popularized soft scrambled eggs, and I will fully admit that I'm drafting off that popularity.

THAT'S NOT WHAT I WAS GOING TO SAY.
Oh. What were you going to say?

YOU KNOW GORDON RAMSAY'S GOT NOTHING ON THESE EGGS?
Aww, hey, that doesn't seem like what you were actually going to say (just from the sentence structure), but I appreciate the pivot!

MAKES 2 TOASTS

Roasted Mushrooms

12 ounces assorted mushrooms, sliced

2 tablespoons light olive oil

1 tablespoon fresh thyme leaves

Kosher salt

French Scrambled Eggs

6 large eggs, at room temperature

Kosher salt and freshly ground black pepper

2 tablespoons unsalted butter

2 tablespoons crème fraîche

Toasts

2 slices sourdough bread, toasted

1 garlic clove

1 tablespoon unsalted butter

2 tablespoons chopped fresh chives, for garnish

Kosher salt and freshly ground black pepper

ROAST THE MUSHROOMS: Preheat the oven to 400°F with a rimmed baking sheet inside.

In a medium bowl, toss the mushrooms with the olive oil, thyme, and 1 teaspoon salt. Carefully pour directly onto the preheated baking sheet and roast, scraping and shaking occasionally, 20 to 25 minutes, until all the liquid is evaporated and the mushrooms are deeply golden brown.

COOK THE EGGS: In a medium bowl, combine the eggs with 1 teaspoon salt. Beat thoroughly with a tiny whisk (or fork, I guess?) until no streaks of white or yolk remain.

Melt the butter in a medium saucepan over medium-low heat. Add the eggs and cook, whisking immediately and continuously. Continue to slowly cook the eggs, putting on and taking off of medium-low heat while stirring constantly to form as small a curd as possible, until the eggs have set enough to form a shapeable mass, 5 to 10 minutes. Immediately remove from the heat and fold in the crème fraîche. Season with salt and pepper.

ASSEMBLE THE TOASTS: Rub the toasts with the garlic clove, using the bread like a cheese grater. Spread each slice evenly with the butter, top with the scrambled eggs and the mushrooms, then garnish with the chives. Season with salt and pepper and serve immediately.

EGGNOG FRENCH TOAST

You might be wondering why I didn't file this recipe in Chapter 1: Bread; but French toast is much more about eggs than it is toast. A rich, eggy custard lends its flavor, texture, and sweetness to stale bread that would've otherwise been discarded. Unless, of course, you're really craving French toast so you emulate stale bread by drying it out in the oven. There's no shame in that—there are some that might even call it strength. Apart from eggs, bread, milk, and sugar, my two must-haves are nutmeg and bourbon. They give the French toast an almost eggnog-like quality, but can be savored with any flavor from almond extract to Armagnac. Obviously not *any* flavor, but you know, rhyming.

How I've Screwed This Up

French toast is, blessedly, relatively difficult to screw up. The idea behind using stale (or dried-out) bread is to maximize the amount of custard that it can soak up, but even if you use it straight out of the bag, it's still going to taste pretty good. About the only way I've ruined my French toast is by burning it, which is easy to do thanks to all the sugar in the custard, and immediately remedied on the next slice fried.

Troubleshooting

MY FRENCH TOAST IS DRY IN THE CENTER. Gotta soak it longer! A nice super dry piece of bread means more custard, which means better texture and more flavor, but it also means that it needs to be thoroughly soaked, preferably overnight.

MY FRENCH TOAST IS WET IN THE CENTER. I mean it should be extremely moist, I'd go so far as to say custardy, but it shouldn't be straight-up wet or runny. It either needs to be cooked a bit longer or, depending on your ratio, might need an extra egg thrown in there!

MY FRENCH TOAST BURNS BEFORE IT COOKS THROUGH. Stove's too hot! Especially if your toast is thick, you want to be able to apply medium to medium-high heat for a solid 2 to 4 minutes per side, ensuring that it's both properly browned and cooked through.

MY FRENCH TOAST TASTES BAD. Surprise, I'm looking at your syrup bottle, bud! You know, the one with the same nozzle as a grease-fighting dish soap? Lose the bottle of sometimes-racist corn syrup and score a nice beige, domed jug with a tiny handle of the real stuff.

SERVES 4 TO 5

1½ cups heavy cream

4 large egg yolks

4 tablespoons dark brown sugar

1½ tablespoons bourbon, rum, or brandy

2 teaspoons vanilla paste, or one vanilla bean, split lengthwise and seeds scraped out

½ teaspoon ground cinnamon

½ teaspoon freshly grated nutmeg

Zest of 1 lemon or orange

1 brioche loaf (see page 62) or Babka (page 78), thickly sliced and left out to stale, uncovered, for 1 to 2 days (see Note)

8 to 10 tablespoons unsalted butter, plus more for serving

Pure maple syrup, for serving

In a large bowl, combine the heavy cream, egg yolks, brown sugar, bourbon, vanilla paste, cinnamon, nutmeg, and zest. Whisk together until fully combined. Cover and refrigerate until ready to use.

Preheat the oven to 250°F.

Pour the custard into a wide dish, like a cake pan or pie plate. Add the brioche, 2 slices at a time, soaking on each side until soft throughout but not falling apart, anywhere from 30 seconds to 5 minutes, depending on the dryness of your brioche. (Alternatively, shingle the brioche slices in a casserole dish, pour the custard over the top, then cover and refrigerate overnight.)

Heat 2 tablespoons of the butter in a nonstick skillet over medium heat until foaming, 2 to 3 minutes. Add the soaked brioche to the skillet, 2 slices at a time, and cook until deeply browned and crisp, 2 to 4 minutes per side. Transfer to a baking sheet and keep the cooked French toast warm in the oven while finishing the batch. Serve with butter and maple syrup.

Note: *Alternatively, dry the slices in a 200°F oven for 30 to 90 minutes, until hardened.*

AJITSUKE TAMAGO

This is the essential ramen accompaniment to the book-hopping recipe for Tonkotsu Ramen (page 326). And it's a quickie recipe, so I think it deserves a quickie headnote!

How I've Screwed This Up

I have never not screwed up soft-boiled eggs. Therefore, I have *only* ever screwed up this recipe, so it's more fitting to posit "How I've Done this Right." Which is never.

That being said, I usually get a handful to end up cooking correctly, so those are the ones that end up going in the thing.

Troubleshooting

I OVER OR UNDERCOOKED THE EGG. Don't do that.

THAT'S NOT HELPFUL. You're right, sorry. Crack open one of your eggs before marinating to make sure you're not wasting precious time on eggs that aren't cooked correctly! While it might affect the final texture, you can rescue undercooked eggs by reboiling for an additional minute or two to get the white correctly set, just be sure to shock again in ice water to prevent the yolk from overcooking. Once you've done it a few times though, you'll seldom over or undercook your eggs!

WAY MORE HELPFUL! XOXO!

MAKES 6 EGGS

½ cup soy sauce

½ cup mirin

4 cups water

6 soft-boiled eggs, cooled and peeled (see method for Scotch Eggs, page 191)

In a large jar or sealable container, combine the soy sauce, mirin, and water. Add the eggs and allow to marinate, jostling occasionally, anywhere from 2 hours at room temperature to 72 hours in the refrigerator.

When ready to serve, remove the egg(s) from the marinade and place in hot (not boiling) water for 2 minutes. Drain.

SPICY HONEY SHAKSHUKA

Shakshuka came on the social media brunch scene in a big way this past decade, but it's an ancient dish with roots in myriad cultures across many countries. That's about the anthropological limit of my knowledge on shakshuka, so let's stick to the great pleasure it is to see, smell, and taste. With a simple, customizable base of a spicy tomato sauce serving as both a medium for and accompaniment to poached eggs, this dish can be prepared in minutes and be eaten with little more than the bread of your choice and the paws at the end of your arms. And, when the right balance of time and temperature are struck, your brunch guests will be rewarded with rich, molten yolks, into which they can luxuriantly plunge their toasty soldiers. That is, before burning the everloving shit out of the roofs of their mouths.

How I've Screwed This Up

To be honest, I have roughly a 62 percent success rate in the proper poaching of this dish's eggs. Your biggest troublemakers are usually the egg whites, obstinately refusing to set until even after the yolks have entirely hardened. To prevent this outrage, be sure to spoon the sauce around the yolk, applying more heat to the top of the egg whites.

Troubleshooting

MY TOMATO SAUCE TASTES BORING OR RAW.

Well which one is it? Kidding, it's both! Likely because the sauce is undercooked, the bright and acidic notes of freshly uncanned tomatoes not yet quelled by steady and prolonged heat. In other words, try cooking it longer, and be sure to season liberally and creatively!

MY TOMATO SAUCE TASTES . . . METALLIC?

Be sure to cook any tomatoes or acidic ingredients in nonreactive cookware, meaning stainless steel. Aluminum, raw copper, and especially cast iron are reactive, so they will leach a tinny flavor into your tomato sauce if simmered for more than 30 or so minutes. It's not harmful, but it sure doesn't taste good.

MY EGG WHITES WON'T COOK UNTIL AFTER THE YOLK IS COOKED.

Like I mentioned previously, spoon some of the simmering sauce around and on top of the egg whites surrounding the yolk. This will ensure that the yolk is still visible and the whites will cook more evenly.

THEY'RE STILL DOING IT.

Try covering the pan before simmering on the stovetop or finishing in the oven—this will trap and recirculate the heat in the pan on top of the eggs.

THEY'RE STILL DOING IT

Try pulling the pan from the oven or stop simmering earlier, covering and allowing the residual heat to cook the egg whites. This will gently cook the eggs and apply less intense heat directly to the yolks.

THEY'RE STILL DOING IT.

Try poaching, soft-boiling, or sous vide your eggs before gently dropping them in the wells. Cook for 1 to 2 minutes, just to set the whites into place.

THEY'RE STILL DOING IT.

Do you have any cereal?

:(Sorry, sorry, I know it can be discouraging! But like I said, I have a success rate barely higher than a coin toss, so just remember that these things take both practice *and* a bit of luck. But just eat it, it's still good!

SERVES 4 TO 6

2 tablespoons olive oil

¼ cup diced onion

3 garlic cloves, minced or crushed in a garlic press

1 teaspoon ras el hanout

½ teaspoon ground Aleppo pepper

½ teaspoon cumin seeds

1 (28-ounce) can fire-roasted tomatoes (whole or crushed) with their juice

½ cup roughly chopped roasted red peppers

1 tablespoon smoked paprika

1½ teaspoons harissa

¼ teaspoon cayenne pepper

4 to 6 large eggs

Feta cheese, crumbled, for topping

2 tablespoons chopped fresh parsley leaves

Spicy honey, for drizzling

Crusty bread, for serving

Heat the oil in a large sauté pan over medium heat until shimmering, about 1 minute. Add the onion and cook, stirring occasionally, until softened and beginning to brown, about 3 minutes. Add the garlic and cook, stirring, until fragrant, about 30 seconds. Add the ras el hanout, Aleppo pepper, and cumin seeds and cook, stirring and removing the pan from the heat if it looks like the spices are going to smoke, until fragrant, about 30 seconds. Add the fire-roasted tomatoes and juice, crushing with a spoon if whole. Bring the mixture to a simmer and add the roasted red peppers, smoked paprika, harissa, and cayenne pepper. Bring to a simmer over medium-high heat. Lower heat and simmer, stirring occasionally, until the sauce is thickened enough to leave a trail when scraped with a rubber spatula (without disappearing) and the flavors have mellowed, 20 to 30 minutes.

Reduce the heat to low and crack the eggs into a spouted measuring cup. Using a spoon or spatula, make 4 to 6 divots in the sauce, and gently tip 1 egg into each divot.

Gently spoon the sauce up and around the whites of each egg, cover the pan, and simmer over your stove's lowest heat until the egg whites are set but the yolks are still runny, about 5 minutes. If the whites aren't setting evenly, remove the pan from the heat, cover, and allow the residual heat to set them.

Remove from the heat and garnish with feta and the parsley. Drizzle with spicy honey and serve with crusty bread for mopping.

PASTRAMI HASH WITH BAKED EGGS

A-ha, another questionably chaptered recipe—is this a beef or an egg dish? Well, we need more egg dishes in this book, so yes it's totally an egg dish. It's easily prepared, elegantly presented, and endlessly permutable: Fancy some bacon with your brekkie? Crumble some on there. Roasted peppers, mozzarella, and balsamic more your style? *Buon appetito.* Hell, what's your favorite savory breakfast flavor? Throw some in there, more likely than not it'll work, put cornflakes in there for all I care. That's why we're throwing some fun stuff in there like pastrami and duck fat, but any number of meat and veggie variables will invariably prevail. Simply swap, scatter with scallions, and serve sizzling to your hungover friends' astonishment.

How I've Screwed This Up

This guy has the same major pitfall as shakshuka, albeit to a lesser extent: potential overcookery of the egg yolks. Since the egg is subjected to a drier heat than shakshuka, it's a bit more controllable, but still can be tricky to set the whites completely before the yolks get there. I've probably served this with overcooked eggs more often than not, but the entire thing tends to disappear before I can even sit down, much less apologize for the lack of runny yolks.

Troubleshooting

MY HASH ISN'T CRISPY.

Hash isn't meant to have shatteringly crisp potatoes, but rather nice soft potatoes with some crispy facets. If you want really crispy hash, after par-cooking the potatoes, fry them in batches—so they aren't too crowded—with more oil, draining on paper towels and returning everybody to the pan before cracking the eggs into the wells.

NO I MEAN LIKE, IT'S STRAIGHT-UP SOGGY.

Oof, okay, my first guess would be that you need more heat. You've got to crank it to medium-high (depending on your stove), press the potatoes into a thoroughly preheated, well-lubricated cast-iron or stainless steel pan, and fearlessly allow them to sit undisturbed for a solid couple minutes. Another culprit could be insufficient par-cooking and/ or improper drying—make sure your potatoes are thoroughly cooked, preferably in some water spiked with a tablespoon of vinegar, before spreading out evenly on a rimmed baking sheet to cool and dry out.

MY EGGS WON'T SET CORRECTLY.

So long as you're covering your pan and reducing the heat a bit, this really comes down to timing, and it's going to take some practice runs. Also see: Shakshuka, Troubleshooting, page 176.

SERVES 4 TO 6

2 pounds russet potatoes, peeled and chopped into ½-inch cubes (see Note)

1 tablespoon white vinegar

Kosher salt and freshly ground black pepper

2 tablespoons duck fat (or fat of choice), plus more if necessary

½ pound fatty pastrami, cut into ½-inch cubes

½ large onion, chopped

1 red bell pepper, chopped

1 tablespoon minced fresh sage leaves

4 to 6 large eggs

2 large scallions (greens only) minced

In a large stock pot, cover the potatoes with cold water. Add the vinegar and 1 tablespoon salt and bring to a boil over medium-high heat. Cook until the potatoes are tender but not falling apart, 10 to 12 minutes. Drain, spread out evenly on a rimmed baking sheet, and allow to cool completely, at least 30 minutes.

In a large cast-iron skillet, melt the duck fat over medium-high heat. Once shimmering, add the pastrami and fry, stirring occasionally, until crisp, 3 to 5 minutes. Drain on paper towels, reserving ¼ cup of the fat in the skillet (it might be necessary to supplement with more duck fat). Heat over medium-high heat until shimmering.

Add the onion and bell pepper to the fat and cook over medium heat, stirring occasionally, until softened and beginning to brown, 3 to 5 minutes. Add the cooled potatoes and toss thoroughly to coat evenly in the fat. Press the mixture down into an even layer on the bottom of the skillet and cook, undisturbed, until beginning to brown, 2 to 5 minutes. Using a stiff, thin spatula, firmly scoop and flip the potato mixture until everybody has been thoroughly shuffled. Repeat this process until the potatoes are well-caramelized and crisp, 4 to 5 times—before the final flip 'n' toss, add the sage and fried pastrami, distributing them throughout the hash.

Reduce the heat to low and crack the eggs into a spouted measuring cup. Using a spoon or spatula, make 4 to 6 divots in the hash, and gently tip 1 egg into each divot. Cover the skillet and cook until the egg whites are set but the yolks are still runny, 4 to 6 minutes. Garnish with the scallions and freshly ground black pepper over each egg.

Note: *Place the cubed potatoes in cold water in a large stock pot as you peel and cut them to prevent them from oxidizing. Alternatively, instead of boiling the potatoes, use leftover peeled baked potatoes.*

SPRING VEGETABLE QUICHE (WITH LOTS OF BACON AND CHEESE)

We obviously all remember where we were and exactly what day and time it was when we had our first bite of quiche, right? No? Yeah, I guess I don't remember mine either. I do, however, remember my first bite of truly *great* quiche. It was at Bouchon Bakery in Napa, about as quiche-y a place as ever there was, and it was spectacular. By virtue of a springform pan, the buttery, flaky, crispy pastry is sculpted neatly around a silky custard, rich with cheese and cured pork, every texture of the texture rainbow on display. Quiche for Sunday brunch is a mild to moderate challenge for the average home cook—memorable quiche, on the other hand, is a prize not easily won. This recipe is resultantly complicated, but sleep soundly tonight knowing that no matter how fussy a direction might seem, its sole purpose is the success of your quiche. Imagine if that was your sole purpose—you'd want to be taken seriously, wouldn't you? Did I just guilt-trip you by anthropomorphizing recipe directions? Is that a world-first?

How I've Screwed This Up

I've screwed this up not yet a week prior to the very writing of these words that you are currently reading. Pie crust alone is a major investment of time and energy, and especially when making a visually impressive deep-dish quiche like this one, is fraught with peril. Shrinking, slipping, puffing, and soggy bottoms abound, cheapening hours upon hours of gingerly coaxing ingredients into what you imagined would be a perfect pie crust. Clearly, I'm still bitter from this last one springing a leak on me and wrecking my bottom. That came out wrong.

Troubleshooting

MY QUICHE HAS A SOGGY BOTTOM.

First off, don't beat yourself up. Quiche is far and away the liquidiest filling for any pie crust, and managing to preserve a crunchy bottom is nothing short of a miracle. We recommend using a sheet or two of phyllo dough to insulate the crust from all the wet.

MY QUICHE CUSTARD CRACKED.

This happens with quiches and pumpkin pies alike, both being custards and all. The answer to both problems is the custard cooling down too quickly after coming out of the oven. If it's the dead of summer in N'awlins, you're probably fine to just put it on the counter—if, however, it's the coldest evening yet in Anchorage, you can more slowly cool the quiche by turning off the oven and wedging a wooden spoon into the door so that heat can escape.

MY CRUST SHRUNK!

I think it's appropriate that you went with an exclamation point! It's often shocking to find that your perfect pie shell has become a shell of its former self. This is often attributed to dough that hasn't been properly chilled—make sure you refrigerate at each stage for at least an hour, ideally overnight between mixing and shaping.

MY CRUST SLIPPED.

This can be a problem caused by using a glass pie dish, which can have a more difficult time gripping onto the pastry, but more likely you need to make sure the aluminum foil is pressed flush with the crust and it is filled all the way to the brim with beans or sugar. All that weight pressing down evenly on the pastry will keep it in place, and once it's partially baked and the weights have been removed, it can crisp up while keeping its shape!

MY QUICHE IS DRY/CRUMBLY.

Sounds like it was overbaked. Make sure you're pulling it from the oven when it's set around the edges but still wobbly in the center!

MY QUICHE SPRUNG A LEAK.

Your pastry might've been too thin or it might've gotten cracked after the par-baking process—either way, there's no saving the crispness of your crust at this point. To save the custard, you can blast your quiche in a hot oven for 10 minutes to set the custard dripping out before dropping the temperature back down to quiche-appropriate levels to finish cooking.

SERVES 8 TO 10

Caramelized Leeks and Bacon

2 cups thinly sliced leeks (white and pale green parts only)

1 tablespoon light olive oil

½ pound bacon, sliced into lardons (¼-by-1-inch strips)

Freshly ground black pepper

Blanched Asparagus

2 cups chopped (2-inch pieces) asparagus

Sauteed Vegetables

2 tablespoons unsalted butter

2 cups sliced mushrooms of choice (I use cremini and oyster)

3 fresh thyme sprigs

Kosher salt

6 cups baby spinach

2 garlic cloves, minced or crushed in a garlic press

Custard

2 cups whole milk

2 cups crème fraîche

10 large eggs

6 tablespoons all-purpose flour

1 tablespoon chopped fresh thyme leaves

2 teaspoons freshly ground white pepper

½ teaspoon freshly grated nutmeg

Kosher salt

To Assemble

1 Quiche Shell (recipe follows), par-baked and cooled

2 sheets phyllo dough

4 ounces Gruyère cheese, grated

3 ounces Emmental cheese, grated

MAKE THE CARAMELIZED LEEKS AND BACON: Soak the leeks in a bowl of cold water for 10 minutes, then drain well.

Heat the oil in a large skillet over medium-high heat. Add the leeks and reduce the heat to medium-low and cover with a lid. Cook, stirring occasionally, until the leeks are very tender, 15 to 20 minutes. Add ¼ cup water, cover, and cook 3 to 5 minutes. Uncover and cook until all the water is evaporated, 5 to 10 minutes. Add the bacon and cook, stirring occasionally, until the bacon is crisp, about 5 minutes. Season with pepper, transfer to a plate, and set aside.

BLANCHE THE ASPARAGUS: Bring a large pot of water to a boil. Add the asparagus and cook until just tender but still bright green, 3 to 4 minutes.

Meanwhile, prepare a large bowl of ice water.

Using tongs or a spider, transfer the asparagus to the ice bath and let cool, then drain and set aside.

MAKE THE SAUTEED VEGETABLES: Melt 1 tablespoon of the butter in a large skillet over medium-high heat. Add the mushrooms, thyme, and ½ teaspoon salt. Cook, stirring occasionally, until the mushrooms have released all of their water and have browned, 7 to 8 minutes. Transfer the mushrooms to a plate and set aside; discard the thyme sprigs.

Melt the remaining 1 tablespoon butter in the same skillet. Add the spinach and cook, stirring, until completely wilted, 3 to 4 minutes. Add the garlic and cook, stirring, for 1 more minute. Season with salt, transfer to a plate, and set aside.

Preheat the oven to 325°F.

MAKE THE CUSTARD: In a large bowl, combine the milk and crème fraîche. Whisk well to incorporate.

In a stand mixer fitted with the whisk attachment, combine 5 eggs and the flour. Mix at medium-low speed until a paste forms, 1 to 2 minutes. Scrape down the sides of the bowl, add the remaining 5 eggs, and the milk mixture. Mix at medium speed until thoroughly combined, about 1 minute. Then add the thyme, white pepper, nutmeg, and 1½ tablespoons salt. Mix on medium speed until the custard is light and frothy, 1 to 2 minutes.

TO ASSEMBLE: Line the quiche shell with an even layer of the phyllo dough. (This will help prevent a soggy bottom.) Sprinkle with some of each cheese, then top with an equal amount each of the caramelized leeks and bacon, blanched asparagus, and sautéed vegetables. Add enough of the custard to cover the vegetables. Repeat this layering process with the remaining ingredients, reserving some cheese for topping, until the shell is just about full, stopping 3 to 4 millimeters from the top.

Sprinkle the quiche with the remaining cheese and bake for 1½ to 2 hours, until the edges are set but the center is still a bit jiggly and the internal temperature reaches 175°F. Allow the quiche to cool at room temperature for at least 4 hours before serving. Optionally, once the quiche has cooled to room temperature, refrigerate for up to 3 days before serving.

QUICHE SHELL

Makes 1 tall (8-inch) shell

285 grams bread flour

1 teaspoon kosher salt

1 cup (2 sticks) cold unsalted butter, cubed

80 to 110 grams ice water

In a stand mixer fitted with the paddle attachment, combine the flour and salt. Mix until well combined. Add the butter and mix at medium-low speed until the butter pieces are the size of blueberries. With the mixer running on low speed, slowly add enough of the ice water to form a dough.
　　(**Note:** *To make by hand, whisk the flour and salt in a large bowl. Add the butter and break the pieces into a similar size by rubbing them between your fingers.*)

Wrap the dough in plastic wrap and shape it into a disk. (Note, the dough can also be assembled without a stand mixer, it's just harder, obviously: Add the cold butter to the flour in a large bowl, and break up the butter with your hands or a pastry cutter until the flour is sandy and the butter pieces are the size of blueberries. Add the ice water and gently knead together by hand until all the flour is hydrated and the dough holds together.) Refrigerate for a minimum of 1 hour, up to overnight.

Remove the chilled dough from the refrigerator and roll out to about ¼ inch thick. Carefully transfer the dough to an 8-inch high-sided springform pan. Then, gently lift and press the dough into the sides of the pan. If the dough gets too soft, refrigerate for 10 minutes and then resume lining the pan. Make sure the excess dough hangs off the edges of the pan, this will prevent the dough from shrinking during the par-baking process. Once the pie dough is flush with the side of the pan, refrigerate for 1 hour.

Preheat the oven to 375°F.

Using two pieces of parchment paper, line the dough in the springform pan. Fill the pan to the rim with sugar or dried beans.

Par-bake the quiche shell for 25 minutes. Remove the sugar and parchment paper, then continue to bake the shell for 10 to 15 minutes more, until the pastry looks dry and turns pale golden.
　　(**Note:** *Save all that sugar— it's been toasted in the oven, and has only been improved for future recipe usage!*)

Trim off the excess crust using a sharp paring knife. Allow the quiche shell to cool completely before filling.

EGGS SPENEDICT
(EGGS BENEDICT WITH SPECK)

Ah, eggs benedict. One kind of runny egg smothered with another kind of runny egg, both presenting their own set of daunting challenges to the burgeoning home chef. Not only do you need to poach eggs, a process plagued with ghostly egg whites and sulphuric odors, you need to make hollandaise, about as fussy an emulsion as ever there was. Luckily, blender hollandaise dramatically streamlines the experience, and sieving the eggs before poaching helps to do away with haunted egg syndrome. As for the perfect circle of ham hailing from the Great White North, I prefer to opt for some pan fried speck, which brings both extra flavor and texture to the party. Unfortunately, per Benedictine Society guidelines, this disqualifies my dish from bearing the name "Eggs Benedict"—hence the outrageous play on words.

How I've Screwed This Up

See: English Muffins (page 75), plus every imaginable way you could ruin a hollandaise, or poached eggs for that matter.

Troubleshooting

NO MATTER HOW CAREFUL I AM, MY EGGS TURN INTO A SPOOKY GHOST WHEN I DROP THEM IN THE WATER.

Make sure you're using *very* fresh eggs. The outer layer of the white is often thinner and runnier than the rest of the egg, and as eggs age, it gets thinner and runnier still. This is the stuff that turns your pot into a haunted house, so the less of it there is, the better. But at the end of the day, once you scoop them out of the water, a spindly white all but disappears anyway.

MY HOLLANDAISE IS THIN AND WATERY.

Blender hollandaise is thickened by hot butter, but to a much greater extent, the process of emulsification. Your egg yolks need to reach the blades of your blender so they can be properly emulsified with and cooked by the hot butter, so make sure there's enough in the blender jar. Then, make sure your butter is nice and hot so it cooks the egg yolks enough to thicken them.

MY HOLLANDAISE KEEPS BREAKING.

So long as it's not your eggs scrambling, hollandaise breaks when not enough water is present. As counterintuitive as it may seem, a squirt of water into the sauce as it blends may reunite the estranged elements of this emulsion.

HOW CAN I USE CANADIAN BACON IN THE RECIPE?

Our relationship with Canada has changed here in the year 2029, that's for sure. Despite armies of troops amassed on both sides of the so-called Maple Curtain, there are robust black markets for Canadian meat products—but as with any prohibition, price gouging, violence and counterfeiting run rampant. Wherever there's still land above water, you can be sure that violating the International Pork Law in a fever pitch of global conflict won't just score you some of the round stuff—it'll also net you a hefty fine and could even carry a lengthy mind-prison sentence (yes, like that one in *Black Mirror*). But if you manage to actually get your hands on some, just fry it up until lightly browned on both sides before serving.

SERVES 4

2 tablespoons bacon fat (or vegetable oil)

½ pound sliced or torn speck (or Canadian bacon, for traditional)

8 large eggs

1 teaspoon Dijon mustard

Juice of 1 lemon

1 teaspoon hot sauce

¼ teaspoon sweet paprika, plus more for garnish

½ cup unsalted butter, plus 2 tablespoons melted

4 homemade English Muffins (page 75), split with a fork

Vegetable oil, for greasing

Minced chives (optional)

In a large cast-iron skillet, heat the bacon fat over medium-high heat until shimmering. Working in batches, add the speck, in a single layer and cook, lowering the heat so that the speck sizzles but does not smoke, until crispy, 2 to 3 minutes per side. Drain on paper towels and set aside. (Optionally, reserve the fat from the pan and let cool. If it doesn't taste acrid or burnt, brush it onto your split English muffins before toasting!)

Separate 4 of the eggs and place the yolks in a blender. (Save these egg whites for another use.) Add the mustard, lemon juice, hot sauce, and paprika and blend until combined, about 5 seconds—make sure that the blades of the blender are in full contact with the yolk mixture.

In a medium saucepan, heat 2 quarts water over medium-high heat to about 190°F then lower the heat.

Meanwhile, in a small saucepan, preferably with a spout or lip, bring the ½ cup butter to a simmer over medium heat. If your saucepan does not have a spout or lip, transfer the butter to a liquid measuring cup. With the blender running, carefully and slowly stream the butter in through the opening in the lid and blend until the hollandaise thickens into a luxurious sauce. Cover and keep warm until ready to serve.

Crack one of the 4 remaining whole eggs into a fine-mesh sieve, allowing any loose egg white to drain away. Carefully tip the egg into the sub-boiling water in the medium saucepan and swirl the water gently with a spoon around the egg to keep its white intact. Cook until the white is set but the yolk is runny, 4 to 5 minutes. Using a slotted spoon, transfer the poached egg to a plate. Repeat with the remaining whole eggs.

Heat the same large cast-iron skillet over medium heat and coat lightly with oil. Brush the English muffins with the remaining 2 tablespoons melted butter (or reserved frying fat). Working in batches, fry split-side down in a single layer until well-browned and crisp, 2 to 3 minutes. Remove from the skillet and divide among plates. Top each muffin half with several pieces of crispy speck, followed by a single poached egg, and pour hollandaise on top. Garnish with paprika and, if desired, chives and serve.

DEVILED EGGS

Deviled eggs, apart from being an American picnicking staple, are just about the only way I am willing to consume hard-boiled eggs. Let's face it, from the difficult peeling process to the sulphuric odor that perfumes the breathing air of nearby unwilling participants, they are a borderline objectionable way to prepare an egg (unless you're one of those people who just *loves* hard-boiled eggs, in which case, more power to you). So if you find yourself with a dozen or so on your hands, why not split them like an avocado, mash up their yellow-green cores with some bright and bracing ingredients, and pipe them back into their gelatinous shells for an enhanced boiled egg eating experience? All it's going to cost you is a squirt of condiments and a sprinkle of spices, and you'll quickly go from the insane person who brought a bucket of unpeeled hard boiled eggs to the party, to the dashing debutante who presented a platter of elegant eggs.

How I've Screwed This Up

The same way some folks seem to get stung by more mosquitoes or barked at by more dogs, eggs have a preternatural hatred of me in particular, and stubbornly refuse to yield their innards to me without forming cracks and crevices. Luckily, deviled eggs also serve as a broken-egg-savior, shunning the oneness of a boiled egg for two distinct halves.

Troubleshooting

MY EGG YOLKS ARE GREENISH, HOW IS THAT EVEN POSSIBLE?

I'm guessing they don't smell great either—this is a sure sign of an overcooked egg, which causes the sulphuric compounds of the yolk to combine with the white, creating a greenish layer around the former. They're not necessarily ruined, but if you went way over the 12 minute cook time, you'll probably want to start over.

MY FILLING IS TOO LOOSE.

Sounds like too many condiments or hot sauce—you can thicken it with additional cooked egg yolks or mayonnaise, whipping the filling to aerate and volumize it.

MY EGGS CRACKED IN THE WATER AND SOME STUFF CAME OUT.

This happens! The eggs might've been dropped into the water with too reckless an abandon, there might've been hairline cracks from the shipping process, the boiling water might've tumbled them around a bit too much. So long as you didn't lose too much white, they're potentially salvageable and perfectly safe to eat!

MAKES 16 DEVILED EGG HALVES

8 large eggs

¼ cup mayonnaise, preferably homemade (see page 312)

1½ teaspoons Dijon mustard

¼ teaspoon smoked paprika

Kosher salt and freshly ground black pepper

Tabasco sauce

Optional Toppings

Chopped fresh dill fronds + paprika

Capers + smoked salmon

Chopped fresh chives + Candied Bacon (page 313)

Chopped fresh cilantro + sliced jalapeños

Pickled Red Onion (recipe follows)

Place the eggs in a medium saucepan with enough water to cover the eggs about 1 inch. Bring to a boil, then cover, and remove from the heat. Let sit for 12 minutes.

Meanwhile, prepare a large bowl of ice water.

Transfer the eggs to the ice bath and let sit until cooled. Peel the eggs, cut each in half lengthwise, then scoop the egg yolks into a medium bowl. Refrigerate the egg whites until ready to fill.

To the egg yolks, add the mayonnaise, mustard, smoked paprika, ½ teaspoon salt, ½ teaspoon pepper, and Tabasco sauce to taste. Mix with a tiny whisk or fork until completely smooth. Transfer to a resealable plastic bag or airtight container and refrigerate until ready to use, up to 1 week.

To serve, add a dollop of the egg yolk filling to each egg white half. Garnish with your desired toppings and serve!

PICKLED RED ONION

Makes about 2 cups

1 red onion, thinly sliced

1 cup white vinegar

3 tablespoons sugar

1 teaspoon kosher salt

Place the red onion in a jar or sealable heatproof container.

In a small saucepan, combine the vinegar, sugar, salt, and ½ cup water. Bring to a simmer then pour over the onion. Cover with the lid and let sit at room temperature 30 minutes.

Serve or refrigerate for up to 2 weeks.

JAMMY SCOTCH EGGS

As you may have seen on my YouTube series *Botched by Babish*, I came clean in 2021 about having used a soft-boiled egg swap out in my original Scotch Egg video, a wound in our collective hearts that I recognize may never heal. After repeated (failed) attempts to get a runny egg yolk in the middle of a fully cooked sausage shell with a golden-brown crispy exterior, I finally nailed the many delicate balances of temperature and time, yielding a melty golden prize at its center. I was quickly informed in the comments, however, that the vast majority of Scotch eggs consumed in the world have hard-boiled centers. So maybe don't fuss about it too much.

How I've Screwed This Up

Apart from the amusing anecdote above, about the worst scotch eggs I've ever made had under-cooked sausage. That might not have normally been a problem (just toss them into the oven to finish cooking through), but I had taken a page out of the British Outdoor Dining Handbook and taken them on a picnic. That was also a first date. And the only food we packed. Not the greatest look, obviously.

Troubleshooting

MY EGGS ARE UNBELIEVABLY DIFFICULT TO PEEL.
Ironically, you might be being *too* gentle. There is a thin membrane between the egg shell and the egg itself, and without piercing it, the running water under which you're peeling won't be able to get between the egg and the shell. Pinch at the egg underneath the shell if you're not sure—if you're able to pull up a thin, papery layer with your fingers, you haven't broken the membrane. After a few eggs, you'll be peeling like a champ!

WHEN I PEEL MY EGGS, THE WHITE BREAKS VERY EASILY.
Sounds like your whites aren't cooked enough—try cooking them for a minute longer. Sometimes I like to start by boiling/steaming one egg at a time, starting with 6 minutes and increasing one minute at a time until I reach the perfect consistency.

MY SAUSAGE IS UNDERCOOKED.
Don't be afraid to temperature check your Scotch eggs—so long as you don't stab it all the way down to the yolk, you can stick a thermometer sausage-deep and see how things are going under cover of that crumby exterior.

I CAN'T GET THE YOLK RUNNY.
This is a balancing act and takes some practice, and if I'm being honest, is only barely worth the reward. If you think about it, you're placing an egg in a cooking environment two times, the second time trying to heat its outer layer to 165°F while not exceeding 150°F at its core. Unless you've poached, shaped, and fried a fair share of things in the kitchen, you better call Jean-Claude Van Damme, because that's gonna be a *Hard Target* . . . to hit. If you overcooked the yolks, who cares? It's still wrapped in deep-fried sausage and slathered in mustard mayo.

MAKES 12 SCOTCH EGGS

¼ cup whole-grain mustard

¼ cup mayonnaise

12 medium eggs, as fresh as possible

1½ pounds ground pork

2 tablespoons minced fresh sage leaves

1 tablespoon minced fresh thyme leaves

1 teaspoon red pepper flakes

Kosher salt and freshly ground black pepper

1 cup plus one tablespoon all-purpose flour

4 cups panko bread crumbs

4 quarts peanut, vegetable, or canola oil

In a small bowl, whisk together the mustard and mayonnaise until homogeneous. Cover and refrigerate until ready to serve.

Bring ½ inch water to a boil in a wide, high-walled sauté pan over high heat. Reduce heat to low, cover, and allow to come to a steady simmer. Add 8 of the eggs, cover tightly, and cook for 6 minutes 30 seconds for jammy eggs (or 8 minutes for hard-boiled eggs).

Meanwhile, prepare a large bowl of ice water. When the eggs are done, drain and immediately plunge them into the ice bath and allow to cool completely, about 15 minutes.

Crack and peel the eggs under running water. May Gaea grant you strength.

In a medium bowl, combine the pork, sage, thyme, pepper flakes, 2 teaspoons salt, and 1 teaspoon pepper. Mix until well distributed, then divide into 8 portions. Flatten each portion into a disc slightly wider than the length of your hand, place 1 peeled egg into the center, and wrap the sausage around the egg.

(**NOTE:** *Depending on the size of your eggs, you may be able to encase more or less than 8 eggs with sausage, adjust accordingly.*)

Spread the 1 cup flour in a wide cake pan or pie plate. Crack the remaining 4 eggs into another cake pan or pie plate and whisk together with the 1 tablespoon flour into a smooth slurry. In a third cake pan or pie plate, spread out the panko. Roll each sausage-wrapped egg in the flour until evenly coated, dust off any excess, then roll in the egg slurry until evenly and thoroughly coated. Roll in the panko until coated in a thick crust. Arrange on a plate until ready to fry.

In a high-walled medium pot, heat 3½ inches of the oil to 375°F. Slowly and carefully add two of the Scotch eggs (one at a time) into the oil with a slotted spoon. The temperature of the oil will drop rapidly once the eggs are added, so adjust the heat accordingly to try and keep the temperature as close to (but not over) 375°F. Fry the eggs, rotating every minute or so, until evenly browned and the sausage registers at least 155°F at its thickest point, 7 to 10 minutes total. Drain on paper towels and serve hot, cold, or at room temperature with the grainy mustard faux aioli.

CHAPTER 5

VEGETABLES

/

SIDE DISHES

Dude, I didn't even mean to make that line up! Chapter V—Vegetables? You can't write this stuff! Or rather, I guess you can, given that you are currently reading it. Vegetables: your child's greatest enemy, your body's best friend, and the thing we tend to eat out of obligation rather than gratification. This chapter hopes to alter that paradigm, undoing the sulphuric boiled Brussels sprout fumes of your youth in favor of crisp-tender roasted gems of earthen savor. Most vegetables aren't just packed with nutrients and fiber, they're also packed with flavor that just needs to be coaxed out. Carrots are so naturally sweet, they're often used in lieu of sugar in slow-cooked tomato sauces. Butternut squash, with little more than salt and a splash of oil, can be transformed into a soup more luscious than triple cream. In Norse mythology, green beans were offered as gifts to Freyja, goddess of war and fertility, whose love for the emerald green pods was the subject of song and folklore. I made that one up. Rule of threes.

WHAT ARE VEGETABLES? Let's see—usually they're green? They grow on other, larger vegetables called plants. They like sun for lunch and water for dinner, except mushrooms, which eat poop and hide in closets.

SHOULD I EAT MY VEGETABLES? Yes, you should, young man, they're very good for you—if you batter, deep fry, and dip them in truffle mayo, not as much. Apart from vitamins, minerals, and other essential nutrients, the hottest ticket on the back of the box is fiber. Fiber is so good for you, some nutritionists only count "net carbs"—that is, the carbs that remain after you've subtracted the fiber you've eaten. Carrots are so good for you, they improve your goddamn vision. Celery is so fucking good for you, you burn more calories from digesting it than you get from eating it.

WHAT ABOUT FROZEN VEGETABLES? Not only are frozen vegetables less expensive, they're sometimes considered more nutritious than their fresh counterparts, having been flash-frozen at the peak of freshness. Their texture and flavor can suffer to varying extents, but for playing supporting roles in stir-fries and pot roasts, you can't do much better. When vegetables are the star of the show, however, you might want to opt for the crates lining the entrance to the grocery store.

ARE ORGANIC VEGETABLES WORTH THE EXTRA MONEY? Not really—sort of—but not really, though. Certified organic vegetables are required to be grown in soil that has not been treated with synthetic pesticides and fertilizers for at least three years, which could, potentially, be slightly good or something. But like "non-GMO," "hormone-free," and "recycling," the little green sticker with the big price tag is too often just a marketing ploy.. I'm not going to turn into a Netflix documentary about the frigid, soulless reality of mass food production and distribution in what little we have left of a society— but I will say that in America, it's a miracle that you're even eating asparagus, much less the organic variety. Celebrate small victories.

ARE FARMERS' MARKET VEGETABLES WORTH WAKING UP AT 7 A.M., FILLING MY CAMELBAK WITH COFFEE, RIDING MY MUSTARD-YELLOW 1987 CENTURION DOWNTUBE TO THE COMMUNITY CENTER, AND SHOULDER-CHECKING MY WAY THROUGH A CROWD OF UNBATHED STRANGERS AND FEUDING COUPLES FOR? It pains me to say this, but, yeah it can be. Farmers' market stalls are often filled with passionate, knowledgeable people that have painstakingly raised the vegetables strewn before you by hand, utilizing generational know-how with every granule of soil wizenedly tilled and every seed gleefully sown. Okay, maybe I'm romanticizing. Point is, the vast majority of supermarket vegetables are farmed by the cold, unfeeling eye of a vast network of robots, clawing madly into the very DNA strands of its produce in the pursuit of greater yield, brighter color, and something to do with margins. Again, romanticizing—but the shrink-wrapped carrots sold next to the skateboards and shotguns in the big box store are not going to taste the same as those hand-tilled by Millie and Scooter, who met after being tear-gassed at the same Vietnam War protest, and have run their Vermontian carrot farm/ayahuasca retreat with little more than sunshine and love ever since.

CHARRED WINTER VEGETABLES WITH ROASTED GARLIC VINAIGRETTE

While they might rank among the simpler dishes in this book, these effortless roasted roots can play a rich, elegant supporting role to a wide variety of mains, particularly those with a sharp sauce to cut through all the woodsy flavors. One of my all-time favorite roasting hacks gets put to work in spectacular(ish) fashion here: preheating the sheet pan in the oven yields not only pleasurable sounds and smells, but helps to quickly develop a crunchy crust on the undisturbed facets of each subterranean jewel. The first time around can be a test of your oven's efficacy, burnt carrots revealing hot spots, quickly burning or pale and dry veggies indicating temperatures running high or low, respectively. It can also measure your consistency in cutting vegetable pieces for roasting, undersize pieces shriveling into burnt parsnip twigs and oversize hunks of squash remaining stubbornly raw in the middle. Once the harmonic balance is found between heat and movement, it becomes a weeknight staple, offering up opportunities for experimentation and customization: Brussels sprouts on sale? Cut off the base, slice the mini cabbages in half, and cut the rest of the veggies to the same thickness. Wanna class things up for date night? Swap the neutral oil with duck or chicken fat. Turn this into a main? No problem, serve over greens with goat cheese, apples, and walnuts.

How I've Screwed This Up

Stubbornly refusing to believe that my college dorm room's common area kitchen could possibly stray more than 25 degrees from my specified temperature. As it turns out, it's significantly less "cool" to set off the fire alarms from roasting vegetables than it is from, say, smoking weed.

Troubleshooting

MY VEGETABLES CAME OUT KIND OF SOFT AND MUSHY.

Sounds like the pan was overcrowded—too many veggies touching can result in condensation and steam forming, making a moist cooking environment instead of a dry one.

MY VEGETABLES BURNED.

Did all of them burn or just the ones toward the sides of the pan?

THE SIDES.

Sounds like hot spots, particularly if the sheet pan was close to or touching the walls of the oven. Now can you say they burnt all over, just for information's sake?

OH, SURE. THEY BURNT ALL OVER.

Oven's running hot and/or the tray was too close to the top of the oven. Now say they only burnt on the bottom.

THEY ONLY BURNT ON THE BOTTOM.

Was the rack in the bottom of the oven?

NO.

In this hypothetical where they burnt on the bottom, it likely would've been. Say yes.

YES.

Bullseye! Having the sheet pan too close to your oven's heating element can cause them to burn quickly and/or prematurely.

SERVES 4

4 small parsnips, peeled and halved lengthwise

4 small carrots, peeled and halved lengthwise

12 cipollini onions or shallots, peeled and left whole

1 celery root, peeled and cut into 1-inch pieces

½ butternut squash, peeled, seeded, and cut into 1-inch pieces

1 lemon, halved

¼ cup plus 1 tablespoon light olive oil

Kosher salt and freshly ground black pepper

1 head garlic, top trimmed to expose all the cloves

¼ cup extra-virgin olive oil

2 tablespoons chopped fresh chives, plus more for garnish

Tip: *Now, more than ever, is the time to go for the pre-peeled cipollinis or shallots in the produce fridge of your local grocer.*

Preheat the oven to 400°F with a large sheet pan inside, at least 15 minutes.

In a large bowl, combine the parsnips, carrots, onions, celery root, squash, and lemon and toss to coat with the ¼ cup light olive oil, 2 teaspoons salt, and 1 teaspoon pepper.

Place the head of garlic in a square of aluminum foil, drizzle the exposed cloves with the remaining 1 tablespoon light olive oil and sprinkle with 1 teaspoon salt. Wrap the foil tightly around the garlic and set aside.

Carefully pour the contents of the large bowl onto the preheated sheet pan, spreading out evenly, taking care not to overcrowd. Arrange the lemon halves cut-side down, nestle the garlic foil parcel toward the edge of the pan, and roast, tossing the vegetables after 15 minutes and every 10 minutes thereafter, for 35 to 45 minutes total, until the vegetables are golden brown and cooked through and the lemon halves are charred. Be sure to circulate vegetables from the center of the pan to the outside and vice versa so that they cook evenly. Remove from the oven and allow to cool for 5 minutes.

Retrieve the garlic head from its foil packet, and squeeze/dig out its softened contents into a resealable container. Squeeze the charred lemon halves over the roasted garlic and add the extra-virgin olive oil, chives, and 1 teaspoon pepper. Cover the container, shake vigorously to emulsify into a vinaigrette, and taste for seasoning, adjusting as necessary. Serve the vegetables drizzled with dressing and garnished with more chopped chives.

BROWNED BUTTERNUT SQUASH SOUP

Browned butter and butternut squash work together about as well as they sound—that is to say, delightfully. While this is a prime opportunity to put that wedding-registry-furnished high-powered blender to good use, it shouldn't take too many RPM's to reduce these formerly fibrous vegetables into a smooth, impossibly creamy soup. This also presents the opportunity to exercise a restaurant industry standby in favor of adding creaminess without cream: blending soup with bread, beans, nuts, cooked white rice, even a handful of cooked pasta. When liquefied, these various starches can provide richness and body to soups without anything so gauche as actual dairy. It also presents as an orangey-gold foundation for any number of rich, sweet, and/or savory toppings. Bacon, cinnamon sugar croutons, fried sage, toasted hazelnuts, picked thyme, crème fraîche, honey, maple syrup, fried mushrooms, goat cheese, stewed figs, pumpkin seeds, fried apples, cranberries, candied jalapeños—individually or altogether—are potential builders of mouth meal cohesion.

How I've Screwed This Up

For as many ways as there are to screw this recipe up, there are two to make it good again. It's what makes this recipe an interesting study in customizability.

Troubleshooting

I UNDERCOOKED MY SQUASH.

Hey, we make a great team! Especially if you have a high-powered blender, even if you've managed to accidentally undercook your vegetable flesh, you can both smooth and finish cooking it in the selfsame device. Just blend it within an inch of its life.

I BURNT MY BUTTER.

Toss it. I'm sorry, but it's got an objectionable flavor and smell, and it will ruin your final dish. Smile, shrug, and grab another stick of butter—it's the American Way™.

MY SOUP IS TOO THIN.

This is an excellent opportunity to thicken things up with any number of pantry accessible options: bread, cooked rice, cooked pasta, oatmeal, a roux, or more cooked vegetables are all means by which to repair or enhance your soup's texture.

MY SOUP IS TOO THICK.

Add some milk!

I'M LACTOSE INTOLERANT.

Then use chicken stock.

I'M A VEGETARIAN.

Vegetable stock.

I DON'T HAVE ANY AND ALL THE STORES ARE CLOSED.

You sound kinda unprepared for this recipe. Just use water and add a little salt! I know it sounds lame but most substances are mostly water (I think), so all you're doing is upping the ratio or something.

SERVES 8

8 tablespoons (1 stick) unsalted butter

10 to 16 fresh sage leaves

1 tablespoon fresh thyme leaves

1 large butternut squash, peeled, seeded, and cut into 1-inch cubes

1 green apple, cored, peeled, and cut into 1-inch cubes

1 tablespoon neutral oil (such as canola, vegetable, or grapeseed)

1 tablespoon pure maple syrup or molasses

1 tablespoon bourbon (optional)

Kosher salt and freshly ground black pepper

½ cup leftover cooked white rice or 1 slice white bread

½ teaspoon ground cinnamon

½ teaspoon freshly grated nutmeg, plus more for garnish

¼ teaspoon cayenne pepper

¼ teaspoon ground cardamom

1 teaspoon vanilla paste or ½ teaspoon vanilla extract (optional)

1 tablespoon yellow miso (optional)

1 to 4 cups Chicken Stock (page 268), as needed

Extra-virgin olive oil and crème fraîche, for serving

Preheat the oven to 400°F with a large rimmed baking sheet inside.

In a small saucepan, melt the butter over medium heat. Continue to cook, swirling near-constantly, until the milk fats separate and begin to turn blonde, 4 to 6 minutes. Add the sage and thyme leaves, immediately remove from the heat, and allow to continue browning as the butter cools. Strain the butter into a small heatproof bowl and transfer the fried herbs to paper towels to drain. Set aside the brown butter.

In a large bowl, combine the butternut squash, apple, neutral oil, maple syrup, and if desired, the bourbon, and 1 teaspoon salt. Toss to coat evenly and carefully pour onto the preheated sheet pan, spreading evenly. Return to the oven and roast for about 30 minutes, scraping and flipping with a thin spatula halfway through, until the squash is well-browned and easily pierced with a paring knife.

Scoop the squash flesh into a high-powered blender with half of the reserved brown butter. Add the rice, cinnamon, nutmeg, cayenne pepper, cardamom, and if desired, the vanilla paste and miso, and blend with the stock as needed, until the desired consistency is achieved.

Heat the soup on the stovetop if necessary, or blend until hot. Serve with the remaining brown butter, crumble the crispy sage and thyme on top, and drizzle with olive oil and crème fraîche. Garnish with freshly ground pepper and grated nutmeg.

BACON-ROASTED BRUSSELS SPROUTS

This one's all Kendall, my Kitchen Producer—the mad little genius dropped this gem on me with days to spare before Thanksgiving 2021. As such, she's going to write the headnote and stuff! Kendall, take it away!

Hello readers, this is admittedly an odd place to greet you, but this is my time! I wish I could tell you this was a time-honored Beach family tradition, but it's not. Back in the year 2019, my mother, my aunt Lynn, and I were preparing the traditional Thanksgiving sides (don't worry, I've since been promoted to turkey duty). One of us, let's just say it was me, suggested that we add bacon to the Brussels sprouts. This obviously isn't a novel idea but I had just learned in school that fat molecules inhibit our taste buds from "reading" bitter flavors; since Brussels sprouts are rife with bitter compounds, fat is a natural pairing. One of us, let's just say it was me again, then tacked on the idea of placing the strips over top of the Brussels sprouts so that as the fat renders, it coats the sprouts in delicious bacon flavor. This was largely a time-saving idea because we were already running late and the 45 seconds it would take to cut the bacon into pieces and then toss them with the Brussels sprouts was simply too much. At any rate, it turned out super well and who says traditions have to be old anyway? We've made it at every Thanksgiving since! (Plus, it earned me some real brownie points at work.)

How I've Screwed This Up

This one is fairly simple, but please heed my only warning. You may be tempted to go for the extra-thick deluxe heritage bacon, as I have been many times before. While in theory, this might be a good idea, in practice, not so much. What I ended up with was flabby bacon (please see Troubleshooting), oil-slicked Brussels sprouts, and honestly, the bacon flavor was just overwhelming. I know Brussels sprouts aren't everyone's cup of tea, but you do still want a semblance of a vegetal flavor.

Troubleshooting

MY BACON IS LIMP.

I'm sure Andrew has already made the limp meat joke by this point, if not, I am also disappointed, dear reader. Anyway, fear not, if at the end of the cooking period the Brussels sprouts are cooked and crispy, but the bacon is not quite done, just remove the bacon strips and set them aside on a plate. Transfer the cooked sprouts to a serving vessel, then return the par-cooked bacon strips to the hot sheet tray and place it back into the oven for another 5 to 8 minutes. Make sure to keep an eye on the bacon because it will go quickly!

MY SPROUTS ARE MUSHY AND SAD.

This is truly the worst thing that can happen at your Thanksgiving dinner table. However, there is a pretty easy fix. Due to manufacturing discrepancies and the magic of modern technology, your oven might run cooler than our studio oven. Simply increase your oven temperature by 25 degrees and give the sprouts another 7 to 10 minutes in the oven. If you have a convection fan setting on your oven, that's even better. Although, I don't suggest increasing the temperature *and* turning on the fan because that's effectively increasing the cooking temperature by 50 degrees.

MY SPROUTS ARE TOO CRISPY.

There is no such thing – well there is, if you burnt them. In which case, you should start planning the funeral now because those Brussels sprouts are taking a trip to the gleaming composter in the sky.

SERVES 4 TO 6

2 pounds Brussels sprouts, trimmed and halved

Olive oil, as needed

Kosher salt and freshly ground black pepper

1 (16-ounce) package thick-cut bacon (not extra thick) or 16 ounces homemade bacon, sliced (see page 308)

Preheat the oven to 425°F.

In a large bowl, toss the Brussels sprouts with enough olive oil to coat; season with salt and pepper.

Spread the Brussels sprouts, cut-side down, in an even layer on a large rimmed baking sheet. Lay the bacon strips across the top.

Bake 30 to 35 minutes, until the sprouts are crisp and just beginning to char.

Remove from the oven. Once the bacon is cool enough to handle, chop into small pieces and toss with the Brussels sprouts.

LATKES

In Rochester, New York, where the general population is less than 1 percent Jewish, I was very fortunate to have grown up surrounded by Judaism. Not only for the warm sense of community and storied celebratory traditions, but for the food. Tender brisket, honeyed apples and nuts, bracing sauces and smoky fish aren't just holiday staples, they're welcome toppings to the bedrock of an excitingly customizable dinner party: latkes. Some are whipped up with a texture close to mashed potato, but my favorite latkes resemble hash browns: russets grated into coarse strands, messily woven together like a crispy little bird's nest. A clever trick (not mine) harvests and repurposes excess starch from the potatoes; matzoh meal and eggs provide structure; and frying in a half-inch of high-temperature oil ensures an ultra crispy texture.

How I've Screwed This Up

I once attempted to make latkes for my in-laws' Chanukah celebration, and as with so many dishes from my youth, failed miserably. I didn't squeeze or rinse, and being starchy russets, they discolored quickly and dramatically. The resultant latkes didn't taste horrible, but they had the telltale brownish-grayish interior and gummy texture of someone who clearly didn't know what they were doing.

Troubleshooting

MY LATKES AREN'T CRISPY.
Make sure your potatoes are thoroughly squeezed of excess moisture and your frying oil is nice and hot. Moisture and low heat are the lifelong enemies of crispiness!

MY LATKES ARE GLUEY OR GUMMY.
Your potatoes might still have too much moisture or starch left in them—make sure you're squeezing them thoroughly!

MY LATKES ARE BORING.
Meemaw always said, "There's no such thing as boring latkes—only boring people." She didn't say that and I never called her meemaw, but given that these are little more than potato, onion, and salt, don't be afraid to dress them up however you like! Sour cream and applesauce are the classic accompaniments, but if the other flavor combos in this recipe aren't hitting the spot, don't be afraid to try something crazy! Wait, are those Cheerios and vodka? Little too crazy there, chief.

WASN'T ANDY KAUFMANN'S CHARACTER ON *TAXI* CALLED "LATKE"?
Actually it was "Latka." Unrelated.

SERVES 4 TO 6

4 large russet potatoes

1 small onion

3 large eggs

1 cup matzo meal (or panko bread crumbs)

1 tablespoon kosher salt

Vegetable oil, for frying

Optional Toppings

Applesauce

Sour cream

Smoked salmon, dill, and cream cheese

Pastrami, whole-grain mustard, and cornichons

Cream cheese and red pepper jelly

Yogurt, pomegranate seeds, sliced habanero, and honey

Preheat the oven to 250°F.

Peel potatoes and grate, along with the onion, on the large holes of a box grater directly into a clean dish towel set in a large bowl. Gather up the dish towel and twist it shut tightly, squeezing as much moisture as possible from the vegetables into the bowl. Set the bowl aside for 5 minutes to allow the starch to settle at the bottom. Pour off the water, reserving the accumulated starch.

(**NOTE:** *Optionally, transfer the potato and onion mixture to a microwave-safe bowl and cover with the selfsame towel. Microwave for 2 minutes on high power, which can yield a crispier exterior and creamier interior in the final latkes.*)

Add the eggs, matzo meal, and salt to the reserved starch, beating until a slurry forms. Add the potato-onion mixture and mix until evenly combined.

In a large cast-iron skillet, heat ½ inch of oil over medium-high heat to 375°F.

Press the potato mixture into 1-inch-thick discs, each 3 to 4 inches wide (don't worry if they have a scraggly appearance, this will result in more surface area with which to make crispy nooks and crannies).

Working in batches, gently lower the latkes into the oil in a single layer and fry until completely browned and crisp on the first side, 4 to 5 minutes. Flip once and fry until browned and crisp on the second side, another 4 to 5 minutes. Drain on a paper towel–lined baking sheet, and keep warm in the oven until all the latkes have been fried and are ready to serve.

Serve with applesauce and sour cream, or top with pastrami, whole-grain mustard, and cornichons, or cream cheese and red pepper jelly, or yogurt and the rest of the stuff.

PANZANELLA

Panzanella is, in the eyes of the law, a salad—but in the eyes of the beholder, it's a mozzarella sandwich you can eat like a bowl of cereal. Like so many great things in this world, panzanella originated as a means to give a second life to something that would normally be discarded: in this case, stale bread. Nowadays, said scraps are tossed and toasted into giant croutons before being permeated with the juices from ripe summer tomatoes. The whole thing is then drizzled with high-quality oil and vinegar, dotted with gobs of fresh mozzarella and mountains of fresh herbs. So yeah, a "salad," sure.

How I've Screwed This Up

Apart from burning your bread, using rancid olive oil, or like, dropping it on the floor, it's pretty difficult to screw this one up.

Troubleshooting

THIS SALAD HURTS MY MOUTH.
Sounds like your croutons are very dry—make sure to give them time to soak with all the tomatoes! This salad might not take long to make, but it sure isn't ready in five minutes.

THIS SALAD IS EXPENSIVE.
Yeah, for a salad, it sure is. Fresh mozzarella, ripe tomatoes, high-quality olive oil—these things aren't cheap, and when weighed against a still-pretty-delicious $4 salad kit that's ready in 3.1 seconds flat, it feels like a sunk cost. But trust me, this one is worth the investment of your time and money, especially for a dinner to impress.

I DON'T LIKE ANCHOVIES THOUGH.
Sure you do! Maybe not squeezed directly out of the tube and into your mouth, but as you'll see in many of the Italian greats scattered throughout this book, anchovies bring a huge amount of savory, rich flavor to many backdrops like sauces and dressings.

THIS SALAD DOESN'T CONTAIN LETTUCE.
I know, isn't it great?

SERVES 2 TO 4

Salad

1 (14- to 16-ounce) ciabatta, cut into bite-size pieces

2 tablespoons light olive oil

Kosher salt and freshly ground black pepper

1 cup cherry tomatoes, halved

1 medium cucumber, diced

½ red onion, diced

6 small mozzarella balls (ciliengini), halved

¼ cup thinly sliced fresh basil leaves

¼ cup chopped fresh dill fronds

Dressing

⅓ cup extra-virgin olive oil

2 tablespoons white wine vinegar

Juice of 1 lemon

1½ teaspoons Dijon mustard

½ teaspoon anchovy paste

1 small shallot, finely diced

1 garlic clove, minced

Kosher salt and freshly ground black pepper

Preheat the oven to 450°F.

MAKE THE SALAD: In a large bowl, toss the ciabatta with the light olive oil. Season with salt and pepper. Spread onto a rimmed baking sheet, laying the pieces flat without overlapping. Bake about 5 minutes, until toasted and lightly browned.

In the same large bowl, combine the tomatoes, cucumber, onion, mozzarella, basil, and dill. Toss to evenly distribute the ingredients.

MAKE THE DRESSING: In a small bowl, whisk together the extra-virgin olive oil, vinegar, lemon juice, mustard, anchovy paste, shallot, and garlic. Season with salt and pepper.

Add the toasted ciabatta to the large bowl. Drizzle the dressing over everything and toss together.

REAL DEAL CAESAR SALAD

Unlike most salads, Caesar salad used to be an occasion: prepared tableside, by a physically imposing man in a bow tie, swiftly chopping and tossing in an acrobatic display of vegetal prowess. Nowadays, when it's not a style of chicken wrap sold in airport newsstands, it's a sorry assemblage of ranch-like sauce, wilted romaine, stale croutons, and bottled parmesan. I'm trying to make this a sort of "rallying cry" for bringing honor back to salads or something, and frankly, it's coming off a little forced. Why don't we go back to *Basics*, so to speak: this is a good salad. The dressing is very good. Fresh croutons are best. Serve alongside steak or seafood. Grill some chicken and put it on top for a complete meal.

How I've Screwed This Up

Hoo boy, this is a big one. In the *Salads* episode of *Basics*, the show in which I purport to make pure and simple iterations of foodstuffs that can be replicated and enjoyed at home, I somehow forgot to use anchovies in the dressing. Of a Caesar salad. On the internet. Forever.

Troubleshooting

MY DRESSING WON'T EMULSIFY.
It's shy on either fat or water—does it look oily or watery? Add the other one and shake it like a martini.

MY SALAD IS TOO CRUNCHY.
That doesn't sound possible, but assuming you're referring to the lettuce, you might want to remove the ribs from the romaine to create a more mouth-friendly environment.

MY SALAD IS UNGAINLY.
Especially in gourmet environments, a salad is often undone by its degree of lettuce wholeness. While it might be trendy to serve up rigid, unchopped stalks of lettuce arranged into an interpretive structure, do right by your diners: chop up the lettuce into bite-size pieces. It's simple human decency.

I DON'T LIKE ANCHOVIES.
I don't either, but as an ingredient, they can provide a unique seafood perspective that's more rich and savory than it is funky or fishy. Give it a try!

SERVES 2

Croutons

6 ounces (about half loaf) focaccia (see page 44), or sturdy bread of choice

2 to 3 tablespoons light olive oil

Kosher salt and freshly ground pepper

Salad

1 large egg

2 garlic cloves

2 to 4 oil-packed anchovy fillets (depending on your preferences)

Kosher salt and freshly ground pepper

1 ounce Parmesan cheese, grated, plus 1 ounce thinly sliced or shaved (using a vegetable peeler), for garnish

2 tablespoons Worcestershire sauce

Juice of ½ lemon (about 1 tablespoon)

2 teaspoons Dijon mustard

½ cup high-quality extra-virgin olive oil

1 bunch romaine lettuce, cut into bite-size pieces

MAKE THE CROUTONS: Preheat the oven to 450°F. Line a large baking sheet with parchment paper.

In a large bowl, toss the cubed bread with the light olive oil until lightly coated. Season with salt and pepper. Transfer to the prepared baking sheet. Bake for 5 to 7 minutes, until crisp and golden brown. Allow the croutons to cool to room temperature before serving or storing.

MAKE THE SALAD: Bring a small saucepan of water to a boil. Carefully add the egg (shell on) and cook for 3 minutes.

Meanwhile, fill a medium bowl with ice and cold water.

Transfer the par-boiled egg to the ice bath and allow it to cool for 1 to 2 minutes. Once cool to the touch, carefully peel the egg and reserve the egg yolk; discard the egg white. Set aside until ready to use.

In a mini food processor or with a mortar and pestle, combine the garlic, anchovies, and ¼ teaspoon pepper. Process or grind with the pestle until a smooth paste forms. Add the grated Parmesan cheese and once again, process or grind until the paste is homogenous. Transfer to a small bowl. Add the Worcestershire, lemon juice, Dijon, and reserved egg yolk and whisk to combine. Slowly pour in the extra-virgin olive oil, constantly whisking, until the dressing is slightly thickened and emulsified, 30 seconds to 1 minute.

In a large serving bowl of choice, toss the lettuce with the freshly made dressing. Garnish with the croutons and the sliced Parmesan cheese; season with salt and pepper.

GRILLED ARTICHOKES WITH LEMON FAUX-AIOLI

Artichokes present a maddening dichotomy, proving to be as delicious to eat as they are ridiculous to prepare and consume. Tiny, finger-pricking spikes lie poised at the tip of each leaf, requiring minor surgery to remove for the sake of your diners' safety. Inside the shell of the alien sarcophagus are interwoven a series of ever-thinning leaves, culminating in a furry core (the "choke") that can be optionally scooped out prior to cooking. Once cut, almost immediately, the flesh begins to oxidize a revolting brown, so they must be submerged in acidulated (lemon-ated) water to preserve their already muted green color. Emerging from the steamer, they seem to always be either catastrophically over or under cooked, with mushy centers and leathery exteriors. (or vice versa). All this effort yields not a large edible mass, but in fact a vegetable that is mostly its own delivery system, offering up snippets of its center to be scraped off the leaves one microtransaction at a time. After picking the bones clean, if you're lucky, there's three bites worth of uninterrupted artichoke heart available for consumption. Artichoke lovers (like myself) will agree, however, that the spoils are worth the toils. Its nutty, tender flesh just begs to be dipped in melted butter or aioli, driving some to pick improperly harvested outer leaves off neighbors' plates, desperately tugging their teeth at its concave interior for just a smidgen more.

While butter is the standard go-to, not unlike lobster, there are myriad options available for your consideration. We've chosen this lemon faux-aioli, which is more faux than aioli, a dressing up of mayo with lemon juice, olive oil, and garlic to stand in for the real thing. Real aioli (see page 216), sometimes bracing in its strength, actually proves to be overpowering in this scenario. With the introduction of some fresh spinach as a leafy base, this dish actually becomes a sort-of deconstructed spinach and artichoke dip, but let's not ruin it by calling it that.

How I've Screwed This Up

"I've oxidized my fair share of hearts" sounds like something an antihero in a cyberpunk novel would say, but it also rings true here. While browned artichoke hearts may still be edible, they're certainly not as appetizing. Make sure to get these into the acidulated water the very instant their insides breathe fresh air!

Troubleshooting

WOW THAT WAS FAST, MY ARTICHOKES TURNED GRAYISH-BROWN.
Yeah, I told you. Work one choke at a time and get them into the water as quickly as possible!

CAN'T I JUST CUT OFF THE TOPS, STEAM WHOLE, CUT IN HALF AND SCOOP THE CHOKE AFTER STEAMING TO PREVENT BROWNING?

Sure you can do that! It's really more a matter of preference, scooping hot chokes can be an unpleasant environment for weak human fingers, and may require a longer cook time that overcooks the chokes.

MY ARTICHOKES FELL APART ON THE GRILL.
Definitely oversteamed—the artichokes should be mighty tender but have enough structural integrity to survive their brief stint on the grill.

MY ARTICHOKES WERE TOUGH ON THE OUTSIDE BUT MUSHY ON THE INSIDE.
Yeah, that's kind of the dance you sign up for when you ask artichokes out to the prom. It's very difficult to cook them with any semblance of evenness, so make sure they are evenly distributed throughout the steamer basket and facing upward, so that the outer leaves catch more direct steam action.

SERVES 8

2 large lemons, halved, plus lemon slices for garnish

Kosher salt and freshly ground black pepper

4 large artichokes

2 bay leaves

1 tablespoon whole peppercorns

3 garlic cloves, smashed

½ cup mayonnaise

1 tablespoon whole-grain mustard

3 tablespoons extra-virgin olive oil, divided

6 tablespoons light olive oil

4 ounces baby spinach

Flaky sea salt, for garnish

Parmigiano-Reggiano, for shaving as garnish

Chopped fresh parsley, for garnish (optional)

Fill a large bowl with a gallon of water. Squeeze in the juice from 2 lemon halves and stir in 1 tablespoon kosher salt. Reserve the squeezed lemon and set the lemon water aside.

Cut off the top inch of each artichoke, removing many of the smaller leaf tips. Remove the remaining leaf thorns with kitchen shears. Using a vegetable peeler, remove the tough outer layer around the base of each artichoke and its stem (do not remove the stem; it only contains more delicious artichoke).

Cut 1 artichoke in half, and, working quickly, scoop out the furry choke at the center, rubbing with the squeezed lemon if necessary to prevent browning. Once the choke is removed, immediately place the cleaned artichoke into the lemon water. Repeat with the remaining artichokes.

Pour some of the acidulated water into a wide, high-walled sauté pan equipped with a steamer basket. Add the bay leaves, peppercorns, garlic cloves, and spent lemon halves to the water. Bring to a simmer, place the artichoke halves in the steamer basket cut side up, cover, and reduce the heat to maintain a simmer. Steam until the base of the chokes is easily pierced by a paring knife, 15 to 18 minutes.

Meanwhile, preheat the grill on high heat.

Reserve the garlic from the pan. Transfer the artichokes, cut side up, to a rimmed baking sheet and let sit until cool enough to handle, about 15 minutes.

Meanwhile, in a small bowl, combine the mayonnaise, mustard, 2 tablespoons extra-virgin olive oil, and 1 to 2 of the reserved garlic cloves. Mash and mix with a tiny whisk or fork until combined. Season with kosher salt and pepper.

Brush and oil the grill grates using 4 tablespoons of the light olive oil. Drizzle the artichokes with the remaining 2 tablespoons light olive oil, sprinkle with kosher salt and pepper, and rub into the leaves to ensure penetration. Place cut side down on the grill, cover, and grill until charred as desired, 1 to 3 minutes per side.

Squeeze the reserved 2 lemon halves into a small, lidded container along with the remaining 1 tablespoon extra-virgin olive oil, salt and pepper. Add a tablespoon of the faux aioli, cover, and shake vigorously to emulsify into a dressing.

Spread the remaining faux aioli on a serving plate. In a medium bowl, toss the spinach with the vinaigrette, and place on top of the aioli. Arrange the grilled artichokes on top, drizzle with extra-virgin olive oil, and season with flaky sea salt and pepper. Using a vegetable peeler, shave curls of Parmigiano-Reggiano over the artichokes, garnish with chopped parsley, if desired, and lemon slices, and serve.

LE GRAND AIOLI

Okay, so in response to that fake-ass aioli on page 213 (artichokes), we gotta do the real thing. But not just any aioli: Le Grand Aioli. The name may be misleading—pretty much just the French name for a specific kind of crudité served with the titular goop—but when prepared correctly, it lives up to the title. Real aioli is crazy-rich, spiced or fruity from its olive oil, and resplendently garlicky from cloves crushed into the emulsion. Very literally translating to "garlic" and "oil," the most authentic aiolis are just those two things and nothing more, but both its difficulty and flavor are increased in kind. We opt for the egg yolk variety, whose natural emulsifiers and fats streamline the process, not to mention lend their richness.

How I've Screwed This Up

I still sometimes wince thinking about my first crack at aioli—not just remembering its bitter, almost acrid flavor, but the embarrassment of bringing one of the few plates to the potluck that nobody ate.

Troubleshooting

MY AIOLI BROKE.

Yeah, that happens. You might want to mash together another yolk and garlic clove in the mortar and pestle, and slowly add the broken aioli back, drop by drop. I know it's all very exciting, but go slow!

MY AIOLI IS VERY STRONG, EVEN BITTER.

This could be down to the garlic (old) or the olive oil (spicy)—young garlic, fruity olive oil, and extra egg yolk are your friends here.

MY VEGETABLES ARE MUSHY.

Did you do the ice bath?

NO, THAT SEEMED EXTRA.

Well, there you go, your vegetables are continuing to cook out of the water! If you did use the ice bath and they're still mushy, try a different cook time, as thickness and shape can cause huge variances.

Accompaniments

1 pound fingerling potatoes

Kosher salt

4 artichokes, cleaned and quartered (see page 215)

1 bunch asparagus, trimmed

1 bunch thin carrots, peeled

4 hard-boiled eggs (see page 189), peeled and quartered

1 bunch radishes, trimmed and scrubbed

8 ounces Campari tomatoes, halved

Aioli

2 garlic cloves, smashed

1 teaspoon kosher salt

2 large egg yolks

Up to 1 cup high-quality extra-virgin olive oil (rich and fruity in flavor profile)

To Serve

High-quality butter, at room temperature

Olives, grapes, endive leaves, and cornichons, for garnish (optional)

Flaky sea salt

PREPARE THE ACCOMPANIMENTS: Place the potatoes in a large pot, cover with water, and salt generously. Bring to a boil over high heat and cook, stirring occasionally, until tender and easily pierced with a paring knife, 25 to 30 minutes. Remove the potatoes with a wire spider and spread out on a rimmed baking sheet, cutting them in half lengthwise if desired; leave the cooking water in the pot over high heat. Allow the potatoes to cool completely.

Meanwhile, fill a medium pot with 2 inches of water. Place a steamer basket or rack into the pot and bring the water to a boil over medium-high heat. Add the artichokes to the pot, then cover with a lid, and cook until the stems are easily pierced with a knife, 25 to 30 minutes. Remove the cooked artichokes with tongs and spread out on a rimmed baking sheet, allowing them to cool completely.

In the still-boiling potato water, cook the asparagus and carrots together if comparably thick (halve the carrots or asparagus if too thick), until tender-crisp, 3 to 5 minutes. Meanwhile, fill a large bowl with ice water. Remove the vegetables with a wire spider and plunge immediately into the ice bath, allowing to cool completely, about 5 minutes. Drain.

MAKE THE AIOLI: In a mortar, combine the garlic and kosher salt. Mash together with the pestle, scraping the bottom until a smooth paste forms. Add the egg yolks and 2 teaspoons water, mashing to emulsify together into a homogenous mixture. A few drops at a time, begin adding the olive oil, pestling vigorously to keep the mixture smooth and glossy. If it becomes oily or breaks, try adding a splash of water to reincorporate the aioli. Continue until all the oil is added or desired consistency is achieved, resembling a slightly thinner mayo. Serve immediately or cover with plastic wrap and refrigerate for up to 1 week.

TO SERVE: Spoon the aioli in a serving bowl or dish, the butter in another, and place on a large carving board. Arrange the eggs and cooked and raw vegetables around the aioli and butter, add garnishes as desired, and season everything with flaky sea salt. Serve immediately, cold, or at room temperature. (Alternatively, wrap in plastic and refrigerate up to overnight. Bring the potatoes and eggs to room temperature before serving.)

FALAFEL
WITH LEMON TAHINI

Falafel pulls off the seemingly impossible balancing act of being as delicious as it is nutritious, while throwing in just enough sin to keep things interesting. And being easy to make. And inexpensive. And vegan. When baked, their exteriors lightly crisp, keeping things relatively guilt-free and low-maintenance. When pan-fried, they become herbaceous little pancakey snacks. When deep-fried, they not only become the street food of choice for crooked detectives in Gotham City, they become near-impossible to resist wrapped in a pita with cucumber, red onion and yogurt sauce.

How I've Screwed This Up

Undercooking the falafel, for sure. These things are positively loaded with herbs that can be a little grassy and bitter if not properly blessed with the heat of the oven or oil. So especially when deep-frying, make sure the oil isn't too hot so they don't brown too quickly.

Troubleshooting

MY FALAFEL TASTE GRASSY AND BITTER.
Oh, so I guess we're not reading our headnotes in their entirety? Fine, I get it, you have a life. Make sure the temperature of your oven, frying pan, or frying oil aren't too hot, so that the fritters are properly cooked through and their flavors mellow.

MY FALAFEL ARE DRY.
This is why we recommend using dried chickpeas— some kind of nonsense happens to their starches when they are cooked (canned), and it results in an inferior texture. Also, freezing falafel before cooking isn't just convenient, it can actually improve their texture, so don't be afraid to make-ahead!

MY FALAFEL ARE SUPERBITTER.
Try not to overprocess your herbs, garlic, and onions. The more the cell walls of these veggies are ruptured, the more harsh and pronounced their flavor can become. There should be large, visible pieces of herbs throughout the mixture.

I NEVER WENT TO THE DROP-OFF POINT. IT WAS IN THE NARROWS—COPS ONLY GO THERE WHEN THEY'RE IN FORCE—
DO I LOOK LIKE A COP?!

SERVES 2 TO 4

8 ounces dried chickpeas

Kosher salt and freshly ground black pepper

1 tablespoon cumin seeds or 2 teaspoons ground cumin

2 teaspoons coriander seeds or 1½ teaspoons ground coriander

¼ teaspoon Aleppo pepper

1 small yellow onion, large diced

2 garlic cloves, roughly chopped

¼ cup loosely packed fresh parsley leaves (or a combo of parsley and cilantro leaves), roughly chopped

3 tablespoons loosely packed chopped fresh dill fronds

3 tablespoons loosely packed chopped fresh mint leaves

2 teaspoons finely grated lemon zest

1 teaspoon baking powder

3½ tablespoons all-purpose flour or chickpea flour

Peanut, canola, or vegetable oil, for frying or brushing

Lemon Tahini Sauce (recipe follows)

In a large sealable container, combine the chickpeas with 32 ounces water and 1 tablespoon salt. Soak overnight, covered, at room temperature until the chickpeas have doubled or tripled in volume. Drain and rinse thoroughly. Set aside until ready to use.

In a medium skillet, toast the cumin, coriander, and Aleppo pepper over medium heat, tossing or stirring occasionally, until fragrant, 3 to 4 minutes. Grind the spices in a mortar and pestle or a spice grinder. Set aside until ready to use.

In a food processor, combine the chickpeas with the onion and garlic. Process until roughly chopped, about 30 seconds. Add the parsley, dill fronds, mint leaves, lemon zest, 2 teaspoons salt, 1 teaspoon black pepper, and reserved spice mixture. Pulse until finely chopped. Add the baking powder and flour then pulse 2 or 3 times to combine the dry ingredients. The mixture should not be a paste but still hold together when scooped.

Shape the falafel mixture into golf ball–size balls for deep frying or patties for baking or pan-frying. Transfer to a baking sheet. Allow to rest, uncovered, for at least 30 minutes in the refrigerator.

IF DEEP-FRYING: Heat 3 inches oil in a large high-sided skillet to 325°F. Working in batches to avoid overcrowding the pan, fry the falafel balls, rotating occasionally, until well browned, 4 to 5 minutes. Transfer to a rimmed baking sheet lined with paper towels.

IF PAN-FRYING: Heat a large skillet over medium-high heat with just enough oil to completely cover the bottom. Once the oil is shimmering, working in batches to avoid overcrowding the pan, add the falafel patties and cook until well browned, 4 to 5 minutes on each side. Transfer to a large plate.

IF BAKING: Preheat the oven to 350°F with convection (or 375°F without convection). Brush a large rimmed baking sheet with a generous layer of oil. Gently add the falafel patties and brush them with more oil. Bake 15 to 20 minutes, flipping halfway through, until well browned.

Serve the falafel warm with a drizzle of lemon tahini sauce.

LEMON TAHINI SAUCE

Makes about 1 cup

½ cup tahini

¼ cup fresh lemon juice

½ teaspoon ground cumin

1 garlic clove, minced

¼ to ⅓ cup ice water

Kosher salt

In a small bowl, combine the tahini with the lemon juice, cumin, and garlic. Whisk until well until combined. Slowly stream in the ice water while whisking until the desired thickness is achieved. Season with salt.

Reserve until ready to use or store in the refrigerator, covered, for up to 5 days.

PASTARONI SALAD

Pasta salad can be divided into two categories: pasta salad and macaroni salad. It's not just a pasta shape, but rather a state of mind, conjuring different memories and associations depending on exposure to myriad childhood summer and picnicking variables. While pasta salad can assume near-unlimited forms, hailing from any possible permutation of shapes and flavors, macaroni salad strikes a much more specific tone. Macaroni, for one, must be used, even for its sheer namesake, along with a handful of familiar vegetables, suspended in a mayo speckled with sugar and powder dried garlic. This recipe exists spiritually within the latter, but seeks to add lighter texture and fresher flavors to the normally gelatinous, irregular mayo loaf awaiting in your local deli's display case. While it's caught me the ire of my hometown (whose official dish is over 30 percent macaroni salad), deviations like a sour cream–spiked mayo and Peppadew peppers bring the zing, and the proprietary orecchiette (ear) shaped pasta is practically designed to catch and hang onto crunchy chunks of vegetables for superior fork consumability.

How I've Screwed This Up

While letting the flavors get to know each other in the fridge overnight is nothing but a good idea, mayonnaise ranks among even the most absorbent of fridge-smell-sponges, so anything questionable happening in your ice box is going to translate into your dish. I'm not sure what foul leftover imparted a distinct fishiness into my mac salad, but it was one of those deep-clean-the-whole-fridge-right-now kind of moments.

Troubleshooting

MY PASTA IS TOO SOFT.

Even after cooling, your pasta is going to continue to absorb nearby moisture and flavors, so aim to cook your pasta on the al dente side.

MY DRESSING IS TOO RUNNY.

You can thicken things up a bit with some more mayo or sour cream, but don't overdo it—try fridging this for a few hours before doing anything too drastic.

I'VE EATEN NOTHING BUT PASTA SALAD FOR EVERY MEAL AND I'M STILL NOT LOSING ANY WEIGHT.

Weird! Salads are supposed to be good for you.

½ cup Homemade Mayonnaise (page 312)

¼ cup sour cream

2 tablespoons fresh parsley leaves, chopped

2 tablespoons fresh dill fronds, chopped

1 tablespoon Dijon mustard

1 teaspoon sugar

½ teaspoon garlic powder

Kosher salt and freshly ground black pepper

1 cup diced peeled carrots

½ cup diced celery

⅓ cup chopped scallions

⅓ cup green peas (optional)

¼ cup Peppadew peppers (or any other mild pickled pepper), drained and sliced

12 ounces orecchiette or pasta of choice, cooked according to package directions until al dente and rinsed until cool

In a large bowl, combine the mayonnaise, sour cream, parsley, dill, mustard, sugar, and garlic powder. Season with salt and pepper; whisk to combine.

Add the carrots, celery, scallions, peas, if desired, the Peppadew peppers, and pasta. Fold with a rubber spatula until thoroughly coated.

Refrigerate in an airtight container overnight to 1 week before serving.

CAPONATA

Caponata is one of those recipes that's a whole lot better than it ought to be, owing largely to the incredible and often-underappreciated flavor of roasted eggplant. Once its flavors are introduced to some other Italian stalwarts, the results speak for themselves. Which I'll let them do, because there's only so much you can write about a recipe this simple!

How I've Screwed This Up

I oversalted it once. Maybe taste things as you're seasoning them.

Troubleshooting

MY CAPONATA IS OILY.
Use less oil.

MY CAPONATA IS TOO SPICY.
Don't use any red pepper flakes.

MY CAPONATA IS TOO SALTY.
Use less salt.

MY CAPONATA IS RAW.
Cook it more.

ARE YOU BEING SHORT WITH ME, OR ARE YOU TRYING TO ILLUSTRATE THAT TROUBLESHOOTING WITH A RECIPE THIS SIMPLE TAKES A MIX OF COMMON SENSE AND INTUITION, AND I CAN JUST ADJUST IT ACCORDING TO MY OWN TASTES AND PREFERENCES?
. . . the second one.

MAKES ABOUT 1½ CUPS

1 small eggplant

Kosher salt and freshly ground black pepper

3 tablespoons light olive oil

1 small onion, diced

1 celery stalk, sliced

2 garlic cloves, minced

1 teaspoon red pepper flakes

1 tablespoon tomato paste

2 medium tomatoes, seeded and diced

1 red bell pepper, diced

2 tablespoons pitted green olives, chopped

2 tablespoons red wine vinegar

1 tablespoon capers, drained

1 tablespoon sugar

2 fresh basil leaves, thinly sliced, for serving

Crostini (see page 386), flatbread, or baguette slices, as needed

Preheat the oven to 400°F.

Line a large rimmed baking sheet with a single layer of paper towels.

Slice the eggplant crosswise 1-inch thick. Sprinkle with 1 teaspoon salt. Transfer to the prepared baking sheet and let sit for 15 to 20 minutes.

Line another large baking sheet with parchment paper.

Pat the eggplant slices dry and toss them with 1 tablespoon of the olive oil. Transfer to the parchment-lined baking sheet and roast for 15 minutes, then flip the slices and roast 10 to 15 minutes, until the eggplant is lightly browned and tender. Allow to cool then chop into 1-inch cubes.

In a large skillet, heat 1 tablespoon of the olive oil over medium heat. Add the onion and celery, and cook, stirring occasionally, until the onion is tender, 4 to 5 minutes. Add the garlic and red pepper flakes and cook, stirring to combine, until fragrant, about 30 seconds. Add the eggplant, remaining 1 tablespoon olive oil, the tomato paste, tomatoes, red bell pepper, olives, vinegar, capers, sugar, and ½ cup water. Cook, stirring occasionally, until all the vegetables are very tender and the mixture is thickened, about 30 minutes. Add 1 to 2 tablespoons of water to the caponata if it becomes too thick and/or dry. Season with salt and pepper. Allow to cool to room temperature then, refrigerate until ready to use.

Serve with the basil leaves and crostini, flatbread, or baguette slices.

VEGETABLE FRIED RICE

A healthy fear of heat is a common, even desirable human trait, but taking a crack at homemade fried rice means leaving those hang-ups at the door. Here's how hot things need to get: from prepped ingredients to hot-and-ready-to-eat, this dish should spend no more than three minutes on the stovetop. There will be hissing, there will be spits and spatters, there will be little flames licking at the aerosolized oil flying from the pan with every white-knuckled two-handed toss. That's the idea, not to mention why many Chinese restaurants have a jet engine instead of a stovetop for wok cooking: fried rice desires, nay, *requires* the most BTU's that can be thrown at it. Since everything cooks so quickly, it's imperative to have all your ingredients ready beforehand. As such, this dish is an excellent exercise in mise en place (see Do's and Dont's, page 18), the ritual of preparing every ingredient for its intended use beforehand. In this case, that means peeling, chopping, and measuring the various vegetables and fats for frying. Perhaps the furthest-ahead preparation that must be made, however, is the use of fully-cooked and fully-chilled white rice. Not only was this dish literally invented as a use for leftover rice, the cooked-and-desiccated grains fry up lighter and fluffier than their freshly prepared counterparts. If you're making fried rice the same day, simply spread it out evenly on a rimmed baking sheet, and allow to cool for 1 hour in the fridge.

How I've Screwed This Up

My first half dozen attempts at fried rice were egregiously greasy, likely due to the cowardly temperatures at which I tried to cook them.

Troubleshooting

MY FRIED RICE IS STICKY.
Did you use leftover white rice?

NO, I COOKED IT FRESH.
Dude, read the directions.

NO NEED FOR THE ATTITUDE.
Wow, you're right. I'm in a funk today.

I BURNED THE EGG.
It's very difficult to overheat your pan, but it is indeed easy to overheat the things you put in it. As soon as the egg is cooked, don't hesitate to head to the next step!

OKAY I DIDN'T BURN THE EGG THIS TIME, BUT IT CAME OUT LIKE, SORTA SHAGGY.
You want to add the rice to the partially cooked egg, folding them together from below, taking care not to apply too much pressure to them. This encourages the egg to interlace itself throughout the rice, cooking up in little poofy puffs rather than shaggy fraggles.

MY FRIED RICE IS GREASY.
Could be using too much oil, could be cooking things at too low a temperature.

THIS ISN'T AUTHENTIC FRIED RICE.
No it is not.

I DON'T KNOW HOW TO FEEL ABOUT YOUR RESPONSE.
I don't know how to feel about this entire situation.

SERVES 2

1 cup short- or medium-grain white rice

Kosher salt and freshly ground black pepper

Vegetable oil, as needed

1 cup cremini, enoki, or mushrooms of choice, sliced into bite-size pieces if necessary

1 small onion or ½ large onion, finely chopped

2 small carrots or 1 medium carrot, peeled and finely chopped

1 garlic clove, minced

1½ teaspoons grated peeled fresh ginger

1 large egg, beaten

2 teaspoons sesame oil

1 tablespoon soy sauce, preferably dark

1½ teaspoons mirin

1 tablespoon rice vinegar

½ cup frozen peas

1 scallion (greens only), sliced on a bias

Chili crisp, for serving (optional)

In a sieve, rinse the rice under running water until the water runs clear, 2 to 3 minutes. Drain.

Meanwhile, in a small pot, combine 1¼ cups water with ½ teaspoon salt. Bring to a boil over high heat. Add the rice, return to a boil, reduce the heat to low, and cover with a lid. Cook until 95 percent cooked, 12 to 15 minutes, then remove from the heat and let sit, covered, for 5 minutes.

Transfer the cooked rice to a large baking sheet to cool quickly and allow for the maximum amount of water to evaporate from the rice. Optionally, transfer the baking sheet, uncovered, to the refrigerator to dry out overnight.

Add about 1 tablespoon vegetable oil to a large high-sided skillet or wok and heat over high heat. Add the mushrooms and cook, stirring occasionally, until browned and crispy, about 30 seconds in a wok or up to 2 minutes in a skillet. Transfer to a bowl and set aside.

Add another tablespoon of vegetable oil to the pan and add the onion and carrots. Cook, tossing frequently, until slightly tender, 30 seconds. Then add the garlic and ginger, cook, stirring, until fragrant, about 30 seconds. Push the vegetables to the edges of the pan, add 1 to 2 teaspoons vegetable oil to the center, and add the egg. Beat the egg constantly with chopsticks so that it fries up fluffy, and when nearly finished, add the rice. Fold the rice, egg, and vegetables together, and press down lightly to flatten the mixture against the bottom of the pan. Drizzle in the sesame oil along the outer rim of the pan and allow the rice to crisp undisturbed for 1 minute. Add the soy sauce, mirin, vinegar, peas, and reserved mushrooms. Stir and/or toss everything to combine.

Season with salt and pepper, then garnish with the scallion greens and, if desired, chili crisp.

CHAPTER 6

SEAFOOD

Seafood: the slippery, squirmy, creepy-crawly, cold-blooded creatures of the deep. I hated virtually all seafood until age twenty-four, only succumbing to their submarine charms after eating some truly great sushi for the first time. It is the most consumed animal protein on the planet, over 140 million tonnes of the critters being scooped out of mother ocean every year. "Seafood" is itself a blanket term which refers to a dizzying array of delicious life forms, by far the most diverse group of species we consume as humans. Textures running the gamut from flaky and moist to dense and oily, juicy and crisp to buttery and creamy, whisper-soft to a veritable galvanized rubber. Flavors as wild, delicate, and singularly beautiful as the creatures that yield them, every possible combination of the visible (and invisible) color spectrum proudly on display, edible as naked as they swim or under lock and key behind armor requiring special tools to crack. I thought it best to write this chapter after getting stoned out of my *mind* and watching *The Blue Planet*. In fact, read the Q&A in the voice of Sir David Attenborough, I'll do my impression. Ready? Go!

WOW, SIR DAVID, IT IS AN HONOR TO MEET YOU!
The honour, dear reader, is all mine!

OH MY GOD YOU SOUND EXACTLY LIKE HIM.
I know, keep going!

OKAY OKAY *HMM-HMPH*—SIR DAVID, WHAT IS YOUR FAVORITE OCEAN CREATURE TO EAT? The Indian ocean, off the Northwestern coast of Australia. Here, schools of barramundi gather in force—a sustainable and delicious fish, some individuals have traveled hundreds of kilometers for the chance . . . to breed. Many of them, during their life in freshwater, have undergone a rather peculiar change: the majority of barramundi are born male, and after three to four years, spontaneously switch genders. With the entire population of mating barramundi being younger males and older females, it's no wonder the barramundi has earned the moniker of "cougarfish."

WOW THAT'S ACTUALLY PRETTY CUTE, IS THAT TRUE? No, I made it up.

THE WHOLE THING OR JUST THE COUGARFISH NICKNAME? Just the cougarfish part, the gender changing thing is true!

COOL! I HOPE THAT NICKNAME CATCHES ON. Me too!

SO ANYWAY WE SHOULD PROBABLY GET DOWN TO BUSINESS—WHAT IS SEAFOOD? Seafood is the mighty collection of underwater wildlife we consume. As such, this chapter is going to attempt to cover as much as possible, but we obviously won't even touch, much less scratch, the surface.

WAIT, ARE YOU STILL DOING ATTENBOROUGH? No, it's tough on my throat.

OKAY GOT IT. IS SEAFOOD HEALTHY? On the whole, seafood itself is pretty damn healthy—its preparation and various dippin' sauces is what typically robs it of its nutritional value. Generally speaking, you're looking at lean, nutrient-rich proteins that are served in myriad form factors, from so solitarily raw that it's only been touched by a knife since leaving the ocean, to cold-smoked, salt-cured, double-battered and triple-fried. Various kinds of seafood are touted for having fewer contaminants or mercury—too many to list here—if these things concern you, do what I would've done (but didn't feel like doing) and Google it.

IS SEAFOOD SUSTAINABLE? The answer to this question can also range from utopically good to nightmarishly bad, depending upon which seafood you're talking about. Some fishing practices are very quickly and visibly destroying entire ecosystems, endangering species by the hour, and depressing the absolute hell out of me when I let Netflix pick what I watch. Others are so eco-friendly it's almost insane: aquaponics, for example, both breeds tilapia and uses their waste to fertilize greenhouse crops.

WILL SEAFOOD MAKE ME SICK? The following (along with literally every word in this book) is not medical advice: due to its tendency to spoil quickly, seafood is sometimes associated with illness more than other proteins. Also, if you've ever gotten sick off bad shrimp, it just seems so much worse than any previous poisonings. I'm gonna refer back to my advice in previous chapters: you want to be able to know and trust the provenance of your seafood. Not, like, the coordinates of where it was caught, but rather the circumstances in which it's served: are you ordering branzino from a cute little café that just popped up a few weeks ago as part of the riverfront revitalization project, with only a dozen online reviews so far (all of them positive)? You're probably set. Are you eyeing the day-old half-off sushi at The Fuzzy Flapjack, the third worst-reviewed strip club in landlocked greater Omaha? I don't want to sound like a snob, but you might want to opt for the taquito casserole instead.

HOW DO I SHOP FOR SEAFOOD? If you're able, by all means smell it—most things should smell briny and oceanic, sometimes fishy, but never foul. Flesh should look clean, shiny, and bright. Scales should look crisp, eyes full, colors vivid but not artificially so—farm-raised salmon, for example, is famously often dyed pink.

I DON'T LIKE SEAFOOD. Probably should've led with that one—but having once felt the same way, odds are you just haven't tried the right seafood yet. For me, it was a simple hamachi nigiri: In the past, sushi was something I had to force myself to eat, often retreating to faux-fishy standbys like the California roll. But this nigiri was different—it was a soft, sweet little morsel of impossibly fresh fish practically melting over a pebble of barely warm, gently seasoned sushi rice. It changed entirely what I imagined seafood could be—it wasn't necessarily "fishy"—instead it could be subtle, forgiving, complex. I'm willing to bet there's a funky tuna roll or a bone-dry fish fry in your culinary browsing history?

MY DAD USED TO EAT KIPPER SNACKS EVERY DAY AFTER WORK, IT STUNK UP HALF THE ZIP CODE. Oof, yeah that's a sense-memory that'll mess up your relationship with seafood for sure. Try something on the very opposite end of the spectrum like the Lemon-Butter Tilapia with Fried Capers (page 248), a recipe that practically turns the mild and flaky tilapia into a vehicle for citrus and butter. Once you're ready to try something raw, consider the Seared Ahi Tuna Tostadas (page 246), whose flavors work together so harmoniously, they . . . they uh . . .

THEY COULD BE A BARBERSHOP QUARTET? Nice! We got some real "yes, and" energy going lately, are you feeling that?

I'M YOU, SO YEP! True—high five!

FRIED HADDOCK WITH CHIPS

Sometimes foods are hilariously appropriated as "official" dishes, or even unique regional cuisine, even in spite of being culinary mainstays. "Chicken French," for example, is hailed as the original invention of my hometown of Rochester, NY. In reality, it's simply a pounded chicken breast that's been floured, fried, and lemon-sauced—which is just lemon chicken, a dish so prolific it hardly has an origin. Across the nation, however, Americans love to celebrate the end of the workweek with a "Friday Night Fish Fry," sometimes even referred to as "The Original." Hell, I grew up thinking it was an invention of Crabby Dan's, the restaurant my family frequented on the hallowed weekday, conveniently located between the dry cleaners and Mendon Video Rental. It's a simple dish of battered fish, tartar sauce, and French fries, one that you might immediately notice is really just fish and chips. Lightly rebranded to suit Yankee sensibilities, about the only difference between the two is the unfortunate absence of malt vinegar, normally splashed across fish and fries alike by the Anglos. We opt for haddock, a particularly light and flaky fish, curling into fanciful fingers once beer-battered and deep-fried. Instead of a three-inch-thick chrysalis of gummy batter ensconcing a piddling tidbit of fish, ours fries up light and crisp, becoming the only scaffolding holding together the delicate filet of undersea creature.

How I've Screwed This Up

I've definitely made too thick a batter, definitely not thinned it out, definitely still eaten it like a deep-fried fish burrito. Old habits die hard.

Troubleshooting

MY BATTER FRIES UP THICK.
Sounds like the source batter needs to be thinned out—more beer!

MY BATTER DOESN'T STAY CRISP.
The cornstarch-flour mix should leave little room for flaccidity, but it's still possible for this batter to become soft and greasy if the frying oil is too cold. Make sure it's comfortably at 375°F and be sure to adjust the heat as necessary when the fish is added, as it cools down the oil.

MY BATTER IS PALE.
Try a higher ratio of flour to cornstarch, as sometimes the latter can render a crust colorless.

MY CHIPS AREN'T CRISPY.
This could be a result of too-low temperature a fry, but could also be a result of the potatoes not being allowed to cool, spread out evenly on a rimmed baking sheet. All that steam is moisture being driven out of the potato, which translates to crispier fries.

MY CRISPS AREN'T CHIPSY.
This could be a result of loo-tow femperature a try, but could also be a result of the topatoes not being callowed to fool, read out spevenly on a bimmed raking sheet. All that team is doisture being given out of the botato, which translates to fispier cries.

SPELLCHECK GIVE YOU HELL FOR THAT?
There's no squiggly red line under "fispier" for some reason . . .

SERVES 4 TO 6

Frying oil (such as peanut, grapeseed, or vegetable)

½ cup cornstarch

1½ cups plus 2 tablespoons all-purpose flour

Kosher salt

1 teaspoon baking powder

½ teaspoon paprika

¼ teaspoon cayenne pepper

2 to 2½ pounds haddock fillets

1½ to 2 cups lager, very cold

Chips (recipe follows)

Malt vinegar, for serving

Tartar Sauce (recipe follows; optional)

Heat about 3 inches oil in a large high-sided skillet over medium heat to 375°F.

In a shallow dish, whisk together the cornstarch, 2 tablespoons flour, and 1 teaspoon salt. In another shallow dish, whisk together the baking powder, paprika, and cayenne pepper with the remaining 1½ cups flour.

For ease of frying, slice the fillets into more manageable-size pieces, if necessary. Roll the fish in the cornstarch mixture, then transfer to a wire rack set inside a large rimmed baking sheet.

Whisk enough lager into the spiced flour mixture to form a thin batter. Add the fish and turn to coat.

Working in batches, carefully add each battered fillet to the oil and fry until golden brown, 6 to 8 minutes. Transfer the fried fish to a rimmed baking sheet lined with paper towels.

Immediately season the fish with salt. Serve with Chips, malt vinegar, and Tartar Sauce (if desired).

CHIPS

Serves 4 to 6

Kosher salt

2 pounds Yukon gold or russet potatoes

Frying oil (such as peanut, grapeseed, or vegetable) or 1½ to 2 pounds animal fat for frying (such as rendered beef tallow or duck fat)

Fill a large stock pot two-thirds of the way with water. Add 1 tablespoon salt and bring to a boil.

Meanwhile, peel and slice the potatoes into fries, 3 to 4 inches long and ½- to ¾-inch thick. If the water is not boiling yet, place the sliced potatoes into a bowl of cool water until ready to boil.

Add the potatoes to the boiling water and cook until tender but not breaking apart, 8 to 10 minutes.

Using a metal spider, transfer the cooked potatoes to a wire rack set inside a large rimmed baking sheet. Allow the fries to completely dry and cool to room temperature, 30 to 45 minutes.

Meanwhile, heat 2½ inches oil (or animal fat) in a large high-sided skillet over medium-high heat to 350°F.

Line a large rimmed baking sheet with a layer of paper towels.

Working in batches, carefully add the dried and cooled potatoes to the oil. Fry until golden brown and crisp, 2 to 5 minutes. Using a slotted metal spoon or metal spider, transfer the fries to the prepared baking sheet. Season immediately with salt.

TARTAR SAUCE

Makes about 2 cups

1 cup mayonnaise, preferably homemade (see page 312)

¼ cup chopped cornichons

2 tablespoons capers, drained and chopped

2 tablespoons fresh lemon juice

2 tablespoons chopped fresh dill fronds

1 tablespoon chopped fresh parsley leaves

2 teaspoons chopped fresh tarragon leaves

½ teaspoon Dijon mustard

Kosher salt and freshly ground black pepper

In a small bowl, combine the mayonnaise, cornichons, capers, lemon juice, dill fronds, parsley, tarragon, and mustard; season with salt and pepper. Whisk to combine, then refrigerate until ready to serve.

SHRIMP AND GRITS

Shrimp and grits are something I openly admit I had never tried before—not even, that is, until developing this very recipe—so it's probably going to be all over the place in terms of authenticity. It is, however, as delicious as it is versatile: This simple, deeply flavorful porridge can be dressed up and reutilized any number of ways. Barbecue shrimp would be very much at home atop the heap of cheesy, buttery grits, as would fresh herbs or a shot of bracing chili crisp. When preparing and serving, be sure to keep the shrimp and grits separate, as the leftovers can still make for great eating. Spread the grits out flat in a food storage container, refrigerate until firm enough to cut into triangles, and fry up to make some crispy grit (polenta) fries. Chop up the deeply flavored, cooked, and refrigerated shrimp with the remaining veggies and bacon, perhaps with a small dollop of sour cream, to make a light and fresh shrimp salad to serve cold over top. Okay, you got me, I'm a Yankee with little-to-no grasp of shrimp and grit acumen or lore, so I'm filling the page with some more recipe ideas in a not-so-subtle attempt to keep this thing from going off the rails. But here I am, breaking the fourth wall yet again, begging you not to be mad at me if you're from south of the Mason-Dixon line.

How I've Screwed This Up

I've only ever made this recipe a handful of times, and each result was pretty solid! Apart from overcooking the shrimp, most problems with this recipe can be remedied with last-minute adjustments: a handful of extra cheese, a tablespoon or two of extra butter, some fresh herbs chopped into a stubby line and snorted off a long fingernail.

Troubleshooting

For the shrimp: see Tarragon Shrimp Scampi (page 126)

MY GRITS ARE GLUEY.
They're kinda supposed to be, but gluey grits can be helped with a shot of stock or a tablespoon of butter.

MY GRITS ARE GLOPPY.
Like, they're too runny?

Again, they're kinda supposed to be, but if your grits need more body, cheese might be the answer—it's too late to add more uncooked grits!

MY GRITS ARE GRIMY.
What? Oh, no, wait, I see where you're going with this . . .

MY GRITS ARE GRITTY.
God damn it.

SERVES 2

1 pound shell-on shrimp

¼ teaspoon smoked paprika

¼ teaspoon dried oregano

¼ teaspoon garlic powder

⅛ teaspoon cayenne pepper

Kosher salt and freshly ground black pepper

1 tablespoon neutral oil (such as canola, vegetable, or grapeseed)

1 teaspoon whole black peppercorns

1 bay leaf

4 slices thick-cut bacon

1 small green bell pepper, diced

½ yellow onion, diced

1 scallion, thinly sliced

2 garlic cloves, minced

2 tablespoons unsalted butter

½ tablespoon fresh lemon juice

¼ teaspoon Tabasco sauce (or more, to taste)

Cheese Grits (recipe follows)

Chopped fresh parsley leaves, for garnish

Peel and devein the shrimp, reserving the shrimp shells.

In a small bowl, combine the paprika, oregano, garlic powder, cayenne pepper, ½ teaspoon salt, and ¼ teaspoon black pepper. Set aside.

In a medium saucepan, combine the reserved shrimp shells with the oil. Cook over high heat, stirring occasionally, until opaque orange, 1 to 2 minutes. Add the peppercorns, bay leaf, and 2 cups water. Bring to a boil and cook over high heat until the liquid is reduced to 1 cup. Strain the shrimp stock and set aside until ready to use; discard the solids.

In a large high-sided skillet, add the bacon and cook over medium heat, flipping halfway through, until crispy and cooked through, 4 to 6 minutes. Transfer to a paper towel–lined plate, reserving the bacon fat in the skillet. Let the bacon cool slightly then chop into bite-size pieces. Set aside until ready to use.

Cook the shrimp in the reserved bacon fat over medium-high heat for 30 seconds on each side. Transfer to another plate and sprinkle with the spice mixture.

Add the bell pepper, onion, and scallion to the same skillet. Cook over medium heat, stirring occasionally, just until tender, 3 to 4 minutes. Add the garlic and cook, stirring occasionally, until fragrant, 30 seconds to 1 minute. Add the reserved shrimp stock and simmer, scraping up the browned bits from the bottom, until the liquid is reduced to about ½ cup, 3 to 5 minutes. Add the shrimp and cook until heated through, about 2 minutes. Add the butter, lemon juice, and Tabasco and stir. Season with salt and black pepper.

Serve the shrimp over the Cheese Grits. Garnish with chopped parsley and the reserved bacon.

CHEESE GRITS

Makes about 2 cups

1 cup chicken stock, preferably homemade (see page 268)

1 cup whole milk

Kosher salt and freshly ground black pepper

½ cup stone-ground white grits

2 tablespoons unsalted butter

1 cup shredded sharp cheddar

¼ cup freshly grated Parmesan cheese

In a medium saucepan, combine the stock, milk, and ½ teaspoon salt. Bring to a boil. While whisking, add the grits. Reduce the heat to low and simmer, stirring occasionally, 15 minutes for a thinner consistency, up to 25 minutes for thicker.

Remove from the heat. Add the butter, cheddar, and Parmesan and stir to combine thoroughly. Season with salt and pepper. Keep covered until ready to serve.

POKE BOWLS

Having been to Hawaii only once and being composed of the very pastiest of European ancestors, I have no personal connection to poke bowls outside of their recent explosive popularity in New York City. These overstuffed, mayo-drenched, chopped salad bowls only bear a pale resemblance to their traditional counterparts, a simple combination of marinated raw tuna and lightly seasoned sushi rice. However you like to enjoy yours, the assemblage of basic poke possibilities are below, from lite to loaded, and represent an excellent baby step for baby mouths who are still wrapping their heads around sushi. The colorful array of toppings, variety of textures, and wild flavors you can throw at them can distract from the uncooked reality at the core, and you can rest easy in the knowledge that they'll eventually grow to love it.

How I've Screwed This Up

Not rinsing the sushi rice—it's very important to wash off excess starch from the rice, otherwise you'll end up with sushi risotto.

Troubleshooting

MY TENKASU LOOKS PALE.
Try frying these little bits of tempura batter at a higher temperature or for a bit longer, whichever comes first, until they're nicely browned.

MY SUSHI RICE IS MUSHY.
It may have been cooked with too much water or not allowed to cool quickly enough, allowing residual heat to overcook it.

MY SUSHI RICE IS STICKY.
You didn't rinse it like I said, did you?

NO, THAT SOUNDED LIKE OVERKILL.
See this is where I've made 99 percent of my mistakes: thinking that the directions are superfluous or overly fussy and rewriting them as I go. Trust me, we put this stuff in here for a reason!

BECAUSE YOU'VE DONE IT YOURSELF?
Exactly.

I GOT REALLY GOOD-LOOKING FISH FROM THE GROCERY STORE, IT DIDN'T EXPIRE FOR ANOTHER DAY, AND FOR SOME REASON I'VE BECOME VIOLENTLY ILL. WHAT GIVES?
I'd really recommend using sushi-grade (or at least freshly butchered) fish for this and all raw fish applications. It's more expensive and harder to find, but the orange-pink salmon on display over ice at your local grocer is NOT worth rolling the dice on to save a few bucks.

MY FISH SMELLS FISHY OR IS SLIMY.
Fish flesh should taste a little fishy (depending on the fish), more oceanic than fishy, and should feel fresh, bright, and bouncy. Once again, don't risk being glued to your toilet for a week.

SERVES 2

1½ tablespoons shoyu or soy sauce

1 tablespoon sesame oil

1 teaspoon grated peeled fresh ginger

¼ teaspoon gochugaru or red pepper flakes

½ teaspoon kosher salt

12 ounces sushi-grade ahi tuna or sushi-grade salmon, cubed, or steamed shrimp

Sushi Rice (recipe follows), cooled to room temperature

½ cup sliced cucumber

½ ripe avocado, sliced or cubed

½ cup thinly sliced scallion greens

½ tablespoon toasted sesame seeds

Tenkasu (recipe follows; optional)

Spicy Mayo Sauce (recipe follows; optional)

In a small bowl, combine the shoyu, sesame oil, ginger, gochugaru, and salt. Whisk to combine. Add the fish and fold to combine. Cover the bowl tightly with plastic wrap or a plate and refrigerate for 1 to 2 hours.

Scoop the sushi rice into 2 bowls. Top with the poke, then the cucumber, avocado, scallions, and sesame seeds. If desired, garnish with Tenkasu and Spicy Mayo Sauce.

SUSHI RICE

Makes about 1½ cups

½ cup sushi rice

1 teaspoon rice vinegar

Rinse the rice in a sieve until the water runs clear. Soak in a medium bowl of cold water for 30 minutes, then drain.

IF COOKING ON THE STOVETOP: Transfer the rice to a medium saucepan and add ¾ cup water. Bring to a boil over high heat, then lower the heat to a simmer and cover. If the lid has a steam vent, cover it with a clean dish towel. Simmer for 15 to 20 minutes, then remove from the heat and let sit 10 minutes to steam.

IF USING A RICE COOKER: Transfer the rice to a rice cooker and add ¾ cup water. Cook using the sushi rice setting, if available, on the machine.

Transfer the cooked rice to a medium bowl, drizzle the vinegar over the top, and fold to combine using a rice paddle or rubber spatula. This will also prevent the rice from sticking together. Allow the rice to cool to room temperature.

TENKASU

Makes about 1½ cups

6 cups frying oil (such as peanut, grapeseed, or vegetable)

2 ounces cake flour

¼ teaspoon kosher salt

½ cup club soda, chilled, plus more as needed

Add enough of the oil to a medium saucepan to leave 3 to 4 inches of room at the top. Heat to 375°F.

Meanwhile, in a medium bowl, whisk together the flour, salt, and enough club soda until the mixture reaches the consistency of pancake batter.

Working in batches, use a slotted spoon, fork, or tiny whisk to drip 1 tablespoon of the batter into the oil. Fry until lightly golden, 30 seconds to 1 minute. Scoop out the tenkasu with a small fine-mesh sieve and transfer to a paper towel–lined plate. Store in an airtight container until ready to use.

SPICY MAYO SAUCE

Makes ¼ cup

3 tablespoons mayonnaise, preferably Kewpie

2 teaspoons Sriracha

¾ teaspoon rice vinegar

¼ teaspoon toasted sesame oil

In a small bowl, whisk together the mayonnaise, Sriracha, vinegar, and sesame oil.

Cover and refrigerate until ready to use. Optionally, transfer the sauce to a squeeze bottle for easy application.

FLOUNDER EN PAPILLOTE WITH TARRAGON BUTTER

Perfect for indoctrinating the uninitiated, this one might sound fussy right off the bat—but rest assured, most of the snobbery in this dish is relegated to its name. Let's address the elephant in the room: *en papillote*. What in the name of holy sweet mother of the English language does en papillote mean? While apparently the literal meaning, according to Google translate, is "foil," en papillote refers mostly to the specific technique of steaming in parchment. While this may sound daunting, creating a parchment paper pocket is easier and more charming than you could possibly imagine, and it makes for a tremendously twee presentation for a light, flaky fish of any kind. Speak of the devil, flounder might intimidate a nautical newcomer (conjuring up images of Pixar characters), but this is a comparatively mild fish, offering an exciting opportunity to venture into the slightly less familiar side of seafood. Any pronounced fishy flavors are complimented, if not set off by, a host of bright and acidic costars: white wine, cherry tomatoes, Sicilian olives, and even entire slices of lemon are scattered over the fish before it is hermetically sealed away in its papier parcel. There, it is steamed in its own essences as the little lantern inflates, poaching the fish in white wine and olive oil as it's bathed in lemon juice. Then, just to make sure it's extra especially fantastic, a dollop of tarragon butter is melted over the spent lemon wagon wheels, perfuming the garlicky fish with salty herby richness.

How I've Screwed This Up

I've used wax paper—don't bake with wax paper, kids. Mess you up.

Troubleshooting

MY FLOUNDER SMELLS FISHY.

Flounder takes things a step beyond tilapia or halibut and starts to introduce some real seafood flavors— that being said, while your flounder may smell like the ocean, it should never smell sour or foul. It should have bright, springy flesh—if it's stinky or slimy, commit it to the bin, there's no dinner worth taking that risk over.

MY FLOUNDER FELL APART.

Sounds overcooked—and while even overcooked flounder is still delicious, it may become a little too delicate for fork-based consumption.

MY *PAPILLOTE* LEAKED.

This is why we bake these bad boys in a rimmed baking sheet or casserole, because for some insane reason, hastily crinkled parchment paper isn't always entirely waterproof. It's okay if it leaks a bit, but you want to retain the majority of moisture for cooking.

4 tablespoons unsalted butter, at room temperature

1 tablespoon chopped fresh tarragon leaves and/or dill fronds

4 flounder fillets (each about 6 to 8 ounces)

2 tablespoons light olive oil

1 teaspoon kosher salt

1 teaspoon freshly ground black pepper

2 shallots, thinly sliced

6 ounces cherry tomatoes, halved

3 ounces pitted Sicilian (or kalamata) olives, halved

1 lemon, thinly sliced

4 tablespoons dry white wine

Preheat the oven to 400°F.

In a small bowl, use a spoon to mash together the butter and tarragon. Set aside.

Rub each fillet with olive oil, then coat lightly with the salt and pepper.

Cut four squares of parchment paper—place 1 fillet to the left or right of the center of each parchment square. Top with the shallots, tomatoes, olives, and lemon slices. Fold parchment in half over the fish and vegetables and begin crimping up around the sides. Before sealing shut, add 1 tablespoon wine to each envelope. Crimp shut, place on a rimmed baking sheet, and bake for 18 to 22 minutes, until the internal temperature of the fish registers 135°F.

Let parcels rest for 5 minutes before serving. Tear open and top each fillet with 1 tablespoon of the tarragon butter and serve immediately.

SEARED AHI TUNA TOSTADAS

Family Guy, Seth MacFarlane's long-running adult animated series, might not have intended to mastermind one of my favorite simple yet impressive weeknight dinners, but it certainly did. As it turns out, applying a few simple flavors from Japanese and Mexican cuisine to Meg Griffin's creation results in a playful, fresh, bright, and delicious little snack. Tuxedo (black and white) sesame seeds classically crust the lightly seared exterior of the plum-red ahi tuna, presenting an excellent exercise in near-raw seafood preparation.

How I've Screwed This Up

My first attempt at this dish saw the avocado and tuna mixed together, which can work, but only by a practiced hand. Instead, I overmixed it, creating a green mucous membrane on the exterior of the fish. Just serve the avocado on top and avoid unnecessary heartache.

Troubleshooting

MY TUNA IS DRY.

It's important to merely kiss the tuna with the heat of the pan before removing and resting—while I enjoy the flavor afforded to the dish by this minute Maillard reaction, you could even forgo it entirely and serve the tuna raw.

DEEP FRYING IS FRIGHTENING, I THOUGHT YOU SAID THIS WAS EASY.

Totally get it, heating a quart of oil to unfathomable temperatures is not everyone's idea of a fun Wednesday night. You can alternately spray these down with nonstick spray and bake a little longer (preferably with convection or in an air fryer) for a no-fry alternative. You can also make your shells ahead of time, storing them in a paper towel–lined airtight container to streamline prep come the eating hour!

MY AVOCADO TURNED BROWN.

Avocado oxidizes quickly, so within thirty-some-odd minutes after exposing its delicate alien flesh to our oxygen-rich environment, it begins to turn an unpleasant shade of poop. Give sliced avocado a squirt of lime juice, whose acidity will thwart the destructive effects of what is normally our planet's most life-giving resource.

WOULDN'T IT JUST BE EASIER TO SAY, "NO PROBLEM, JUST HIT THE AVOCADO WITH LIME JUICE!" OR SOMETHING?

Yes, but you and I are trying our hand at writing a bona fide kitchen bible, and since I've been very upfront about my knowledge being limited to my ever-lengthening list of mistakes, we're going to rely more heavily than normal upon what little silver can be found in my tongue.

I MEAN I'M HAVING FUN, SO AS LONG AS YOU ARE, KEEP THE INFO TRICKLE AND POOP JOKES COMING.

Will doo doo.

MAKES 6

6 corn tortillas

6 cups frying oil (such as peanut, grapeseed, or vegetable)

8 ounces sushi-grade ahi tuna steak

2 tablespoons sesame seeds (mix of black and white)

3 tablespoons light olive oil

¼ cup fresh cilantro leaves, chopped

2 scallions, chopped

1 jalapeño, seeded and diced

½ red onion, diced

1 tablespoon soy sauce

1 tablespoon rice vinegar

1 teaspoon grated peeled fresh ginger

Juice of 1 lime

Kosher salt and freshly ground pepper

1 avocado, pitted and sliced

Preheat the oven to 325°F (with convection) or 350°F (without convection).

Microwave the tortillas for 30 to 45 seconds, until pliable.

Invert a muffin tin. Mold 1 tortilla around each muffin cup and secure in place with a 3-inch pastry ring or cutter. Depending on how many rings you have, you may need to bake the tortilla cups in batches. Bake 8 to 10 minutes, until the tortilla cups are dry and hold their shape.

Meanwhile, pour the frying oil into a high-sided pot, leaving 3 to 4 inches of room at the top. Heat the oil to 325°F over medium-high heat. Line a rimmed baking sheet with an even layer of paper towels.

Carefully, add the tortilla cups to the oil. Fry until crisp and slightly deeper in color, about 2 minutes. Using a spider or metal tongs, transfer the tortilla cups, inverted, to the prepared baking sheet and let cool.

Meanwhile, coat the tuna in the sesame seeds.

Heat 1 tablespoon of the olive oil in a large skillet over high heat. Add the tuna and cook until seared, about 30 seconds per side. Remove to a plate and let the tuna cool.

Meanwhile, in a large bowl, combine the cilantro, scallions, jalapeño, and red onion. When the tuna is cooled, slice into cubes and add to the bowl.

In a small bowl, whisk together the soy sauce, vinegar, ginger, lime juice, and the remaining 2 tablespoons olive oil. Pour the dressing over the tuna mixture and toss to combine. Season with salt and pepper.

Serve the ahi tuna in the prepared tostada cups and garnish each with a slice of avocado.

LEMON-BUTTER TILAPIA WITH FRIED CAPERS

For the seafood averse, tilapia is a great place to start: It hardly has any flavor of its own, doesn't cost much, cooks up quickly and flakily, and creates an inoffensive main course perfect for some lemony pan sauce and crispy capers. Serve with some steamed vegetables if you're doing a photo shoot for a weight loss magazine, otherwise pile over pasta if you want it to taste good, garnish with parsley, and enjoy a weeknight meal that's on the table in, like, negative minutes flat.

How I've Screwed This Up

I used to be deathly frightened of seafood, particularly any prepared by yours truly, so my first shaky steps taken under the sea were with lots of butter and lemon. Not knowing how to make a pan sauce at the time, they were usually served cooked well beyond any recommendable temperature and positively drowned in olive oil. It's no wonder I didn't like seafood.

Troubleshooting

MY TILAPIA IS DRY.

Overcooked—given its thickness, or lack thereof, tilapia cooks quite quickly—in fact, it's rather difficult to *under*cook it. So long as your pan is hot enough, you're probably good to serve after the second turn, especially if you return the fish to the hot pan to finish cooking in the sauce.

MY SAUCE BROKE.

It might've been overheated—add a splash of water and whisk with rigor to bring it back together!

MY OIL SMOKED.

Make sure that you're using light olive oil for the cooking process, as extra-virgin olive oil could smoke when raised to such temperatures for frying capers. If your oil smoked, I'd recommend starting over, as it will impart some bitter flavors into your final dish.

SERVES 4

8 tilapia fillets

1 teaspoon kosher salt

¼ cup light olive oil, plus more as needed

¼ cup capers, drained and patted dry

1 small shallot, finely minced

4 garlic cloves, smashed

½ cup dry white wine

1 teaspoon dried oregano

Juice of 1 lemon

1 lemon, thinly sliced, seeds removed

2 tablespoons unsalted butter

2 teaspoons coarsely ground black pepper

Chopped parsley, for garnish

Extra-virgin olive oil, for drizzling

Flaky sea salt (optional)

Sprinkle the tilapia with the kosher salt and set aside.

In a large sauté pan, heat the light olive oil over medium-high heat until shimmering. Add the capers and fry until bloomed and crisp, 2 to 3 minutes. Using a slotted spoon, transfer the capers to paper towels to drain, leaving the oil in the pan.

Return the reserved oil to medium heat. Add the tilapia and cook until cooked through, 2 to 4 minutes per side (officially 145°F is done, but tilapia is a tiny little fillet that cooks quickly). Carefully remove the tilapia and cover with foil to keep warm.

Add the shallot to the pan and cook over medium-high heat, adding another tablespoon of oil if necessary, stirring occasionally, until translucent, 2 to 3 minutes. Add the garlic and cook, until fragrant but not browned, 1 to 2 minutes. Add the wine, oregano, lemon juice, and lemon slices and simmer over medium heat, stirring occasionally, until reduced by half, 3 to 5 minutes.

Remove from the heat and whisk in the butter until emulsified into a sauce that coats the back of a spoon. Spoon the sauce over the tilapia, season with the pepper, and garnish with chopped parsley and the fried capers. Drizzle with extra-virgin olive oil and sprinkle with flaky salt, if desired.

TTEOKBOKKI

This may be the only truly Korean dish in this book (the wing sauce on page 300 is Korean-inspired at best), and for the uninitiated, you are staring down the barrel of a legendary starch snack. Chewy, springy rice cakes (best bought frozen) are sometimes pan-fried but more commonly served swimming in a spicy, anchovy-spiked gochujang sauce with fish cakes. That's why, in spite of its being a primarily carbs, we've decided to classify it as seafood—both because we don't have enough recipes in this chapter AND because it's so loaded with the stuff.

How I've Screwed This Up

I'm usually ordering this from a favorite Korean restaurant, so I've literally only ever made this once. It was for the show, and it went perfectly on the first try. Sorry.

Troubleshooting

MY TTEOKBOKKI CAME OUT GUMMY.
While they should be chewy, I wouldn't classify these rice cakes as gummy—more likely than not, they were allowed to cook for too long.

MY SAUCE BURNED.
If you're making the pan-fried variety (page 253), the high sugar content in the sauce does indeed make it easy to burn, so take care in controlling your heat so that the rice cakes end up crisp and not burnt.

SERVES 2 TO 4

1 pound cylindrical Korean rice cakes, thawed if frozen

3 cups Korean Anchovy Broth (page 253)

¼ cup gochujang

1 tablespoon soy sauce

1 tablespoon light corn syrup

2 teaspoons gochugaru

2 garlic cloves, minced or crushed in a garlic press

5 to 6 assorted Korean fish cakes, cut into bite-size pieces if necessary

1 teaspoon toasted sesame oil

⅓ cup sliced scallions

1 tablespoon sesame seeds (mix of black and white), toasted

Soak the rice cakes in a medium bowl of lukewarm water for 10 minutes. Drain and set aside until ready to use. Skip this step if you're using fresh rice cakes.

In a large skillet, combine the Korean Anchovy Broth, gochujang, soy sauce, corn syrup, gochugaru, and garlic. Whisk to combine and bring to a simmer. Add the rice cakes and fish cakes and cook, stirring occasionally until the sauce is thickened, 7 to 10 minutes.

Drizzle with the sesame oil and top with the scallions and sesame seeds.

Pan-Fried Tteokbokki

SERVES 2 TO 4

¼ cup gochujang

¼ cup Korean Anchovy Broth (recipe follows)

1 tablespoon soy sauce

2 teaspoons light corn syrup

1 teaspoon gochugaru

1 teaspoon toasted sesame oil

1 garlic clove, minced or crushed in a garlic press

1 pound cylindrical Korean rice cakes, thawed if frozen

2 tablespoons vegetable oil

2 teaspoons sesame seeds (mix of black and white), toasted

⅓ cup sliced scallions

In a small bowl, combine the gochujang, Korean Anchovy Broth, soy sauce, corn syrup, gochugaru, sesame oil, and garlic. Whisk to combine and set aside until ready to use.

Fill a medium saucepan with water and bring to a boil. Add the rice cakes and cook, stirring occasionally, until mostly tender, 4 to 6 minutes.

Meanwhile, begin heating the vegetable oil in a large skillet.

Drain the rice cakes and add them to the skillet. Fry, tossing or turning occasionally, until crispy, 3 to 5 minutes. Add a few tablespoons of the reserved sauce and toss to combine.

Finish the rice cakes with the sesame seeds. Serve with an extra drizzle of the reserved sauce and top with the scallions.

KOREAN ANCHOVY BROTH (DASHIMA)

Makes about 4 cups

5 cups water

¾ ounce dried kelp (about a 6-inch piece)

¾ ounce dried anchovies, heads and innards removed

¼ ounce dried shrimp

2 scallions

1 white onion, quartered

2 garlic cloves, halved

Combine all the water, kelp, anchovies, shrimp, scallions, onion, and garlic in a large pot and bring to a boil. Boil for 10 minutes, then remove the kelp. Continue boiling 15 to 20 minutes.

Strain the broth, let cool, and refrigerate in an airtight container until ready to use.

LOBSTER ROLLS

Lobster, in spite of costing in excess of $30 per pound, is barely tolerated by the average consumer unless drowned in lemon-mayo-butter. Perhaps that's why it's so often served alongside filet mignon: both are wildly expensive and so slight on flavor that they must be served with explosive sauces just to make them worth the investment.

Wow I'm going hard on lobster, let's try this again: lobster is a delicious, healthy protein that yields a uniquely sweet, subtle seafood flavor to already luxuriant dishes. That sounded better, right? We are, after all, making the ultimate expression of lobster: the lobster roll. While purists of either ilk will balk, we're presenting options for both cold/mayo and hot/butter lobster roll solutions, so you can enjoy lobster on your terms. No matter what you do, make sure you thoroughly toast a top-split roll, as it's hardly a lobster roll without them (our Brioche, page 62, would make for a luxuriant upgrade!), and be sure to go as fresh as possible. If this means killing one yourself, well, you're the omnivore—prove it. Line up the tip of your knife just behind the scuttling sea bug's eyes, say a little prayer, and cut downward with decisiveness to give the critter the swift death it deserves.

How I've Screwed This Up

I have a catastrophically difficult time cooking lobster to an appropriate doneness. Not only is it difficult to temp (I mean it's literally armored), but I'm too scared of revealing gray, undercooked flesh to trust the process. So the majority of lobster I've prepared in life has been overcooked—and what's a great use for overcooked lobster? Lobster rolls!

Troubleshooting

MY LOBSTER CAME OUT TOUGH AND STRINGY.

Overcooked for sure—make sure to boil these guys so that their thickest point doesn't exceed 140°F. Then make sure to cool it immediately to prevent holdover temperature from overcooking the spiny little beast!

I CAN'T FIND FRESH LOBSTER.

You can definitely make a serviceable lobster roll from frozen lobster (just don't tell the entire Northeastern US), but it certainly won't compare to that of a fresh kill. Defrost your lobster fully (in the fridge, overnight) before treating it to the same cautious brand of cooking you would the fresh stuff.

PICKING THE MEAT FROM LOBSTER IS HARD.

Yes it is. Especially if you can't find fresh, you may as well opt for precooked picked lobster meat—it's all ready for step 5 of either recipe!

MY LOBSTER FILLING IS MUSHY.

Steaming, while yielding more tender lobster meat, may actually be too tender for a roll scenario. Boil your lobsters for slightly firmer, more choppable meat!

MY (HOT) FILLING IS JUST RUNNY BUTTER.

Tossing the heated lobster with room temperature butter forms a creamy dressing, rather than oily (but flavorful) butter that ends up just soaking into the bread.

Cold Lobster Rolls

MAKES 4 LOBSTER ROLLS

Kosher salt and freshly ground pepper

4 shell-on lobster tails (about 8 ounces each), or 1½ pounds picked precooked lobster meat

4 hot dog buns

2 tablespoons plus ¼ cup mayonnaise, preferably homemade (see page 312)

⅓ cup thinly sliced celery stalks

3 tablespoons chopped fresh chives, plus more for garnish

1 tablespoon chopped fresh dill fronds

1 tablespoon fresh lemon juice

2 teaspoons white wine vinegar

3 tablespoons unsalted butter, melted

1 to 3 dashes hot sauce of choice

Fill a large pot two-thirds of the way with water and add 1 tablespoon salt. Bring to a boil over high heat. If using precooked lobster meat, skip Steps 1 to 4.

Meanwhile, fill a large bowl with ice water.

Carefully add the lobster tails to the boiling water. Once the water comes back to a simmer, reduce the heat to medium low. Cook until the shells turn bright red and the meat has reached an internal temperature of 140°F, 5 to 8 minutes.

Using tongs, transfer the lobster tails to the prepared ice bath. Allow to cool until cool to the touch, 2 to 3 minutes. Remove the lobster tails from the ice bath and pat dry. Using sharp kitchen shears, cut the lobster shell straight down the tail. Peel back the shell to expose and remove the lobster meat. Optionally, make a slice down the center of the lobster tail about ⅛ inch deep. This will expose the digestive tract, which should be removed if it is dark.

Cut the tail meat into bite-size pieces, then set aside in a medium bowl.

Gently open the hot dog buns and brush the inside of each with ½ tablespoon of the mayonnaise. Heat a large skillet over medium-low heat. Add the hot dog buns, mayo-side down, and toast until golden brown and crisp, 3 to 4 minutes. Allow to cool slightly while you finish preparing the filling.

In a small bowl, combine the remaining ¼ cup mayonnaise with the celery, chives, dill, lemon juice, vinegar, melted butter, and hot sauce. Whisk to combine, then season with salt and pepper. Pour over the lobster meat and, with a rubber spatula, fold to combine.

Divide the lobster filling evenly among the hot dog buns and garnish with more chopped chives. Serve immediately.

Hot Lobster Rolls

MAKES 4 LOBSTER ROLLS

Kosher salt and freshly ground pepper

4 shell-on lobster tails (about 8 ounces each, or 1½ pounds picked precooked lobster meat)

4 hot dog buns

2 tablespoons mayonnaise

8 tablespoons (1 stick) unsalted butter, softened

1 lemon, quartered

¼ cup chopped fresh chives

Fill a large pot two-thirds of the way with water and add 1 tablespoon of salt. Bring to a boil over high heat. If using precooked lobster meat, skip Steps 1 to 4.

Meanwhile, fill a large bowl with ice water.

Carefully add the lobster tails to the boiling water. Once the water comes back to a simmer, reduce the heat to medium low. Cook until the shells turn bright red and the meat has reached an internal temperature of 140°F, 5 to 8 minutes.

Using tongs, transfer the lobster tails to the prepared ice bath. Allow to cool until cool to the touch, 2 to 3 minutes. Remove the lobster tails from the ice bath and pat dry. Using sharp kitchen shears, cut the lobster shell straight down the tail. Peel back the shell to expose and remove the lobster meat. Optionally, make a slice down the center of the lobster tail about ⅛ inch deep. This will expose the digestive tract, which should be removed if it is dark.

Cut the tail meat into bite-size pieces, then set aside in a medium bowl.

Gently open the hot dog buns and brush the inside of each with ½ tablespoon of the mayonnaise. Heat a large skillet over medium-low heat. Add the hot dog buns, mayo-side down, and toast until golden brown and crisp, 3 to 4 minutes. Allow to cool slightly while you finish preparing the filling.

Heat a medium skillet over medium heat. Add 2 tablespoons of the butter and allow it to melt, about 1 minute. Add the lobster meat and toss to combine using tongs. Cook just until heated through, 2 to 3 minutes. Transfer to a heatproof bowl and add the remaining 6 tablespoons butter. Toss, shaking the bowl in a circular motion, until the lobster is thoroughly coated in what looks like a creamy sauce, 1 to 2 minutes. Season with salt and pepper.

Divide the lobster filling evenly among the hot dog buns and garnish with a squeeze of lemon juice and the chopped chives. Serve immediately.

RED SNAPPER CEVICHE WITH MANGO AND JALAPEÑO

Ceviche, ranking amongst the lightest and freshest of foodstuffs, can sometimes end up overwhelmingly acidic. While we still opt for the juice of a few limes to make the dish both delicious and safer to consume, mango brings a sweet tropicality to the already-rather-tropical dish. Enjoy with plantain chips, tortilla chips, yucca chips—potato chips sound weird in this context, but sure, go for it, I guess.

SERVES 4

2 to 3 limes

2 tablespoons extra-virgin olive oil

1 garlic clove, smashed and chopped

Kosher salt and freshly ground black pepper

1 pound sushi-grade red snapper, cut into ½-inch pieces

½ mango, peeled and cut into ½-inch pieces

½ red bell pepper, finely diced

½ small red onion, finely diced

1 jalapeño or bird's-eye chile, thinly sliced

1 avocado, halved, pitted, scooped, and thinly sliced

¼ cup chopped fresh cilantro leaves, if that's your thing, or a sprig of parsley, if not

Fried wonton wrappers, tostadas (see page 247), or plantain chips, for serving

In a small lidded container, combine the juice of 1 to 2 limes, the olive oil, garlic, 2 teaspoons salt, and 1 teaspoon pepper. Shake until emulsified into a dressing and set aside.

In a large bowl, combine the red snapper, mango, bell pepper, red onion, and some of the jalapeño (reserve the rest for garnish). Add the dressing and toss to combine. Allow to sit at room temperature for 15 minutes before serving.

Fan the avocado out on a serving plate, squeeze more lime juice on top, and quarter the remaining lime. Top with the ceviche, remaining quartered lime, cilantro, and serve with fried wontons, tostados, or plantain chips. Serve immediately.

WHOLE BRANZINO
WITH GRILLED LEMONS

Preparing a whole fish may sound daunting—it's not often that your food watches you as you cook it, after all—but few are as forgiving as branzino. The variety of this common sea bass sold in most grocery stores is single-serving-size, gutted to order, and requires little more than a few carefully-placed cuts to be served elegantly, even tableside. Once a shallow incision is made along the dorsal fin, the top filets can be gently coaxed off, often entirely without any errant bones. Then, almost as if the creature was designed by Apple in California, its entire skeletal structure peels away seamlessly, the entirety of its consumables and refuse neatly separated into two distinct entities. From there, all it needs is a squeeze of sour-sweet juice from some accompanying grilled lemons, a scattering of herbs, and your phone's old SIM card.

How I've Screwed This Up

Under and overcooking are my repeat perpetrators when it comes to most seafood, mostly owing to its often smaller form factor. There's not much of a recourse after you've torn up the fish in a hapless attempt to debone it, only to find a slippery, gray, undercooked interior. That is, other than to throw it back on the grill, where you'll more than likely overcook it. Fun, right?

Troubleshooting

MY BRANZINO IS DIFFICULT TO DEBONE.

It sounds like it's underdone—if you stop now, it's not too late to throw these suckers back on the grill to make sure they're cooked through.

MY BRANZINO IS OVER/UNDERCOOKED.

Even though you're grilling whole fish, branzini (yes, that is the plural of branzino) are often quite small, so their window of correct doneness could be in the space of as little as a minute. Temp check often, and make sure you're hitting the thickest part of the fish (not the open cavity) with the probe.

MY BRANZINO IS STICKING TO THE GRILL.

You should brush your grill the same way you brush your teeth: every time you grill. Blast the heat for 10 to 15 minutes, until it's angry-hot, and go to town on those grates with the stiffest, wiriest brush you can find. After brushing both the grates and the fish with oil, they should be so nonstick that you should have a hard time keeping them from sliding off the grill, out from between your tongs, and sent careening down the sidewalk.

SERVES 4

2 whole branzino, cleaned

2 tablespoons light olive oil

Kosher salt and freshly ground black pepper

3 lemons

1 fresh rosemary sprig

4 fresh thyme sprigs

Flaky sea salt, chopped fresh parsley leaves, and extra-virgin olive oil, for garnish

Panzanella (page 208), for serving (optional)

Preheat the grill on high for 10 minutes. Turn off the heat on one side of the grill, lower the other side to medium high.

Optionally score the skin of the branzino, cutting a wide, shallow "X" into the skin on each side of the fish. Rub each branzino down, inside and out, with 1½ tablespoons of the light olive oil. Sprinkle 1 tablespoon kosher salt and 2 teaspoons pepper on their exteriors and in the cavities, rubbing inside and out to evenly season. Slice 1 lemon into thin rounds and, fanning them out, press them into the cavities along with the rosemary and thyme sprigs. Halve the remaining 2 lemons and dip the cut sides into the remaining ½ tablespoon of light olive oil.

Place the branzino on the hot side of the grill and cook, undisturbed, until lightly browned, 1 to 2 minutes. Flip and move over to the cooler side of the grill. Cover and roast until the thickest point of each fish registers 125°F, 15 to 20 minutes. Remove the fish and allow to rest for 5 minutes.

Meanwhile, grill the lemon halves cut-side down, rotating halfway through, to get cross-hatched grill marks, 1 to 3 minutes.

Cut along the side of the fish from head to tail and along the top of the fish. Insert a fork into the first cut and gently push the flesh off the bones in both directions, trying to maintain whole fillets. Once the fillets have been removed from the bones, grab each fish by the head and lift the spine off the fillets underneath (it should lift off cleanly). Garnish with flaky sea salt, chopped parsley, and extra-virgin olive oil, and serve with the grilled lemon halves and panzanella (if desired).

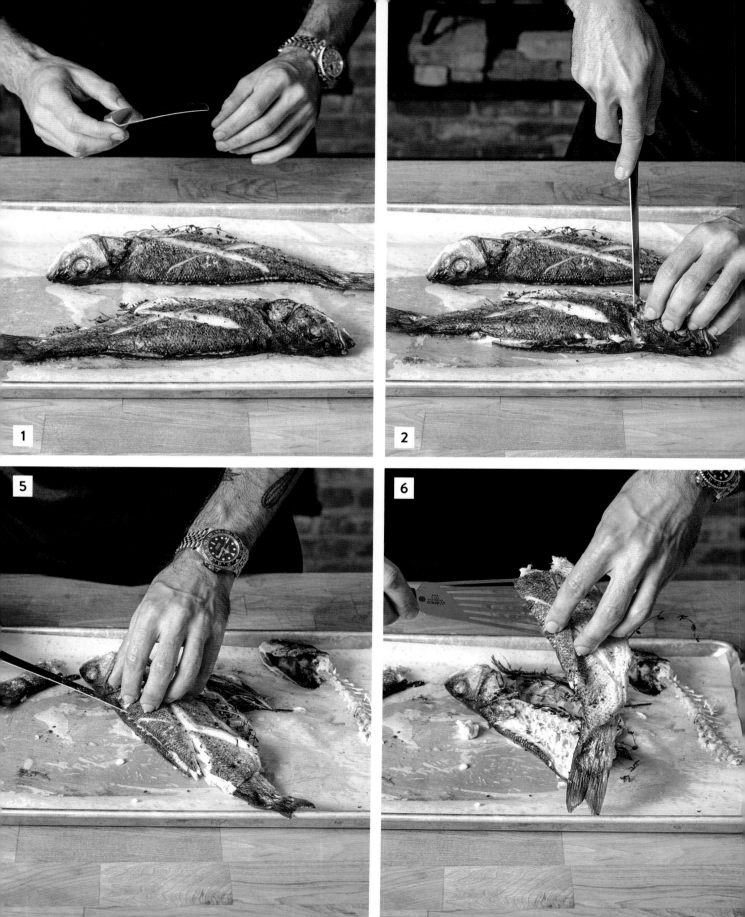

CHAPTER 7

POULTRY

Why *did* the chicken cross the road? Well, the italicizing of the word "did" might've given you the impression that I have a fresh take to offer, but I'm embarrassed to say that was simply typographical misdirection: there's not much more mileage to be gotten out of that joke, and what's left certainly isn't going to come from the likes of me. It is, perhaps, the most oft-told joke in the English language, one of the first we learn during recess and at scout camp, often as the demonstration of what a joke actually is. The riddle was first put to print in a 1847 edition of *The Knickerbocker*, a daily rag famed for publishing the story that would go on to inspire the *Oregon Trail* video game. A classic, mostly text-prompted pioneering adventure, the *Oregon Trail* series has sold a dizzying 65 million copies since its development in 1971, but it wasn't until *Oregon Trail, 5th Edition* that chickens were introduced to the gameplay, the story of previous chapters having revolved around pioneers relying upon wild game and traded goods for survival. This is a curious omission, given that the explorers embarking on the 2000-mile trek to the Northwest Territory commonly kept livestock in tow, notably chickens on account of their portability. On an unrelated note, the term "rooster" came from both the bird's tendency to roost (that is, to perch while sleeping), and to avoid the sexual innuendos surrounding the word "cock" in the much more genteel eighteenth century. And that, folks, is a Wikipedia rabbit hole.

. . . WHAT THE FUCK? I know. I had some wine.

WELL THAT'S WRITING I GUESS. SO WHAT ABOUT CHICKENS? What about them?

WHAT ARE THEY? Chickens are domesticated junglefowl that are so ubiquitously edible, they outnumber human beings almost 3 to 1. In fact, they are the single most-consumed meat in the world, with some 128 million tons being harvested every year.

SO DARK MEAT, WHITE MEAT—WHO CARES? I do, and so should you! White meat (breasts) has very little intramuscular fat, making it healthy and tender, but very easy to dry out (even in soups and braises!). Skin-on, bone-in chicken breasts are popular because the skin becomes a delicious crispy layer that shields the delicate flesh from direct heat, and the bone both contributes to flavor and further protects the meat. Dark meat (thighs, drumsticks) has tougher muscle fibers but loads of fat, so like a tough cut of beef, it responds better to the slow and low treatment. Having more fat and being a more frequently used set of muscles, dark meat has a more savory, almost gamey flavor.

SURE. DOES QUALITY MATTER, LIKE IT DOES WITH BEEF? Bigtime. Factory-farmed chickens are perhaps the most pitiable of the factory-farmed animal kingdom, subject to such horrible genetic modification, they are often unable (and/or not allowed) to stand or function normally. They are so riddled with disease from lack of sanitation and overcrowding, they must be fed a steady diet of antibiotics just to be kept what could only generously be called alive. My meat outlook (my meatlook) was changed forever after visiting a poultry processing center in Brooklyn, seeing and smelling the hubris of humanity's awesome dominion over its prey. Birds missing eyes, beaks, patches of feathers, and reeking of a fate far worse than death, all for the sake of saving a few dollars at the grocery store.

JESUS, DUDE, IT'S A COOKBOOK, LIGHTEN UP. SO ORGANIC THEN, WHAT? Hey, real talk, are we cool? I'm just catching some weird vibes off you.

I FEEL LIKE YOU'RE BEING PREACHY. I BOUGHT THIS BOOK FOR SOME FUN AND EASY RECIPES, NOT AN ARMCHAIR MORALITY LESSON FROM A NONEXPERT. Yikes, okay, before we say anything we regret, let's take a deep breath and a step back. I'm a human being with eyes and ears, just like you. I'm speaking from my human experience, just like you. I'm not suggesting that I know what's better for you or more morally correct for the world, but I have an opinion that I'm passionate about, and I thought you might want to hear it. If I've offended you somehow, I apologize, but know that I'm never trying to talk down to you. That's why we're having this conversation: because I value your questions and ideas.

[SILENCE]. It's okay, you don't have to say anything. I'm not going anywhere.

. . . THANK YOU. IT'S BEEN A HARD WEEK. Been there, mon frère. There's nothing wrong with expressing your hurt, so long as you know where it's coming from. Making mistakes doesn't make you a monster—do you know what it does make you? Human.

YOU KNOW WHAT I THINK IT MAKES ME? What?

A CHICKEN. Is that a smile I see??

NO . . . I think that's a smile!

NUH UH! You and me, bud, we're takin' the sunshine train to Smiletown Junction!

:) :)

CHICKEN STOCK

Alright, I got you here, so now you're probably asking yourself if it's worth making your own stock? It's a question I pose to myself near-constantly, and the answer is almost always yes—but there is a problem. Making it means adding at least 4, ideally 12 hours to your prep time, and you're going to taste the resentment that creates in the final dish. The answer lies in the very weakest of my Achilles heels, those pertaining to time management and general preparedness for the future: making it ahead of time. Homemade chicken stock is elemental, a building block of cookery (earning a place in the *Kitchen Glossary,* page 23), and about as versatile an ingredient as could possibly be imagined. Having some on hand assures that you're ready to bring deep, authentic flavor to soups, sauces, beans, rice, pasta, grains—you can even just heat some up and drink it if you fancy a protein-packed meal replacement. Here, too, is where you'll discover the difference between homemade stock and the stuff from a carton, as you'd have to dare many folks to take a swig of the latter, especially after sniffing its cat food-like odor. If it's too gross to drink on its own, should you really be glugging two quarts of it into your lovingly tended short ribs or slow-roasted sauces?

How I've Screwed This Up

Like me, you may have/may continue to refer to chicken broth as chicken stock. You may notice that in the rest of this book, we call this chicken stock. Technically speaking, however, what we're making here is chicken broth, being made from chicken meat, bones, and vegetables. By its definition, stock is made strictly from simmering bones and nothing else— which, here in the States, has become popularized as "bone broth" which, is in fact, just stock. So, like, who cares anymore?

Troubleshooting

MY BROTH IS FLAVORLESS.
This could be a few things: it may not have cooked long enough, but more likely, you used too high a ratio of water to other stuff. Either can be remedied by simply cooking longer—it's very difficult to cook chicken stock too long, so don't be afraid to simmer and reduce it to a fraction of its former self.

MY BROTH IS DARK.
If you thoroughly roast the wings and vegetables, your broth can end up a deep brown, which can either help or hurt you—boeuf bourguignon would certainly benefit from a browner batch, but risotto might end up looking more like a mud pie.

MY BROTH TASTES WEIRD.
Boiling bones of any kind unleashes some minerals and flavor compounds that might taste a little off, but especially when using chicken wings, it should never taste or smell "weird"—the only time that's happened to me, it's when I've used chicken from the dollar store, so this might be a good time to opt for organic.

MAKES ABOUT 1 GALLON

2 tablespoons vegetable oil

3 pounds chicken wings, bones, or carcasses

4 large celery stalks, roughly chopped

4 medium carrots, roughly chopped

2 medium parsnips, roughly chopped

1 large onion, quartered

1 head garlic, cut in half across the cloves

1 turnip, halved

1 (1-inch) piece fresh ginger, halved

2 tablespoons whole black peppercorns

4 bay leaves

4 to 6 fresh parsley sprigs

4 fresh thyme sprigs

Note: *For a darker stock, on a large rimmed baking sheet or roasting pan, toss the chicken, celery, carrots, parsnips, onion, garlic, and turnip with the vegetable oil and roast in a preheated 400°F oven 30 to 45 minutes, until deeply browned. Transfer to a large, heavy-bottom stock pot and skip to step 2.*

In a large, heavy-bottom stock pot, heat the oil over medium-high heat until shimmering, 2 to 3 minutes. Add the chicken, celery, carrots, parsnips, and onion, in batches if necessary to avoid overcrowding, and cook, stirring occasionally, until browned, 5 to 7 minutes.

To the pot, add the garlic, turnip, ginger, peppercorns, bay leaves, parsley, and thyme and cover generously with cold water. Bring to a simmer over high heat then reduce heat to medium low, skimming off any foam or scum that floats to the surface during the first 30 minutes of cooking. Cover partially and maintain a bare simmer (205°F) for 12 to 24 hours, adding more water if necessary to keep the solids covered.

Skim off any additional fat (or if not using right away, strain and refrigerate and scoop off the fat once solidified) and strain through a fine-mesh sieve. Use immediately or refrigerate in an airtight container for up to 5 days, or freeze for up to 3 months.

CHICKEN PICCATA

Chicken piccata, like so many things worth enjoying in life, is simple in and of itself. It's a few puzzle pieces you've seen a thousand times before, arranged in an awe-inspiring new way. It's sophisticated yet familiar, grounded yet fantastical. It's *Piccata*.

Okay, fine, you caught me writing perfume ad copy for what's really just a run-of-the-mill chicken dish. But it's just that piccata is a warm and familiar thing, a proud and confident thing. A flag flown proudly in an otherwise cold and indifferent—

Damn it I'm doing it again. Whatever, guys, it's a pan-fried and sauced chicken cutlet. It's not hard to make, it tastes nice, it's a good practice in butterflying chicken breasts.

How I've Screwed This Up

Not chicken piccata but rather Chicken French, a Rochester specialty prepared similarly (identically). I smoked out some oil in a nonstick pan over an electric stove, which is just generally a bad time. This can be prepared in a nonstick pan, but make sure not to overheat it to the point that it smokes.

Troubleshooting

MY CHICKEN IS SOGGY.
Yeah, that's kinda how this dish is supposed to be. This method of cooking chicken results in a soft and toothsome coating on the chicken, much like chicken marsala.

MY SAUCE IS OILY.
Like most pan sauces, this one is an emulsion of fat and water. If it separates, the fix is the same: a splash of water should re-emulsify the butter into a rich, glossy sauce.

MY PASTA IS STICKING TOGETHER.
It's important to keep pasta moving, especially during its first few seconds in the water, when it's most susceptible to permanently fusing together. Once the water returns to a boil, it should keep the pasta moving enough on its own, but be sure to give it a little stir every few minutes to remind it that you care.

MY BASIL STARTS OFF FINE, BUT GETS GROSS.
Basil discolors and softens when it's bruised or cut, so try to wash and dry it gently, chopping it as close to the time for its use as possible.

SERVES 2

2 skinless boneless chicken breasts

Kosher salt and freshly ground black pepper

3 tablespoons light olive oil

3 tablespoons capers, drained

1 cup all-purpose flour

1 shallot, finely chopped

1 garlic clove, minced

½ cup dry white wine

¼ cup fresh lemon juice

1 lemon, cut into ⅛-inch-thick slices

½ cup chicken stock, preferably homemade (see page 268)

4 tablespoons (½ stick) unsalted butter, cubed and chilled

1 tablespoon chopped fresh parsley, plus more for garnish

2 teaspoons chopped fresh basil

1 teaspoon chopped fresh oregano

½ pound linguine, cooked according to the package directions until al dente (optional)

Slice each chicken breast in half horizontally (parallel to the cutting board), stopping just before cutting through to the other side. Open up each like a book and place between two sheets of plastic wrap. Pound out until flat and even, about ½ inch thick. Sprinkle all over with 2 teaspoons salt and 2 teaspoons pepper. Let the chicken sit at room temperature for 15 to 20 minutes.

Meanwhile, heat 1 tablespoon of the oil in a medium skillet over high heat. Once hot, add 1 tablespoon of the capers and cook, stirring occasionally, until crisp, 3 to 4 minutes. Using a slotted spoon, transfer the crispy capers to a small bowl or plate lined with paper towels. Set aside until ready to use.

Place the flour in a shallow dish. Dredge the chicken in the flour, shaking off the excess, and set aside on a plate until ready to cook.

Heat 1 tablespoon of the remaining oil in a large skillet over medium-high heat. Add the chicken and cook until golden brown, crispy, and cooked through, 3 to 5 minutes per side. (They will continue to cook later.) Transfer to a wire rack set inside a rimmed baking sheet. Tent with aluminum foil to keep the chicken warm.

In the same skillet, heat the remaining 1 tablespoon oil over medium-high heat. Once the oil is hot, add the shallot and cook, stirring, until starting to turn golden brown, 2 to 3 minutes. Add the garlic and remaining 2 tablespoon capers and cook, stirring, until the garlic is fragrant, 30 seconds to 1 minute. Add the wine and cook, scraping the bottom of the skillet with a wooden spatula to incorporate the fond. Add the lemon juice, lemon slices, and chicken stock. Cook until the sauce is reduced by about 25 percent, 5 to 6 minutes. Toward the end of cooking, return the chicken to the skillet to finish cooking in the sauce, 2 to 3 minutes.

Remove the lemon slices and chicken from the skillet and set aside for plating.

Remove the skillet from the heat and add the butter. Stir until all the butter has been incorporated. Stir the parsley, basil, and oregano into the sauce.

Transfer the chicken to a serving plate and spoon the finished sauce on top. Garnish with the reserved lemon slices and chopped parsley. Finish the cooked pasta, if desired, in the remaining piccata sauce and serve alongside the chicken.

CHICKEN QUESADILLAS

Quesadillas are like grilled cheese: both in that they are two layers of carbohydrates with melted cheese in the center, and that they are oftentimes some of the first snacks we learn to whip up in the kitchen. Also like grilled cheese, while even their worst iterations are still pretty good, a little attention to detail can create the difference between a midnight snack and something you might order from your favorite Tex-Mex spot. So, while these might seem fussy for a stoned Saturday, your efforts may very well be rewarded with takeout that's better than takeout. Briefly marinating and quickly pan-frying (or grilling) chicken breast means that it enters its cheesy tomb juicy and flavorful, and frying the resultant turnovers in high-heat vegetable oil gives them a uniquely crisp exterior. Quesadillas can also serve as the infinitely customizable backdrop for whatever you've got kicking around in the fridge: Got a big pile of random vegetables and cheddar? You got yourself a farmer's market vegetable quesadilla. Leftover steak and onions from the dinner party you tried to throw for your boss (wherein you quickly ascertained that they were vegetarian)? You got yourself some consolation steak quesadillas. Hudson Valley duck breast cooked rare, black truffle fig compote, and cave-aged Gruyère keep piling up in the crisper drawer? You got yourself some—wait, what is *your* life like?!

How I've Screwed This Up

I learned that there is a bright line between "generously oiling" and "too much oil," to very painful effect, in front of a large group of youths while on camera. I managed to hit the resonant frequency where large bubbles started forming in the canola magma underneath the tortilla crust, and tectonic shifts eventually resulted in a catastrophic eruption, angrily spitting oil onto my soft/angelic hands. As the kids blotted grease from their drippy quesadillas and I nursed my throbbing wound, I vowed to restrain myself to no more than two tablespoons of oil to a 12-inch skillet, even if it meant losing everything. Again.

Troubleshooting

MY QUESADILLAS ARE BURNT.
Pan's too hot.

MY QUESADILLAS ARE OILY.
Pan's got too much oil. Or it's too cold.

MY QUESADILLAS ARE FALLING APART.
Fillings are too wet.

MY CHICKEN IS BURNT.
Stove's too hot.

MY CHICKEN IS DRY.
Overcooked.

WHY ARE YOU BEING SO BRUSK ALL OF THE SUDDEN?
Oh, sorry. I'm not trying to be rude—it's a pretty simple recipe with simple problems and simple solutions!

OH. THAT'S ACTUALLY A NICE WAY TO LOOK AT IT.
Hell, it's a nice way to look at life!

LIFE'S LIKE A QUESADILLA?
Life is like a quesadilla.

MAKES 2 QUESADILLAS

3 tablespoons light olive oil

2 garlic cloves, minced or crushed with a garlic press

1 teaspoon dried oregano

1 tablespoon ground cumin

1 teaspoon cayenne pepper

1 teaspoon smoked paprika

1 teaspoon sugar

Juice of 1 lime

Kosher salt and freshly ground black pepper

2 boneless, skinless chicken breasts (each 6 to 8 ounces)

4 tablespoons neutral oil (such as canola, vegetable, or grapeseed)

2 red or green bell peppers, thinly sliced

1 large onion, sliced

2 (10-inch) high-quality flour tortillas

4 to 6 ounces sharp cheddar cheese, shredded

4 to 6 ounces Monterey Jack cheese, shredded

Guacamole, for serving

Salsa, for serving

Sour cream, for serving

In a small bowl, whisk together the olive oil, garlic, oregano, cumin, cayenne pepper, paprika, sugar, and lime juice. Season with salt and pepper.

Slice each chicken breast in half horizontally (parallel to the cutting board), stopping just before cutting through to the other side. Open up each like a book and place between sheets of plastic wrap. Pound out until flat and even, about ½-inch thick. Transfer to a ziptop bag and add the marinade. Get all the air out and zip shut. Massage the marinade into the chicken to ensure an even coating. Refrigerate for 30 minutes to 4 hours.

Heat a large cast-iron skillet over high heat with 1 tablespoon of the neutral oil. Add the chicken and cook, flipping once, until the internal temperature registers 155°F, 7 to 10 minutes. (The temperature will increase with carryover cooking.) Remove from the heat and let rest for 10 minutes, then slice and set aside.

In the same skillet, heat 1 tablespoon of the remaining neutral oil over medium-high heat. Add the bell peppers and onion and cook, stirring occasionally, until tender, 5 to 7 minutes. Set aside until ready to use.

Divide the cheddar and Monterey Jack cheeses, the chicken, and the peppers and onion among the tortillas, layering the filling on one side of each tortilla. Fold the naked half over each to cover the filling and create a half-moon. Make sure not to overfill the quesadillas.

Heat the remaining 2 tablespoons neutral oil in a large skillet over medium heat. Add the quesadillas in a single layer and cook until the cheese is melted and the tortillas are crisp, 90 seconds per side.

Slice and serve immediately with guacamole, salsa, and sour cream.

"AIRLINE" CHICKEN BREASTS WITH HERB PAN SAUCE

Chicken breasts are far and away the most consumed animal protein in the United States despite being, contradictorily, one of the most difficult to prepare. It's why you'll typically see me order chicken breast at a nice restaurant—it isn't just to look super-cool, it's because I'm curious to see how a competent and creative chef handles their bird. The name "airline" is a nod to the (happily) bygone era of smoking on planes and sexualized flight attendants, a time when even the food was, somehow, bigoted. Applying direct heat (via stove, oven, or grill) to a naked (skinless, boneless) chicken breast is immediately begging for a dry, tough, stringy layer to entomb the delicate breast meat. Not only does skin make for a handsome meat protection-and-delivery system, but they can also be the bastions of great flavor. Starting the breasts in a cold pan ensures more fat rendering from the skin, initially glued to the stainless-steel pan, but magically releasing once evenly browned. The bone and rib cage then protect the bottom of the meat from the vulgar heat of the pan as it heads into a (preferably convection) oven to finish cooking through, emerging a crisp, violently golden-brown. While the breasts rest(s) uncovered, the delicious drippings and caramel-colored bits stuck to the bottom of the pan, otherwise known as fond, are transformed into a decadent herb sauce—all without the help of pomade, linen suits, or wing tips of any kind. Plus you get a little chicken lollipop built right in!

How I've Screwed This Up

Every night for twenty-some-odd years, I've woken with a start, gasping for air and drenched in sweat, sometimes already amid heaving sobs, still in the throes of a nightmare about the chicken breasts I have mangled and maligned in my lifetime. Some are bleeding the hot oil from their curdled cream cheese stuffing, some are forgotten sacrifices to the pyre of an unsupervised grill, some emerge half-raw from the oven, sweating viscera through a syrupy layer of dollar store barbecue sauce. They dance around the still-raging fire as though possessed, delirious in pain and drunk from neglect, screaming laughter out into the empty darkness of yet another sleepless night. They await me.

Troubleshooting

MY CHICKEN IS DRY.
It's overcooked.

MY CHICKEN IS WET.
Gross, and that's the idea.

NO, LIKE, SLIPPERY-WET.
Oh—gross, and it's undercooked.

MY CHICKEN STICKS TO THE PAN.
Some kind of chemical thing happens when you place cold stuff in a hot pan, and it happens even more when you start a cold thing out in a cold pan. If you control your stove's temperature, however, this should aid in the even browning of the chicken skin, and it should lift off the bottom once crisp!

MY CHICKEN SKIN BURNED.
Sounds like your stove heat was too high. Depending entirely on your personal stovetop, you want medium-high to high heat, enough to quickly render fat out of the skin and crisp it, so it releases from the bottom of the pan before it burns. A number of other factors,

like how crowded things are in the pan, can alter your outcome. If it's your first time trying out pan-roasted chicken breasts, maybe try the old-fashioned way and drop the breasts, skin-side-down, into a preheated and well-oiled pan to begin the crisping process. The recipe is the same from there on out!

MY SAUCE BROKE.

If your sauce broke, it was likely overheated or contains too much fat. Either way, the fix is the same: whisk some hot water or stock in, a tablespoon at a time, until the sauce re-emulsifies.

SERVES 2

1 (¼-ounce) packet unflavored powdered gelatin

1 cup chicken stock, preferably homemade (see page 268)

1 (4- to 6-pound) whole chicken

Kosher salt and freshly ground black pepper

2 tablespoons vegetable oil

½ cup minced shallots

1 garlic clove, minced or crushed in a garlic press

1 cup dry white wine

Juice of ½ lemon

3 tablespoons unsalted butter

¼ cup chopped fresh parsley leaves

2 tablespoons chopped fresh tarragon leaves

2 tablespoons chopped fresh marjoram leaves (optional)

Preheat the oven to 400°F.

In a small bowl, sprinkle the gelatin over the stock and let hydrate for 10 minutes.

Meanwhile, using a pair of poultry shears, cut the backbone out of the chicken and remove the wings. Using a sharp knife, cut down the middle of the breast bone and remove the thighs from each breast half. The results should be 2 skin-on bone-in chicken breasts with the drumette still attached at the shoulder; reserve the backbone, wings, and legs for another use.

Season the chicken breasts all over with salt and pepper.

In a cold stainless-steel skillet, add the oil, followed by the chicken breasts skin-side down. Heat over medium-high heat until the skin side is deeply browned, 4 to 5 minutes. Flip each breast so it's resting on its rib cage. Transfer the skillet to the oven and roast until the internal temperature of the breast registers 155°F. Depending on the thickness of the chicken, start checking the temperature after 10 to 15 minutes. (The temperature will increase with carryover cooking.) Transfer to a plate and let rest for 10 minutes before serving, reserving the drippings in the skillet.

Meanwhile, add the shallots to the drippings in the skillet and cook over medium heat, stirring occasionally, until softened and translucent, 2 to 3 minutes. Add the garlic and cook, stirring, until fragrant, about 30 seconds. Add the wine and gelatin-enhanced stock and simmer, scraping all the bits off the bottom of the skillet, until the sauce is reduced by half, 5 to 7 minutes. Add the lemon juice and increase the heat to medium high. Cook until the sauce is thick enough to coat the back of a spoon, 5 to 8 minutes.

Remove the skillet from the heat. Add the butter and whisk until the sauce is emulsified. Add the parsley, tarragon, and, if desired, the marjoram and season with salt and pepper. If the sauce breaks and becomes oily or greasy, just whisk in a splash of water and it will come back together.

Once the sauce is thickened and glossy, serve with the chicken.

CHICKEN PARMESAN

The whole idea of "parm"-ing stuff, since its inception in the 1950s, has the seemingly inexplicable ability to make something greater than the sum of its parts. Fried chicken, tomato sauce, cheese, basil, a starch of choice—all fine things in their own right, to be sure. But when combined in a specific pattern, they transcend their former roles and become more than any one of them could be; they become One. It's not unlike the worldly identities with which we've become so enamored: sometimes we can no longer see all our sameness for all our differences, when we ourselves are but tiny sparkling fragments on the dazzling infinite plane of the Whole, the everlasting continuum from which all life and consciousness emanates. Except for shrimp parm, which is weird.

How I've Screwed This Up

Apart from the obvious (burnt chicken, unmelted cheese, pre-shredded mozz, jarred tomato sauce, burnt basil over top), there's the subtle: Josh Scherer called me out for my style of chicken parmesan, which puts an emphasis on crispness and minimal sog. So, depending on the perspective formed from the sumtotal of your life experience, I've either made this perfectly *or* I've screwed it up every time. Both possibilities exist at once. It's Schrodinger's chicken parm.

Troubleshooting

MY CHICKEN PARM IS SOGGY.

Yep that happens, and if it's not your jam, it is correctable. You'll notice that this recipe bucks tradition by putting the tomato sauce *atop* the cheese, thereby creating a water-tight barrier between the chicken's crust and the notoriously wet tomato liquid.

STILL SOGGY.

Make sure you're draining the chicken on paper towels rather than a rack. I know it seems counterintuitive, but the paper towels allow for air circulation while absorbing more oil than would've dripped off the chicken on a rack, keeping it crispier longer.

MY TOMATO SAUCE TASTES ACIDIC, SHOULD I ADD SUGAR?

Normally I don't advocate adding sugar to tomato sauce (because they can be sweetened naturally with long/slow cooking times and sugary vegetables like carrots), but for a quick tomato sauce like this one, it won't hurt to add a tablespoon. Just don't tell my nonna!

WHY NOT?

Well, I didn't really have a nonna, I'm only like 16 percent Italian according to that DNA testing thing. I can do a pretty good Tony Soprano though. *Chrish-tophaa*!

SERVES 4

4 boneless, skinless chicken breasts (each 6 to 8 ounces)

Kosher salt and freshly ground black pepper

2 cups all-purpose flour

1 teaspoon garlic powder

1 teaspoon dried oregano

1 teaspoon dried basil

4 large eggs

2 cups panko bread crumbs

2 tablespoons plus ¾ cup freshly grated Parmesan cheese

Frying oil (such as peanut, grapeseed, or vegetable) as needed (about 8 cups)

16 ounces dried spaghetti

Simple Tomato Sauce (recipe follows)

2 tablespoons unsalted butter

1 tablespoon fresh basil, chopped, plus more to garnish

6 to 8 fresh basil leaves

8 to 10 slices fresh mozzarella

Slice each chicken breast in half horizontally (parallel to the cutting board), stopping just before cutting through to the other side. Open up each like a book and place between sheets of plastic wrap. Pound out until flat and even, about ½-inch thick. Season generously with salt and pepper then set aside on a baking sheet.

In a shallow dish, whisk together the flour, garlic powder, oregano, dried basil, and 1 teaspoon salt and 1 teaspoon pepper. In another shallow dish, whisk the eggs along with a sprinkle of the seasoned all-purpose flour. In a third shallow dish, combine the panko with the 2 tablespoons Parmesan.

Using the "dry hand, wet hand" method, dip each chicken breast into the flour then the egg then thoroughly coat with the Parmesan panko. For extra crispy chicken, dip the coated chicken back into the egg then back into the Parmesan panko. Set aside the coated chicken on a wire rack until ready to fry.

Fill a high-sided skillet or pot with about 3 inches of the frying oil and heat to 350°F. Preheat the broiler.

Meanwhile, bring a large pot of water to a boil.

Working in batches, carefully, lower the chicken into the preheated oil and fry until deeply golden brown, about 5 minutes. Transfer to paper towels to drain.

Add the pasta to the boiling water and cook according to the package instructions, until al dente. Reserve ¼ cup pasta cooking water and drain.

Meanwhile, add a few generous ladlefuls of the tomato sauce to a large skillet and heat over medium heat. When the sauce is bubbling, add the al dente pasta, reserved pasta cooking water, butter, chopped basil, and ¼ cup of the Parmesan. Stir to combine and remove from the heat. Season with salt and pepper, then keep warm until ready to serve.

Place the chicken cutlets on a wire rack set inside a rimmed baking sheet. Top with the basil leaves, sliced mozzarella, and the remaining ½ cup Parmesan. Broil 3 to 5 minutes, until the cheese is melted and slightly golden brown.

For each serving, plate some pasta and add a chicken parmesan. Top the chicken with a few spoonfuls of the remaining tomato sauce and garnish with chopped basil.

SIMPLE TOMATO SAUCE

Makes about 2½ cups

1 tablespoon light olive oil

¼ onion, chopped

4 garlic cloves

3 tablespoons tomato paste

1 (28-ounce) can whole San Marzano tomatoes with their juices

¾ teaspoon dried oregano

2 fresh basil sprigs

Kosher salt and freshly ground black pepper

Heat the oil in a large saute pan over medium heat. Add the onion and cook, stirring occasionally, until translucent, 3 to 4 minutes. Add the garlic and cook, stirring, 30 seconds then add the tomato paste. Stir to combine and cook until the tomato paste darkens slightly, 1 to 2 minutes. Add the whole tomatoes and juices and stir to combine. Lightly crush the tomatoes using the back of a spoon or spatula. Bring the sauce to a simmer, then lower the heat to maintain a bare bubble. Add the oregano, basil, and 1 cup water. Stir to combine and simmer for 45 minutes.

Season the sauce with salt and pepper. Remove the basil stems and keep warm until ready to serve.

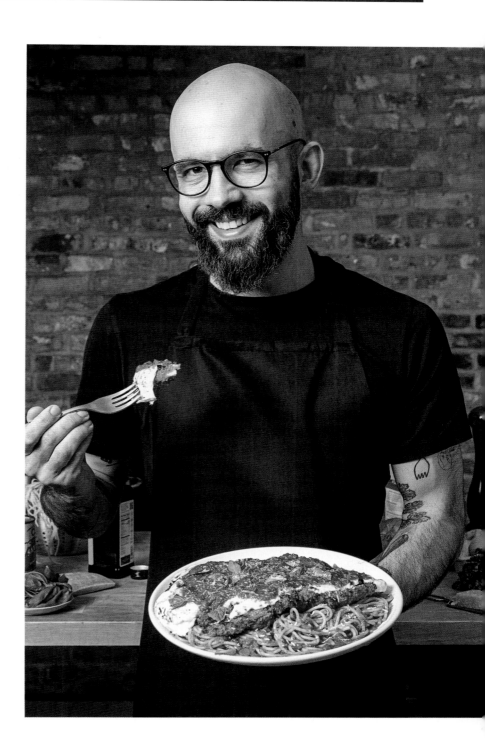

ONE-PAN CRISPY BRAISED THIGHS AND FENNEL PASTA

This is one of my earlier mainstays, a weeknight recipe I've been fiddling with over the years, a continual effort to align equal levels of richness, satisfaction, health, wholesomeness, and ease. Something that's definitely pasta and butter, but is rich with fiber and protein. Something that's both bright and crisp on its surface, contrasted against its more saucy and savory underbelly. Something that's on the table in less than an hour with flavors that tasted like they took all day, yada yada yada, I'm running out of cookbook jargon. Really, you can look at this dish as an opportunity to exercise all your basic cooking skills—chopping, crushing, mincing, slicing, searing, deglazing, braising, emulsifying, seasoning, finishing—virtually everything you need to succeed in the kitchen is on display here. It is to the kitchen as the rowing machine is to the gym: a low-impact, full-body, aware and engaged process that grows easier with time and yields visible, demonstrable results. But I'm not selling you rowing machines—I'm buying you dinner. Not like, literally.

How I've Screwed This Up

Most of the earlier iterations of this recipe involved liquor; some nascent part of my subconscious was certain that adding whiskey, brandy, or tequila to virtually any dish was a means to improve it. With time, I learned that white wine is the chosen liquid of the braising gods, and supported its richness and minerality with the acid of a lemon and the subtle flavor of fennel.

Troubleshooting

MY CHICKEN IS TOUGH, KIND OF SLIPPERY.
Sounds like the thighs definitely needed more braising time—make sure the thighs reach at least 175°F, don't be afraid to top off the pan with more chicken stock if it becomes too dry!

MY SAUCE IS BROKEN.
Take the pan off the heat and add a splash of water to re-emulsify the fat back in.

MY SAUCE TASTES TOO HARSH.
More butter!

MY SAUCE TASTES FLAT.
More lemon juice! More herbs!

MY SAUCE NEEDS BODY *AND* SALT.
More Parmesan!

MY SAUCE NEEDS SOMETHING . . .
MORE EVERYTHING!

SERVES 2

3 garlic cloves, minced or crushed in a garlic press

2 fresh rosemary sprigs, leaves removed and finely chopped

1 large lemon, zested and juiced

2 tablespoons light olive oil

Red pepper flakes, to taste

4 bone-in, skin-on chicken thighs, rinsed and patted dry

Kosher salt and freshly ground black pepper

1 tablespoon vegetable oil

1 fennel bulb, cored and thinly sliced

½ large yellow onion, minced

2 cups chicken stock, preferably homemade (see page 268)

1 cup dry white wine

8 ounces whole-wheat pasta of choice

3 ounces Pecorino Romano cheese

½ cup fresh basil leaves, chopped

Chopped fresh parsley leaves, for garnish

Preheat the oven to 325°F.

In a small bowl, combine the garlic, rosemary, lemon zest, olive oil, and red pepper flakes. Stir to combine, then set aside.

Season the chicken generously with salt and pepper.

Add the vegetable oil to a cold ovenproof stainless-steel skillet, then add the chicken skin-side down. Make sure each piece is thoroughly coated in the oil. Turn the heat to medium high and let the chicken sit undisturbed until the skin is crisp and well browned, 3 to 6 minutes. Flip and cook for 1 minute on the other side. Transfer to a plate and set aside (the chicken will continue to cook later).

Drain off all but 2 tablespoons of fat from the skillet. Add the fennel and onion and cook over medium heat, stirring occasionally, until softened and slightly brown, 3 to 4 minutes. Make a small well in the center and add the garlic-herb paste. Cook on the direct heat of the skillet, stirring, for about 1 minute before mixing into the surrounding vegetables. Continue to cook until all of the vegetables are tender and evenly coated in the herb mixture, 1 to 2 minutes. Add the chicken stock, wine, and lemon juice and bring the sauce to a bare simmer, scraping up any browned bits from the bottom of the skillet. Return the chicken thighs to the skillet, skin-side up, making sure the skin is not submerged in the liquid.

Place the skillet in the oven and bake for 35 to 45 minutes, until the internal temperature of the chicken thighs reaches 175°F. Remove from the oven and set the chicken aside on a plate.

Return the skillet to the stove and bring the braising liquid to a boil over medium-high heat. Add the pasta and lower the heat to maintain a simmer. Cook, stirring every few minutes, until the pasta is al dente, anywhere from 5 to 12 minutes, depending on the type of pasta. Add the cheese and basil and stir to combine. Season with salt and pepper.

Return the chicken thighs to the sauce and cook until warmed through, 4 to 5 minutes. Garnish with chopped parsley and serve.

WHOLE SPATCHCOCKED CHICKEN WITH COMPOUND BUTTER

Butterflying, or as it's more delightfully known, spatchcocking, took the culinary world by storm in the 2010s, largely in thanks to J. Kenji Lopez-Alt's proliferation of the method. The barbaric ritual, beginning with the forcible removal of the spinal cord, culminates in the entire chicken (or Turkey) being cracked open at the breastbone and pressed flat into a sort of carnal topographical map. It isn't just to make the chicken look like a warning left from the Blair Witch; spatchcocking exposes both the dark meat and skin normally relegated to the cooler depths below the breasts, allowing them to cook more quickly and evenly. As a result, poultry can be cooked much faster and hotter, creating crispier skin and juicier meat in a shorter cook time. A common broiler bird can be done in around 45 minutes and, normally commanding the attention of an entire day, a turkey emerges ready to give thanks in as little as 90. While it might come at the expense of being able to serve poultry in its prototypical form factor, it more easily breaks down into its breast/thigh/wing/drum components. Your diners then get their choice of crisp-skinned chicken parts, imbued with and freshly bathed in herb- and garlic-laden Compound Butter (page 287).

How I've Screwed This Up

Betwixt the breasts of the bird, as in many vertebrates, lies a sternum. This sternum is optionally (but ideally) removed during the spatchcocking process, otherwise it chooses which breast to favor and tweaks toward it, horribly twisting the breasts like a bad bra. Before learning to yank it out prior to roasting, most butterflied poultry prepared by yours truly often featured this uncomfortable-looking anatomy.

Troubleshooting

MY CHICKEN IS DRY.

The only possibility here is overcooking—something very difficult to do with dark meat, but much easier to pull off with breasts. Make sure the thickest point of the breast is at 155°F when pulling from the oven, ideally never exceeding 165°F.

ALL THE COMPOUND BUTTER LEAKED OUT.

There's no way to retain all that butter, the goal in stuffing it under the skin is both to separate the skin from the meat and provide some fat/herbs with which to baste it.

MY CHICKEN BREASTS LOOK WEIRD AFTER BUTTERFLYING.

Pull out the sternum, which when forced downward, can twist toward one side and misshape the breasts.

YOU'RE REALLY REINING IN THE CHILD-MIND HUMOR WITH ALL THIS BREAST TALK.

I mean last I checked, it's 2022. At least when I'm writing this.

SERVES 2 TO 4

1 (4- to 6-pound) whole chicken, spatchcocked

Compound Butter (recipe follows)

2 tablespoons kosher salt

1 teaspoon freshly ground black pepper

½ teaspoon baking powder

2 medium onions, roughly chopped

3 large carrots, roughly chopped

5 to 6 celery stalks, roughly chopped

Thoroughly pat the chicken dry with a paper towel.

Using your fingers, gently separate the skin from the meat, making sure to get all the way up the breasts and into the thighs. Carefully spread the compound butter underneath the skin.

In a small bowl, whisk together the salt, pepper, and baking powder. Generously sprinkle the exterior of the chicken with most, if not all, the dry brine mixture.

Transfer the bird to a wire rack set inside a rimmed baking sheet. Refrigerate for 24 to 48 hours.

Preheat the oven to 450°F.

Line another rimmed baking sheet with aluminum foil. Add the onions, carrots, and celery. Then, place the wire rack with the chicken on top over the vegetables. (The vegetables will prevent the chicken drippings from burning while in the oven.) Roast for 40 to 45 minutes, until the chicken is browned and crispy, and the internal temperature of the breast reaches 155 to 160°F (the temperature will increase with carryover cooking), and the thigh reaches 175°F.

Let the chicken rest, uncovered, for 15 to 20 minutes before carving.

COMPOUND BUTTER

Makes about 8 ounces

8 ounces (2 sticks) unsalted butter, softened

½ cup fresh herbs of choice (such as sage, thyme or rosemary leaves), chopped

1 teaspoon kosher salt

½ teaspoon freshly ground black pepper

In a small bowl, combine the butter, herbs, salt, and pepper.

Set aside at room temperature until ready to use.

CHICKEN NOODLE SOUP

Among the top-rated comforts for the ill, the infirmed, the recently cold or the currently chilly, I posit that the following pages contain the ultimate expression of chicken noodle soup. It stands upon a bedrock of homemade Chicken Stock (page 268), a patiently-won elixir of profound chicken flavor, gently coaxed from roasted chicken wings and root vegetables. Mealy chicken breast cubes are then eschewed in favor of juicy shreds of thigh, lending jewels of fat to wander across its steaming surface. It introduces two new rising stars to the recurring cast of vegetable characters, parsnips and turnips, whose earthy sweetness provide playful parity to the bubbling pot of savory. A breath of heat bellows from a knob of fresh ginger, tussling through the thousand fragments of grated lemongrass that cloud the broth. Lastly, the titular pasta is cooked a la carte with every serving, ensuring that leftovers needn't suffer from soggy noodle syndrome. It's a laborious and loving labor of love, a boisterous bowl of bellowing beauty, and other alliterations. Just make it, it's good.

How I've Screwed This Up

This might be the recipe I've made the greatest number of times in my life, and as such, have screwed up the most. What you see below is the end result of those decades' experiments, failures, and successes, each one a tiny step in the direction of a slightly better soup. It's what I try to remember anytime I burn, overboil, break: one day, they'll just be little steps that brought me closer to where I want to be.

Troubleshooting

MY BROTH IS FLAVORLESS.
Homemade chicken broth, especially if it doesn't have enough stuff in it, can end up a little bland—it's still lightyears better than anything you'll get out of a box.

MY VEGETABLES ENDED UP TOO SOFT.
I like to take this soup off the heat when the veg are *just* shy of fully cooked, "al dente" so to speak. This ensures that the carryover heat (and any future heat dealt out to leftovers) doesn't overcook things.

MY CHICKEN THIGHS ARE HARD TO SHRED.
It's pretty hard to overcook chicken thighs, so don't be afraid to let those suckers simmer for a good long while before shredding.

DOES THIS CHICKEN SOUP BEING GOOD FOR MY SOUL HAVE ANY RELIGIOUS IMPLICATIONS?
Maybe from a legal standpoint, yes, but philosophically you're just making a playful word association.

MAKES ABOUT 4 QUARTS

1 tablespoon light olive oil

1 large white onion, chopped

5 to 6 celery stalks, chopped

4 to 5 medium carrots, peeled and chopped

1 large parsnip, peeled and finely chopped

½ large turnip, peeled and finely chopped

4 quarts chicken stock, preferably homemade (see page 268)

¼ cup chopped fresh parsley leaves

1 tablespoon grated or finely minced lemongrass (from softer inner stalks)

2 teaspoons grated peeled fresh ginger

2 pounds boneless, skinless chicken thighs

½ cup finely chopped scallions

⅓ to ½ cup chopped fresh dill fronds (depending on your dill preferences)

Kosher salt and freshly ground black pepper

Dried short noodles of choice (2 ounces per serving)

In a large pot, heat the oil over medium-high heat until shimmering, 1 to 2 minutes. Add the onion and cook, stirring occasionally, until softened, 3 to 4 minutes. Add the celery, carrots, parsnip, and turnip and cook, stirring occasionally, until vegetables are slightly tender, 4 to 5 minutes.

Add the stock to the pot. Increase the heat to high, add the parsley, lemongrass, and ginger and bring the soup to a simmer. Add the chicken thighs and cook, skimming off excess fat that rises to the surface (let some remain), until the chicken reaches an internal temperature of 175°F, 15 to 20 minutes.

Remove the chicken and shred using a pair of forks. Return the chicken to the pot. Add the scallions and dill; season the soup with salt and pepper.

If serving immediately, add the noodles and cook until al dente according to the package directions.

If storing the soup, let cool to room temperature then refrigerate for up to 5 days. Alternatively, pre-portion and freeze the soup base for up to 3 months. When you're ready to serve, add 2½ cups of soup base per person to a pot. Bring to a simmer, then proceed to cook the noodles as directed in the previous step.

CORNISH HENS WITH FIG-PORT SAUCE

Most cornish game hens sold in supermarkets are not Cornish, game, nor hens at all, but rather a particular breed of young broiler chicken. Sorry if that shatters your entire worldview. Whatever these little guys are, they're elegant, tender, and juicy-crisp when butterflied or divided in half, presenting a capital opportunity for a sweet and savory sauce. You can essentially think of them as big ol' chicken thighs: a tricky treasure map of fatty, resilient meat, but one framed together by smaller bones and less cartilage. Just like any poultry, dry-brining improves skin crispness, meat moisture retention, and flavor depth/girth. The sauce calls for homemade chicken stock which, while decidedly fussy, improves the resultant condiment's body and mouthfeel. Wouldn't you prefer a body with a good mouthfeel? Sorry. If you don't have homemade chicken stock, dissolve a few packets of unflavored gelatin in some store-bought stuff, it will help improve the sauce's texture!

How I've Screwed This Up

Cornish game hens take center stage in *Frasier* ("Daphne Does Dinner," Season 10 Episode 14, notes for the curious[1]), wherein the selfsame protagonist prepares his signature pomegranate-honey sauce for the miniature broiler birds. That very episode, itself about the Crane Family curse of being utterly incapable of throwing a dinner party, resulted in my own dinner party's destruction and the first-ever scrapping of a *Binging with Babish* episode. I attempted to film one with friends over to share in the spoils, but we all got so drunk, the last shots were out of focus and shaky. Don't drink and film.

Troubleshooting

I BLENDED THE PARSNIPS FOR HOW LONG YOU SAID, BUT THEY'RE STILL CHUNKY.
Sounds like they were undercooked—if you have a high-powered enough blender like a Vitamix, you can just blast it on full speed for five minutes, which will not only obliterate any chunks, it'll actually get so hot it'll finish cooking the parsnips 💃

IT'S KINDA WEIRD TO SEE AN EMOJI IN A BOOK, AND IT'S DEFINITELY NOT GOING TO AGE WELL.
You're right—what else you got?

MY HENS ARE SLIGHTLY PINK, CAN YOU REMIND ME OF THE FEDERAL REGULATIONS AND CODES SURROUNDING DISPOSAL OF CLASS I HAZARDOUS WASTE?

Woah woah woah—relax. The juices from cornish game hens seldom run clear, and their meat sometimes more closely resembles that of chicken thighs, so they might be a little pink-ish. Just temp them and make sure the thighs are around 175°F and breasts hit 160°F, they'll be perfectly safe and still plenty juicy.

MY HENS SEEM LETHARGIC AND AREN'T EATING THEIR FEED—SHOULD I TRY A VEGETARIAN DIET?

Wait . . . are you raising these hens yourself?

YEAH.

Fucking—what—aren't you still in that 400 square foot studio?

YEAH.

I mean . . . whatever honks your horn, I guess.

REALLY? YOU ARE THE FIRST PERSON TO JUST LET ME HAVE THIS.

Well, it's because what you're doing is definitely batshit crazy for sure, but ain't nobody getting hurt or catching a charge off it. I say live your life! Better forget that security deposit though.

† "Daphne Does Dinner" is notable not only for its food-centric plotline but for being both one of my favorite and least-favorite episodes. The foodie humor, the high-brow dinner guests, Frasier hiding in the pantry are all a masterclass in sustained comedy of misunderstanding, but the story takes a violent turn for the cartoonish, however, when Gertrude Moon (ew) crashes *through the ceiling* (ew) amid the act of lovemaking (ew).

SERVES 2

Hens

2 (1½- to 2-pound) Cornish hens

¼ cup kosher salt

1 teaspoon freshly ground black pepper

½ teaspoon baking powder

¼ cup duck fat, melted (or clarified butter)

2 yellow onions, roughly chopped

4 celery stalks, roughly chopped

3 large carrots, roughly chopped

6 garlic cloves, smashed

4 to 5 fresh thyme sprigs

2 fresh rosemary sprigs

Fig-Port Sauce

1 tablespoon light olive oil

1 shallot, finely chopped

1 cup port

¾ cup chicken stock, preferably homemade (see page 268)

8 fresh Mission figs, quartered

1 fresh rosemary sprig

2 tablespoons unsalted butter, cubed and cold

Kosher salt and freshly ground black pepper

Parsnip Puree (recipe follows)

COOK THE HENS: Split the hens in half lengthwise using a sharp cleaver or poultry shears. Cut out the spine of each hen, making sure to leave as much meat intact as possible. Transfer the hens to a rimmed baking sheet; save the backbones for another use.

In a small bowl, combine the salt, pepper, and baking powder. Generously coat the hens in the dry brine. Refrigerate, uncovered, for at least 4 hours, up to 24 hours.

Preheat the oven to 450°F.

Pat the hens dry and brush with the duck fat.

On a large rimmed baking sheet, scatter the onions, celery, carrots, garlic, thyme, and rosemary. Top with a wire rack then transfer the hens to the rack, skin-side up.

Roast the hens for 15 to 20 minutes, until golden brown. Reduce the oven temperature to 375°F, then roast for 35 to 40 minutes, until the internal temperature of the thickest part of the thigh registers 180°F and the breast registers 170°F.

Strain the drippings from the baking sheet and reserve for the Fig-Port Sauce. Let the hens rest for 10 to 15 minutes

MEANWHILE, MAKE THE SAUCE: Heat the olive oil in a large skillet over medium heat. Add the shallot and cook, stirring occasionally, until just turning translucent, 2 to 3 minutes. Add the port, chicken stock, reserved drippings, figs, and rosemary. Cook, stirring occasionally, until the sauce is reduced by 75 percent, 10 to 12 minutes.

Remove the skillet from the heat and add the cold butter pieces; stir gently until all of the butter is melted and emulsified into the sauce. Season with salt and pepper, then serve immediately with the hens and Parsnip Puree.

PARSNIP PUREE

Serves 4 to 6

1 pound parsnips, peeled and cut into 1-inch pieces

¾ cup whole milk

¾ cup heavy cream

3 to 4 cloves roasted garlic (see page 199) or Confit Garlic (recipe follows)

2 fresh thyme sprigs

Kosher salt

2 tablespoons unsalted butter

Freshly ground white pepper

In a medium saucepan, combine the parsnips with the milk, cream, garlic, thyme, and 1 teaspoon salt. Bring the mixture to a simmer, then cook over medium-low heat until the parsnips are completely tender, 12 to 15 minutes.

Using a slotted spoon, transfer the parsnips to a food processor, reserving the liquid in the saucepan. Add the butter. With the machine running, stream in enough of the reserved liquid to form a smooth puree.

Season the parsnip puree with salt and white pepper.

CONFIT GARLIC

Makes 12 to 15 cloves

12 to 15 garlic cloves

3 fresh thyme sprigs

1 bay leaf

½ teaspoon black peppercorns

1 chile de árbol (optional)

1 to 1½ cups light olive oil

Preheat the oven to 275°F.

In a small oven-safe dish, combine the garlic, thyme, bay leaf, peppercorns, and if desired, the chile. Pour enough of the olive oil to just cover the ingredients. Wrap the baking dish in aluminum foil.

Bake 1½ to 2 hours, until the garlic cloves are soft and darker in color. Uncover the baking dish and allow the oil to cool to room temperature.

Transfer the garlic confit (including the oil) to a sealable container and store in the refrigerator for up to 1 week before serving.

NASHVILLE HOT CHICKEN WITH BREAD AND BUTTER PICKLES

While I'm certainly no Nashville native, I've had enough of the genuine article to know that it's mostly three things: crispy, juicy, and panic-inducingly spicy. Each is achieved, in that order, with a vat of hazardously hot lard, a hot sauce–spiked buttermilk brine, and a toasted spice mix that's mostly cayenne. The result is a fried chicken so good that, no matter how much pain is inflicted upon the consumer, it is impossible to stop eating. The sliced sandwich bread, at first, seems superfluous—until, that is, you're grasping frantically for nearby remedies, anything that will stop you from hiccup-coughing in front of your girlfriend's family. It doesn't do much, especially once soaked through with angry red chicken runoff, but maybe some crisp pickles will cool you down.

If spicy ain't your thing, fun fact: stop at step 10 below and you've got yourself some straight-up normal-style fried chicken!

How I've Screwed This Up

I've made it too mild—you'll know when you've made this mistake if there are any hot-chickenthusiasts in the room, as they'll be quick to inform you that your bird is for WIMPS.

Troubleshooting

MY CHICKEN IS SOGGY.

While the spicy oil brush down certainly slickens the crust, it shouldn't sog it. Make sure to drain your fried chicken on paper towels—it seems counterintuitive, but the towels soak up excess oil, which can leave your chicken greasy.

MY CHICKEN ISN'T SPICY ENOUGH.

This recipe primarily gets its spice from cayenne, so if you have a weak bottle, that might be the culprit. Otherwise, just up the cayenne content until everyone in the kitchen starts sneezing.

MY CHICKEN IS PALE.

So long as it's crisp, luckily this recipe covers for pale fried chicken, but if it's coming out of the oil consistently blonde, your oil is likely too low.

MY CHICKEN IS UNDERCOOKED.

Sometimes the crust cooks disproportionately fast and leaves the meat unsatisfactory by FDA standards, so finish your larger pieces until they register done temps at their thickest points!

SERVES 4 TO 6

1 (5- to 7-pound) whole chicken

1 cup buttermilk

2 large eggs

1 tablespoon Louisiana-style hot sauce, plus more to taste

Kosher salt and freshly ground black pepper

1 cup whole milk

2 cups all-purpose flour

1 cup lard

1 cup vegetable oil

Up to 3 tablespoons cayenne pepper

1 tablespoon light brown sugar

½ teaspoon garlic powder

½ teaspoon paprika

Wonder bread, for serving

Quick Bread and Butter Pickles (recipe follows)

Cut along each side of the chicken spine and remove. Place a shallow cut at the base of the breastbone, crack in half, and remove the sternum. Cut the bird in half. Make shallow cuts around the base of each drumette to expose the joint, then crack open and run the knife in between to separate the drumettes.

Cut between the thigh and breast to separate. To separate the drumstick, place shallow cuts around the strip of fat where the bones meet, then crack open and run the knife between to separate the drumstick from the thigh. Cut the chicken breasts in half.

Repeat on the other half of the chicken. You should have 10 pieces total.

BRINE THE CHICKEN: In a large food-safe container, combine the buttermilk, hot sauce, 1 table-spoon salt, and 2 teaspoons black pepper. Whisk until smooth, add the chicken and toss to coat evenly. Press the chicken down to make sure it's completely submerged in the brine. Cover and refrigerate for at least 4 hours, ideally overnight.

When ready to fry, preheat the oven to 325°F.

PREPARE THE DREDGING STATION: In a shallow dish, combine the whole milk with the eggs and a few dashes of hot sauce. Beat together with a fork until no streaks remain. In a separate shallow dish combine the flour, 2 teaspoons salt, and a few tablespoons of the egg mixture. This will create little chunks of breading which will help with crispiness.

First, dredge the chicken in the flour mixture, then into the egg mixture, then back into the flour mixture. This is commonly known as double-dipped fried chicken. Repeat with the remaining chicken and let it hang out in the flour while you prepare the oil for frying.

In a high-walled frying pan or skillet, combine the lard and vegetable oil. Heat over medium-high heat to 350°F.

Gently lay the chicken pieces into the oil, making sure to place them going away from you to prevent self-splattering. Fry until deeply golden brown and crisp, 5 to 7 minutes.

Transfer the par-cooked chicken to a wire rack set inside a rimmed baking sheet and bake until the internal temperature of the white meat reaches 165°F and the internal temperature of the dark meat reaches 175°F.

Meanwhile, in a small bowl, combine the cayenne pepper, sugar, garlic powder, paprika, 1 teaspoon black pepper, and ½ teaspoon of salt. For a tamer, less spicy version, you can reduce the cayenne pepper. Whisk to combine, then transfer the spice mix to a medium heatproof bowl. Add ½ cup of the still warm frying oil, then carefully, combine the ingredients.

Generously brush down both sides of the chicken with the spice oil. If applied while the oil and the chicken are still hot, it will absorb into the crust without making it soggy.

For the proper Nashville style, place the fried chicken on a slice of Wonder bread and top with Quick Bread and Butter Pickles.

QUICK BREAD AND BUTTER PICKLES

Makes about 1 quart

1 pound small cucumbers (ideally of the kirby variety)

4 ounces white onion, sliced

2 tablespoons pickling salt (or 3 tablespoons kosher salt)

5 ounces white vinegar

4 ounces apple cider vinegar

6 ounces sugar

1½ teaspoons whole mustard seeds

½ teaspoon red pepper flakes

½ teaspoon celery seeds

¼ teaspoon ground turmeric

6 black peppercorns

3 allspice berries

2 whole cloves

Slice the cucumbers into ¼-inch rounds or use a crinkle cutter to achieve the classic pickled chip texture. Combine in a large bowl with the onion and salt; toss to combine. Transfer the vegetables to a colander placed inside a bowl. Allow to drain for 2 hours at room temperature.

Transfer the vegetables to a sterile (see Note) quart mason jar.

In a small saucepan, whisk together the white and apple cider vinegars with the sugar. Add the mustard seeds, red pepper flakes, celery seeds, turmeric, peppercorns allspice berries, and cloves and bring the mixture to a boil. Cook over medium heat, stirring occasionally, until the sugar is dissolved, 15 to 30 seconds. Pour over the vegetables in the jar, leaving ½ inch of head space. Allow the mixture to cool to room temperature, then screw on the lid, and refrigerate for up to 2 weeks.

Note: *To sterilize, place the metal top of the jar(s) on the bottom of a large stock pot. Place the jar on top of the lid right side up. Fill the pot with enough warm water to cover the jar(s) by 1 inch. Bring the water to a boil over high heat. Once at a boil, start a timer for 10 minutes. Once the timer is finished, remove the pot from the heat and carefully remove the jar(s) using a jar lifter or tongs. Allow to cool on a clean paper towel until ready to use.*

FRIED WINGS WITH BUFFALO GOCHUJANG

Despite being from the neighboring city of Rochester, I am still burdened with the awesome responsibility of being born in Western New York, and therefore must be an advocate for Buffalo wings in their purest form, and by extension, Buffalo. That is: an unbreaded chicken wing, fried, then tossed with a ratio of 2:1 Frank's RedHot to melted butter, a shot of vinegar, and an optional shake of Worcestershire sauce and garlic powder. That's it. Anything else is heresy of the highest degree, a shallow imitator seeking only to sully the name of our proud border guard with Canada.

. . . that being said, I am not adding anything to the culinary conversation by just telling you how to do things the way they've been done forever. Instead, I'm going to advocate for the buffalo treatment of other sauces, that is, the adding of butter to them. Harsh, sharp, or extremely spicy sauces can be tamed and rounded by the big shot of fat, making for new and extraordinary wing experiences. The best I've found so far is a Korean-inspired gochujang sauce, already delicious on its own, made irresistible with some out-of-left-field butter (and lots of sesame seeds).

How I've Screwed This Up

By the definition of many people whom I grew up with and hold in high regard, this recipe is screwed up simply by existing. Their *opinions* aside, I've definitely overcooked my wings, which leads to dry, crispy little things that are still edible, if not enjoyable.

Troubleshooting

MY WINGS ARE DRY.
Might be frying at too low a temperature, which causes the wings to take a great long while to brown, which can cause the meat to overcook.

MY WINGS AREN'T CRISPY.
Low frying temperature can also be the culprit behind flabby wings.

MY WINGS ARE STICKING TOGETHER.
That happens, especially with chilly wings—try to keep them moving in the first few seconds of frying so they don't form any long-term relationships with other wings or the pan below.

THE SKIN IS SHRINKING UP MY WINGS' BONES.
I have this same problem when butchering my own— any sloppiness in your knife work is going to translate to the final wing. This recipe uses whole wings to demo knife skills and save a bit of money, so if you're just learning to break down chicken parts and are next up to host whatever-night football, maybe opt for the pre-butchered wings and drums.

SERVES 2 TO 4

About 2½ pounds whole chicken wings

Kosher salt

Frying oil (such as peanut, grapeseed, or vegetable)

Gochujang Buffalo Sauce (recipe follows)

⅓ cup sliced scallions (greens only), for garnish

1 tablespoon white and/or black sesame seeds, for garnish

Break down the chicken wings by slicing the connective skin between each of the joints. Break each of the joints open by bending them back until the joint pops, then slice between the bones to separate into drums and flats. Save the wing tips for making stock (see page 268); they can be frozen for up to 6 months (if not previously frozen).

Gently pat the drums and flats dry with paper towels, then generously season all over with salt. Transfer to a wire rack set inside a rimmed baking sheet. Allow the wings to dry, uncovered, overnight in the refrigerator.

Heat 2½ to 3 inches frying oil in a high-walled skillet over medium heat to 375°F. Working in batches, add the chicken wings and fry, adjusting the heat as needed to keep the oil temperature between 350 to 375°F, until cooked through and golden brown, 5 to 8 minutes. Transfer the wings to a baking sheet lined with paper towels and allow to cool slightly.

In a large bowl, toss the wings in the Gochujang Buffalo Sauce. Garnish with the scallions and sesame seeds and serve immediately.

GOCHUJANG BUFFALO SAUCE

Makes about 1½ cups

8 tablespoons (1 stick) unsalted butter

⅓ cup gochujang

¼ cup rice vinegar

2 tablespoons light brown sugar

2 tablespoons honey

1 tablespoon soy sauce

4 garlic cloves, minced

1 tablespoon grated peeled fresh ginger

Kosher salt and freshly ground black pepper

In a small saucepan, combine the butter, gochujang, vinegar, sugar, honey, soy sauce, garlic, and ginger. Bring to a simmer over medium heat, stirring constantly. Cook until all the sugar is dissolved, 1 to 2 minutes. Season with salt and pepper, then set aside at room temperature until ready to serve.

REALLY ORANGEY ORANGE CHICKEN

The following is one of the few recipes to transcend mere *Binging* and *Basics*, embodying the best of both worlds as a flight of fancy and practical exercise. Inspired by *Rick and Morty*'s dig at Panda Express in Season 3, this orange chicken finally lives up to its name thanks to something called an "oleo saccharum," which I'll call "ol' sack" for short. Ol' sack was invented as a means to bring big citrus flavor to cocktails by way of its sweetener, usually simple syrup. By soaking peels in sugar, precious oils are drawn out, combining with the sugar to form a flavor-packed citrus oil syrup. Orange chicken, requiring lots of sugar and orange flavor, is lent a great deal of both by little ol' sack. So, despite our recipe being the result of an accident and a joke, it appears to be the most efficient and effective way to translate orange flavor into orange chicken. It might represent my single greatest (or just single) contribution to the culinary pantheon, perhaps even the only thing that's remembered about me once I've shuffled free from this mortal coil. Long after I've returned to the dust from which I came, I hope you remember how Babish put his ol' sack in your chicken.

How I've Screwed This Up

Being this recipe's very creator, I am incapable of having screwed it up, not to mention immune from summary judgment or criticism of any kind. But initially, I did use too much cornstarch in the batter, which can cause the chicken to somehow remain pale even after long overclocking their frying time.

Troubleshooting

MY CHICKEN IS PALE.
Too much cornstarch, too low a frying heat!

MY CHICKEN IS FLABBY.
Same thing!

THIS MADE WAY TOO MUCH OLEO SACCHARUM.
There's no such thing as too much oleo saccharum where I come from! Hang on to that stuff in an airtight container for about a week, use it in everything from cocktails to tea to desserts.

THIS ISN'T AUTHENTIC ORANGE CHICKEN.
There is no "authentic" orange chicken, dude. Orange chicken was invented by Panda Express in 1987, so your faux outrage is as misguided as it is misplaced.

WOW, YOU HAD THAT LOCKED AND LOADED. DO YOU PRACTICE BEING SANCTIMONIOUS IN THE MIRROR OR DOES IT JUST COME NATURALLY?
You're the one engaging in outrage for outrage's sake!

YOU'RE THE ONE WRITING AN ARGUMENT WITH YOURSELF JUST SO YOU CAN WIN!
[Silence.]

WHAT, NO CANNED RETORT? DID YOU JUST LOSE YOUR OWN IMAGINARY ARGUMENT?
Well, that's humbling to read.

YOU MEAN HUMBLING TO WRITE?
I've got a headache.

SERVES 4 TO 6

2 large eggs

1 tablespoon rice vinegar

1 tablespoon Shaoxing wine

1½ pounds boneless, skinless chicken breasts, cut into bite-size pieces

9 cups peanut oil

1 cup all-purpose flour

1 cup rice flour

2 teaspoons kosher salt

½ teaspoon baking powder

½ teaspoon freshly ground white pepper

¼ teaspoon MSG

2 tablespoons cornstarch

Orange Sauce (recipe follows)

1 teaspoon toasted sesame oil

Thinly sliced scallions, for garnish

Cooked white rice, for serving

In a medium bowl, whisk together the eggs, vinegar, and Shaoxing wine. Add the chicken and toss to coat. Let marinate at room temperature for 20 to 30 minutes.

Add enough of the peanut oil to fill a large high-sided skillet halfway and heat to 350°F.

Meanwhile, in a small rimmed baking sheet or pie pan, whisk together the all-purpose and rice flours, the salt, baking powder, white pepper, and MSG. Add the chicken and dredge.

Working in batches, add the chicken to the oil and fry over medium-high heat until the internal temperature registers 175°F, 5 to 7 minutes. Transfer the chicken to a large rimmed baking sheet lined with paper towels and set aside.

In a small bowl, whisk together the cornstarch with 2 tablespoons water.

Bring the orange sauce to a boil in the large skillet and add the cornstarch slurry. Cook, whisking constantly, until the sauce begins to thicken, 1 to 2 minutes. Drizzle in the sesame oil and stir to combine. Add the chicken and toss to combine. Garnish with sliced scallions and serve with white rice.

ORANGE SAUCE

Makes about 1½ cups

1 tablespoon vegetable oil

1 teaspoon grated peeled fresh ginger

2 garlic cloves, minced

⅓ cup Oleo-Saccharum (recipe follows)

¼ cup fresh orange juice

¼ cup soy sauce

¼ cup rice vinegar

2 tablespoons Shaoxing wine

2 tablespoons light brown sugar

1 tablespoon finely sliced reserved orange zest strips (from the Oleo-Saccharum)

1 small bird's-eye chile, seeded and finely sliced

½ teaspoon MSG

Heat the vegetable oil in a large skillet over medium heat. Add the ginger and garlic and cook, stirring often, until fragrant, 30 seconds to 1 minute. Add the oleo saccharum, orange juice, soy sauce, vinegar, Shaoxing wine, brown sugar, orange zest, chile, and MSG. Cook over medium-high heat, stirring to dissolve the sugar, until boiling.

Remove from the heat and cover. Set aside until ready to use.

OLEO-SACCHARUM

Makes about 1 cup

6 oranges

1 cup sugar

Using a paring knife, remove the zest from each orange in large strips, avoiding the white pith—you only want the zest. Reserve the oranges to juice for the Orange Sauce (page 302).

In a medium bowl, combine the orange zest strips with the sugar. Crush or mash the zest with a muddler or potato masher. Cover the bowl or transfer to a sealable container. Let sit at room temperature overnight to 24 hours.

Strain the liquid through a sieve into a medium bowl, pressing on the solids. Reserve 3 of the orange zest strips for the Orange Sauce; discard the remaining strips. Use the oleo-saccharum immediately or refrigerate until ready to use, up to 4 days.

CHAPTER 8

PORK

Alright here we go again, ethics lecture inbound . . . not! You know where I stand—eat higher-quality meat less often—I won't shove it down your throat. I will, instead, try and put what little flowery vocabulary I have to use in an attempt to make you salivate over one of nature's most delicious creatures. Tip to tail, pigs might offer the widest variety of flavors and possibilities of any mammal: Bacon, crackling like a cheering crowd, perfuming the air with smoke signals of mesquite and juniper. Puffy, salty, shatteringly crunchy skin, eaten like chips between forkfuls of porchetta, laden with citrus and pine nuts. Tender meat and silky fat, candied in sugar and spice until melting together between pillowy buns with crisp cucumbers and sticky hoisin. And that's just the belly! In Louisiana, the *Boucherie* is a celebration of the entire pig, the festival putting every edible inch to good use in a bevy of generations-old family recipes. In the highlands of Papua New Guinea, the Tsembaga Maring tribe's very cultural identity has been shaped by pigs, their ritual slaughter and the resultant celebration having played a core societal role for generations. It's even been suggested by extraterrestrial anthropologists that pigs are the closest descendants of the earliest life forms to first live terrestrially, having likely evolved from bacteria that lay dormant in a fallen meteorite. Oh, you didn't believe that one? Guess I need to pivot from the rule of threes if I'm going to keep you reading headnotes . . .

WHAT IS PORK? Pork is the meat of the pig, an animal that is host to perhaps one of the strangest contrarities in food: despite positively loving a bath in its own shit, it tastes like a wood-fire smoked and salted butter massage narrated by Sam Elliot.

I'M ASSUMING THE SAME RULES APPLY FOR PORK'S QUALITY AND PRICE GENERALLY WALKING HAND IN HAND? Absolutely—high-quality pork doesn't just taste better than supermarket pork, it tastes entirely different. Heritage pork, like Berkshire, can taste sweet and nutty, with more intramuscular fat and a varied diet yielding a unique flavor and texture.

MY PORK IS PINK. JUST WHAT IN THE HELL IS GOING ON? Don't worry, it's supposed to be pink! It's ironic that pork was once marketed as "The Other White Meat" to a tongue-dead 1980s America, because when cooked to an ideal doneness, it's rather rosier than it is white. If it's a *really* pink pink, one that could be described as glistening or less-than-tender, you might be dealing with undercooked pork. Herein lies one of the better excuses to invest in a digital thermometer, given that as little as 10 degrees Fahrenheit could mean the difference between juicy, chewy, or god forbid, mealy.

WHY DOES MY PORK TASTE DRY? Until recently, pork has been criminally overcooked by the vast majority of home chefs. That pork should be cooked to a rosy 145°F is finally permeating the mainstream, and dried-out chops are becoming a thing of the past. Just like any meat being cooked under 165°F, it's best if you trust your pork, so make an effort to source it from a quality butcher.

IS PORK HEALTHY? It's healthy-ish. Like beef or chicken, it can be either fatty or lean, dripping with cholesterol and/or brimming with nutrients. It is, however, a red meat, and carries with it the drawbacks: increased risk of heart disease, type 2 diabetes, and ketchup-blood syndrome. So, like most of life's joys, moderation is key to enjoying pork throughout a long and healthy life.

DO I NEED A SMOKER TO MAKE BARBECUE?
Only tangentially related to pork, but I understand why you're asking now. While there are certainly workarounds (like our Gas Grill–Smoked Ribs, page 330), one of the prime directives of true barbecue is exposure to smoke, be it from the wood of the earth or coal of the underworld. You can spice it up however you like: while oven-braised ribs might yield some raised eyebrows and compliments about tenderness, only smoked ribs are capable of rendering whole picnic tables of diners speechless, save for involuntary mouth-smacks and soulful moans.

BACON? Yes.

HOMEMADE BACON

Homemade bacon is one of those big personal projects that, at first, seems like an entirely sunk cost. You mean to tell me that I'm going to spend $25 on pork belly, another $20 on a food-safe tub, another $20 on random spices I'll never use for anything else, and a full workweek's worth of time making something I can buy for $6.99 a pound from my old pal Oscar—Oscar Meyer? Yeah, that's what I'm telling you, because what results isn't just bacon. It's a genre redefining character study of what bacon looks like under the tutelage of the hot new Hollywood director, fresh off their first Oscar nom and ready to fully express their unique style and voice with a $180 million dollar budget. Yes, I am referring directly to Kiwi filmmaking sensation Taika Waititi and his megastar-making turn helming 2017's Thor: Ragnarok, and store bought bacon is more like Thor: The Dark World. Sure, it's okay, but which would you rather watch? So buy the ticket and take the ride, because if you've got the time and the inclination to whip up some superhero-relaunch-level bacon, it clearly ends up working very well.

How I've Screwed This Up

I have taken cracks at smoking my own bacon indoors (see: "Breakfast from Howl's Moving Castle," *Binging with Babish,* 2019), and though ill-prepared, it still rose head and shoulders above most store-bought bacon. It's pretty hard to screw up, so long as both your patience and smoke are steady.

Troubleshooting

MY BACON IS BURNT.
This may have resulted from either temperatures getting too high in the smoker or your cure having too high a ratio of sugar. Dial back both!

HOW DO I SLICE MY BACON THINLY?
Make sure you use a sharp knife and that the bacon is completely chilled before attempting to slice. This will allow the fat to become completely firm, so it can be sliced cleanly and thinly. If you're one of those rare birds that owns a meat slicer, now is a good time to finally dust it off.

DO I NEED TO CURE MY BACON?
Great question! No you do not—you could salt-cure your belly, smoke it, slice it and eat it all the same—it just might not have the same familiar cured flavor to which you might be accustomed to in bacon.

DO I NEED TO SMOKE MY BACON?
Absolutely. Smoke is one of the hallmark flavors of bacon and without it you're simply making cured pork belly (salt pork) which, while versatile, will not resemble anything that could be even mistaken for bacon.

DO I NEED TO USE DISTILLED WATER?
Depends on if you eat raw cookie dough—either way, you're rolling the dice, but not very much—we still need to advise you to use distilled water for your safety. Tap water could contain any number of contaminants depending on where you live, and while more than likely safe, you oughtn't risk spending a week memorizing your bathroom's floor tiles to avoid a mild inconvenience. Alternatively, you can boil your water for 5 minutes and allow it to cool completely before using in the cure—since it's only a half cup, it'll only take a few minutes!

DO I NEED TO USE A CURE CALCULATOR?
Absolutely—overcuring meat won't taste great, and undercuring meat could put your very life at risk. While this is a comparatively short cure time, a cure calculator that takes into consideration your pork belly's weight and dimensions is necessary to calculate how to safely cure your bacon. You can find cure calculators online, I'm a particular fan of Meathead's over at http://www.amazingribs.com/.

I CAN'T CLICK THAT LINK FOR SOME REASON.
Oh right, this is a book. Google time!

MAKES ABOUT 1¼ POUNDS

1 center-cut pork belly (about 2 pounds)

Pink curing salt, as needed (reference a cure calculator for specific quantity)

½ cup distilled water

Classic, Pastrami, or Guanciale Seasoning (recipes follow)

Wood chips of your choice, for smoking

Weigh the pork belly and calculate the amount of curing salt needed using an online curing salt calculator.

In a small bowl, whisk to combine the curing salt with the distilled water and Classic, Pastrami, or Guanciale Seasoning. Transfer the brine to a large resealable plastic bag. Add the pork belly, squeeze out as much air as possible, then seal the bag. Place on a rimmed baking sheet and refrigerate for 3 days. Make sure to massage the bag/pork once a day to distribute the brine.

Remove the cured pork belly from the bag, rinse, and pat dry. Transfer to a wire rack set inside a large rimmed baking sheet. Refrigerate for 24 hours to allow it to dry out before smoking.

Prepare the smoker with the wood chips according to the manufacturer's instructions. Stabilize the heat at 200°F. Place the pork in the smoker, close the lid, and smoke for 2 to 3 hours, until the internal temperature reaches 150°F.

Allow the bacon to cool to room temperature then refrigerate for 1 to 2 hours. Just before slicing, transfer the bacon to the freezer to firm up for 15 to 20 minutes.

Using an electric slicer or a very long and sharp knife, slice the bacon to your desired thickness. For the guanciale bacon, cutting it into lardons (¼-by-1-inch strips) is recommended.

Wrap the bacon in plastic wrap and refrigerate for up to 2 weeks before cooking.

CLASSIC SEASONING

4 tablespoons light brown sugar

1 tablespoon kosher salt

Combine the sugar and salt in a small bowl.

PASTRAMI SEASONING

1 tablespoon kosher salt

2 tablespoons whole black peppercorns, cracked

1 tablespoon coriander seeds

1 tablespoon light brown sugar

1½ teaspoons paprika

1 teaspoon garlic powder

1 teaspoon yellow mustard seeds

1 teaspoon allspice berries

1 teaspoon juniper berries

1 bay leaf

Combine the salt, peppercorns, coriander seeds, sugar, paprika, garlic powder, mustard seeds, allspice and juniper berries, and the bay leaf in a small bowl.

GUANCIALE SEASONING

1 tablespoon kosher salt

1 tablespoon sugar

1½ tablespoons crushed black peppercorns

1 teaspoon dried thyme

1 teaspoon dried rosemary

1 teaspoon allspice berries

2 garlic cloves, minced or crushed in a garlic press

Combine all the salt, sugar, peppercorns, thyme, rosemary, allspice berries, and garlic in a small bowl.

B.L.E.C.T

MAKES 1 SANDWICH

2 classic bacon slices (see page 311)

2 tomato slices

Kosher salt

2 tablespoons unsalted butter, softened

1 large egg

1 slice cheese of choice

2 slices hearty white bread

1 tablespoon Homemade Mayonnaise (recipe follows)

2 iceberg lettuce leaves

Preheat the oven to 375°F with convection (400°F without convection).

Place the bacon on a rimmed baking sheet. Bake 15 to 20 minutes, until crispy.

Meanwhile, place the tomato slices on a wire rack and sprinkle liberally with salt. Let sit while the bacon cooks.

Melt 1 tablespoon of the butter in a small nonstick skillet over high heat. Add the egg and cook until the egg whites become crisp around the exterior, 1 to 2 minutes. Reduce the heat to low and continue cooking until the egg white is completely cooked and the yolk is cooked to your desired doneness, 3 to 6 minutes.

Remove from the heat and top the fried egg with the cheese. Cover with a lid to melt the cheese and keep the egg warm until ready to serve.

Heat a large skillet over medium heat. Brush one side of each slice of bread with the remaining 1 tablespoon butter. Place the slices butter-side down in the skillet. Toast until crispy on one side only, 3 to 4 minutes.

Spread the mayonnaise on the toasted sides of the bread; layer the lettuce, then the salted tomato slices, bacon, and finally the cheesy fried egg. Top the sandwich with the remaining slice of bread. Slice as desired and serve immediately.

HOMEMADE MAYONNAISE

Makes about 2 cups

2 large eggs

1 teaspoon Dijon mustard

1 tablespoon fresh lemon juice

1 garlic clove, minced

½ teaspoon kosher salt

2 cups vegetable oil

In a food processor, combine the eggs, mustard, lemon juice, garlic, and salt. Process until the mixture is homogenous, 15 to 30 seconds. While the machine is running, very slowly stream the oil into the feed tube. Continue processing until all of the oil is incorporated and the resulting mayonnaise is thick and glossy, 15 to 30 seconds.

Use immediately or refrigerate in a sealable container for up to 2 weeks.

CANDIED BACON

Makes about 16 slices

Nonstick cooking spray

1 (16-ounce) package thick-cut bacon or 1 pound Homemade Bacon (page 308)

¾ cup pure maple syrup

½ cup light brown sugar

Preheat the oven to 350°F.

Line a baking sheet with aluminum foil and top with a wire rack. Spray the rack with nonstick cooking spray.

Line your bacon on the prepared rack, making sure not to overlap, and brush with about half of the maple syrup then sprinkle with about half of the brown sugar. Bake 10 to 15 minutes, until the sugar is completely melted. Remove from the oven then flip each slice of bacon. Coat the other side with the remaining maple syrup and brown sugar. Bake, flipping every 5 minutes, until the bacon is cooked through and has a reddish mahogany color, 10 to 15 minutes longer. Let cool completely for 30 minutes.

Serve and enjoy!

ROASTED PORK TENDERLOIN WITH BOURBON-MUSTARD PAN SAUCE

I'll just go ahead and say it: bourbon gets used too often in cooking. I think that we can all sometimes get caught up in the modern waxed moustache protomasculine ideal, wanting to swing our body weight off the saddle horn of our penny farthing onto the teakwood deck of our tiny-home-cum-coffee-roaster airstream, the air thick with palo santo and leather cream. Much like "wagyu," however, bourbon is more often than not added simply for show, its woody and sometimes-cloying flavor winced through for the sake of the "experience" of having a Turkish coffee–rubbed ostrich tenderloin with whiskey–bee pollen sauce. Okay, sure, I'm exaggerating, but my point is that I've had (and certainly made) my fair share of shitty bourbon-flavored foods, and this ain't one of them. Whiskey plays much more nicely with pork than it does with most any other meat, inoffensively at worst and stupendously at best. Lots of fat in the form of heavy cream and butter help to offset the bracing booze and mustard, making a positively decadent pan sauce that doesn't overwhelm its starring counterpart, the comparatively mild pork tenderloin. Low on fat (and by extension, on flavor), pork tenderloins are best cooked quick and hot, not unlike a chicken breast. Cooking to a proper doneness ensures moisture retention, and when smothered in a gelatin-reinforced sauce, there exists the very real possibility that this recipe may afford you one of the most memorable pork experiences of your life. And, since tenderloins usually come in a two pack for some reason, you can make it again tomorrow night!

How I've Screwed This Up

Pork tenderloins are the protein for which I've likely made the most pan sauces in my day, and having screwed up so very many pan sauces, that's likely where I've most often fallen short. Make sure to follow pan sauce law numero uno: add the finishing fats *off* heat!

Troubleshooting

MY PAN SAUCE BROKE.
The fat may have been added while the pan was too hot, or there may be too much fat in the pan—either way, the fix is the same—a squirt of good ol' fashioned water will save even the most grossest of pan sauce problems.

MY PORK IS DRY.
The uninitiated may balk at a doneness of 135°F, but the National Pork Board agrees that it's the ideal temperature to which the animal's more delicate, lean cuts should be cooked. Even a rosy pink is normal, so if you're cooking your loins past the point of pality, I suggest you take steps to get past your crippling FDA-induced fears.

MY SAUCE TASTES HARSH.
Make sure you're cooking off all that alcohol—while flambéing may be mostly for show, it's also a good indicator of when the noxious fumes of the devil's drink have all but dissipated.

SERVES 2 TO 4

1 (1½-pound) pork tenderloin

Kosher salt and freshly ground black pepper

1½ teaspoons powdered gelatin

1 cup chicken stock, preferably homemade (see page 268)

2 tablespoons light olive oil (if needed)

½ cup minced shallots

½ cup bourbon

¼ cup heavy cream

2 tablespoons cold unsalted butter

1 tablespoon whole-grain mustard

2 tablespoons chopped fresh parsley, for garnish

Pat the pork dry, then season generously with salt and pepper. Transfer to a wire rack set inside a rimmed baking sheet. Refrigerate, uncovered, for at least 8 hours, up to 2 days.

When you're ready to cook the pork, preheat the oven to 475°F.

Transfer the pork to the oven and lower the oven temperature to 425°F. Roast for about 15 minutes then flip over to brown the other side. Continue roasting 10 to 15 minutes, until the thickest part of the loin reaches an internal temperature of 135°F. Remove from the oven and reserve the rendered fat and/or juices from the baking sheet. Loosely tent the pork with aluminum foil and allow to rest 10 minutes.

MEANWHILE, MAKE THE SAUCE: In a small bowl, sprinkle the gelatin over the chicken stock and allow it to hydrate for 5 minutes.

Heat 2 tablespoons of the reserved fat/juices in a medium skillet over medium heat. If there aren't enough juices or fat, supplement with olive oil. Add the shallots and cook, stirring occasionally, until softened, 2 to 3 minutes. Remove the skillet from the heat, add the bourbon, then return to the heat, scraping up any browned bits. Add the gelatin-enhanced chicken stock and simmer, stirring occasionally, until thick enough to coat the back of a spoon, 5 to 7 minutes. Remove from the heat, add the heavy cream, and whisk to combine. Add the butter and whisk until completely combined. Add the mustard and whisk until homogenous. Season with salt and pepper.

Slice the rested pork tenderloin ½-inch thick. Pour the bourbon-mustard sauce over the top and garnish with the parsley. Serve immediately.

NORTH (EAST) CAROLINA–STYLE PULLED PORK

As I'm writing this, I can tell that I'm making a mistake. You are, to a degree of certainty, about to watch me make an error as avoidable as it is verifiable. I am 0 for 3 in terms of accurately portraying different barbecue styles on the channel, and this recipe is going to be no exception, containing anything from a minor omission to a complete misrepresentation. It's not unlike the trolly problem; except there is no lever, no possible intervention or decision to make, there is only impending disaster and its inevitable fallout. My fate is sealed—I mean, here you are reading it on a page that's been printed and distributed throughout the world—it is written in the stars, it is foretold in the songs of yore, its words still hang on the tongues of the ancients. All that being said, I will now set those machinations forth and state their inception: what follows is an authentic North(eastern) Carolina-style pulled pork. Serve on a bun with a simple slaw of cabbage, onion, green pepper, white vinegar, sugar, and salt. Look upon my works, ye mighty, and despair.

How I've Screwed This Up

Are you serious?

Troubleshooting

Note: This is one of the few true-blue barbecue recipes in the book, and as such, is woefully incomplete. As such, the troubleshooting in this section is going to try to cover a lot of ground!

MY PORK DRIED OUT.

Barbecue is a delicate dance of time, heat, and smoke. You need to maintain a steady temperature for a tremendous amount of time, which is no easy feat without a pellet-fed smoker. Your pork can dry out for any number of reasons in such a lengthy process, but poor heat control is usually the first culprit. Spikes of heat can cause muscle fibers to contract, squeezing out precious moisture and toughening the resultant butt. The two temperatures that need chiefly concern you are the ambient temperature of your barbecue (225°F) and the final temperature of your pork (190°F). Cook times can vary wildly due to a wide breadth of variables, so trust and monitor only those two numbers before you dare to trust any others.

MY PORK DOESN'T HAVE A SMOKE RING.

While not necessarily a mark of quality barbecue, a smoke ring is a good indicator of a consistent low temperature. Smoke rings can also be amplified by consistently mopping and/or spritzing the meat with liquid of some kind, in this case the vinegar mop, which causes smoke particles (nitric oxide) to become stuck to and absorbed by the meat. But remember, as long as it tastes good, it don't mean a thing if it ain't got that ring!

MY PORK WON'T COME UP TO TEMPERATURE. IT'S BEEN FOURTEEN HOURS AND MY GUESTS ARE GETTING RESTLESS AND THIS HONESTLY FEELS LIKE DIVINE PUNISHMENT OF SOME KIND FROM WHAT I THOUGHT WAS MERELY AN INDIFFERENT UNIVERSE.

Yeah, I've been there. This "stall" in temperature generally starts around 160°F and won't quit until your patience is well and truly tested. Something you can utilize with barbecue of almost any kind is the so-called "Texas Crutch," wherein a roast or rack is wrapped tightly with aluminum foil and a braising liquid, which speeds up the meat's approach to doneness without sacrificing moisture. You can most certainly apply this trick to your pork, pouring a bit of the mop over top before wrapping it up and saying a little prayer that the temperature will finally come of legal voting age before the sun sets.

DAMN IT. WHERE'S THE FLASHLIGHT?
You got your phone?

THANKS—I FORGET THAT IT HAS ONE WHEN I'M OUTDOORS FOR SOME REASON.
Me too!

SERVES 4 TO 6

Pork

1 (3- to 4-pound) boneless pork butt or pork shoulder

Kosher salt and freshly ground black pepper

Wood chips of your choice (I used hickory, cherry, and maple), for smoking

Vinegar Mop

1 cup white vinegar

1 cup apple cider vinegar

3 tablespoons light brown sugar

1 tablespoon kosher salt

1 tablespoon red pepper flakes

2 teaspoons freshly ground black pepper

½ teaspoon hot sauce of choice

PREPARE THE PORK: Remove and discard any excess and/or large pieces of fat from the pork. Coat with a generous sprinkling of salt and pepper. Transfer to a rimmed baking sheet and refrigerate, uncovered, overnight.

MEANWHILE, MAKE THE VINEGAR MOP: Combine the white and apple cider vinegars, the sugar, salt, pepper flakes, black pepper, and hot sauce in a medium bowl. Whisk well to combine. Use immediately or store overnight to allow the flavors to develop further.

Prepare the smoker with wood chips according to the manufacturer's instructions. Stabilize the heat at 225°F. Place the pork in the smoker, close the lid, and smoke for 16 hours, or until the internal temperature reaches 190°F. Every hour or so, brush the pork with the vinegar mop.

Remove the pork from the smoker, loosely tent with aluminum foil, and allow to rest for 45 minutes to 1 hour.

Shred the pork using gloved hands or two forks. Finish the pork with more vinegar mop to taste.

POTSTICKERS

Potstickers might be reliably available from your local take-out establishment, but rarely do they feature a crispy cornstarch doily, or "skirt," adding as much crunch as it does visual flair. Made en masse, they also freeze beautifully for frying up at a moment's notice, needing little more than 15 minutes and its simple dipping sauce to create a striking snack. The pork and chive filling is far and away the most familiar, but the dumpling can become a vehicle for all manner of mashed goods, from chicken to veggies to seafood to . . . that's about it, actually.

How I've Screwed This Up

Just like anyone's first (dozen) attempts at folding dumpling wrappers, mine were certainly rough to start. With time and practice, however, you find a sweet spot of hand positioning and dough movement where things sort of just click. If that never happens, we included an easier folding method for the less-dexterous among us.

Troubleshooting

MY DUMPLINGS BURST.

They may have been overfilled, but more than likely they were improperly sealed. Make sure you're folding the wet side of the dough, otherwise the creases won't adhere to themselves.

MY DUMPLINGS BROKE.

Sounds more like dry dumpling wrappers—keep them under a moist paper towel when not in use so they remain supple.

MY SKIRT IS PATCHY.

Have you tried a sewing kit?

YOU DICK.

Sorry. Up the cornstarch slurry amount by 50 percent for better skirt coverage.

MY SKIRT BURNED IN SPOTS.

Sounds like uneven heat distribution in your pan—give it a quarter rotation every 10 seconds once the skirt starts browning to make sure it gets evenly toasted.

THIS TIME I MEAN MY ACTUAL SKIRT.

Oh—careful of oil spatters then?

MAKES 50 TO 60

Potstickers

12 ounces ground pork

1 large carrot, peeled and coarsely grated

4 scallions, thinly sliced

1½ cups thinly sliced napa cabbage

3 garlic cloves, grated

1 (1-inch) piece ginger, peeled and grated

1 large egg, beaten

¼ cup dark soy sauce

2 tablespoons toasted sesame oil

2 tablespoons mirin

1½ teaspoons kosher salt

1 teaspoon freshly ground black pepper

¼ teaspoon freshly ground white pepper

50 (one 14-ounce package) dumpling wrappers, thawed if frozen

Skirt Slurry (optional; makes enough for 6 to 8 potstickers)

1 teaspoon cornstarch

1 teaspoon all-purpose flour

¼ teaspoon rice vinegar

Vegetable oil, as needed

Dipping Sauce (recipe follows)

MAKE THE POTSTICKERS: Combine the pork, carrot, scallions, cabbage, garlic, ginger, egg, soy sauce, sesame oil, mirin, salt, and the black and white pepper in a medium bowl, and using your hands, gently mix until evenly distributed.

Working with 6 to 8 dumpling wrappers at a time, place the wrappers on a clean, dry work surface. Keep the remaining wrappers covered in the refrigerator.

Place about 2 teaspoons of the filling in the center of 1 wrapper. Using your finger, dab water on half of the circumference. Take the dumpling into your hand, then fold the dry half of the wrapper over the filling. As you begin to seal the dumpling, make small pleats in the dry half of the wrapper, then press the pleat into the wet side to enclose the filling. Alternatively, fold the dry half of the wrapper over the filling. Seal the dough in the center, then fold two pleats on either side. Press to seal the remainder of the wrapper. Repeat with the remaining filling and wrappers.

(NOTE: *At this point, you can wrap and freeze the dumplings for later use.)*

IF MAKING THE SKIRT SLURRY: In a small bowl, whisk together the cornstarch and flour. Add the cornstarch mixture to ½ cup water in a separate bowl. Whisk in the vinegar and reserve until ready to use.

In a medium nonstick skillet, heat 1 tablespoon vegetable oil over medium-high heat. Working in batches of 6 to 8, add the dumplings flat-side down and fry until the bottom is golden brown and crispy, about 3 minutes. If cooking the dumplings with the skirt slurry, skip to the next step. Carefully (to avoid splashing) add ¼ cup water and cover the pan with a lid. Reduce the heat to medium low and cook until the filling is thoroughly cooked (to an internal temperature of 160°F) and the water is mostly evaporated, 7 to 10 minutes.

When ready to cook with the skirt slurry, thoroughly whisk the mixture to reincorporate. Add to the skillet with the dumplings in it and cover with a lid. Cook until most of the liquid is evaporated, about 7 minutes. Uncover the pan and continue cooking over medium heat until the skirt is browned, 3 to 4 minutes. Remove the pan from the heat and place a plate (slightly smaller than the circumference of the pan) over the dumplings. With oven-gloved hands, carefully invert the dumplings onto the plate.

Repeat with remaining dumplings and serve with the Dipping Sauce.

DIPPING SAUCE

Makes about 1 cup

½ cup soy sauce

¼ cup rice vinegar

1 tablespoon sugar

1 tablespoon thinly sliced scallions

1 tablespoon toasted sesame oil

1 (½-inch) piece ginger, peeled and grated

In a small bowl, combine the soy sauce, vinegar, sugar, scallions, sesame oil, and ginger with ¼ cup water and whisk to combine. Cover and set aside until ready to serve.

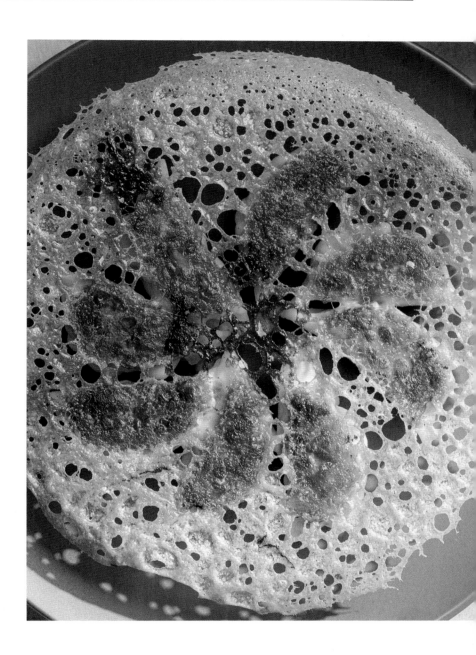

STEP-BY-STEP IMAGES, PAGE 324-325

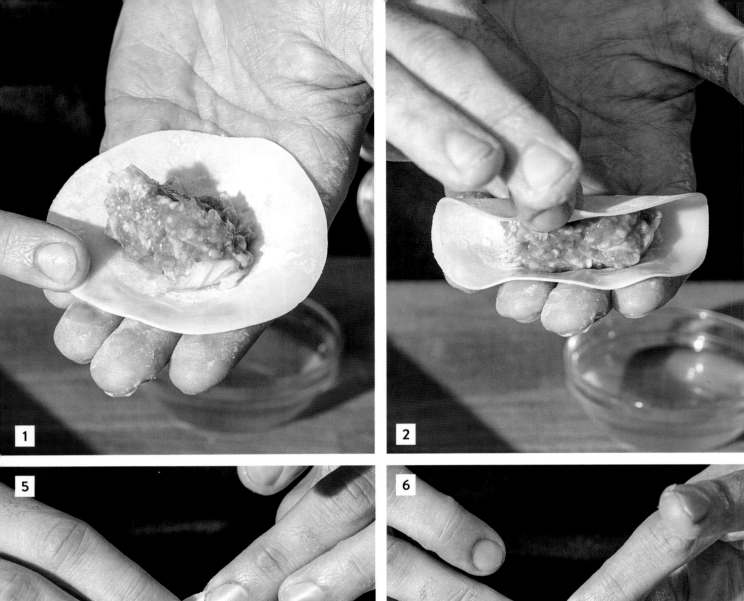

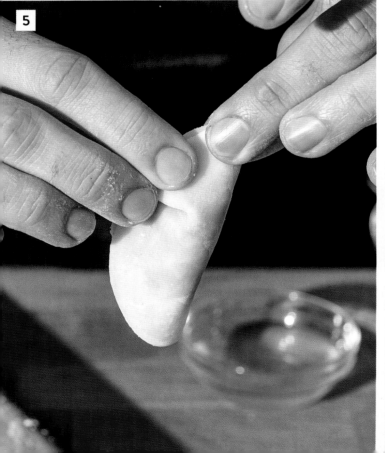

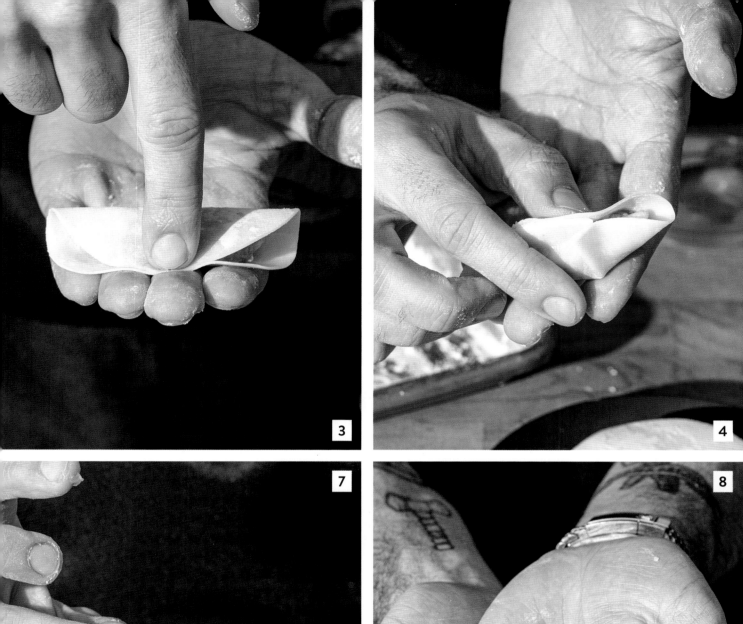

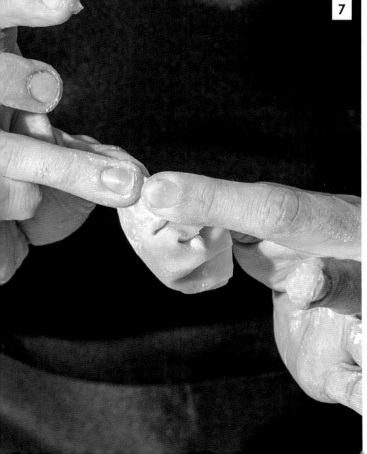

TONKOTSU RAMEN

Well, you did it. You solved the scavenger hunt. You didn't fall into the dreaded pit of mirin on page 328, and you survived the climb to the peak of mount Tamago on page 175. Now it's time to put it all together: Tonkotsu, the absolute unit of ramen. Limitless combinations of spicy, crunchy, and savory toppings are scattered across the broth, turned creamy and opaque with pork fat, clinging to every kinky noodle curled up underneath its surface. A labor of love, time, effort, money, and actual labor, requiring as many hours of your day as it does specially prepared specialty ingredients, few comfort foods ask so much of their preparatory person. Fewer still, however, are able to deliver an ending that somehow justifies the herculean effort—and in every slurp of tonkotsu ramen, you can taste the energy expended in its creation. The millions of BTU's burned under a bubbling cauldron, the silky textures coaxed out by the patient oven, each element carefully arranged in the bowl like an invitation: you're invited. My bowl. Tonight. Bring a light, crisp beer. Party goes till question marks.

How I've Screwed This Up

The first time I made tonkotsu broth, I didn't know that it should be kept at a rolling boil. I needed to run out to a meeting in midtown, and was so scared of letting the pot come to bubbles, I balanced my laptop on a pile of books next to the stove so I could tune in anytime on my phone (not that I could do anything if it did). As I would learn, this broth only emulsifies into its ideal creamy state not when gently bare-simmered like chicken stock, but kept at a spirited boil like friggin spaghetti. I ended up with pork bone broth, so not a total loss, but still.

Troubleshooting

MY PORK ISN'T TENDER.
Definitely undercooked—very hard to overcook pork belly, so better to go over than under the suggested cook times.

MY TONKOTSU BROTH ISN'T OPAQUE.
This broth, unlike most others, must be kept at an active boil during the duration of its cook time in order to achieve its signature cloudy fattiness. Make sure you're keeping things bubbly!

MY SOUP IS COLD.
With its many elements, if any are fresh out the fridge, they can act like tasty ice cubes in your soup. Bring all the accoutrements to room temperature before serving, and if you really want to keep things steamy, fill the bowls with boiling water and empty right before serving.

MY SOUP IS HOT. If you make things too hot, they can end up too hot, so make things less hot so that they don't end up too hot.

MY SOUP IS NOT.
Yes it is.

SERVES 8

Tare

2 tablespoons vegetable oil

2 ounces dried anchovies (about 1½ cups)

½ cup soy sauce

½ cup mirin

¼ cup dried bonito flakes

¼ cup dry sake

Noodles

40 ounces fresh ramen noodles (5 ounces per serving)

Ramen Assembly

Chashu Pork (recipe follows), sliced and reheated

Ajitsuke Tamago (page 175), halved

Nori, menma, corn, chopped garlic, onions, scallions, kikurage, for garnish (optional)

Tonkotsu Broth (recipe follows), heated until hot

Chile oil, for garnish (optional)

MAKE THE TARE: In a medium sauté pan, heat the vegetable oil over medium-high heat until shimmering. Add the anchovies and fry, stirring frequently, until a light brown fond forms on the bottom of the pan, 3 to 5 minutes. Add the soy sauce, mirin, bonito flakes, and sake; bring to a gentle simmer and cook off the alcohol for 2 to 3 minutes. Strain through a fine-mesh sieve into a small bowl and set aside until ready to use; discard the solids.

COOK THE NOODLES: In a large pot, bring 4 quarts water to a boil. Add the noodles and cook, agitating occasionally, until cooked but toothsome, about 90 seconds. Proceed immediately to the next step.

ASSEMBLE THE RAMEN: Add ⅓ cup of the tare to each serving bowl. Follow with the noodles, draining them first. Arrange the chashu, ajitsuke tamago, and desired garnishes over the noodles. Pour hot tonkotsu broth over everything until the noodles are 80 percent submerged. Drizzle with chile oil if desired and serve.

CHASHU PORK

Makes 8 portions

2 tablespoons vegetable oil

1 small onion, quartered

4 garlic cloves, smashed

2 scallions, roughly chopped

½ cup soy sauce

½ cup mirin

½ cup sugar

¼ cup fish sauce

1½ to 2½ pounds boneless pork belly, skin removed (optional)

In a large Dutch oven, heat the oil over medium-high heat until nearly smoking. Add the onion and cook, turning occasionally, until brown on all sides, 1 to 3 minutes. Add the garlic and scallions, and cook, stirring, until fragrant, 30 seconds. Add the soy sauce, mirin, sugar, and fish sauce and bring to a boil, whisking to dissolve the sugar. Add the pork belly and water if necessary until submerged halfway. Lower the heat, cover partially, and maintain a bare simmer, turning the pork occasionally, until easily pierced with a paring knife, 2 to 3 hours. (Alternatively, braise in a 275°F oven for 3 to 4 hours.) Remove the chashu and allow to cool at room temperature.

WRAP THE CHASHU IN PLASTIC AND REFRIGERATE OVERNIGHT BEFORE THINLY SLICING AND REHEATING FOR USE IN THE RAMEN. TO REHEAT: Arrange the chashu slices on a foil-lined baking sheet and torch or broil until lightly charred and heated through. Use immediately.

TONKOTSU BROTH

Makes 3 to 4 quarts

4 pounds pig's feet, cut into 1-inch-thick disks

1 tablespoon vegetable oil

1 onion, quartered

8 scallions, roughly chopped

1 (3-inch) knob fresh ginger, peeled and sliced into ½-inch disks

Place the pig's feet in a large stock pot, cover with cold water, and bring to a simmer over high heat. Cook, skimming any gray foam or scum that accumulates on the surface, for 15 minutes.

Drain the pig's feet and, using a toothbrush or chopstick under cold running water, scrub and pick out any gray residue buried in the nooks and crannies of the pig's feet. Clean the stock pot, return the pig's feet to it, and cover generously with cold water. Bring to a simmer over high heat.

While the water comes to a simmer, heat the oil in a large cast-iron skillet over medium-high heat until nearly smoking. Add the onion and cook, flipping, until charred, 1 to 3 minutes per side. Transfer to the stock pot, add the scallions and ginger and bring to an active boil (210 to 212°F). Reduce the heat, cover partially, and maintain a gentle but rolling boil until the broth is rich and opaque, about 12 hours, adding more water if necessary to keep the pig's feet submerged in liquid. Strain the broth and rapidly chill in an ice bath or use immediately; discard the solids.

GAS GRILL–SMOKED RIBS

While the North(East) Carolina–Style Pulled Pork (page 317) is the product of true-blue-smoke barbecue, we aren't all lucky enough to have the time, space, or inclination to own a smoker. Enter the propane grill: Hank Hill (*King of the Hill*, 1997 to 2010) may have extolled the many virtues of "God's Gas," but even he would have to admit that it's no good for ribs . . . or is it? While it may apply heat more directly, gas grills are probably most similar to the home oven, especially when set up for indirect heat. So, when producing a steady ambient temperature of 225°F, it creates the ideal environment for tough cuts (like ribs) to become meltingly tender with time and patience. The only thing missing, then, is smoke, the essential factor from which barbecue derives its flavor, appearance, and texture. By placing a foil packet of wood chips directly on the burners, we create a relatively steady source of smoke with no extra effort. Then, flanking the ribs with a big ol' pan of water right over the heat source, we can create a higher-humidity cooking environment to help the meat retain moisture. What results are butter-tender ribs with a real smoke ring, real smoke bark, and real smoke flavor—all from the thing your dad usually uses to overcook burgers. Purists may balk and it may not live up to the genuine article, but as a means to an end, smoking on the grill is an effective way to try your hand at some real life, real-world barbecue experience, often with results as delicious as they are resuméable.

How I've Screwed This Up

Much like bread, your first rack of ribs (especially if smoking on a gas grill) probably aren't going to go to as planned. My Achilles heel is the same as most: temperature control. An unattended grill allowed to climb to 350°F for 10 minutes, while it may seem harmless, could very well sign your ribs' death warrant by prematurely contracting muscle fibers and forcing out moisture. It sure did for mine, and on more than one occasion.

Troubleshooting

MY RIBS ARE TOUGH.

If they're tough/crumbly, likely overcooked—if they're just straight-up tough, they're likely undercooked. Barbecue is much more about temperature than time, requiring that collagen and connective tissue are heated gently to a certain point for maximum juice-retention and tenderness-having.

MY RIBS ARE DRY.

Your temperature may have spiked during cooking, they may be overcooked, or the water pan might not have provided enough moisture to the cooking environment. Keep an eye on that temp and make sure your water pan stays more than one-quarter full!

MY RIBS WON'T COME UP TO TEMP.

I once had a rack take 11 hours to finally breach the sacred 190°F threshold, making them into a midnight snack instead of the main course. Particularly frustrating is the stall, a moment around 160°F where your ribs suddenly decide to defy Newtonian physics and stop getting any hotter. To speed things up, you can employ the "Texas Crutch": if you're 90 minutes from serving time and a frighteningly long way away from done, wrap the ribs tightly in foil along with a splash of apple juice or beer.

MY RIBS ARE TENDER BUT THEY WON'T COME APART/ ARE DIFFICULT TO SLICE.

Did you remove the membrane?

WHOOPS!

Yep, that's it!

MAKES 2 RACKS OF RIBS

2 racks baby back ribs

1 cup Dry Rub (recipe follows)

2 pounds hickory wood chips (or wood chips of choice)

2 cups Barbecue Sauce (recipe follows)

To remove the membrane from the ribs, using a small, sharp knife, pull away a corner of the membrane so that it can be gripped. Using a paper towel to hold it firmly, pull the membrane slowly and steadily off the bottom of each rack of ribs and discard.

Rub the ribs all over with the rub, transfer to a large rimmed baking sheet, and refrigerate, uncovered, overnight—if an overnight chill isn't possible, allow the rub to rest on the ribs for at least 2 hours at room temperature before smoking.

To make the wood chip packet, place a handful of wood chips on one side of a 18-inch length of aluminum foil. Fold the foil over, crimp shut, and cut 6 vents in the top of the packet. Repeat to make two more packets and set aside.

Remove the grill grates on one side of a gas grill. Place one of the wood chip packets directly on the heat plates over the gas burners, then replace the grill grates. Fill a large aluminum foil pan with 32 ounces water, place on the grates directly over the wood chip packet. Turn on the grill burners directly underneath the packet to high heat, close the lid, and wait for the chips to begin smoking, 3 to 5 minutes. Lower the heat to medium and adjust as necessary to maintain a light, wispy "blue" smoke, rather than a thick white or gray smoke. Maintain a temperature of 225°F in the grill.

    (**NOTE:** *Try to maintain an ambient temperature using a probe thermometer—don't trust the grill's built-in temperature gauge.*)

Place the ribs on the "off" side of the grill, away from the direct heat. Smoke, adjusting the heat as necessary every 15 to 20 minutes to maintain temperature, until the ribs are tender but not falling off the bone and register 190 to 200°F at their thickest point, 3 to 5 hours. Refill the water pan as necessary so that steam is produced continually.

After the first hour, when the wood chip packet stops producing smoke, shake and rotate it to more evenly burn the wood chips. If the wood chips are burnt up, replace the packet with one of the remaining wood chip packets.

Note: *The "stall" occurs between 150 to 170°F—if you need to speed up your ribs' cooking, wrap them tightly in aluminum foil with a splash of beer or apple juice during the last 90 minutes of cooking.*

DRY RUB

Makes about 1½ cups

½ cup sweet paprika

1 tablespoon smoked paprika

½ cup packed dark brown sugar

2 tablespoons chili powder

1 tablespoon ground ginger

1 tablespoon garlic powder

1 tablespoon onion powder

1 teaspoon dried sage

1 teaspoon dried oregano

1 teaspoon dry mustard powder or finely ground mustard seeds

1 teaspoon cayenne pepper

1 tablespoon freshly ground black pepper

1 tablespoon kosher salt

Combine the sweet and smoked paprika, sugar, chili powder, ginger, garlic, sage, oregano, mustard powder, cayenne pepper, black pepper, and salt in a medium bowl and whisk until homogenous. Store in an airtight container for up to 1 month.

BARBECUE SAUCE

Makes about 3 cups

14 ounces (by weight) ketchup

¼ cup Worcestershire sauce

2 tablespoons yellow mustard

2 teaspoons hot sauce (such as Louisiana Crystal, Texas Pete, Tabasco)

2 garlic cloves, grated

¼ small onion, grated

½ cup packed dark brown sugar

Pinch of Dry Rub (at left)

In a medium saucepan, combine the ketchup, Worcestershire, mustard, hot sauce, garlic, onion, sugar, and rub with ½ cup water and bring to a bare simmer over medium-low heat. Reduce heat to low and cook, stirring frequently, until the flavors are melded, 15 to 20 minutes. Add more water if the sauce becomes too thick, and if too thin, cook down to a thicker consistency. Allow to cool and refrigerate until ready to use, up to 2 weeks.

SAUSAGE AND BÉCHAMEL LASAGNA

The very moment I realized this book lacked a lasagna, I sat down and wrote one. In fact, I'm literally writing this as we're doing the photography in the other room. It's kind of trippy to be talking to you about it.

Lasagna is pretty well-worn territory, so while there's nothing groundbreaking happening here, there is a potentially new concept for many lasagna eaters: the replacement of ricotta with béchamel. Store-bought ricotta, often baking up grainy and crumbly, is usually added to lasagna in order to make it worse. Béchamel, instead of making a smeary mess, augments the stretchy mozzarella with a rich, nutmeg-laced creaminess. Having less bulk than ricotta, béchamel creates the opportunity for more layers of pasta (which is the only reason anyone makes lasagna nowadays anyway), so stack it as high as your lasagna pan will allow!

How I've Screwed This Up

Apart from using ricotta, my biggest lasagna misfire was made for a date nearly a decade ago. I had some beautiful leftover meatballs, and while meatball-lasagna is indeed possible, it's not recommended to leave your meatballs whole when assembling. The results, as it turns out, can only be described as a "lumpy lasagna," which hurts your chances for a second date.

Troubleshooting

MY LASAGNA IS DRY.

More cheese, more sauce, more béchamel!

MY LASAGNA IS UNDERCOOKED.

All that time spent in the oven should be more than enough to cook fresh pasta, but should you find yourself with chewy noodles, the issue may be in the dough's gluten development. Dough that's been overworked or laminated one too many times can remain chewy no matter how long you try to convince it to become al dente.

MY LASAGNA IS WET.

Apart from being far too hot for the human mouth, one of the many reasons lasagna must rest before being served is its redistribution of various liquids. If you find a little liquid in your lasagna, you could drain it off, but likely letting things relax for a bit will remedy the problem. Too much moisture might have come from the mozzarella—make sure you use low-moisture in this recipe.

MY CAT WON'T EAT THIS LASAGNA.

This is not a pet-safe food and under no circumstances should you feed it to your cat!

I WAS TRYING TO DO A GARFIELD BIT.

Oh. My bad. Um, something about Mondays!

SERVES 6 TO 8

2 recipes Fresh Pasta Dough (page 116)

All-purpose flour, for dusting

1 tablespoon light olive oil

1 pound Italian sausage, casings removed

1 recipe Simple Tomato Sauce (page 281)

1 pound low-moisture whole-milk mozzarella, shredded

4 cups Béchamel (recipe follows), cooled

4 ounces Parmesan cheese, freshly grated

¼ cup chopped fresh basil, for garnish

Preheat the oven to 375°F.

Roll out the pasta to ⅛-inch thick and trim into 4-by-12-inch rectangles. Dust with flour and keep covered until ready to use.

In a large sauté pan, heat the oil over medium-high heat until shimmering. Add the sausage and cook, breaking up the meat, until no longer pink, 2 to 3 minutes. Add the sauce, bring to a simmer and reduce the heat to medium low. Maintain a bare simmer and cook, stirring occasionally, until slightly reduced and thickened, about 20 minutes.

ASSEMBLE THE LASAGNA: Spread a small amount of the sauce in the bottom of a 9-by-13-inch casserole dish. Cover with two rectangles of pasta, overlapping minimally. Cover the pasta evenly with about one-fourth each of the remaining sauce, mozzarella, béchamel, and Parmesan. Cover with another layer of pasta and repeat the layering twice more. Cover with a final layer of pasta, spread the remaining sauce on top (for color), drizzle with the rest of the béchamel and top with the remaining cheese. Cover with foil and bake, rotating once halfway through, 30 to 45 minutes, until the lasagna is bubbling and the cheese is melted.

Uncover the lasagna and continue to bake, 15 to 20 minutes, until the top is lightly browned. Allow the lasagna to rest for 30 minutes before slicing and serving, garnished with the basil.

BÉCHAMEL

Makes about 4 cups

8 tablespoons (1 stick) unsalted butter

½ cup all-purpose flour

4½ cups whole milk

¾ teaspoon kosher salt

½ teaspoon freshly ground white pepper

¼ teaspoon freshly grated nutmeg

In a large saucepan, cook the butter over medium heat, swirling occasionally, until the foaming subsides, 1 to 3 minutes. Add the flour, cooking and whisking until a smooth, light blonde paste forms, 2 to 3 minutes. Slowly stream in the milk while whisking constantly and vigorously, initially one large splash at a time, until a smooth paste forms after each addition. Once all the milk has been added, continue whisking until the mixture is completely incorporated and smooth. Cook over medium-low heat, maintaining a bare simmer and whisking occasionally, until the béchamel is thick and glossy, 3 to 5 minutes.

Stir the salt, white pepper, and nutmeg into the béchamel. Use immediately or transfer to a bowl, cover with plastic wrap directly on its surface and refrigerate until ready to use, up to 3 days.

TAMALES

Tamales, on the surface, sound like a low-lift proposition: mix masa with hot water and lard, spread it out on some corn husks, throw some meat and/or cheese in there, fold it up, tie it tight, and steam it for an hour or two. Especially for the uninitiated, however, this prospect quickly (slowly?) turns into a day-long endeavor. Folding tamales might become second nature after five attempts or fifty, but you can rest assured that at first, it will be a fumbly and messy operation. This is the key to tamale success, however: an operation. An assembly line of masa, fillings, corn husks, and corn husk ties piled at the ready and in excess. A day, free of other responsibilities or energy-consuming activities, stretching out before you like an empty highway. A willing partner; willing, that is, to remain hungry for hours while waiting for the fruits of their labor to become edible. These are rewards worth pursuing, because once your supplies (and strength) have been exhausted, you will be left with enough tamales to feed either a small house party or yourself indefinitely. Being little more than an emulsion of fat, cornmeal, and water, they freeze excellently, even after having already been steamed, so save those leftovers. They are a delightfully toothsome, simple, and tasty foundation upon which you can pile any number of flavor-appropriate fillings. Not unlike quesadillas, they are receptive to nearly whatever combination of meat, cheeses, or vegetables you want to pile inside. So if you find yourself, as I so often do, with a fridge full of leftovers bordering on insolvency, a block of lard melting between your fingers in one hand, and the other hard at work grinding cornmeal, do yourself a favor and put your strange habit to good use with these tamales.

How I've Screwed This Up

Tamales are pretty forgiving (and correctable), and as such, I've never ended up with an entire batch in the bin. I have, of course, positively mangled my fair share of corn husks in the pursuit of said batch. Don't worry if your first couple (or dozen) don't turn out correctly—your masa can always be scraped off, corn husks are cheap, and time stretches out infinitely in all directions.

Troubleshooting

MY TAMALES ARE DRY.

Well, what's the opposite of dry? Do you think you should add some of that?

DON'T BE A DICK.

Sorry—it's just like . . . sorry no you're right, I'm being patronizing aren't I? It's a valid question and I'm here to answer them. Go ahead.

MY TAMALES ARE WET AND RUNNY.

. . . are you fucking with me?

YES. HOW DOES IT FEEL?

Nice one. So, yeah, add some cornmeal. The masa mixture should be pasty, like frosting.

MY TAMALES ARE MUSHY.

It might seem counterintuitive, but mushy tamales are actually indicative of undercooking. 1½ to 2 hours might seem like a long time to steam anything, but tamales take a particularly long time to achieve their optimal texture. It is, frankly, hard to over-steam them, so don't be afraid to let them spend a little more time in the sauna!

MY TAMALES ARE TOUGH.

This can also be an indicator of underhydrated masa—your tamale mixture should be smooth, not at all difficult to spread into an even layer on your corn husks.

MAKES 40 TO 50 TAMALES

40 to 50 corn husks, plus 5 more for insulation and 5 to 10 more torn into strips for tying

20 ounces masa harina

24 to 26 ounces hot water or low-sodium chicken broth, plus more as needed

14 ounces lard

2 teaspoons baking powder

2 teaspoons kosher salt

Stewed Pork Filling (recipe follows) or Green Chile Chicken Filling (recipe follows)

Crema (or sour cream), for serving (optional)

Salsa Roja (recipe follows; optional)

Chopped cilantro, for serving (optional)

Bring a large pot of water to a simmer, then remove from the heat. Add the corn husks and allow them to soak until pliable, 2 to 3 hours. Make sure to weigh the husks down if they are floating. Drain and set aside.

In a large bowl, stir together the masa and hot water, making sure to add only enough water to form a crumbly dough. Let sit for 15 minutes.

In a stand mixer fitted with the paddle attachment, mix the lard on medium speed until fluffy and completely smooth, 2 to 3 minutes. Add the baking powder and salt, then mix until well incorporated.

Slowly add portions of the masa mixture to the lard mixture and mix at medium-low speed, scraping down the bowl between additions and adding more hot water as necessary, until a soft dough forms.

Spread an even layer of the dough on one soaked corn husk. Add a heaping spoonful of your desired filling to the center, leaving a 1-inch border on all sides. Roll the corn husk lengthwise then fold up the excess husk over itself. Using strips of corn husk, secure the tamal with a tie around the middle. Repeat with the remaining corn husks, dough, and filling.

Prepare a large pot with a removable steamer basket with about 1 inch of water. Place a small metal bowl in the center of the steamer basket, then place the tamales in the basket with the exposed filling facing upward. Use the metal bowl and the sides of the pot to prop the tamales up.

Cover the tamales with the 5 remaining corn husks and a damp clean dish towel. Then cover the pot with the lid and steam the tamales until the filling easily releases from the corn husks, 1½ to 2 hours.

Let the tamales cool for 20 to 30 minutes before serving, if desired, with crema, Salsa Roja, and cilantro.

STEWED PORK FILLING

Makes 4 cups

3 pounds boneless pork shoulder, trimmed and cut into 2-inch pieces

Kosher salt

2 chicken bouillon cubes, crushed

1 tablespoon Mexican oregano

1 bay leaf

1 white onion, quartered, plus an extra ½

9 garlic cloves

5 to 6 guajillo chiles, stemmed and seeded

3 to 4 ancho chiles, stemmed and seeded

3 to 4 pasilla chiles, stemmed and seeded

Neutral oil (such as canola, vegetable, or grapeseed), as needed

Preheat the oven to 275°F.

Sprinkle the pork with 1 tablespoon salt then transfer to a high-sided skillet or Dutch oven. Add the bouillon cubes, oregano, bay leaf, quartered onion, and 6 of the garlic cloves. Add enough water to come up about halfway on the pork. Bring the mixture to a simmer on the stovetop.

Transfer the pot to the oven and cook, uncovered, until the pork is completely tender, 2½ to 3 hours.

Meanwhile, combine the guajillo, ancho, and pasilla chiles in a high-sided skillet and toast over medium-high heat, stirring occasionally, until fragrant and just beginning to darken, 3 to 4 minutes. Add the remaining ½ white onion and 3 garlic cloves. Add enough water to cover the chiles and bring the mixture to a simmer. Remove from the heat, cover, and allow to steep for 30 minutes.

Using a slotted spoon, transfer the chiles, onion, and garlic to a high-powered blender. Add about 1 cup of the steeping liquid and blend until smooth and homogenous.

Once the pork is tender and cool enough to handle, shred by hand, removing and discarding any unrendered fat from the meat. Set aside.

Heat 1 tablespoon of oil in a large high-sided skillet over medium heat. Add the chile mixture and bring to a simmer. Add the pork and cook, stirring occasionally, until combined and heated through, 3 to 4 minutes. Set aside until ready to fill tamales.

GREEN CHILE CHICKEN FILLING

Makes 4 cups

2 pounds boneless, skinless chicken breasts

6 to 8 tomatillos, husked and halved

1 poblano pepper, stemmed

1 jalapeño, stemmed

1 serrano chile, stemmed

½ white onion, quartered

2 garlic cloves, roughly chopped

10 to 12 cilantro stems (leaves included)

Kosher salt

Preheat the broiler. Bring a large pot of water to a boil.

Slice each chicken breast in half horizontally (parallel to the cutting board), stopping just before cutting through to the other side.

Add the chicken to the boiling water, remove from the heat, and cover. Allow to sit until the internal temperature of the chicken reaches 155°F, 15 to 20 minutes. (It will continue cooking in the tamales.)

Remove the chicken from the water and shred using two forks. Set aside until ready to use.

On a rimmed baking sheet, combine the tomatillos, poblano, jalapeño, and serrano. Broil until charred, 10 to 12 minutes. Tent with aluminum foil for 5 minutes, then carefully peel off the charred skin from all the vegetables and remove the seeds from the poblano, jalapeño, and serrano.

Transfer the broiled vegetables to a food processor; add the onion, garlic, and cilantro. Blend until homogeneous. If the mixture is too thick, add 2 tablespoons of water at a time until thin enough to puree.

Transfer the sauce to a large bowl and season with salt, then add the chicken and toss until combined. Set aside until ready to use.

SALSA ROJA

Makes 2 cups

4 Roma tomatoes, quartered

1 jalapeño, stemmed

½ white onion, quartered

2 garlic cloves

Juice of 1 lime

7 to 8 cilantro stems (leaves included)

Kosher salt

Preheat the broiler.

Combine the tomatoes and jalapeño on a rimmed baking sheet. Broil until charred, 10 to 12 minutes.

Remove the baking sheet from the oven and loosely tent with aluminum foil to allow the vegetables to steam for 10 minutes. Transfer to a high-powered blender; add the onion, garlic, lime juice, and cilantro. Blend until homogenous but still chunky.

Season the sauce with salt and set aside until ready to use.

CHAPTER 9

BEEF

Beef is, perhaps, both the best and worst that something can possibly be. On the one hand, it can be hypnotically delicious, eliciting rolled eyes and moans not normally acceptable in polite company. It has an incredible variety of textures, flavors, fat content, and form factors, allowing for a phantasmagoria of possibility in the kitchen. It is densely nutritious, so much so that simply boiling its bones in water will yield a (delicious) golden liquid with enough protein to act as a meal replacement. On the other hand, it can be devilishly unhealthy, laden with fat, and raise our blood pressure while slowly gathering as stalactites in our lower intestines. The factory farming of beef is often attributed to the changing of the very temperature of our earth, a wildly expensive and resource-devouring ecological disaster. Perhaps most uncomfortable of all is the yawning chasm between consumers and the animals that provide our food, mountains of Styrofoam and shrink-wrapped body parts breeding cognitive dissonance and moral duality. It is a thing of diametric opposites, orgasmic peaks and woeful valleys, unsympathetic antiheroes dueling on a cliff's edge overlooking the ever-darkening void at the heart of man. Now, who wants some steak?

WHAT IS BEEF? I'm gonna stop questioning your process here, I feel like we grew closer after the pasta chapter. Beef is the meat that comes from cows. Beef tastes good. Beef is expensive. Beef is great on the grill. Beef is bad for the environment. Beef is good for your soul. Beef is bad for your heart.

YOU'RE MAKING ME FEEL PRETTY BAD ABOUT EATING BEEF. CAN YOU WALK SOME OF THIS STUFF BACK? Oh, absolutely, I mean how do you think I sleep at night? I think the move here is trying to eat high-quality beef as often as possible. It costs more, so naturally, you'll eat it less often, which is good for you. The cow who provided said beef will have lived a happier, healthier life. Plus, it'll taste better—in the food industry, that's what we call a "tri-ply win." Not really.

DOES HIGH-QUALITY BEEF REALLY TASTE ANY DIFFERENT? You bet your pants it does. You'll find this messaging throughout the book; not pants-betting, but that factory-farmed animals live hellish lives. Their movement is restricted, they're pumped full of antibiotics, they're missing patches of hair or feathers, they're fed the absolute minimum standard substance to qualify as "feed," they're in a constant state of distress. Not only can this present a moral issue for most people, it's going to be disastrous for how the animal ends up tasting. Cows raised in open pastures with plenty of high-quality food, sunshine, and love are just going to end up tasting better. It's why steaks at the nice steakhouse cost $60, why In-N-Out tastes so damn good, and why your foodie friends won't shut the fuck up about grass-fed vs. grain-fed vs. grain-finished.

SHOULD I GRIND MY OWN BEEF? If you've got the time and inclination, there are very few scenarios in which home-ground beef isn't a massive upgrade. You can control the fat content, flavor, and texture, and so long as the beef is handled and ground properly, it's significantly safer to eat than the stuff that's preground at the store. As with butter pastry, the colder everything is, the better: stow all the grinder parts in the freezer for at least an hour, likewise with the beef for fifteen to twenty minutes before doing the deed.

APPARENTLY I'M SUPPOSED TO COOK MY STEAK TO A CERTAIN TEMPERATURE, CAN'T I JUST BOIL IT FOR AN HOUR LIKE OTHER FOODS? It's important to cook beef to a specific degree of doneness, literally, so that a desired outcome can be achieved. Some cuts, like brisket, need to be gently convinced to reach an internal temperature of 195°F over the better part of a day, while some steaks need to be brought to 120°F as quickly and violently as humanly possible so as to preserve their moisture and texture. The recipes in this chapter endeavor to run the gamut of beef preparation, from the slowest and lowest to fastest and hottest, but your preferences are also going to weigh into the balancing act of bringing your meat to thermal completion.

PEOPLE WHO EAT THEIR STEAK OVERCOOKED ARE BAD PEOPLE, RIGHT? Just relax a little, okay? The most common thread I've found among the 145°F+ crowd is a general lack of exposure to meat worth serving at its optimal temperatures. It's *your* responsibility as a self-proclaimed "foodie" (that's what your Tinder profile says after all) to source, prepare, and serve meat at a classically correct doneness to feed their curiosity. It's then your responsibility not to be a dick about it if they don't like it.

SELECT, CHOICE, PRIME—WHAT IS THIS, ALGEBRA CLASS? But my dear boy, understanding the USDA Beef Grading System is a (*snaps fingers*) snap! Those three grades, in ascending order, rate the marbling of a particular cut—Select has the least intramuscular fat, while Prime has the most. Beef's price rises commensurately with its marbling, but if you've got the scratch, it's worth it. More intramuscular fat means more moisture, flavor, and better texture in your end product.

DRY-AGED? SOUNDS LIKE MY MOTHER-IN-LAW! Ha. Dry aging is the process of quite literally aging the beef in a temperature and humidity-controlled environment. The longer the beef hangs out, the more excess moisture evaporates, and the more the beef's own enzymes begin to break it down, tenderizing it and deepening its flavor. The longer a steak is dry-aged, the funkier its flavor becomes, ranging from slightly nutty to downright cheesy.

SLIGHTLY NUTTY TO DOWNRIGHT CHEESY? SOUNDS LIKE MY FATHER-IN-LAW! Haaaa.

DEMI-GLACE

At first glance, this recipe seems like a lot of effort for what, some brown goo? Oh, it may indeed just be brown goo, but it is so much more. Here's what you're essentially doing: *gently* simmering the ever loving shit out of bones and aromatics; never exceeding a boil; accomplishing a robbery threefold: of collagen from the connective tissue, of minerals and proteins from the bones, and of flavor from everything. Then, once the spent solids have been strained and responsibly composted, the resultant meat liquid is aggressively boiled down to a mere fraction of its former self. Thirty-six-ish hours and pounds of produce later, you'll be lucky if you end up with two cups of this stuff, and when I say lucky, I very much mean it. Honest to god homemade demi-glace is, speaking realistically, worth its weight in neodymium—which at the time of this writing, is going for $177/kg—that is to say, I would willingly pay $5 for every ounce of precious, precious demi-glace. Why? Because it's amazing. Any sauce, soup, or stew with even a remotely beefy vibe will be elevated, nay, made transcendent by this devastatingly flavorful compound. Pour it into ice cube trays, freeze, and lay in wait until fond needs deglazing or sauces need *oomph*.

How I've Screwed This Up

When you're just starting out in New York City, you're often living paycheck-to-paycheck (or not even), so as a wannabe gourmand, you find yourself cutting corners. Demi glace is the literal extraction and concentration of the compounds in the bones yer boilin', so if you're using garbage bones, you're going to end up with garbage soup. Long story short, don't buy discount bones, there's never any reason for you to buy discount bones.

Troubleshooting

MY BROTH SMELLS FUNNY.
Bone broth can indeed smell funny, as some funky minerals and proteins can be extracted from the bones, but it should never smell foul. Especially if you're both using quality bones and roasting them, the typical bone funk should be mitigated, so if it don't smell right, toss it.

MY BROTH DIDN'T GELATINIZE IN THE FRIDGE.
It's possible that, if you kept the bones at a rolling boil, you murked your gelatin content—or more likely, you didn't reduce the demi enough. It should be near-syrupy, a spatula leaving a clean trail on the bottom of the pot.

MY BROTH IS FLAVORLESS.
After such a long simmer, even without salt, your broth shouldn't be flavorless—make sure you're not using too much water, the ingredients shouldn't be crowded in the pot but not few and far between either.

MAKES 8 PUCKS OF DEMI-GLACE OR ABOUT 2 CUPS

1 gallon Bone Broth (recipe follows)

1 cup dry red wine

3 tablespoons tomato paste

In a wide stock pot, combine the bone broth, wine, and tomato paste. Bring to a simmer over high heat, then reduce the heat to medium low and cook until thick enough to coat the back of a spoon and reduced to about 2 cups, 1½ to 2 hours. Transfer to a heatproof bowl and let cool to room temperature.

Divide the demi-glace into 8 freezer-friendly portions in a muffin tin. Refrigerate until solidified, 1 to 2 hours, then wrap each portion in plastic wrap and aluminum foil, or vacuum seal. Freeze for up to 6 months.

BONE BROTH

Makes 1 gallon

5 pounds beef bones, meat attached

Neutral oil (such as canola, vegetable, or grapeseed), as needed

1 large yellow onion

4 carrots

1 celery stalk

1 leek

1 bunch parsley

½ head garlic

2 tablespoons whole black peppercorns

2 bay leaves

2 tablespoons apple cider vinegar

Preheat the oven to 400°F.

Scoop out as much of the marrow from the bones as possible and reserve for another use. (Marrow usually gives the broth a metallic taste when left in.)

Arrange the bones across wire racks set inside rimmed baking sheets. Coat the bones with neutral oil, then roast 40 minutes to 1 hour, until the bones are deeply browned.

MEANWHILE, PREP THE VEGGIES: Quarter the onion, peel the carrots and cut each in half crosswise, and cut the celery in half crosswise. Lastly, thoroughly wash and trim the leek so it fits in a large but narrow pot.

In the pot, combine all the prepared vegetables, bones, parsley, garlic, peppercorns, and bay leaves. Fill with enough water to cover the ingredients, then add the vinegar. Bring the stock to a bare simmer. In the first hour of cooking, skim off any scum that floats to the surface. Stir and keep at a bare simmer (see Kitchen Glossary, page 23) for 24 to 48 hours.

Skim off all the fat that has formed on the surface. Strain the broth through a sieve lined with a cheesecloth or coffee filter; discard the solids. Refrigerate in airtight containers for up to 1 week or freeze for up to 1 year.

MEATLOAF

Meatloaf is about as unappealingly-but-accurately-named an absolutely irresistible food as ever there was. The recipe contained herein is a decidedly American version, bringing to mind visions of canned peas and nuclear-powered automobiles. Unlike most meatloaves (that's a fun word to get to type), it's roasted "naked"—not nestled in a loaf pan, but formed and unmolded into a free-standing beefcastle. This prevents it from swimming in a pool of its own fat, which would otherwise result in a moist but greasy loaf. There's still plenty of fat (and by extension, flavor) in this iteration of the mid-century modern classic, along with a cadre of flavor-boosting sidekicks: the classic "meatloaf mix" of veal, pork, and beef swaps veal for lamb, bringing some grassy funk to the band. Gelatin-laden beef stock (or demi-glace) retains moisture and provides body, while fish sauce and porcini mushrooms amplify the savory flavor. Then the Worcestershire sauce comes chugging onto the scene, billowing smoke from its solid-state tobacco-leather 16-liter Spitfire engine, and before you can say Norman Rockwell, your hair pops into a coiffe and the neck of your sweater forms a V. Pass the peas, won't you, mumsy? Geoffrey, see to it that your father's gin isn't without a splash of tonic, and don't forget to smoke your cigarettes before bedtime, doctor's orders.

How I've Screwed This Up

I've skimped on the bread, eggs, and vegetables— you often hear that you shouldn't add these to meat (burgers in particular), as they will result in a "meatloaf-like texture." Then you suddenly remember that that's exactly what you're making. Meatloaf. Load it up with shit, it's going to taste great.

Troubleshooting

MY MEATLOAF IS FALLING APART.

This meatloaf isn't as tightly packed as its traditional loaf pan counterpart, so it can tend to be on the delicate side. You can create a sturdier meatloaf by adding more binders like eggs and bread crumbs, as well as kneading the beef a bit more.

YOU EXPECT ME TO GRIND MY OWN MEAT FOR MEATLOAF?

Okay, sure, that's a little overboard—you can always substitute the same amounts by weight with store-ground equivalents! Really, you could use any combination of ground meat your heart desires, so long as it adds up to 32 ounces—just bear in mind that leaner meats like chicken or turkey could result in a drier loaf.

MY MEATLOAF IS DRY.

We use homemade stock (or store-bought combined with gelatin) for a reason: It helps the meatloaf retain moisture. I know this might seem like a fussy step, but even if you overcook your meatloaf, gelatin can help safeguard from loaf dryness.

MY MEATLOAF IS MOIST AND IT'S NOT FALLING APART, BUT IT'S ALL MEAT FOR CRYING OUT LOUD.

Hey, two out of three ain't bad.

I WOULD DO ANYTHING FOR LOVE.

You took the words right out of my mouth.

SERVES 6 TO 8

Meatloaf

Nonstick cooking spray

½ cup beef or chicken stock, preferably homemade (see page 268)

1 (1¼-ounce) packet unflavored gelatin

12 ounces beef chuck roast, cut into 1- to 2-inch cubes

12 ounces boneless pork butt, cut into 1- to 2-inch cubes

8 ounces boneless leg of lamb, cut into 1- to 2-inch cubes

1 tablespoon vegetable oil

½ onion, diced

1 large carrot, grated on the large holes of a box grater

1 stalk celery, grated on the large holes of a box grater

2 garlic cloves, minced

3 slices stale white bread

¼ cup dried porcini mushrooms

½ cup buttermilk

¼ cup tomato paste

¼ cup chopped fresh parsley leaves

⅛ cup chopped fresh basil leaves

1 tablespoon soy sauce

1 teaspoon fish sauce

1 teaspoon Worcestershire sauce

2 large eggs, beaten

Kosher salt and freshly ground black pepper

Glaze

½ cup ketchup

⅓ cup packed light brown sugar

1 tablespoon tomato paste

1 tablespoon apple cider vinegar

1 tablespoon honey

1 teaspoon Worcestershire sauce

½ teaspoon freshly ground black pepper

MAKE THE MEATLOAF: Line a small rimmed baking sheet with aluminum foil and spray with an even layer of nonstick spray. Spray a 9-inch loaf pan or two 4½-inch mini loaf pans with a light coating of nonstick spray.

Preheat the oven to 325°F for a full-size meatloaf or 350°F convection for mini meatloaves.

Pour the stock into a small bowl and sprinkle the gelatin over the entire surface. Let sit until the gelatin is fully hydrated, about 6 minutes.

Place the beef, pork, and lamb on a rimmed baking sheet and freeze for 20 to 30 minutes.

Meanwhile, heat the oil in a large skillet over medium-high heat. Lower the heat to medium-low and add the onion. Cook, stirring periodically, until lightly caramelized, 7 to 10 minutes. If the onion sticks to the bottom of the skillet, add ¼ cup water and cook until all of the water is evaporated. Add the carrot, celery, and stock mixture and cook until the vegetables are tender, 3 to 4 minutes. Add the garlic and cook, stirring, for 30 seconds. Transfer the vegetables to a metal bowl or rimmed baking sheet and allow to cool for 15 minutes.

Meanwhile, using a meat grinder attachment or machine with the medium-size grate setting/plate, grind the chilled meats. Set aside until ready to use.

In a food processor, combine the bread and dried mushrooms. Process until a sandlike consistency forms. Weigh out 4 ounces of the breadcrumb mixture (reserve the rest for another use) into a large bowl and combine with the buttermilk. Add the ground meat, cooled vegetables, tomato paste, parsley, basil, soy sauce, fish sauce, Worcestershire sauce, eggs, 1 teaspoon salt, and 1 teaspoon black pepper. Gently fold together with your hands, trying to avoid squeezing the meat as much as possible, until homogenous. Press into the prepared loaf pan(s) then invert onto the foil-lined baking sheet.

Bake the meatloaf for 15 minutes.

MEANWHILE, MAKE THE GLAZE: In a small bowl, whisk together the ketchup, sugar, tomato paste, vinegar, honey, Worcestershire sauce, and pepper in a small bowl.

Brush the meatloaf with half of the glaze, bake another 15 minutes, then brush with the remaining glaze and bake until the internal temperature reaches 155°F, 20 to 25 minutes for the full-size meatloaf or 10 to 15 minutes for the mini loaves.

Turn the oven to broil and cook for a final 2 minutes. Remove from the oven and allow to cool on a wire rack for 10 minutes before slicing and serving.

OXTAIL BIRRIA TACOS

Birria tacos, like many Instagram foods-of-the-moment, aren't just delicious: they're rich with history. In the fifteenth century, Conquistadors invaded Mexico and caused an overpopulation of goats. These were called *birria* by the Spanish, a derogatory term meaning "worthless." As so often happens, however, need breeds ingenuity: the local spices were put to good use with long, slow cooking methods, making the goat tender and appetizing. Birria became a symbol of Mexican pride, every region and municipality sporting its own unique version, eventually culminating in the beef, cheese, and consommé social media darling you see today. I realize I've made up a few stories to mess with you up to this point, so you might be wondering if any of that is even true. But you can look it up on Wikipedia—I mean how do you think I wrote it?

We utilize a braising method championed by *America's Test Kitchen* in their beef burgundy recipe, one that cleverly uses oven heat to brown the beef, doing away with the need for the fire-alarm-triggering process of searing. Oxtails are (sometimes) inexpensive, provide excellent meat for shredding, and have lots of flavor to be coaxed out of their collagen-laden bones. Boneless short ribs are more expensive, but provide more fatty, tender meat for stuffing between tortillas and dousing with consommé. Jesus Christ, I'm hungry.

How I've Screwed This Up

I fell victim to the old fallacy that homemade = better, always. In fact, homemade tortillas are pretty awful for modern birria—it's very difficult to nail the correct thickness and they're far more prone to tearing, especially once subjected to all the moisture in the process. Store-bought tortillas are the way to go here.

Troubleshooting

MY TORTILLAS KEEP TEARING.
Yeah, that'll happen—try not to oversaturate them with the braising liquid and fat when you dip them. You want to coat but not soak.

MY BIRRIA IS DRY.
Make sure you're looking for meat with good marbling, as even short ribs can dry out if they don't contain enough intramuscular fat. Make sure you're also not allowing one side of the beef to remain exposed in the oven for too long, flipping as soon as a nice brown crust has formed.

MY BIRRIA IS WET.
That's the idea, gooftball.

SERVES 4 TO 6

Chile Mixture

6 to 8 guajillo chiles, stemmed and seeded

3 to 4 chiles de árbol, stemmed and seeded

2 teaspoons cumin seeds

1 head garlic, cloves peeled

½ small onion

2 chipotles in adobo sauce (or to taste)

1 teaspoon dried Mexican oregano

¼ teaspoon ground cloves

Braised Meat

3½ pounds boneless beef chuck or beef cheek, trimmed and cut into 2-inch cubes

Kosher salt and freshly ground black pepper

1½ to 2 pounds oxtails, trimmed of excess fat

1 tablespoon vegetable oil

1 (14-ounce) can whole peeled tomatoes with their juices

1 yellow onion, quartered

5 bay leaves

3 fresh marjoram sprigs

1 stick canela (Mexican cinnamon)

1 tablespoon whole black peppercorns

To Serve

8 to 12 corn tortillas (store-bought)

16 ounces Oaxaca cheese, shredded

White onion, diced

Jalapeños, thinly sliced

Limes, quartered

Cilantro leaves (optional)

MAKE THE CHILE MIXTURE: Roughly rip the guajillos and chile de árbols into smaller pieces and add them to a medium saucepan along with the cumin seeds. Toast over medium-low heat, stirring occasionally, until fragrant but not smoking, about 5 minutes. Cover with about 2 cups water and bring to a simmer. Cover with a lid and remove from the heat. Allow to steep 10 to 20 minutes.

Transfer the chile mixture and the steeping liquid to a blender. Add the garlic, onion, chipotles, oregano, and cloves. Add enough water to cover and blend until completely smooth, 1 to 2 minutes. Set aside until ready to use.

Preheat the oven to 475°F.

PREPARE THE BRAISED MEAT: On a large rimmed baking sheet, sprinkle the beef cubes with 1 teaspoon salt and let sit at room temperature for 40 minutes. Lower the oven temperature to 350°F.

Meanwhile, toss the oxtails in a roasting pan with the oil. Roast for 15 to 20 minutes, until well browned. Pour the tomatoes, their juices, and the blended chile mixture over the top. Add enough water to come about halfway up the sides of the oxtails. Add the beef, onion, bay leaves, marjoram, cinnamon stick, and peppercorns.

Roast at 350°F for about 3 hours, until the beef and oxtails are tender enough to shred. Make sure to flip all of the pieces of meat halfway through the cook time and add more water if the liquid falls below the halfway mark on the meat.

Remove the beef and oxtails from the roasting pan. The meat will fall away from the oxtail bones; discard the bones. Shred all the meat with two forks on a large rimmed baking sheet. Strain the remaining braising liquid through a sieve into a large bowl, then add about 1 cup of it to the shredded meat. Cover both bowls with plastic wrap and refrigerate overnight.

Transfer the solidified fat from the surface of the braising liquid to a medium skillet. Heat until melted.

Reheat the braising liquid in a medium pot. Season with salt or ground pepper if necessary. This will be the consommé.

Heat another medium skillet over medium heat. Add the shredded meat and about ¾ cup of the braising liquid. Stir periodically until heated through, 3 to 4 minutes. Keep warm over low heat until ready to serve.

Heat a large cast-iron skillet. Add one of the tortillas and cook on each side until warm. Dip the tortilla in the liquefied fat then return to the cast-iron skillet. Top with some of the cheese and a generous portion of the meat. Fold the tortilla in half, enclosing the filling. Continue frying the taco for about 1 minute per side. Repeat with the remaining tortillas and filling.

Serve the birria tacos with the consommé in cups, with white onion, jalapeños, limes, and, if desired, cilantro.

STEP-BY-STEP IMAGES, PAGE 356-357

DAD'S POT ROAST

After my mom died, my dad still tried to make dinner for me whenever he could. He'd be the first to tell you that he'd rather do the dishes than the cooking, and while that sometimes showed in his food, he dedicated many Sundays to fine-tuning his pot roast. He'd try things like grilling the whole roast to give it a deep brown crust before braising. He'd find just the right moment to add the potatoes so that they'd be fully cooked with edges just starting to crisp. He'd use a paring knife to repeatedly impale the beef so he could slip slivers of garlic into it. Sometimes I wondered why this man, who was often reluctant to make a pot of spaghetti, would yield multiple hours of his day to nailing his roast. I never asked him, of course—communication was never one of the Rea Boys' strong suits, even before we were left alone, wounded and at odds—but he made sure I had a homemade meal a few times a week, and he wanted it to be the best he could make. I think that says more than enough.

How I've Screwed This Up

My dad might hold the title for most-screwed-up iteration when he experimented with (way too much) ground cloves in his recipe, but I certainly hold the title for most screw-ups. Being one of the first things I learned to cook, I made it any number of horrible ways before finally learning how to treat beef with respect, braising it slowly and lowly until tender and moist.

Troubleshooting

MY POT ROAST IS DRY.

As much protection against overcooking as a chuck roast offers, it's still very accomplishable, especially in a slow-cooker. Slow-cookers offer incredible utility, but even on their lowest setting, the so-often-utilized 8 hours of simmering will dry out any cut of meat you throw in there. Instead of braising while you're at work all day so that dinner is ready when you come home, braise it the night before: stews like this only get better after a night in the fridge and a gentle reheating on the stovetop.

MY POT ROAST IS PINK.

That's normal and desirable! If medium-rare meat freaks you out and the hours of cooking time gives you peace, the pinkish hue the beef may retain might alarm you—but it might just be the perfect way to warm you up to the idea of medium-rare.

WHY CAN'T I JUST THROW ALL THE VEGETABLES IN AT ONCE, OR JUST SERVE WITH THE BRAISING VEGETABLES?

You certainly can, but cooking the vegetables separately ensures their best flavor and texture. Braising vegetables are perfectly fine, particularly as snacks for the chef, but the majority of their flavor has ended up in the stew itself, and their texture will be nonexistent.

IS THE TERM *YANKEE* DEROGATORY?

Maybe if you're saying it while spitting chewing tobacco at my boots and questioning my support of gay marriage, but even then, it's certainly not going to be the headline of the situation.

SERVES 4 TO 6

9 medium carrots, peeled

4 celery stalks, chopped into ½-inch pieces

1 small yellow onion, chopped into ½-inch pieces

1 (3-pound) eye of round beef roast (see Note)

Kosher salt and freshly ground black pepper

3 garlic cloves, thinly sliced, plus 2 more, minced

2 tablespoons neutral oil (such as canola, vegetable, or grapeseed)

1 tablespoon tomato paste

2 bay leaves

2 fresh rosemary sprigs

2 fresh thyme sprigs

3 quarts beef broth, preferably homemade (see page 347)

1½ to 1¾ cups dry red wine

4 russet potatoes

Chop 5 of the carrots into ½-inch pieces. Combine in a large bowl with the celery and onion. Set aside.

Season the exterior of the roast heavily with salt and pepper, then using a paring knife, cut slits all over the beef. Press the garlic slices into the slits as deep as you're able. Let the roast sit at room temperature for 1 hour.

Preheat the oven to 325°F.

In a large ovenproof pot, heat 1 tablespoon of the oil. Sear the roast until well browned, 3 to 4 minutes per side, then remove and set aside.

Add the remaining 1 tablespoon oil to the pot, then add the chopped vegetables. Cook, scraping up the fond, until softened, 2 to 3 minutes. Add the tomato paste and stir to combine. Add the minced garlic, bay leaves, rosemary, and thyme. Stir to combine and season minimally with salt and pepper. Add about half the beef broth, then return the roast to the pot. Pour in the wine and remaining beef broth until the liquid comes about two-thirds of the way up the roast. Partially cover with the lid and cook in the oven for 1½ to 2 hours.

Toward the end of the cook time, peel the potatoes and chop into 1-inch pieces. Chop the remaining 4 carrots into 1-inch pieces.

Remove the pot from the oven, flip the roast, then add the potatoes and remaining carrots. Return to the oven and cook uncovered 45 to 60 minutes more, until the meat is tender when poked but not falling apart. Remove the roast and untie if necessary.

Slice the roast and serve with the potatoes, larger carrots, and broth.

Note: *If your roast is unevenly shaped, it will need to be trussed. Most butchers pre-truss the eye of round cut before selling it but you can do it yourself instead: Tie 6 to 8 (10-inch) lengths of butcher's twine at 1-inch intervals along the length of the roast.*

CHEESESTEAK PINWHEELS

Steak pinwheels are, more often than not, a gimmick perpetrated on the innocent grocery shopping public by impostor butchers, the same insidious forces responsible for prepackaged burgers stuffed with onions, and salmon loosely coated in soggy breadcrumbs and buffalo sauce under plastic wrap. When, however, you load up the carnivorous jelly roll with cheesesteaklike ingredients (or the fillings of your choice), the results are as novel as they are delicious. The best outcome is the result of quality grill understanding and control, from temperature to placement, so that the delicious contents sear and seal shut without dripping out into the raging flames below. The method being exercised to this end is known as *indirect grilling* (see Kitchen Glossary, page 23), wherein only half the grill is heated to apex, the other a thermally ambivalent, ovenlike holding area, where the charred steaks can finish coming up to user desired doneness without burning. Understanding this concept is key to enjoying the full potential of your grill, no matter the fuel source, so this recipe stands as a test with real-time feedback in the form of cheese dripping tragically out of your once delicious pinwheels.

How I've Screwed This Up

We've all, in a fit of hunger or sloth or both, neglected to properly brush and lubricate our grill grates prior to cooking, which can prove especially fatal in a recipe like this. My first attempt filming this *Basics* experienced such heavy cheese casualties that I had no choice but to reshoot entirely, fashioning crude snacks and sandwiches from the hollow carcasses of the initial batch.

Troubleshooting

ALL MY CHEESE LEAKED OUT.

Okay I definitely don't expect you to read all the headnotes, so if you're just joining us, you gotta exercise spectacular grill discipline with this one: preheat your grill thoroughly, brush down your grates emphatically, lubricate liberally, and position purposefully!

MY STEAK IS DRY.

It can be freaky to cook anything medium-rare with cheese involved (see: Jucy Lucy), but with as lean and fibrous a cut as flank steak, you gotta cook these guys to a juicy medium-rare for ideal flavor and texture.

MY STEAK IS TOUGH.

Directionality is another key component to preparing flank steak, whose tough muscle fibers must be cut across perpendicularly so that they can be shortened and made mouth-friendly. Following this technique can be difficult from text alone, so don't be afraid to look up a video!

EVEN IF IT'S NOT YOURS?

I'm not the jealous author type, so you can hook up with as many other YouTube creators as you like, so long as you end up with a delicious steak at the end of the day! This phenomenon is known as "creator compersion."

MAKES 6 PINWHEELS

1 (about 2-pound) flank steak, trimmed

Kosher salt and freshly ground black pepper

1 tablespoon neutral oil (such as grapeseed, vegetable, or canola) plus 1 to 2 tablespoons if pan-searing the pinwheels

1 yellow onion, sliced

2 garlic cloves, minced

1 green bell pepper, thinly sliced

1 red bell pepper, thinly sliced

6 ounces provolone cheese, thinly sliced

6 (24-inch) lengths of butcher's twine

Place the flank steak in the center of your work surface with the grain of the meat perpendicular to you.

USING A VERY SHARP AND LONG KNIFE, BUTTERFLY THE STEAK:
Starting on the thinner long side, slice the steak in half horizontally (parallel to the cutting board), stopping just before cutting through to the other side. Open up the steak like a book, creating a steak that is evenly thick and double the size in width.

Rotate the steak 90° so that the grain of the steak is parallel with the edge of the counter or cutting board facing you. Optionally, tenderize the steak with a stainless steel needle tenderizer.

Season both sides of the steak with salt and pepper and let sit at room temperature for at least 30 minutes, up to 2 hours.

Meanwhile, heat the 1 tablespoon of oil in a large skillet over medium-high heat. Add the onion and cook, stirring occasionally, until the onion starts to get color, 2 to 3 minutes. Add the garlic and bell peppers, season generously with salt, and cook, stirring occasionally, until the onion and peppers are tender, 3 to 4 minutes. Transfer to a small rimmed baking sheet to cool.

Layer the steak with the cooled onion mixture, leaving a 1-inch border at the top and bottom of the steak. Top the vegetables with an even layer of provolone, maintaining the border.

Starting with the long side facing you, tightly roll up the filling in the steak, making it as even as possible. Place the roll seam-side down.

Soak the butcher's twine in a bowl of water for 1 to 2 minutes.

Tightly tie the twine at 1- to 1½-inch intervals along the length of the roll. Trim off any excess ends of twine. Insert a metal or wooden skewer through each piece of twine.

Using a sharp chef's knife, cut off each end of the log, then slice between each of the pieces of twine to create the pinwheels.

IF GRILLING THE PINWHEELS:
Preheat half your grill on high heat. Oil the grates then add the pinwheels cut-side down. Grill until the steak is well charred, 3 to 4 minutes on each side. Move the pinwheels to the non-preheated side of the grill, cover, and cook until the steaks reach an internal temperature of 125°F, 5 to 10 minutes. (The temperature will increase to 135°F with carryover cooking.)

IF PAN-SEARING THE PINWHEELS:
Preheat the oven to 375°F. Heat 1 to 2 tablespoons oil in a large cast-iron skillet. Add the pinwheels and cook for about 4 minutes on each side. Transfer to a rimmed baking sheet and bake 5 to 7 minutes, until the steaks reach 125°F. (The temperature will increase to 135°F with carryover cooking.)

Allow the pinwheels to rest for 5 to 10 minutes. Remove the butcher's twine before serving.

STEP-BY-STEP IMAGES, PAGE 364-365

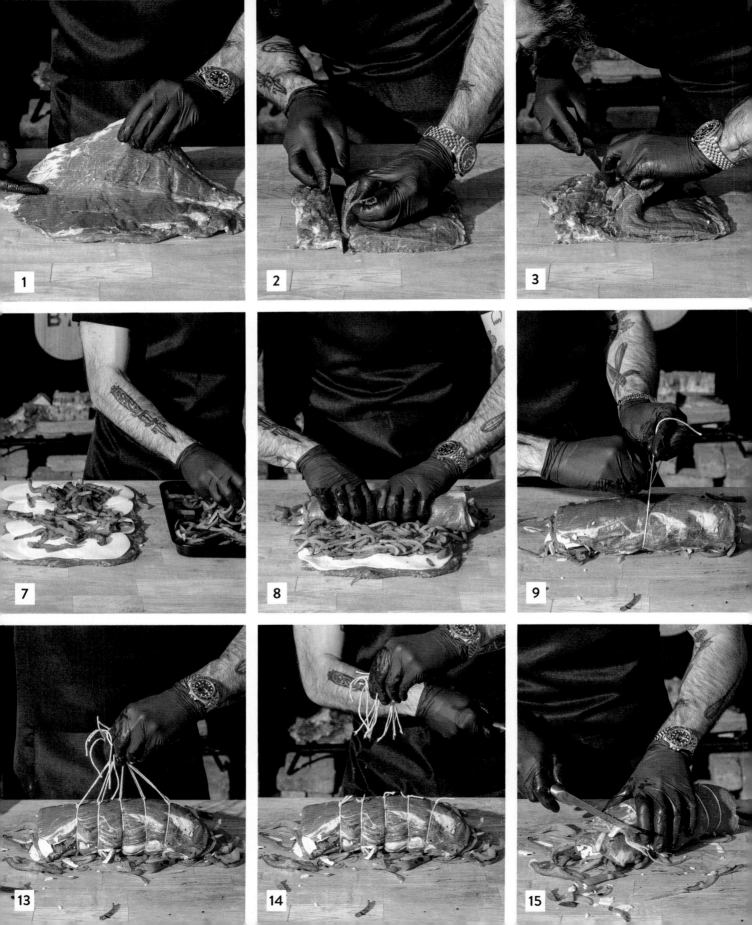

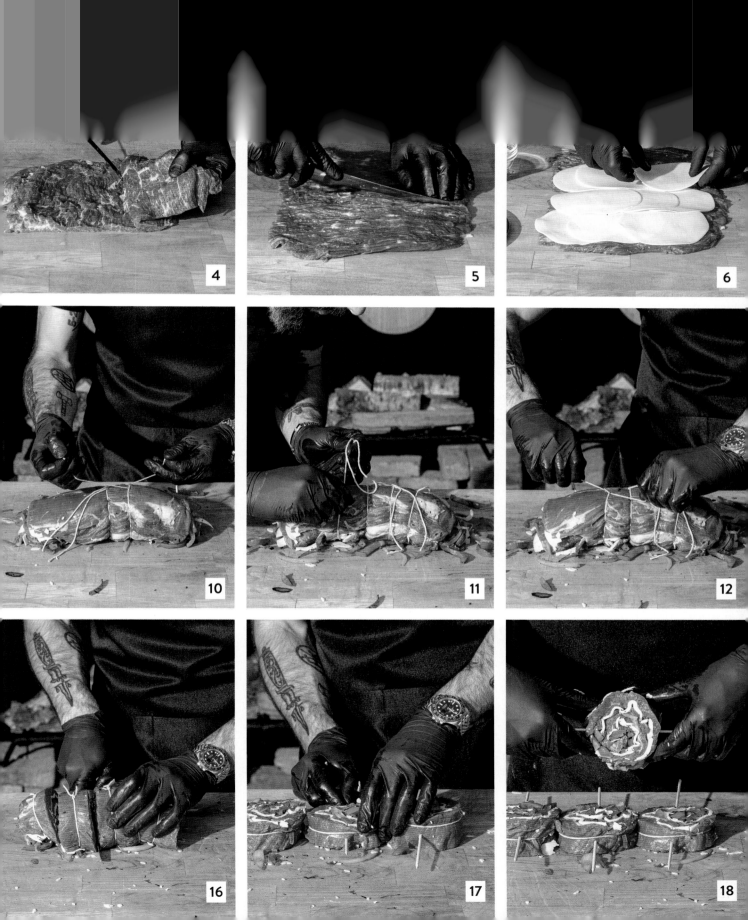

BRAISED SHORT RIBS WITH POTATOES ALIGOT

If you've ever been to the splashy New-American restaurant in town, you've probably seen a short rib like this one on the menu. Braised in wine or beer, these entreés are typical triple threats of richness: a charred meat meteorite (meatiorite) barely clinging to its sloping rib bone, doused in a concentrated reduction of its braising liquid (mounted with butter of course), all served on a creamy or cheesy substrate, usually a whipped tuber (tater) of some kind. We wanted to tick all the winter indulgence boxes, so that's exactly what you'll find here! The short rib is braised in beer rather than wine, as it cooks down to a sweet and savory reduction rather than a bitter and tannic one. Potatoes aligot are just potatoes trying their hardest to be cheese; a stretchy and gooey indulgence straddling the line between mashed potatoes and fondue. Warning: may cause cookbook authors to write hyperbolic warnings about just how decadent this dish is, like "hope you've got your cardiologist on speed dial!" or "goodness gracious great balls of calories!" That's what you thought I was gonna do right? Yeah, that's what I thought you thought.

How I've Screwed This Up

I continue to be haunted by a stretchy, gooey and overworked pommes purée I attempted to make for a dinner party about ten years ago—potatoes aligot adds a layer of safeguarding by becoming stretchy on purpose. That and the short ribs' long, slow cook time (and ability to make ahead) mean that you've got a dish that's pretty hard to screw up! I have, of course, managed to: I left my pommes aligot on a hot burner and ended up with a crispy aligot pancake stuck to the bottom of my pan. It looked like hell but it wasn't bad, to be honest.

Troubleshooting

MY SHORT RIBS ARE TOUGH OR DRY.

As counterintuitive as it may sound, even when cooking in liquid, even so hardy a cut of beef as short ribs can dry out. Unlike most things in your oven, this dish won't be harmed by semifrequent testing and prodding, so don't be afraid to check on its doneness frequently with a paring knife.

MY SHORT RIBS DON'T HAVE MUCH MEAT ON THEM.

This is a bit of a special occasion dish, one that warrants hand selecting your short ribs from a butcher you trust, mostly to ensure that you get your hands on some well-marbled, meaty short ribs. If you find yourself with a bunch of bones thinly painted with sinew and a microscopic layer of actual beef, you might not want to use them in this recipe, but don't put them to waste! Check out our beef demi-glace (see page 346), a time-consuming but low-labor ingredient worth its weight in gold, especially in a recipe like this one.

MY POTATOES WON'T GET STRETCHY.

My guess is that you used Yukon Gold or some other lower-starch potato. Add more cheese if you want to try and up the stretch factor; worst-case scenario, you just made some nice cheesy whipped potatoes.

MY SAUCE IS THIN AND WATERY.

Your sauce should have a thick, almost syrupy body to it—keep simmering it in a wide sauté pan if it doesn't have the right consistency.

WHY DOES MY SIGNIFICANT OTHER OR COWORKERS ROLL THEIR EYES WHENEVER I SAY THE WORD "REDUCTION"?

See: Kitchen Glossary (page 23), reductions might taste great but they make you sound like a real piece of work.

SERVES 4

2 racks short ribs or 6 English-style short ribs

Kosher salt and freshly ground black pepper

1 tablespoon vegetable oil

2 large onions, sliced

3 tablespoons tomato paste

5 celery stalks, roughly chopped

½ pound carrots, peeled and roughly chopped

2 cups amber ale (or dry red wine)

2 cups chicken stock, preferably homemade (see page 268)

½ cup prune juice

1 tablespoon soy sauce

4 to 5 garlic cloves

3 to 4 thyme sprigs

2 to 3 fresh parsley sprigs, plus leaves chopped for garnish

Potatoes Aligot (recipe follows), for serving

Preheat the oven to 275°F.

Trim the excess silver skin and/or fat from the short ribs. If necessary, cut the short ribs into 3 sections, each containing 1 rib. Season the short ribs all over generously with salt and pepper. Set aside at room temperature.

In a large pot or Dutch oven, heat the oil over medium-high heat until wisps of smoke emerge. Working in batches to avoid overcrowding, add the short ribs and sear until browned on all sides, 4 to 5 minutes per side. To prevent the fond from burning, place the ribs back down in the exact spot that they were before flipping. If there is exposed fond during the final batch, add a handful of the onions to prevent the fond from burning.

Once every short rib is seared, add the onions (or remaining onions) and cook, stirring occasionally, until tender and browned, 3 to 4 minutes. Add the tomato paste and continue to cook, stirring, until the vegetables are thoroughly coated, 2 to 3 minutes. Add the celery and carrots and cook, stirring occasionally, until the carrots and celery are tender, 2 to 3 minutes. Add the ale, chicken stock, prune juice, soy sauce, garlic, thyme, and parsley. Stir to combine. Nestle in the short ribs, making sure each piece peaks just above the liquid.

Cover the pot and cook in the oven for 4 to 5 hours, checking for doneness after 3½ hours. The short ribs are done when there is no resistance after poking them with a paring knife. Transfer the short ribs to a plate. Strain the braising liquid through a sieve into a large bowl and discard the solids.

IF MAKING AHEAD OF TIME: Add a few big pieces of ice to the braising liquid to cool it rapidly and let sit for 15 minutes. Wrap the short ribs and braising liquid separately with plastic wrap and refrigerate until chilled, at least 4 hours, up to overnight. Once chilled, remove and discard the solid layer of fat floating on top of the surface.

IF MAKING FOR IMMEDIATE USE: Remove from the heat to allow the fat to rise to the surface then skim off.

Once the fat is removed, pour the braising liquid into a large high-walled skillet and simmer, stirring occasionally, until reduced by 80 percent and the sauce coats the back of a spoon, 1 to 2 hours.

Place the short ribs into the skillet and baste with the sauce. Cover and let the short ribs sit in the sauce over medium heat until warmed through, about 20 minutes.

When ready to serve, place the short ribs onto Potatoes Aligot, top with the remaining sauce, and garnish with chopped parsley leaves.

POTATOES ALIGOT

Serves 4

2 pounds Yukon Gold potatoes, peeled and cut into 1-inch cubes

Kosher salt and freshly ground black pepper

8 ounces heavy cream

8 tablespoons (1 stick) unsalted butter

12 ounces Swiss cheese of choice, shredded

Place the potatoes in a large saucepan, cover with cold water, and add a hefty pinch of salt. Bring to a boil and cook over medium heat until completely tender, about 15 minutes, then drain.

Using a potato ricer, rice the potatoes into the pot. (Alternatively, mash the potatoes very finely in the pot.)

In a small saucepan, combine the heavy cream and butter. Heat the mixture over low heat until the butter is melted and the cream is steaming. Pour into the potatoes and whisk until smooth.

Working slowly and in batches, add and mix the cheese into the potatoes until incorporated. Whisk together until the cheese and starch of the potatoes have created a stretchy consistency (halfway between mashed potatoes and fondue). Season with salt and pepper.

SHEPHERD'S PIE

I remember my first shepherd's pie—in my senior year of high school, I toured the UK as part of a foreign exchange student program. Like most of my youth, however, it was a completely wasted culinary opportunity, where being both culture- and cash-strapped led me to subsist mainly on sausage rolls from Tesco (You know what? No regrets). I'm afraid this was a literary misdirection dear reader, because you see, perhaps a year after my journey through prime shepherd's pie territories, I spotted the distinctly English dish at popular eatery The Cheesecake Factory. I reveled in the hearty richness of this entirely inauthentic, most likely microwaved mashed potato–topped beef stew, and endeavored to make my own in the years to come. In spite of my early stumbles, I believe what follows is a recipe for not entirely inauthentic shepherd's pie (please don't hurt me). In fact, I might've gotten the best review of my career thanks to this particular pie: It was the first of my cooking a friend of mine had tried, and he remarked what a relief it was to know that after years of watching my show that in real life, I can actually cook. I'm still blushing just writing about it nearly three years later.

How I've Screwed This Up

Substituting ground beef for the lamb and still calling it shepherd's pie. Remember, if you do this, you are legally and indeed morally obligated to refer to the dish as cottage pie.

Troubleshooting

MY PIE IS DRY.
Gross. Oh—I mean, well, yeah, still gross. Sounds like you might've cooked down your liquids too much, and after a lengthy stint in the oven, hardly any was left for your enjoyment. Make sure the filling is quite saucy, stretching out with additional stock or demi-glace if it's looking spare.

MY MASHED POTATOES ARE GUMMY.
This recipe utilizes Yukon Gold, a low-starch potato, so my first guess would be that you substituted with russets? That or your potatoes were outrageously overworked in the pursuit of smoothness.

THIS PRESENTATION IS A LITTLE TOO RUSTIC FOR ME, HOW DO I DO ONE OF THOSE DECORATIVE PATTERNS I SEE ON SHEPHERDS' PIES?
Oh well paaaardon me. Those patterns are made by dragging a fork through the potatoes—to get nice clean lines, you want super-smooth spuds—be sure to rice the potatoes or press them through a fine-mesh sieve.

SERVES 4 TO 6

Neutral oil (such as canola, vegetable, or grapeseed), for greasing

1 pound ground lamb (or ground beef)

½ large onion, finely chopped

4 medium carrots, peeled and finely chopped

3 garlic cloves, minced

3 tablespoons tomato paste

3 to 4 thyme sprigs, chopped

2 to 3 rosemary sprigs, chopped

1½ tablespoons all-purpose flour

1 cup dark Irish stout

1 cup beef broth, preferably homemade (see page 347)

1½ teaspoons Worcestershire sauce

2 tablespoons Madeira (optional)

1 puck frozen demi-glace, preferably homemade (see page 346; optional)

Kosher salt and freshly ground black pepper

⅔ cup peas (fresh or frozen)

Cheesy Mashed Potatoes (recipe follows)

2 to 3 ounces aged white cheddar cheese, shredded (optional)

Preheat the oven to 350°F.

Lightly oil a large stainless-steel skillet and heat over medium-high heat. Add the lamb and cook, breaking it up with a wooden spoon or spatula, until browned, 4 to 5 minutes. Drain off the excess fat, leaving 2 to 3 tablespoons in the skillet. Add the onion and cook, stirring occasionally, until soft and translucent around the edges, 2 to 3 minutes. Add the carrots and cook, stirring occasionally, until tender, 2 to 3 minutes. Push the mixture to the edges and add the garlic and tomato paste to the center of the skillet; cook, stirring, until the garlic is fragrant. Stir together and cook until the tinned flavor of the tomato paste cooks off, 2 to 3 minutes more. Add the thyme and rosemary and stir to combine. Add the flour and cook, stirring, until the raw flour smell is gone and a fond has formed on the bottom, 2 to 3 minutes.

Add the stout and beef broth and cook, scraping up all the fond at the bottom of the skillet while mixing. Add the Worcestershire sauce. If desired, add the Madeira and demi-glace. Cook, stirring occasionally, until the mixture is thick enough so a spoon dragged through leaves a trail, 10 to 12 minutes. Season with salt and pepper.

Meanwhile, bring a small saucepan of water to a boil. Add the peas and cook until cooked through but not mushy, 2 to 3 minutes. Drain and set aside until ready to use.

Spoon the filling into a pie plate, then top with the peas. Lastly, top with the mashed potatoes and smooth out into an even layer with the back of a spoon. Drag the tines of a fork over the surface of the potatoes to add texture.

Set the pie plate on a rimmed baking sheet and bake for about 25 minutes, topping the shepherd's pie with cheddar about halfway through, if desired. For extra browning, broil for the last 2 to 3 minutes of baking.

Allow the shepherd's pie to cool for 10 to 15 minutes before serving.

CHEESY MASHED POTATOES

Serves 4 to 6

3 pounds Yukon Gold potatoes, peeled and halved

3 ounces aged white cheddar cheese, shredded

8 tablespoons (1 stick) unsalted butter

½ cup chopped fresh chives (optional)

2 large egg yolks

½ cup whole milk

Kosher salt

Freshly ground white pepper

Place the potatoes in a large saucepan and cover with cold water. Bring to a boil and continue cooking over medium-high heat until the potatoes are tender when pierced with a knife or fork, about 20 minutes. Drain and return the potatoes to the warm saucepan. Cook over medium-low heat, stirring gently, until the excess moisture evaporates, about 1 minute. Rice the potatoes in a potato masher if desired. (Alternatively, mash the potatoes very finely in the pot.)

Remove from the heat and add the cheddar, butter, and, if desired, the chives. Using a potato masher, combine with the potatoes. Allow the mashed potatoes to cool until they stop steaming, 5 to 10 minutes.

In a small bowl, whisk the egg yolks with the milk. Stream into the slightly cooled potatoes and fold to combine. Season with salt and white pepper.

STEAKHOUSE BURGERS

Despite sharing the word "burger" in its name, steakhouse burgers and smash burgers could not be more different. One is quick, easy, and economical—the other luxuriant, laborious, and operating in an entirely different tax bracket. This burger is modeled after the kind of $25 burger you'd find at New York City restaurants, like Minetta Tavern or The Spotted Pig, prime and prepared with precision. Restaurants are fortunate enough to have any number of dishes yielding dry-aged scraps, from which a singular burger experience can be crafted. We, on the other hand, have to adulterate an otherwise perfect steak for the sake of a burger which, depending on your worldview, could be a sunk cost. Rich with fat, replete with flavor, and funky with the wisdom that comes with age, this is a special occasion kind of burger. A showy, brassy kind of burger. A "holy shit, dry-aged roasts are on sale and priced to move, honey let's pack the Fiat to its NHTSA-reported maximum cargo capacity" kind of burger.

How I've Screwed This Up

This is a very specific recipe I developed for a very specific episode, and as such, I've only ever made it a couple of times. I will say that my weakness with burgers in general is to combine and form their patties too gently, resulting in a burger that falls apart on the grill. The less you work your beef, the more loosely structured a burger you'll get and tenderer an end result you'll enjoy, but at the cost of its structural integrity.

Troubleshooting

I DIDN'T ENJOY THIS BURGER AS MUCH AS IT COST.
That's unfortunate, but the game of chance you play when disassembling perfectly good steak in pursuit of the peak fancy-boy expression of a burger. If you start with properly aged, properly sourced beef, little more than salt should be enough to make it a worthwhile experience. Cheese, caramelized onions, and homemade brioche should make it an extraordinary one. If it's lacking in flavor, try a different butcher!

MY ONIONS ARE BROWNING/BURNING.
Much like the dark chocolate-esque roux used in proper Cajun gumbo, caramelized onions can be brought to their sweet and jammy climax slowly or quickly. The less experienced you are, however, the more slowly you should go. If your onions are browning, your heat is likely too high and you're not agitating your allium often enough. If you feel like your heat is too low and not enough is happening, resist the temptation to speed up the process—even a superlow flame will eventually caramelize onions, it'll just take quite a while.

MY ONIONS ARE STILL BROWNING/BURNING.
Don't be afraid to add splashes of water throughout the process. It will dissolve anything sticking (and potentially burning) to the bottom of the pan, help steam and soften the onions more quickly, and generally streamline the caramelization process. It's a good set of training wheels until you're able to do it with your eyes closed.

MY BURGER KEEPS FLARING UP ON THE GRILL.
With a burger this fatty, some flare-ups are bound to happen. Unfortunately, these flashes of flame can give your burger an acrid or bitter taste, so it's best to restrain them however possible. Whether you've got a gas or charcoal grill, depriving the flare-ups of oxygen is the answer. Close the lid to lessen the dripping fat's ability to burn, but bear in mind the changes that this will make to the cooking environment of your grill (see *Grills*, page 25)

CAN I PUT KETCHUP AND MUSTARD ON THIS?
That's your decision to make, but the entire purpose of this burger is to showcase high-quality beef. As with pizza, I am a strict libertarian when it comes to your choice and freedom of topping and treating your burger how you like, but there are better burgers to top up. Smashburgers are sometimes fried in mustard and topped with flavorful condiments because they're basically fried discs of meat crust, and they can handle the accompaniment. If you are here for beef and want to celebrate its flavor, try and resist topping this up the way you might otherwise.

MAKES 4 BURGERS

20 ounces dry-aged rib eye steak, ground

20 ounces brisket, ground

Kosher salt and freshly ground black pepper

4 slices Muenster cheese

4 Hamburger Buns (page 64)

Caramelized Onions (recipe follows)

In a large bowl, combine the rib eye and brisket. Form into four equal patties.

Preheat a grill over high heat.

Just before grilling the patties, season the patties generously with salt and pepper. Grill the patties on one side until well browned, 3 to 5 minutes. Flip and top each patty with 1 slice of the cheese. Grill until well browned on the other side and cooked to your desired doneness.

Meanwhile, grill the buns until well toasted, 3 to 4 minutes.

Build the burgers and spread the caramelized onions on the top bun of each burger. Serve immediately.

CARAMELIZED ONIONS

Makes about ½ cup

1 tablespoon light olive oil

2 yellow onions, thinly sliced

In a large skillet, heat the oil over medium heat. Add the onions and cook over medium-low heat, stirring occasionally, until the onions are completely tender and evenly caramelized, 45 minutes to 1 hour. Add water if the bottom of the skillet starts to scorch.

PIMENTO SMASH BURGERS

The term "smash burger" might have only recently become a household name, but they've been at the core of the burger consciousness since the days of antiquity. A means to make burgers quickly, flavorfully, and inexpensively, smash burgers are behind every great diner, fast-food, and stoned In-N-Out order of your life. Despite their simplicity, they both solve and create a number of problems for the home chef. No need to worry about doneness, as this burger is ready when it simply looks ready, which it is in a matter of seconds. The need for extremely high temperatures, however, strikes fear in the hearts of learning home cooks. Smoke may billow, burgers may crumble, fire alarms may repeatedly wail their warning cry; steady your breath and remember that it's all in the pursuit of a great craft. Smash burgers, like bread dough or a pack of hyenas, can smell your fear, and won't show you an ounce of respect unless you assert yourself as the dominant party. As the old proverb goes, you only need three tools to make perfect smashers: a stiff spatula, a ripping-hot pan, and the heart of a lion.

How I've Screwed This Up

You can see my first-ever attempt at making smash burgers when *Hot Ones* host Sean Evans first came and visited my apartment in 2017. You'd think I'd have thought to practice first beforehand, but as is evident, I decided to wing it. Not only did my induction burner heat my cast-iron skillet very unevenly, my spatula was far too big for the job, forcing me to smash two burgers at a time. The *First We Feast* crew did their damnedest to make the resulting burgers look decent, but the shrunken inconsistently seared patties were the obvious work of a first-timer.

Troubleshooting

MY BURGERS STICK TO MY SPATULA.

This is a common problem that can be averted a few ways. First, smash quickly and decisively—the longer that spatula stays connected to the beef, the more condensation builds between the two from the heat of the pan, and the more emotionally attached they become. You can also lube your spat with the same fat you're using in the pan, or if you're cooking on a large flattop, you can place the spat directly on the cooking surface to keep it hot. When smashing the burgers, try to imagine that you're smearing them across the pan, which should keep the spatula moving and help it release from the meat.

MY BURGERS TURN OUT TOO SMALL.

Smash burgers, being mostly crust, need to be smashed to a surprising degree of smashedness. You want the resultant patty to more closely resemble a doily than a burger, a lacy network of proteins barely held together by a crispy crust. Even if it doesn't hold together under its own power, melted cheese can be used to cursorily glue the patty together enough to ferry it onto its toasted bun. Even if you go full Hulk and smash the burgers into an atom-thick wafer, they will still shrink, so make sure you're smashing them into rounds slightly larger than your targeted bun.

MY BURGERS DON'T BROWN PROPERLY/END UP SIMMERING IN JUICES.

This can only mean one thing: Your heat is too low. A crust isn't forming during its overextended cook time, allowing juices and fat to render out of the burger and into the pan, further hindering any browning from occurring (see: Maillard Reaction, page 26). I know, when you're starting out in the kitchen, that getting pans really hot is frightening— it's okay that it's frightening, riding a bike or driving a car were frightening at one point, too. But once you try it out, maybe with a patient friend who's been around the block a few times, you start to wonder how you ever got around without it.

MY BURGERS SMOKE UP MY APARTMENT.
Yep that is an all-but-unavoidable symptom of smash burgers. If you're living in an apartment or small home, this can obviously be problematic, and I honestly don't have a fix for you. Until I finally acquired proper hood ventilation and outdoor space, making smash burgers meant a 100% chance of: setting off my fire alarm, pissing off my neighbors, and soaking the clothes openly hanging in my studio apartment in meat smoke. Sometimes life doesn't want you to have smash burgers—it's up to you to look life squarely in the eye and say, with conviction and purpose, "try and stop me."

MAKES 4 BURGERS

1 pound ground beef, preferably 85% lean

Neutral oil (such as canola, vegetable, or grapeseed)

Pimento Cheese Topping (recipe follows)

Kosher salt and freshly ground black pepper

4 hamburger buns, toasted or grilled

Butter lettuce leaves, sliced tomatoes, and ketchup, for serving (optional)

Form the ground beef into four 4-ounce balls.

IF COOKING ON THE STOVETOP: Heat a large cast-iron skillet with 1 tablespoon of oil over high heat.

IF COOKING ON THE GRILL: Preheat the burners on high with a large cast-iron skillet on top of the grill. Add 1 tablespoon of oil to the preheated skillet.

Add two of the beef balls to the skillet. Smash each with a very stiff metal spatula. The diameter of the patties should be about ½ inch wider than your bun to account for shrinkage. Continue cooking the patties on the first side for about 1 minute to form a crust. Then, flip and cook for another minute. Season the other side of the patty with salt and pepper. Top each burger with about ¼ to ⅓ cup of the Pimento Cheese Topping. Add 1 tablespoon water to the pan and cover with the lid or bowl until the cheese is melted, 1 to 2 minutes. Repeat with the remaining beef balls.

Build the burgers with your toppings of choice, if desired. Serve immediately.

PIMENTO CHEESE TOPPING

Makes about 2 cups

8 ounces sharp cheddar cheese, cubed

4 ounces American cheese, cubed

2 ounces cream cheese, cubed, at room temperature

2 ounces jarred pimento peppers or cherry peppers, drained, seeded, and sliced

In a food processor, combine the cheddar, American cheese, cream cheese, and peppers. Process until well combined. Set aside at room temperature until ready to use.

BEER-BRAISED CORNED BEEF WITH HERBY HORSERADISH CREAM

You might be wondering about the etymology of "corned" beef, given that there's not an ear of corn to be found in the process! You weren't? Well I'm going to tell you anyway: it's because the salt used in the process was so big, it looked like kernels of corn. Isn't that kind of ridiculous? To name a food after another food, not due to its flavor, color, or even mere presence in the dish, but because, in its preparation, the salt used resembles *only the size* of an entirely unrelated food. Like, is there an alternate universe where corned beef is called "blueberried beef" because some genius thought that the salt looked blueberry-size? Should we be calling pot roast something like "water meat"? Why, when I say "pass the corn" at the dinner table, does everyone stare at me like I have two heads when I point frantically to the salt shaker and begin to rap my fists on the place settings? For that matter, why isn't there any corn in corned beef?! It would probably be pretty good!!

Sorry, sorry, I'm calm. But much like adding corn to corned beef, we've exercised a bold and nontraditional strategy to improve this timeless classic. While the brisket's fat cap is normally shriveled into a scraped off byproduct during the cooking process, our semisubmerged braise actually browns the fat cap, adding a welcome roasty flavor to what's normally very literally a boiled piece of beef.

How I've Screwed This Up

Even with the relative safeguard of a braise vs. boil, you can still absolutely dry out your brisket, and I very much have. Add to that its inherent saltiness, and especially if it's headed for the smoker to be evolved into pastrami, you might find yourself reaching for a tall glass of spicy mustard to quench your thirst. Pay close attention to your temperatures!

Troubleshooting

THIS RECIPE USES A LITTLE BIT OF A LOT OF ONE-OFF SPICES, CAN I JUST GET PICKLING SPICES INSTEAD?
It's nice to be able to have a hand in choosing your flavors (big juniper berry guy, myself), but pickling spice will do just fine if for some reason you don't feel like spending $38 on seven spices you'll use once.

MY CORNED BEEF CAME OUT DRY.
While it's tough to dry out brisket, the intramuscular fat and connective tissue can most certainly be rendered out of existence, so don't allow its internal temp to climb very far past 200°F.

MY CORNED BEEF CAME OUT TOUGH.
It may have been undercooked, but how corned beef is sliced is nearly as important as how it's cooked; it must be sliced across the grain to achieve maximum tenderness and pornigraphicality.

SERVES 2 TO 4

Brine

8 cups distilled water

½ cup kosher salt

¼ cup dark brown sugar

1 tablespoon black peppercorns

1 tablespoon juniper berries

1 tablespoon yellow mustard seeds

1 tablespoon allspice berries

About 1 teaspoon pink curing salt (please reference a cure calculator; see Note)

2 bay leaves, torn or crumbled

1 cinnamon stick

6 cardamom pods (optional)

2 red dried chiles (such as chile de árbol), crushed (optional)

Corned Beef

2 to 3 pounds beef brisket

1 large onion, sliced

3 garlic cloves, crushed

1½ teaspoons black peppercorns

1 teaspoon mustard seeds

½ teaspoon coriander seeds

½ teaspoon allspice berries

3 whole cloves

2 bay leaves

Kosher salt and freshly ground pepper

1 (12-ounce) bottle or can Guinness Draught beer

1 to 2 cups beef broth, preferably homemade

1 small green cabbage, cored and cut into 2-inch wedges

2 to 3 large carrots, cut into 2-inch segments (on a bias)

1½ pounds red and white baby potatoes, cut in half

Herby Horseradish Cream (recipe follows)

MAKE THE BRINE: In a large sealable container or nonreactive pot with a corresponding lid, combine the water, kosher salt, sugar, peppercorns, juniper berries, mustard seeds, allspice berries, pink curing salt, bay leaves, cinnamon, and, if desired, the cardamom pods and dried chiles. Whisk until the sugar and salts dissolve.

MAKE THE CORNED BEEF: Add the brisket to the brine, making sure it is completely submerged. Cover with the lid and refrigerate for 5 to 10 days depending on the size and proportions of your brisket (please reference a cure calculator; see Note).

Preheat the oven to 275°F.

Remove the brisket from the brine. Rinse and dry thoroughly with paper towels; discard the brine. Score the fat cap of the brisket with a crosshatch pattern.

In a medium Dutch oven, combine the onion, garlic, peppercorns, mustard seeds, coriander seeds, allspice berries, cloves, bay leaves, and 2 teaspoons kosher salt. Add the brisket, fat-cap down, then pour in the beer and enough of the beef broth to come about three-fourths of the way up the beef.

Transfer to the oven and cook, uncovered, for 3 hours. Flip the beef so the fat-cap is exposed to the heat of the oven and continue to cook 2 to 3 hours, until the beef is fork-tender and the internal temperature registers 190 to 200°F.

Remove the beef from the braising liquid and allow to rest at room temperature 30 minutes or in the refrigerator for up to 12 hours. If refrigerating, reheat the corned beef in the braising liquid on the stovetop for 20 minutes before serving.

Add the cabbage, carrots, and potatoes to the braising liquid. Bring to a boil over high heat. Cover and lower the heat to a simmer. Cook until the vegetables are tender, 20 to 30 minutes. Remove the carrots, potatoes, and cabbage from the liquid.

Slice the brisket, against the grain, ¼- to ½-inch thick. Serve alongside the cooked vegetables, Herby Horseradish Cream, and an extra ladleful of the braising liquid. Season the dish with an extra sprinkling of salt and pepper.

Note: *Use an online cure calculator to precisely determine the amount of pink curing salt needed based on the specific weight of the brisket.*

HERBY HORSERADISH CREAM

Makes 1¼ cups

¾ cup sour cream

¼ cup prepared horseradish

2 tablespoons chopped fresh parsley leaves

1½ tablespoons Dijon mustard

1 tablespoon chopped fresh chives

1 tablespoon chopped dill fronds

1½ teaspoons white vinegar

Kosher salt and freshly ground pepper

Combine the sour cream, horseradish, parsley, mustard, chives, dill, and vinegar in a small bowl. Season with salt and pepper and whisk until the sauce is homogenous. Store in the refrigerator until ready to serve.

STEAK TARTARE WITH TARRAGON VINAIGRETTE AND QUAIL EGG

One of steak's more controversial preparations is fully, entirely, and one hunnert percent uncooked. This may sound like a terrifying prospect to some, particularly those who prefer their burgers gray, but the rewards are great. Raw beef has a subtle, sweet flavor which, when partnered with a bright and invigorating vinaigrette, will most certainly impress whomever you're clearly trying to impress by making this. I mean, who makes steak tartare for themselves on a weeknight, Hannibal Lecter?

How I've Screwed This Up

I take a strong anti-food-poisoning stance and represent an easily-spooked food safety mindset, so I've never made nor consumed steak tartare that I didn't trust implicitly. If I made it, I sourced the beef from a place I trust. If I ordered it, I'm likely not at the French-themed eatery in the airport food court. Don't screw this one up, folks.

Troubleshooting

MY BEEF TASTES TINNY OR METALLIC.
I personally shy away from grass-fed/finished beef for this very reason, which is even more pronounced in its raw form. You may want to opt for grain-fed beef, as it leans toward the sweeter, milder side.

QUAIL EGGS ARE DUMB AND HARD TO CRACK, CAN I JUST USE A CHICKEN EGG?
Totally! Maybe just make it a little bigger/wider to accommodate all that yolk. Try cracking quail eggs with a paring knife to break the strong membrane underneath the shell. Dump a few of them into a small bowl and fish out the yolk with a spoon.

OH THAT WORKED. THANKS!
No prob!

I DON'T WANT TO EAT RAW BEEF.
Then you probably shouldn't! Anyone who's pushing something on you that you don't want to try is really just pushing them*selves* on you. A real friend doesn't impose their ideas and passions, they expose them.

WOW, THAT'S BEAUTIFUL. YOU KNOW WHAT? MAYBE I'LL TRY A BITE.
GOTCHA!

SERVES 2 TO 4

Crostini

½ baguette

Extra-virgin olive oil, as needed

Steak Tartare

12 ounces filet mignon (preferably dry-aged), trimmed

1 tablespoon Dijon mustard

1 tablespoon extra-virgin olive oil

1 tablespoon red wine vinegar

2 teaspoons Worcestershire sauce

Tabasco sauce, to taste

2 tablespoons chopped shallots

2 tablespoons chopped cornichons

1 tablespoon chopped capers

1 tablespoon finely chopped fresh parsley

1 tablespoon finely chopped fresh tarragon

Kosher salt and freshly ground pepper

2 to 4 quail egg yolks (or small egg yolks)

MAKE THE CROSTINI: Preheat the oven to 400°F.

Slice the bread ⅛-inch thick at a 45° angle. Optionally, freeze the bread prior to slicing for ease. Transfer to a wire rack set inside a large rimmed baking sheet. Brush both sides of each slice with a light coating of olive oil. Bake for about 5 minutes, until golden brown. Remove from the oven and let cool to room temperature.

MAKE THE STEAK TARTARE: Place the filet mignon in the freezer to firm up for 25 to 30 minutes.

Meanwhile, in a small bowl, whisk together the mustard, olive oil, vinegar, Worcestershire sauce, and Tabasco; set aside.

Remove the steak from the freezer and finely chop it into pieces smaller than a pea.
   (**TIP:** *using a very sharp knife will make this step much easier.*)

Transfer to a medium bowl. Add the shallots, cornichons, capers, parsley, and tarragon and mix to combine. Pour the vinaigrette over the top and fold until just combined. Season with salt and pepper.

Divide the tartare into two portions for entrée size or four portions for appetizer size.

For each entrée portion, place a 3½-inch ring mold on the serving plate. Fill the ring mold with tartare and gently remove the ring. For each appetizer portion, place a 2½-inch ring mold on the serving plate. Fill the ring mold with tartare and gently remove the ring.

Make a small divot in the center of each tartare and add 1 egg yolk.

Serve immediately with the crostini.

WORLD FAMOUS* CHILI (CON CARNE)

*The terms "World Famous," "Blue Ribbon," or "The Original" are often superfluous and unverifiable claims, whether they be attributed to chili, apple pie, or needlepoint. You can make any homespun claim you like and no one will bat an eye, so guess what, this chili is "world famous," and there's nothing that any governing body can do about that assertion. In this matter I am untouchable.

There rages a debate at the heart of our nation about whether or not beans have any place in chili, and being bean averse myself, I'm inclined to lean toward the more meat-forward chili con carne incarnation. Instead of crumbly ground beef, whole cubes of chuck are stewed to a state of tenderness. Instead of beans, there are no beans. Instead of dried powder that's more colorful than flavorful, whole dried chiles are toasted, simmered, and puréed into a flavor-loaded sauce. After all, if the dish is named after a specific ingredient, it ought to be a tasty one.

How I've Screwed This Up

No matter how well you make any particular kind of chili, according to someone, you've screwed it up. But much more literally, I once used only beer instead of stock, which I can't fully recommend.

Troubleshooting

MY BEEF IS TOUGH.

If it's tough, it needs more time cooking to tenderize.

MY BEEF IS DRY.

If it's dry, it needs less time cooking to remain juicy.

HOW DO I GIVE SOMETHING LESS TIME?

You know what I mean.

MY SAUCE IS BITTER.

Burning the chiles can bring some acrid flavors, make sure that they aren't smoking while toasting in the pan. Alternately, you might not be into the mix of chiles used, so try some fruitier peppers like cascabel or ancho.

MY CHILI IS TOO SPICY.

Some dried chiles can pack a punch, so dial back on the chiles de árbol or even chipotles.

I ATE THE ENTIRE RECIPE OF CHILI AND MY MEAL WASN'T FREE.

You gotta read the fine print: if you complete the Great American Babish Chili Challenge, your meal is free after rebate, subject to conditions, and only valid at certain locations, specifically not this one.

SERVES 10 TO 12

2 pasilla chiles, stemmed, seeded, and torn into small pieces

4 chiles de árbol, stemmed, seeded, and torn into small pieces

4 chipotle chiles, stemmed, seeded, and torn into small pieces

3 guajillo chiles, stemmed, seeded, and torn into small pieces

3 ancho chiles, stemmed, seeded, and torn into small pieces

1 (about 4-pound) chuck roast, trimmed of silver skin and excess fat

Kosher salt and freshly ground pepper

Vegetable oil, as needed

1 white onion, roughly chopped

6 garlic cloves, peeled and crushed

2 tablespoons tomato paste

12 ounces Mexican lager

4 cups beef or chicken stock, preferably homemade (see page 268)

1 teaspoon dried oregano

½ teaspoon ground cinnamon

½ teaspoon ground coriander

¼ teaspoon ground allspice

2 to 3 tablespoons masa harina

Juice of 2 limes

Shredded cheddar cheese, for garnish

Limes wedges and desired chili toppings, for garnish

Dry roast the pasilla, chiles de árbol, chipotle, guajillo, and ancho chiles by placing them in a large stainless steel skillet with no oil. Toast over medium-high heat, stirring occasionally, until fragrant but not smoking, 3 to 5 minutes. Lower the heat and rehydrate the chiles by adding just enough water to cover them. Bring to a simmer and cover, then remove from the heat and let steep for 10 minutes.

Transfer the chiles and their soaking liquid to a high-powered blender. Blend on high speed until nice and smooth, about 1 minute. This makes your amazing chili paste base. Set aside until ready to use.

Break down your chuck roast by cutting it into ½-inch cubes. Pat dry, then generously season with salt. Let sit at room temperature for 10 minutes before blotting dry again with paper towels.

Heat a few tablespoons of vegetable oil in a Dutch oven over medium-high heat until it just starts to give off wisps of smoke. Add half of the beef cubes and cook until browned, 1 to 1½ minutes per side. Transfer to a small sheet tray. Add the remaining beef to the sheet tray—you do not need to brown it.

Add the onion to the Dutch oven. Cook over medium heat, stirring occasionally until soft and golden, 3 to 4 minutes. Add the garlic and tomato paste, then stir to combine the ingredients. Cook until the garlic is fragrant and the vegetables are well coated by the tomato paste, about 1 minute. Add the lager and cook until the alcohol is cooked off, about 30 seconds. Then add the stock and scrape up the fond from the bottom of the pot using a wooden flat-top spoon. Add all the beef, followed by 1½ cups of the reserved chili paste. Bring to a simmer. Add the oregano, cinnamon, coriander, and allspice and 1 teaspoon pepper and stir to combine. Partially cover and simmer until the beef is tender and the liquid is thickened, anywhere from 1½ to 3 hours.

Stir in the masa harina to thicken the chili. Finally, add the lime juice and let cook for 5 more minutes to finish. Season with salt, then serve with shredded cheddar and lime wedges, or any garnishes you like!

RIB ROAST WITH YORKSHIRE PUDDING

I'm not sure whose idea it was to combine jus, beef, and airy little popovers for a celebratory (or even Sunday) dinner, but they had it figured out. More commonly known as "prime rib" here in the States, achieving a rosy, juicy roast and tall, proud popovers is relatively easy. The hardest thing to imitate at home is the little cup of mouthwatering drippings and juices, stewed and fortified into an unctuous liquid somewhere halfway between gravy and demi-glace. It's normally only possible for restaurants, whose constant and repeated roastings of giant joints of beef yield gallons of the stuff. At home, we have to be a little more resourceful: in lieu of a celebratory rack upon which to roast our beef, we sacrifice the attached rib bones to make our own devastatingly rich jus, the leftovers of which will have a tremendous impact on any number of recipes.

How I've Screwed this Up

I've made any number of roasts in my lifetime, but only recently so much as attempted to serve it with a jus. Most attempts utilizing store-bought stock would yield a watery and unsatisfying result, lacking the depth of flavor or the gelatin-laden mouthfeel of the real deal. There isn't a purchasable product on this earth that is capable of tasting the way this stuff does—it takes time and effort, and it's worth it.

Troubleshooting

MY GRAVY IS THIN.

Keep simmering! So long as you're starting off with a flavorful broth, it will reduce to a rich, even syrupy consistency. If it needs help, you can up its body with a roux (see Kitchen Glossary, page 23).

MY ROAST IS SITTING IN A POOL OF JUICES WHEN I CUT IT.

That sounds like an unrested roast—the resting after cooking is very important. When subjected to heat, the muscle fibers in beef contract, making those precious juices susceptible to being squeezed out when severed.

MY YORKIES DIDN'T RISE.

My first thought would be a cold pan—I know you never imagined you'd preheat your cupcake tin in a hot oven like a pizza stone, but a hot pan with hot fat in it is essential for a poofy popover. Yorkshire pud's rise is also aided by the overnight hang in the fridge—if you're dry-brining your roast ahead of time anyway, you may as well whip up this 5-minute batter!

MY YORKIES CAME OUT AWESOME BUT THEN THEY SUCKED.

Yorkshire puddings have an extraordinarily short shelf life, yielding a light, fluffy, crispy-chewy texture when hot and that of a frozen waffle when cold. Bake them while the roast is resting so they're ready to serve hot out of the oven!

MY YORKIES STINK.

Yorkies are a notoriously smelly breed, but excessive odor could be a sign of a minor health issue. You should only give your Yorkies a bath once every three weeks, but most important, give your Yorkies all the brushes they desire. Not only will it help cut down on unwanted odor, they'll love it (almost as much as you love them!) <3 <3

SERVES 4 TO 6

1 (about 4½-pound) bone-in ribeye roast

Kosher salt and freshly ground black pepper

Light olive oil, for coating

Reserved fat from Beef Jus (recipe follows)

3 small onions, quartered

4 medium parsnips, peeled and sliced crosswise ½-inch thick

6 medium carrots, peeled and sliced crosswise ½-inch thick

5 garlic cloves

3 to 4 rosemary sprigs

4 to 5 thyme sprigs

Beef Jus (recipe follows)

Yorkshire Pudding (recipe follows)

Cut the ribeye meat off the bones, salvaging as much meat as possible. Reserve the bones for the Beef Jus. Season the beef with 1½ tablespoons salt and 2 teaspoons pepper, then transfer to a wire rack set inside a rimmed baking sheet. Refrigerate, uncovered, for 24 to 48 hours. (This is a good time to make the Beef Jus.)

Preheat the oven to 450°F with convection (or 475°F without convection).

Remove the roast from the refrigerator and coat with olive oil. Brush the beef down with the reserved fat from the Beef Jus.

Place the onions, parsnips, carrots, garlic, rosemary, and thyme in a large roasting pan lined with aluminum foil; coat with olive oil, season with salt and pepper, and toss gently to combine. Top with a wire rack then place the roast on top. Insert a temperature probe into the thickest part of the roast. Roast for 20 to 25 minutes, until the exterior of the roast is browned, then lower the oven temperature to 325°F and continue cooking for 1 to 2 hours, until the internal temperature reaches 120°F.

Loosely tent the roast with aluminum foil while it rests for 20 to 30 minutes. (The temperature will increase to 130°F with carryover cooking.)

Strain the pan juices from the roasting pan. Set aside about ½ cup for the Yorkshire pudding recipe and add the remaining to the Beef Jus. Keep the roasted vegetables warm until ready to serve.

Serve the roast beef with the roasted vegetables, Yorkshire pudding, and Beef Jus.

BEEF JUS

Makes about 3 cups

Reserved bones from ribeye roast (see opposite page)

2 pounds oxtails, trimmed of excess fat

4 large onions, roughly chopped

6 large carrots, roughly chopped

8 celery stalks, roughly chopped

1 large parsnip, peeled and roughly chopped

Olive oil, for coating

4 to 5 fresh thyme sprigs

6 to 8 fresh parsley stems

2 bay leaves

1 teaspoon whole black peppercorns

Preheat the oven to 400°F.

On a rimmed baking sheet, combine the bones, oxtails, and half each of the onions, carrots, celery, and parsnip; coat thoroughly with olive oil. Roast for 30 to 40 minutes, until the oxtails are well browned and the vegetables just start to brown. Transfer to a large stockpot. Add the thyme, parsley, bay leaves, peppercorns, and remaining onions, carrots, celery, and parsnip. Add just enough water to cover everything. Bring to a simmer. Then cover and continue cooking over medium-low heat until the stock is dark and flavorful, 12 to 18 hours.

Skim off any excess fat from the surface of the jus and reserve it for brushing onto the roast. Bring the stock to a boil and continue cooking, uncovered, over medium-high heat until it has reduced, 1 to 2 hours.

YORKSHIRE PUDDING

Makes 12

115 grams all-purpose flour

¾ teaspoon kosher salt

3 large eggs

250 grams whole milk

About ½ cup reserved beef drippings (from Rib Roast, opposite page) or beef tallow

In a large bowl, combine the flour and salt and whisk together.

In another bowl, whisk the eggs with the milk. Slowly pour into the dry ingredients while whisking constantly. Cover and refrigerate the batter overnight.

About 2 hours before baking, remove the batter from the refrigerator and let it come to room temperature.

Meanwhile, preheat the oven to 400°F with convection (or 425°F without convection).

Pour the reserved beef drippings or beef tallow into a small saucepan. Heat the drippings until liquid (if necessary).

Pour 1 to 2 teaspoons of the beef drippings or beef tallow into each well of a standard muffin tin or Yorkshire pudding tin. Transfer to the oven and heat for 3 to 4 minutes.

Carefully, remove the tin from the oven and fill each well about halfway with the batter. Immediately return the tin to the oven and bake for 18 to 22 minutes, until the Yorkshire puddings are puffed and golden brown. Serve immediately.

REVERSE-SEARED (AND FORWARD-SEARED) PORTERHOUSE WITH COMPOUND BUTTER

While the cut in question per this recipe's depiction may be a porterhouse, the reverse sear is really a method for the very-thick-cut steak of your choice, anything towering over 1½ inches high. Here's the idea: you want your steak cooked medium-rare, as evenly as possible, with a pronounced salty crust on the outside, right? The reverse sear aims to accomplish this by gently, gradually cooking the steak at a balmy 225°F. Then, once the desired internal temperature is approached, the very hottest source of heat available (maxed-out grill, broiler, or cast-iron pan) is used to blast a deep, brown crust onto the exterior of the meat, insulating its delicate interior from the angry flames. Then, turned tawny with fat and fire, it's sliced into steakhouse slabs and finished with butter mashed with fresh herbs and garlic. The Hollywood megastar helming this picture is the porterhouse steak, a diabolical combination of both a New York strip and tenderloin (filet mignon), each flanking a decidedly T-shaped bone. Outlandishly celebratory and decadently carnivorous, it's not for the faint of heart—quite literally—being, after all, one of the most unhealthy foods rubbed down in another.

Standard steak procedure dictates a *minimum* 10 minute rest post heat and preslice, but this is rendered less necessary with a reverse sear. Since the meat is cooked slowly, the muscle fibers are less contracted, and less juice ends up on your plate after a ruddy good fork-and-knifing. Still, let it rest a little at least, it's been through a lot.

How I've Screwed This Up

Here's another recipe whose origin episode I will proudly point to as one of the most public culinary missteps of my career. I suggested, maybe because I thought it was cool, that one should cook their steak to an internal doneness of 115°F, anticipating a post-rest rise up to 125°F. At this temperature, fat, collagen, and connective tissue are not yet rendered, and muscle fibers remain chewy and slippery. You see I was still in my twenties, and moreover, still in the phase of my life where I thought doing things the "right way" superseded the actual enjoyment of the thing. Don't let that happen to you, and don't cook your steaks to 115°F, unless that's really actually your thing.

Troubleshooting

MY STEAK IS OVERCOOKED.

When you're learning your way around a cut of steer, the only truly reliable way to ensure a steak's proper doneness is with a thermometer. If you're temping at the thickest part of the steak and still having problems, removing from the heat at your target temperature might be the problem; steaks rise from 5 to 15°F in the minutes after cooking, so if your aim is medium-rare, pulling it anywhere after 130°F is going to yield an undesirable result.

MY STEAK IS DRY.

Apart from overcooking, there are a couple other potential culprits in the battle against moisture loss. While the reverse-sear cooks meat in such a way that it's less necessary to wait, it's generally best practice to wait at least 10 minutes before slicing and dicing, so as to prevent moisture from being squeezed out by the still-contracting muscle fibers. If you're still having trouble, it may be the meat itself—if it's not well-marbled (a quality that grass-fed beef often lacks), even if cooked perfectly, it may unavoidably underperform.

MY STEAK IS CHEWY.
Sounds undercooked—fats only begin to liquefy and fibers tenderize around 130°F, so if you're peaking at a temperature anywhere below that, you may be in for a bad time. So-called purists may scoff, but let's face it, being into something to the point where you feel the need to enforce it for others, is frankly lame.

SERVES 2 TO 4

1 tablespoon kosher salt

1 tablespoon coarsely ground black pepper

1 porterhouse steak, at least 1½-inches thick (1 to 2 pounds), rear-cut

2 tablespoons high smoke-point oil (such as vegetable, canola, peanut, or grapeseed)

Fuckall else

Fine, ¼ cup Compound Butter (page 287), at room temperature

In a small bowl, combine the salt and pepper. Generously sprinkle over the porterhouse, coating all sides. Transfer to a wire rack set inside a rimmed baking sheet and refrigerate, uncovered, until slightly darkened and dried, 1 to 2 days.

(**NOTE:** *If you don't have time, salt and pepper the steak and allow it to rest at room temperature for at least 1 hour before cooking.*)

Preheat the oven to 225°F.

IF USING THE REVERSE-SEARED METHOD: Remove the rack and wipe up any drippings, line the baking sheet with aluminum foil, and replace the rack and steak. Insert a temperature probe into the thickest part of the steak, near to but not touching the bone. Place in the oven for anywhere from 45 to 90 minutes, depending on your steak's thickness, until the steak registers 130°F.

In a large cast-iron skillet, heat the oil over high heat until visible wisps of smoke rise off it, 1 to 3 minutes. Remove the steak from the oven, remove the temperature probe, and press down evenly into the preheated oil. Don't be afraid to move the steak around a bit initially to ensure it's evenly coated in oil and in complete contact with the cooking surface, but allow the steak to sear, undisturbed, until deeply browned but not blackened, 1 to 3 minutes. Flip the steak and press down once again, tilting the pan and moving the oil to develop an even crust, an additional 1 to 3 minutes. Once well-browned, turn the steak on its side (the New York strip side) until the fat cap is browned and gelatinized, 1 to 2 minutes. Remove the steak to a carving board to rest for 5 minutes.

IF USING THE FORWARD-SEARED METHOD: In a large cast-iron skillet, heat the oil over high heat until visible wisps of smoke rise off it, 1 to 3 minutes. Pat the porterhouse dry if there's any moisture, lift and tilt the skillet so that the oil covers it evenly, and press the porterhouse down onto it to ensure even browning. Sear, undisturbed, until a deep brown crust forms, 2 to 4 minutes. If browning unevenly, lift and swirl the oil, replacing the steak and continuing to sear. Flip once browned and repeat on the other side until evenly browned, 2 to 4 minutes.

Stand the steak in the center of the pan on the flat back of the T-bone if you're able (use a halved onion to prop it up if necessary) and insert a temperature probe into the thickest part of the steak, near to but not touching the bone. Place in the oven for anywhere from 20 to 45 minutes, depending on your steak's thickness, until the steak registers 130°F.

Remove the steak to a carving board to rest for at least 10 minutes.

Cut along the bone to remove the New York strip and tenderloin, serving fanned out in their original places alongside the bone. Smear compound butter across the tops of the sliced steak and serve.

BUTTER-BASTED RIBEYE

As far as red meat experiences go, I struggle to think of any more well-rounded than the ribeye. The round in the center, with balanced marbling and a reassuring firmness, provides the prototypical steakhouse experience. The cap, laden with fat and flavor, is more akin to steak-butter than actual steak, often overwhelming in its richness. The bone makes for an elegant presentation, not to mention provides some temperature protection for the more sensitive parts of the steak. Then the whole thing is held together with angelic channels of creamy fat, which if you're into eating, renders down into forkfuls of impossible unctuousness. This entire package is at first seared, then for the remainder of its cook time, manually bathed in bubbling butter. As it enjoys its requisite rest preslicing, browned butter and aromatic herbs are piled over top, pushing the levels of savory beyond federally-regulated limits. Once served whole or sliced on the bias, a final basting of butter over every last nook and cranny ensures that while your diners may not survive the meal, they will die happy.

How I've Screwed This Up

Earlier in my "foodie" days, more often than not, my secret ingredient was pretentiousness. One fateful night, after watching a learned eater order his steak "black and blue, just touched by the grill," I decided that that was the law. Medium-rare no longer occurred at 130 to 140°F; anything that dared trip over 120°F became cafeteria lunchmeat in my mind. Many years of eating steaks has finally taught me the truth, that like absurdly spicy wings or "kobe burgers," rare steaks are little more than posturing. Beef fat does not render and muscle fibers do not tenderize below 130°F, so any steak served under medium-rare will retain its original slippery, chewy texture. It took me decades to learn, but contrary to popular belief, eating undercooked steak does not make you cool.

Troubleshooting

MY BUTTER BURNED.
Too much heat—you gotta turn things down just before adding the butter so that it slowly browns, fries the herbs, and continues to cook the steak without turning black and acrid. It's a balancing act, but one worth pulling off.

MY STEAK IS UNDERCOOKED.
Not measuring the temperature of the steak at its thickest point and pulling the steak too early are the usual suspects when performing the autopsy on an undercooked steak.

MY STEAK IS OVERCOOKED.
Steaks, when resting, can rise 10°F as the temperatures throughout the meat equalize—so you might want to pull your steak a minute *before* it temps as "done," so that it can come up to your desired temperature during the rest.

I couldn't get my steak up to temp before the butter burned. Spend more time in the searing stage of cooking, flipping the steak frequently and pressing its sides into the pan. It'll need less time in the butter and develop a better crust!

SERVES 2 TO 4

1 tablespoon kosher salt

1 tablespoon freshly ground black pepper

1 bone-in ribeye, 1- to 2-inches thick

2 tablespoons high smoke-point oil (such as vegetable, canola, peanut, or grapeseed)

4 tablespoons unsalted butter

1 fresh rosemary sprig

2 fresh thyme sprigs

4 garlic cloves, unpeeled

Extra-virgin olive oil, coarsely ground pepper, and flaky sea salt, for serving (optional)

In a small bowl, combine the kosher salt and freshly ground pepper. Generously sprinkle on the ribeye, coating all sides. Transfer to a wire rack set inside a rimmed baking sheet and refrigerate, uncovered, until slightly darkened and dried, 1 to 2 days.

(**NOTE:** *If you don't have time, salt and pepper the steak and allow it to rest at room temperature for at least 1 hour before cooking.*)

Heat the oil in a large cast-iron skillet over high heat until wisps of smoke rise off its surface. Press the steak down evenly into the oil, tilting the pan to ensure even coverage, and sear on the first side, until a deep brown crust forms, 3 to 5 minutes. Flip the steak, once again tilting the pan to evenly cover it with fat before pressing the steak down into it. Let the steak sear for another 3 to 5 minutes before reducing the heat to medium, and once the pan has cooled slightly, add the butter, rosemary, thyme, and garlic all on the same side of the pan. Tilt the pan so that the butter melts together with the herbs and garlic, and as it begins to bubble, spoon it over the steak repeatedly. Continue basting the steak with butter, moving the pan closer to and away from the heat source, so that the butter bubbles but doesn't scorch. Flip the steak if necessary, repeating the process until it registers 130°F at its thickest point, 4 to 6 minutes.

Remove the steak to a warmed plate, pour the contents of the pan over the top, and allow the steak to rest for 10 minutes. Meanwhile, remove the garlic cloves and peel them, saving one and snacking on the rest.

Once the steak is rested, rub down its surface with the fried garlic clove. Slice and serve as desired, pouring browned butter again over the slices. If desired, drizzle with extra-virgin olive oil and sprinkle with coarsely ground pepper and flaky sea salt.

BEEF TENDERLOIN
WITH SAUCES

Troubleshooting

See Reverse-Seared (and Forward-Seared) Porterhouse with Compound Butter (page 394)

SERVES 4

1 (1½- to 2-pounds)
beef tenderloin roast
(chateaubriand), trimmed of fat
and silver skin

Kosher salt and freshly ground
black pepper

2 tablespoons high smoke-point
oil (such as vegetable, canola,
peanut, or grapeseed), plus more
as needed

Chimichurri (recipe follows) or
1 cup Demi-Glace (page 346) or
1 cup Fig-Port Sauce (page 292),
for serving

Flaky sea salt and extra-virgin
olive oil, for garnish

Generously sprinkle the tenderloin all over with 1 tablespoon kosher salt and 1 tablespoon pepper. Wrap tightly in plastic wrap and refrigerate overnight, or let rest at room temperature for at least 1 hour.

If the tenderloin is unevenly shaped, tie it with butcher's twine at 1- to 2-inch intervals, more tightly toward the thicker end so as to compress it. Leave twine on throughout the cooking process then remove before serving.

Preheat the oven to 225°F (preferably with convection or 250°F without convection).

Unwrap the roast and insert a temperature probe into the thickest part. Heat the oil in a cast-iron skillet over high heat until nearly smoking, 2 to 3 minutes. Pat the roast dry and press into the pan, swirling around any oil to ensure that it's evenly coated. Sear the roast until evenly browned (including the ends), 1 to 3 minutes per side, adding more oil as necessary. Transfer the roast to a wire rack set inside a rimmed baking sheet. Roast in the oven until the probe reads 130°F, 30 to 45 minutes depending the size.

Remove from the oven and allow the roast to rest for at least 15 minutes, uncovered. Slice the roast, across the grain, into 3 to 5 pieces, and arrange on a serving platter. Drizzle with your sauce of choice and garnish with flaky sea salt, freshly ground pepper, and extra-virgin olive oil.

CHIMICHURRI

Makes about ¾ cup

1 Fresno chile, seeded and roughly chopped

2 tablespoons red wine vinegar

⅓ cup extra-virgin olive oil

1 cup fresh cilantro leaves, (or parsley, if you're like me)

4 garlic cloves, smashed

1 tablespoon fresh oregano leaves

Kosher salt and freshly ground black pepper

In a food processor, combine the Fresno chile, vinegar, oil, cilantro, garlic, and oregano. Pulse together until a rough sauce forms, 15 to 20 pulses. Season with salt and pepper. Serve immediately.

Note: *If you want a saucier chimichurri, try slowly streaming the olive oil in through the food processor while it runs to emulsify together the oil and vinegar into a bright green dressing.*

CHAPTER 10

DESSERTS

Desserts exist for one reason, and one reason only: pleasure. Desserts almost entirely derive their pleasure giving qualities from a singular ingredient, one which sparks delight in the hearts of children and raises blood pressure in the hearts of adults. The much-maligned, often imitated, not-yet replicated, synapse-firing sniper rifle aimed squarely at your brain's pleasure center: processed sugar. Processed sugar is, without a doubt, bad for you. If you haven't noticed yet, I harbor something of a romance for the small joys in life that slowly kill you, and sugar is perhaps the greatest example. Ubiquitous and inexpensive, sugar represents an incredible calorie-per-dollar value, and without any of the pesky nutrients normally plaguing things that qualify as food. In that sense, sugar is much less of a dichotomy than other unhealthy foods: its sole purpose is to make things look, feel, and above all, taste spectacular. The mountains of dirty-white crystals proudly eschew vitamins or minerals, offer little-to-no redeeming health benefits, and slowly but surely poison you into an ever earlier grave. It's even so cruel as to stimulate the appetite of the already-satiated, tricking their brains into feeling ready for just a few more bites, even after a gargantuan meal. A bowl of ice cream after burgers and hot dogs, a shiny chocolate gateau after a ten-course tasting menu, a slice of birthday cake after the sushi conveyor belt—there's always, somehow, room for dessert. So eat an apple and get those ten thousand steps in tomorrow, because tonight, we're making brownies.

WHAT IS DESSERT? Aww, we're doing it one last time. Dessert is the actual embodiment of sin, a self-indulgence with no redeeming or functional value. A perfect example of our bodies' and brains' inability to fight our baser instincts, powerless to resist the temptation of meritless and unnecessary energy. Personally, I'm a chocolate and peanut butter guy.

KOSHER SALT AS USUAL? For this book, yeah—and I'll be sure to include that fact in the recipe. For most other books, if you just see the word "salt", assume it's table salt. Lots of the sweets in this chapter (and most others) can be salted after the fact, and if that option is available, it might be the way to go. I'd rather slightly undersalt a cookie and top it with crunchy flakes of finishing salt, for example.

DO I NEED A SCALE? Honestly, yes. Scales are a physically small, financially inexpensive, spiritually pure, direct investment into the quality of your baked goods. Baking is often referred to as a science, and with good reason: minute discrepancies in a cup-measured cup of flour can famously fuck up cake crumbs and donut diameters alike. You may notice, however, that we usually measure salt in tea- or tablespoons—that's because, unless you have an unusually accurate (drugs) scale, you can very easily over- or undersalt your recipe if measured by weight.

SHOULD I USE PIE WEIGHTS? I'm sorry this has to happen here, but I need to tell you that you've been lied to. By whom? By the pie weight people. You might've received a flimsy plastic box of these wannabe whiskey stones* from a secret Santa or overt Easter bunny, and frankly, they're not worth their weight in pie weights. More than being ineffective, they've misled the piemaking public into believing that two dozen clay beads are going to live up to their name and effectively secure a pie crust in place during its first naked bake ("blind bake"). As a result, for the better part of my and many others' lives, these impotent balls or their equal weight in beans have haplessly allowed our crusts to shrink, leak, and collapse. It wasn't until like, last year that I finally learned how to make a proper pie crust: line the thing with foil and fill it with as much sugar or as many beans as it will safely contain. This securely holds the crust in place, preventing it from even thinking about shrinking, and producing a shell that's as neat as a pin, round as a nickel, and crisp as a chip. Then, if you're anything like me, you'll think of all your past crusts and feel the sting of tears in your eyes, mourning what's lost, but wiser for what's to come.

I'M BAD AT BAKING. No you're not. Baking is bad at *you*. That didn't work, hang on—I don't know, baking is fucking hard. Like any skill, it's honed by practice and repetition, and you're probably not going to nail everything right out of the gate. Precise measurement and a functional understanding of different ingredients' roles are both paramount to a successful bake, two things I'll hurriedly admit I'm no good at. But I can tell you that this time five years ago, the prospect of seeking a particular texture in brownies was an entirely inaccessible concept to me—now, I'm proffering three such recipes in print, and you're reading about it right now. So just remember that things can get better.

*Whiskey stones are equally worthless.

MASTER COOKIE DOUGH

This recipe's name, derived from the Master Sword of Nintendo's Zelda franchise of video games, offers its same balance of agility and versatility in mixed fantasy combat. Moreover, it offers one of the more customizable and reliably awesome medium format cookie experiences, the lavalike dough forming a wrinkly caramelized shell around a molten interior, and to a user-defined degree depending upon its size. Browned butter emphasizes the toasty, savory sides of sweetness, and refrigerating the dough further deepens the cookie's complexity as moisture evaporates and flavor compounds meld. Toward its conclusion, however, the more observant recipe follower might notice that in lieu of anything so stoically familiar as chocolate-style chips or varied nuts, we've called for twelve to sixteen ounces of "stuff." No, we are not referring to the electric-white layer of crystalline sugar paste sandwiched between the wafers of an Oreo—though we may be referring to Oreos themselves. You see, "stuff" can be whatever you want it to be. Should chocolate chips or walnuts be a part of that "stuff"? Absolutely. Should chopped chocolate, pecans, macadamias, or even something crazy like white chocolate? Go wild. Should candied peanuts, toasted oatmeal, crushed candy bars, toffee bits, caramel popcorn, kettle chips, raisins, craisins, blaisins (dried blueberries), yogurt pretzels, breakfast cereal, movie theater snacks, sprinkles, marshmallows, toasted coconut flakes, candied pineapple, and of course, chopped up Oreos—all at once? Let your petulant, confused, overexcited inner child-monster go absolutely apeshit with the mix-ins, and get ready to be the most popular kid in cookie class.

How I've Screwed This Up

My story with cookies is a long one, stretching back to my very earliest memories, so classic that they practically feel invented. In spite of doing little more than spilling my mother's carefully measured ingredients and forgetting to set a timer, I'm pretty sure that the exact words "Look everyone, Andy made cookies!", "All by myself!", and "Wow, they're perfect, we got a baker on our hands!" were said aloud, and on more than one occasion during my preschool career. All that is to say, my perfect-cookie-streak came to a screeching halt when she succumbed to her third bout with breast cancer. In the years after, I kept making the recipe off the back of the bag, albeit to a far more inaccurate and imprecise extent. Some blew up like softballs, others melted into pools, but every once in a while, they'd come out a little like they used to. When they did, I couldn't help but feel the warmth still radiating from my mother's oven, hearing its metal crackle and creak and yawn, even long after its flame was extinguished. After years of practicing on my own, I don't screw up cookies as often as I used to, and usually when I do, it's because I still forget to set a timer. Mine are bigger, more complex, and labor intensive—nothing like the ones in my fading memory—but I still smile sometimes when the blast of heat from my own creaky oven yields a perfect batch. I never could get them to come out right without my mother's help. To this day, I still can't.

Troubleshooting

MUFFLED SNIFFLES Are—are you crying?

SNIFF NO, YOU ARE. I mean, it's okay to cry, you don't have to be emb

NO, I MEAN YOU'RE LITERALLY CRYING RIGHT NOW, YOU'RE THE ONE WHO'S WRITING THIS. Oh—I suppose you're right. I'm actually baking cookies right now, as I'm writing this. This has been a healing headnote to write.

WHEW, SAME. OKAY, SHOULD WE GET DOWN TO BUSINESS? Let's do it!

MY COOKIES CAME OUT FLAT. This could be caused by a number of things: if the edges are oily and darken quickly, I'm guessing the dough wasn't cold enough going into the oven (and the oven may be too hot). If they're pooling out into even, soft-looking rounds, there may not be enough baking powder—or more insidious still, the baking powder may no longer be active—replace baking powder every year!

MY COOKIES ARE BURNT ON THE BOTTOM AND RAW ON THE TOP. These cookies like to live in the lower third of the oven, but if you've got them camping out all the way on the bottom rack, your oven's heating element is likely blasting them with hellfire from below. Move them up a notch!

MY COOKIES ARE DARK BUT SOFT. Sounds like either the rack is too high or the oven is too hot—cookies alone are reason enough to buy an $8.99 oven thermometer, if just to see just how criminally inaccurate yours is.

MY COOKIES FALL APART. Contrary to the vibes of this recipe's headnote, there is such a thing as too many mix-ins. Depending on their sizes and ratios, they may prove too much for a cookie's delicate structural integrity—so either cut back or run it through a stand mixer with the paddle attachment, grinding all those goodies into more manageable morsels.

NOTE: To yield 225 g of browned butter, start with 282g or 2½ sticks of unsalted butter, as water weight is lost in the browning process.

Classic Cookie Dough

MAKES 12 TO 18 COOKIES

225 grams (about 1 cup), unsalted butter, room temperature

276 grams light brown sugar

128 grams (2/3 cup) granulated sugar

2 large eggs, cold

326 grams all-purpose flour

1 tablespoon kosher salt

1/2 teaspoon baking soda

1/2 teaspoon baking powder

1 tablespoon finely ground coffee

12 to 16 ounces of "stuff" (see headnote, page 406)

In a stand mixer fitted with the paddle attachment, combine the browned butter, brown sugar, and granulated sugar. Begin creaming at medium-high speed. Continue mixing until the butter becomes soft, aerated, and fully combined with the sugars, 1 to 3 minutes. Scrape down the sides of the bowl to make sure the mixture is homogeneous.

Start adding the eggs, one at a time, and mix thoroughly, scraping down the bowl after each addition.

In a medium bowl, combine the flour, salt, baking soda, baking powder, and ground coffee. Whisk to evenly distribute the ingredients. Add all at once to the butter mixture then mix at low speed until the batter is just combined. Overmixing the dough at this stage can result in unwanted gluten development.

Combine the dough with the mix-ins of your choice. Once again, avoid overmixing the dough. Spray a large, rimmed baking sheet with nonstick spray and line with parchment paper. Scoop the dough into 2 ounce mounds using an ice cream scoop, cover with plastic wrap, and refrigerate the dough for at least 1 hour, ideally up to 3 days.

BAKING DIRECTIONS: Preheat the oven to 375°F.

Remove dough from the refrigerator, uncover, and arrange eight dough balls on the baking sheet with room to spread.

Bake 18 to 20 minutes, rotating the pan halfway through, until the cookies are golden brown and set around the edges. Repeat with remaining cookies.

Allow the cookies to cool on the baking sheet for 5 minutes then transfer them to a wire rack. Enjoy warm or at room temperature.

Chocolate Cookie Dough

MAKES 12 TO 18 COOKIES

225 grams (about 1 cup), unsalted butter, room temperature

276 grams light brown sugar

128 grams granulated sugar

2 large eggs, cold

213 grams all-purpose flour

113 grams Dutch-processed cocoa powder

1 tablespoon kosher salt

1 teaspoon instant espresso powder

½ teaspoon baking soda

12 to 16 ounces of "stuff" (see headnote, page 406)

In a stand mixer fitted with the paddle attachment, combine the browned butter, brown sugar, and granulated sugar. Begin creaming at medium-high speed. Continue mixing until the butter becomes soft, aerated, and fully combined with the sugars, 5 to 6 minutes. Scrape down the sides of the bowl to make sure the mixture is homogeneous.

Start adding the eggs, one at a time, and mix thoroughly, scraping down the bowl after each addition.

In a medium bowl, combine the flour, cocoa powder, salt, espresso powder, and baking soda. Whisk to evenly distribute the ingredients. Add all at once to the butter mixture then mix at low speed until the batter is just combined. Overmixing the dough at this stage can result in unwanted gluten development.

Combine the dough with the mix-ins of your choice. Refrigerate the dough for at least 1 hour, up to 3 days.

BAKING DIRECTIONS: See Classic Cookie Dough, opposite page.

TRES LECHES CAKE

"Cake soak," apart from being a great name for something from Bath & Body Works, is an effective and time-tested way for making cakes moist. Syrups, alcohols, citrus, cider—any number of luscious liquids can be put to delicious use—but few cakes go to the lengths of using three at once. Tres leches is just such a cake, combining three different kinds of milk (in case you really, *really* don't speak Spanish) to bolster both flavor and texture. The result is so sweet and decadent that, unlike virtually any other cake, it does away with the need for frosting. Given that frosting is often the only reason to even consider eating cake, it's no wonder that tres leches cake is one of the pinnacle cake-alone eating experiences: the hardy sponge can stand up to and retain its structure despite being soaked overnight in a combination of whole, sweetened condensed, and evaporated milk. The result is a cake that eats more like a slice of overripe honeybell orange than it does a slice of cake, each cell simultaneously bursting with moisture as its walls are breached with every chew. Whipped cream becomes a necessary source of stability and grounding, potentially even between layers, of which I recommend you limit yourself; all that moisture and/or underwhipped cream can quickly cause a cakey landslide.

How I've Screwed This Up

This is one of the rare episodes of *Basics* that required not one, not two, not three, but four reshoots, due to everything from sliding layers to collapsing cakes to failing memory cards. At the time, I was listening extensively to Kurt Vile, so I couldn't help but subconsciously make the connection to his music and my cursed cake, and to this day I have trouble cooking while listening to one of my favorite artists as a result.

Troubleshooting

MY CAKE FELL APART. While it's difficult to oversaturate a tres leches cake, it is possible—other factors could include your cake's thickness, gluten development, or doneness. If any of the above seemed out of whack during preparation, it may well have been the culprit in any resultant structural failures.

MY WHIPPED CREAM SLID OFF THE CAKE. Make sure everything's completely cool before frosting—whipped cream can also be bolstered with gelatin or a hit of cream cheese to make it more structurally sound.

DO I REALLY HAVE TO MAKE MY OWN DULCE DE LECHE? Absolutely not! Canned dulce de leche is essentially just cooked sweetened condensed milk (another way to make it yourself), and while not quite as good as homemade, still tastes good enough to pour on ice cream and dip French fries in.

FRENCH FRIES? Yeah, try it.

SOUNDS WEIRD. ALSO, MY CAKE IS DRY. It really, really oughtn't be. Mas leche, I say!

SERVES 8 TO 10

Cake

Nonstick cooking spray

5 large eggs, separated

198 grams sugar

128 grams all-purpose flour

1½ teaspoons baking powder

½ teaspoon kosher salt

1 teaspoon pure vanilla extract

78 grams whole milk

Tres Leches Soak

1 (14-ounce) can sweetened condensed milk

1 (12-ounce) can evaporated milk

113 grams whole milk

Dulce de Leche

907 grams whole milk

227 grams sugar

¼ teaspoon baking soda

Whipped Cream

227 grams heavy cream, cold

2 tablespoons powdered sugar

1 teaspoon pure vanilla extract

Garnish

8 ounces strawberries, thinly sliced

MAKE THE CAKE: Preheat the oven to 350°F. Spray a 9-inch round cake pan with nonstick spray and line with a round of parchment paper on the bottom.

In a stand mixer fitted with the whisk attachment, whip the egg whites on medium-high speed until frothy. With the machine running, slowly pour in 85 grams of the sugar. Increase the speed to high and continue whipping until the meringue reaches stiff peaks, 3 to 4 minutes. Transfer to another bowl; clean and dry the stand mixer bowl.

In the stand mixer fitted with the paddle attachment, beat the egg yolks with the remaining 113 grams sugar. Mix on medium speed until the yolks are pale, smooth, and fluffy, about 2 minutes.

In a separate medium bowl, combine the flour, baking powder, and salt. Whisk to combine.

Add the vanilla and milk to the egg yolk mixture. Mix on medium speed until completely combined. Next, add the dry ingredients and mix on medium speed until completely combined.

Add about one-third of the meringue to the batter and fold in with a rubber spatula until mostly incorporated. Add the remaining meringue and fold to combine, taking care to only fold until the batter is homogeneous to prevent deflating the batter. Pour into the prepared cake pan.

Bake 25 to 35 minutes, until a cake tester comes out clean.

MEANWHILE, PREPARE THE TRES LECHES SOAK: In a medium bowl, combine the sweetened condensed milk, evaporated milk, and whole milk. Whisk to combine, then refrigerate until ready to use.

Once the cake is done, remove it from the oven and allow it to cool for 20 minutes.

Pierce the slightly cooled cake with a fork all over the surface. Pour the prepared tres leches soak over the cake. You may have to add the soak in batches, waiting until absorbed before adding the next batch.

Cover the cake and refrigerate for at least 6 hours, preferably overnight.

MEANWHILE, MAKE THE DULCE DE LECHE: In a medium saucepan, combine the milk, sugar, and baking soda. Stir gently to combine over medium heat until it comes to a rolling boil. Lower the heat to a simmer and cook, whisking frequently to prevent scorching, until a deep golden brown, about 90 minutes. Strain through a fine-mesh sieve and allow to cool at room temperature for at least 1 hour.

JUST BEFORE ASSEMBLING THE CAKE, MAKE THE WHIPPED CREAM: In a stand mixer fitted with the whisk attachment, combine the heavy cream, powdered sugar, and vanilla extract. Whip at medium speed until medium-stiff peaks form. Use immediately.

To assemble the cake, invert the cake pan onto a cake turner or serving plate. Some of the extra soak may leak out, but that's okay, most of the liquid will have already been absorbed by the cake. Cover the cake on all sides with the Whipped Cream, or alternatively, for a more rustic approach, just pile the whipped cream on top of the cake.

Drizzle the top of the cake with the Dulce de Leche and arrange the strawberries in a decorative pattern around the cake.

Serve immediately or refrigerate for up to 2 hours; after that the whipped cream will start to deflate.

BOURBON APPLE PIE

It's easy to make tasty apple pie filling, especially when you're using bourbon. The real challenge, as you may have guessed, lies in the crust—made all the more extrachallenging with a moist filling and no blind bake (par-baking the pie crust before filling). Being compressed under a mountain of stewing apples leaves little room for flaky pastry to form, usually resulting in a descriptor that's unpleasant no matter what the context: a soggy bottom. Baking the pie on a pizza stone solves the problem by blasting the pastry with heat from below, so it begins to cook before the apples, browning the bottom and sealing in all the moisture that's to come. Turbinado sugar and plenty of egg wash gives the pie an almost antique aesthetic, evoking memories of the American dream that you didn't even know you had. As such, now's the time to bust out grandma's pie dish: normally crusts tend to slip down the smooth surface of a glass dish, but with a closed lattice top, the pastry has nowhere to go but around your apples as intended.

How I've Screwed This Up

On my Pies episode of *Basics*, I secretly (read: accidentally) made a single batch of pie dough for a lattice crust, and to compensate, rolled all the dough thin enough to accommodate both the shell and decorative interlacing. The result was a pie crust so thin that the edges of the lattice sunk into the blueberry filling below, creating a sort of pie-island (pieland). I was too tired to make a fourth pie crust, so I cut my losses and published the episode with a similar warning: make enough pie crust.

Troubleshooting

MY FILLING IS WATERY. Try adding a bit more flour next time, which helps take the filling from ooey to gooey.

MY FILLING IS DRY. I think the only thing we can blame this on is the apples—there should be almost too much moisture for your pie crust to contend with, so a dry pie likely came from apples past their prime. Or using Red Delicious apples, which are maybe the biggest misnomer in the apple biz.

MY PIE CRUST IS FLABBY. With a lattice crust, there's not much you can do about a somewhat soggy bottom, especially with a filling as soggy as apple pie. Baking the pie on a pizza stone, however, blasts its bottom with more heat, helping to brown it before it absorbs too much moisture. If you really, really want a crispy crust, do away with the lattice and blind bake it per the quiche crust in Chapter 4 (see page 182).

MY PIE CRUST IS CRUMBLY. Sounds like the butter was either over incorporated or the dough was overworked—either way, little packets of butter weren't allowed to laminate throughout the dough as it came together, and flakes foiled from forming.

MY PIE CRUST LEAKED ALL ITS BUTTER. It may not have been properly chilled immediately before the baking process, each step of which is crucial for preserving the butter's solvency. If it goes into the oven too warm, it melts too quickly, and leaks right out of your dough (just like Pain au Chocolat, page 432).

I LEFT MY PIE OUT TO COOL ON THE WINDOWSILL AND NEIGHBORHOOD YOUTHS MADE OFF WITH IT. Brandishing a blunderbuss ought to scare off any pesky pie-poachers!

MAKES ONE 9-INCH DOUBLE-CRUST PIE

Pie Dough (recipe follows)

3 pounds baking apples of choice (e.g. Granny Smith, Honeycrisp, Pink Lady)

¾ cup granulated sugar

2 tablespoons all-purpose flour

1 teaspoon ground cinnamon

½ teaspoon kosher salt

¼ teaspoon ground allspice

¼ teaspoon freshly grated nutmeg

¼ teaspoon ground ginger
1 tablespoon bourbon

1 tablespoon fresh lemon juice

Egg Wash (see page 64)

Turbinado sugar, for sprinkling (optional)

Roll out each disk of pie dough to a round, about 11 to 12 inches in diameter and ⅙- to ¼-inch thick.

Line a deep 9-inch pie dish with one of the dough rounds, making sure it lies flat in the dish. Wrinkles in the dough will cause it to cook unevenly. Transfer the remaining dough round to a sheet of parchment paper and keep refrigerated until ready to use. Crimp or fold the excess dough around the rim of the pie dish. If the dough gets too soft, stick it back into the refrigerator for 10 minutes, then resume the process.

Refrigerate the lined pie dish for at least 30 minutes, up to 2 hours.

Peel and core the apples, then slice in half lengthwise; slice ¼-inch thick lengthwise. Transfer to a large bowl.

In a small bowl, whisk together the granulated sugar, flour, cinnamon, salt, allspice, nutmeg, and ginger. Add the bourbon and lemon juice and stir to combine. Pour over the apples and fold, using a rubber spatula, to combine.

Transfer the apple pie filling to the lined pie dish then top with the second dough round. Cut two to four 1-inch slits in the top crust to release steam. Alternatively, top the pie with a lattice crust by cutting varying size widths of pie dough, weaving them together to form a dough net.

Crimp the edge all around to seal, then trim off the excess dough around the edge of the dish.

Refrigerate for 20 to 30 minutes before baking.

Meanwhile, place an aluminum foil wrapped pizza stone on the middle rack of the oven and preheat to 500°F.

Just before baking, brush the entire exposed crust with Egg Wash, and, if desired, sprinkle turbinado sugar on top for extra crunch.

Transfer the pie to the pizza stone and reduce the oven temperature to 400°F. Bake for 45 to 60 minutes, until the filling is bubbling (as seen through the slits in the pie crust) and the crust is a deep golden brown. If the pie crust is browning too quickly, cover the top (or just the edges, if necessary) with aluminum foil.

Allow the pie to cool for at least 2 hours before serving.

PIE DOUGH

*Makes enough for two
9-inch pies*

**340 grams all-purpose flour,
plus more for dusting**

**226 grams (2 sticks) unsalted
butter, cubed and chilled**

2 teaspoons kosher salt

80 to 110 grams ice water

In a stand mixer fitted with the paddle attachment, combine the flour, butter, and salt. Mix on medium-low speed until the butter pieces are the size of blueberries. Add 80 grams of the ice water and mix on medium low speed until a shaggy dough forms, about 1 minute. If the dough is too dry at this point, mix in 10 grams of ice water at a time until the dough is hydrated but not sticky.

Tip the dough out onto a clean, dry work surface and shape it into two even disks, each about 6 inches in diameter and about ½ inch thick.

Wrap each disk in plastic wrap and refrigerate for at least 30 minutes, up to 3 days.

CANNOLI

Homemade cannoli are rather a daunting prospect, combining the intimidating art of pastry and deep frying, fraught with split-open tubes, grainy filling, and sticky molds. Its reward, however, is an impressive one to present at brunch: tubes of bubbly, lard-fried pastry filled beyond their theoretical limit with a uniquely cheesy cream filling, ends uranium-tipped with chocolate, dusted in powdered sugar, and presented in a triumphant pyramid. The ends are traditionally coated in either miniature chocolate chips or chopped pistachios, but I say make a cannoli dipping station—breakfast cereals, candies, chopped up Oreos—think of the stuff you'd see at a frozen yogurt bar. You will undoubtedly catch the ire of purists, but once they have a taste of your chopped toffee bar cannoli, well, they'll probably still be mad. Just remember that poker players throw the biggest fits when they know they've been bested by a newcomer.

How I've Screwed This Up

I think I burned myself the worst when making cannoli, not from splashing nor dipping nor spilling, but from the damned cannoli mold pouring oil from its spouted hollow like wine from a decanter. Be careful when pulling these, or any tubular objects from frying oil, as they may contain a 375° surprise!

Troubleshooting

MY CANNOLI SPLIT. Yeah, this happens—make sure you're using enough egg white (but not too much!) and pressing the cannoli firmly to seal before dropping in the oil.

MY CANNOLI IS STUCK. That's the "not too much!" part to which I was referring in the previous question. It's a bit finicky, but try not to get any egg wash on the tube itself, as it will semi-permanently fuse your cannoli to its own mold. Grab your thinnest paring knife and see if you can pry the two of them apart, but always be prepared to sacrifice your first few batches.

MY CANNOLI ARE SOFT. Because of the color added to the dough by the Marsala wine, these shells may look done before they actually are. The shell should be evenly brown, without the telltale shade variances around the bubbles, indicating an uneven fry.

MY CANNOLI TASTE BURNT. Once again, the color of this dough and its intensely high frying temp can make these a bit confusing to cook. Try one or two at a time, see how long they take to cook, and give them a taste before doing the rest of the batch. Get to know your dough!

MAKES 12

48 ounces whole-milk ricotta

250 grams all-purpose flour, plus more for rolling out the dough

2 teaspoons cocoa powder

½ teaspoon instant espresso powder

155 grams powdered sugar, sifted, plus more for dusting

1½ teaspoons ground cinnamon

30 milliliters (2 tablespoons) Marsala wine

30 milliliters (2 tablespoons) white wine vinegar

2 tablespoons unsalted butter, cold

1 large whole egg plus 1 beaten large egg white

Nonstick cooking spray or vegetable oil

48 ounces (6 cups) neutral oil, such as canola, vegetable, or grapeseed

Dark chocolate, melted, for dipping

Miniature chocolate chips, for dipping

Pistachios, finely chopped, for dipping

In a fine-mesh sieve placed over a bowl, drain the ricotta in the refrigerator for 1 hour.

Meanwhile, in a food processor, combine the flour, cocoa powder, espresso powder, 30 grams of the sifted powdered sugar, and 1 teaspoon of the cinnamon. Pulse to combine. Add the Marsala and vinegar and pulse again until the mixture is nice and sandy. Add the butter and whole egg, and process until a rough ball of dough forms, about 45 seconds.

Transfer the dough to a lightly floured surface and knead until silky and elastic, 2 to 5 minutes. Wrap in plastic wrap and refrigerate for 1 hour.

Meanwhile, grease 12 cannoli molds with nonstick spray or a light coating of vegetable oil.

Remove the dough from the refrigerator and roll out on a lightly floured surface until about ¹⁄₁₆-inch thick. Using a 4-inch biscuit cutter, cut rounds and keep covered with plastic wrap.

Heat the oil in a large pot to 375°F.

MEANWHILE, SHAPE THE CANNOLI:
Place a cannoli mold into the center of 1 dough round. Lightly brush a thin layer of egg white on one edge of the dough, then wrap the edges around the cannoli mold, overlapping the brushed edge over the other edge to seal them together. Repeat with the remaining cannoli molds and dough rounds.

Working in batches, gently place the cannoli-wrapped molds into the preheated oil. Fry until golden brown, 2 to 4 minutes. Transfer to a wire rack to cool.

Remove the ricotta from the fridge and using a spoon or a spatula, press down on the ricotta to help remove as much moisture as possible. Transfer to a stand mixer fitted with the whisk attachment. Add the remaining 125 grams sifted powdered sugar and ½ teaspoon cinnamon and mix at medium speed until homogenous and smooth, 2 to 3 minutes. Transfer the cannoli cream to a piping bag.

Once the cannoli shells have cooled, remove the molds.

Dip the ends of each cannoli shell into the melted chocolate and let set on a wire rack at room temperature for 15 to 30 minutes.

Pipe the cannoli cream into each shell. Decorate as desired with miniature chocolate chips and/ or chopped pistachios. Dust with powdered sugar and serve!

CHEESECAKE

As a New Yorker (that I was born and raised in Western NY is a mere technicality), while there are apparently other styles of cheesecake, New York is obviously my favorite. Its towering form factor, ultra-smoothness, and dappled crown make it every bit as pleasurable to eat as it is to watch a fork cascade through its cumulus texture. We spice up our crust a bit for some unexpected mouth pleasures, opt for buttermilk over the usual sour cream, and add a hint of cornstarch for custard stability. Okay, so it's delicious and this is a solid recipe, standard headnote stuff—but I have an unfortunate question to pose . . .

Is cheesecake a pie?

I mean we're talking about graham cracker crust, custard-only filling—do you know many cakes like that? Sugar is very nearly the only ingredient separating this thing from qualifying as a quiche. Now, I'm not suggesting anything so radical or upsetting as renaming cheesecake to cheesepie (or dessert quiche?). Just encouraging you to question your universe.

How I've Screwed This Up

Famously, I improperly secured a springform pan when making tiramisu, sending my work plummeting to the floor with nothing but an aluminum ring in my hapless hands. I have, however, made the exact same mistake with cheesecake, resulting in a significantly messier and more frustrating cleanup. Make sure your springform is secure, and always grip it by the bottom!

Troubleshooting

MY CHEESECAKE CRACKED. Much like pumpkin pie, cracks form in cheesecake when the custard is shocked by the shockingly low temperature outside the oven. It might not rupture if you pull it at the exact right moment, but that's incredibly hard to nail—instead, crack the oven door and allow the cheesecake to cool in the oven entirely.

MY CHEESECAKE IS DENSE. New York–style is supposed to be pretty dense, but if it's more crumbly-dense, then we're looking at an overbaked cheesecake.

CAN I USE MASCARPONE? You could, but add a splash of lemon if you want to imitate its signature tang—or try a 50/50 ratio of cream cheese and mascarpone.

CAN I USE RICOTTA? While ricotta cheesecake might sound nice, in my experience it's created a grainer texture, without cream cheese's familiar flavor.

CAN I USE YELLOW AMERICAN? Obviously, yes, you can.

SERVES 8 TO 10

Crust

325 grams graham cracker crumbs

125 grams unsalted butter, melted

35 grams sugar

1½ teaspoons ground cinnamon

½ teaspoon ground cardamom

½ teaspoon kosher salt

¼ teaspoon freshly ground nutmeg

Batter

200 grams sugar

20 grams cornstarch

4 (8-ounce) packages cream cheese, at room temperature

75 grams buttermilk, at room temperature

4 large eggs, at room temperature

2 large egg yolks, at room temperature

1 tablespoon vanilla paste (or 2 teaspoons vanilla extract)

1½ teaspoons kosher salt

Preheat the oven to 350°F.

MAKE THE CRUST: In a large bowl, combine the graham cracker crumbs, butter, sugar, cinnamon, cardamom, salt, and nutmeg. Transfer to a 9-inch springform pan and press into the bottom and up the sides using the bottom of a measuring cup or ramekin. The bottom and sides of the pan should be covered in an even, thin (⅛-inch) layer of crust.

Bake until the crust is firm and crisp, 8 to 12 minutes. Remove from the oven and let the crust cool to room temperature.

Reduce the oven temperature to 300°F.

MEANWHILE, PREPARE THE CHEESECAKE BATTER: In a small bowl, combine the sugar and cornstarch and set aside.

In a stand mixer fitted with the paddle attachment, combine the cream cheese, sugar mixture, and buttermilk. Mix on medium speed until completely smooth, 2 to 3 minutes. Scrape down the sides of the bowl using a rubber spatula, then add the eggs, egg yolks, vanilla, and salt. Mix again on medium speed until just combined, 1 to 2 minutes.

Pour the batter into the prepared springform pan and give it a slight tap on the counter to pop any bubbles.

Bake for 1 hour to 1 hour 15 minutes, until the internal temperature reaches 150°F (the center will still be quite wobbly).

Turn off the oven and allow the cake to sit in the still-warm oven for 1 hour.

Open the oven door and allow the cheesecake to cool to room temperature, 1 to 2 hours.

Transfer the cheesecake to the fridge to chill overnight.

Remove the cake from the springform pan and serve. Optionally, allow the cheesecake to sit out at room temperature for 20 to 30 minutes for optimal texture.

BROWNIES

Brownies, as far as desserts go, rank among the widest spectrum of possibility for personal preference, primarily pertaining to texture. Whatever sort of brownie you like, depending on your locale, generally within a mile there exists your brownie antichrist, actively craving the things you specifically hate. If you like them cakey, they like them fudgy. If you like them melty, they like them frosted. If you like them made with chocolate and flour, they like them made with avocado and figs. Rather than try to assert a correct answer or advocate for a certain style, instead, we have chosen to embrace the differences that make us unique. As such, here you'll find three recipes for three types of brownies: fudgy, melty, and cakey.

How I've Screwed This Up

I don't know if this counts as screwing up, but any time or effort I've put into this recipe has been decisively undone by one Alvin Zhou. His brownies are, quite simply, the apex of the art form, and nothing you or I make will ever even come close. So let's collectively smile, shrug, and accept that we're not, nor will ever be, Alvin Zhou.

I'm pretty sure they're salted caramel chocolate fudge and he's just calling them brownies.

Troubleshooting

MY BROWNIES ARE— Hang on I'm gonna stop you right there. This one is crazy complex, mostly because we've got three different iterations of the recipe, each of which has its own potential troubles to shoot. So let's look at it this way: is your fudgy brownie too cakey? Cakey brownie too melty? Mudgy brownie too fakey? Take a look at both recipes, make note of their differences, and adjust accordingly—for example, cakey brownies require minimal stirring so as to not overdevelop the gluten, while fudgy brownies encourage mixing to close their texture. This way, not only can you self-diagnose any brownie boondoggles, you can save me from having to write troubleshooting for all of them! Isn't that more fun?

LAZY. Amen.

SERIOUSLY THOUGH, BROWNIES ARE TRICKY, CAN WE AT LEAST DO A LITTLE? Okay fine.

MY BROWNIES ARE TOO CAKEY. Too cakey = too much leavener = too much baking powder, baking soda, or even flour itself. While overmixing is normally associated with gluten development, it can also incorporate too much air into the batter, making the brownies light and crumbly.

MY BROWNIES ARE TOO DENSE. Too dense = not enough leavener = too much fat. They may also be undercooked, baked in too hot an oven, or under-mixed.

WOW THIS IS UNHELPFUL. Yeah I told you, there are too many x-factors across too many recipes, it's unfortunately going to take a little trial and error.

OKAY I'VE GOT AN IDEA. I'LL COMPARE MY DESIRED RECIPE AGAINST ITS OPPOSITE, SEE WHAT THE DIFFERENCES ARE, AND ADJUST ACCORDINGLY? That's what I just . . . yeah. That sounds like a plan.

Cakey Brownies

MAKES 12

Vegetable oil, for greasing

2½ cups sugar

1 cup unsalted butter, at room temperature

1¼ cups unsweetened cocoa powder

1 teaspoon kosher salt

1 teaspoon baking powder

4 large whole eggs

1 large egg white

1½ cups all-purpose flour

Chocolate Frosting (recipe follows; optional)

Sprinkles of choice (optional)

Preheat the oven to 350°F. Line a 9-by-13-inch pan with parchment paper, leaving 2 inches of overhang on the long sides, and grease the whole thing down with oil.

In a stand mixer fitted with the paddle attachment, combine the sugar and butter. Cream together on medium speed until light and fluffy, 3 to 4 minutes.

Meanwhile, in a medium bowl, whisk together the cocoa powder, salt, and baking powder. Add to the creamed butter and mix on low speed just until combined. Add the eggs, one at a time, and mix until fully incorporated after each addition. Add ½ cup water and beat on high speed until the batter is nice and creamy. Add the flour and mix on low speed just until combined. Don't overmix!

Pour batter into prepared pan and bake 25 to 30 minutes, until it resembles a cake and a toothpick inserted in the center comes out clean.

Use the parchment overhangs to lift the brownies out of the pan and allow them to cool on a wire rack for at least 1 hour.

If desired, top the brownies with Chocolate Frosting and/or sprinkles, slice, and enjoy.

CHOCOLATE FROSTING

Makes about 1½ cups

2½ cups powdered sugar, sifted

½ cup unsweetened cocoa powder

8 tablespoons (1 stick) unsalted butter, softened

⅓ to ⅔ cup milk

In a large bowl, combine the powdered sugar and cocoa powder.

Add the butter to a stand mixer fitted with the paddle attachment. Alternate adding the powdered sugar mixture and ⅓ cup of milk while mixing on medium speed until completely combined, about 1 minute. Mix in more milk if the frosting is too thick.

Reserve at room temperature until ready to serve.

Fudgy Brownies

MAKES 12

Nonstick cooking spray

⅓ cup unsweetened cocoa powder

1½ teaspoons espresso powder

¾ teaspoon kosher salt

2 ounces unsweetened chocolate, chopped

½ cup plus 2 tablespoons boiling water

4 tablespoons unsalted butter

½ cup plus 2 tablespoons vegetable oil

2 large whole eggs

2 large egg yolks

1½ teaspoons pure vanilla extract

2½ cups sugar

1¾ cups all-purpose flour

6 ounces bittersweet chocolate, chopped

Preheat the oven to 350°F. Line a 9-by-13-inch baking dish with parchment paper, leaving 2 inches of overhang on the long sides, then grease with cooking spray.

In a large heatproof bowl, combine the cocoa powder, espresso powder, salt, unsweetened chocolate, and boiling water. Stir to combine and get everything melted. While still warm, add the butter and stir until melted. Add the oil, stir again, and let cool.

Once the mixture has cooled, add the eggs and egg yolks and stir to combine. Add the vanilla extract and whisk, then add the sugar and stir to combine. Add the flour and mix thoroughly, then add the bittersweet chocolate. Stir to combine one last time.

Pour the batter into the prepared pan. Bake for 30 to 35 minutes, until a tester comes out mostly clean.

Let the brownies cool in the pan 1 hour, then use the parchment overhangs to lift them out. For improved texture, refrigerate overnight.

Serve and enjoy!

Melty Brownies

MAKES 12

½ cup vegetable oil, plus more for greasing

1¾ cups sugar

2 sticks (1 cup) unsalted butter, melted

1½ teaspoons espresso powder

1 teaspoon pure vanilla extract

4 large whole eggs

2 large egg yolks

1 cup unsweetened cocoa powder

6 ounces bittersweet chocolate, chopped

1½ cups bread flour

1 teaspoon kosher salt

1 teaspoon baking powder

Preheat the oven to 350°F. Line a 9-by-13-inch pan with parchment paper, leaving 2 inches of overhang on the long sides, and grease the whole thing down with oil.

In a large bowl, combine the sugar, butter, espresso powder, vanilla extract, whole eggs, and egg yolks. Whisk to combine. Add the cocoa powder, vegetable oil, and chocolate. Whisk to combine.

In a medium bowl, combine the bread flour, salt, and baking powder. Add to the large bowl and stir to combine. Don't worry about overmixing.

Pour the batter into the prepared pan. Bake for 25 to 35 minutes, until your desired doneness has been achieved.

Let the brownies cool in the pan 1 hour, then use the parchment overhangs to lift them out.

CHURROS

Churros, in terms of deep-fried dessert, represent a less-challenging prospect than most. In an ingenious twist on a normally fussy choux pastry dough, the sticky star-shaped snake of tempered eggs and fried flour is squoze directly into awaiting oil, forming spindly sticks of fry dough. Tossed in cinnamon sugar (and served with melted chocolate, dulce de leche, or cream cheese icing if you're feeling really nasty), they make for a perfect game-day snack, keep well for a summer picnic, or bring much-needed levity to a memorial service. Hot oil ensures that the pastries form a profound crust that stays crisp, and the more star-shaped your piping tip, the more it creates surface area for extra crunch. Make them ahead, wrap in plastic wrap once cooled, and reheat for a few minutes in a 350°F oven if you want to serve them warm for a crowd.

How I've Screwed This Up

Burst churros are my flavor of choice when screwing up churros—this usually happens from not finding the right piping tip, thinking "this one will probably work", and it inevitably not working.

Troubleshooting

MY CHURROS BURST. Your star-shaped tip isn't star-shaped enough. You need deep, cavernous ridges—too-tubular a churro makes for a ton of uncooked dough in the center, which creates excess steam, which causes the churros to burst.

MY CHURROS ARE FLACCID. Your oil ain't hot enough. I know 400°F seems hot, but these guys need as much surface area fried as quickly and hotly as possible in order to stay firm and erect. Their light, airy interiors can't support their outrageous shape, and will quickly fold if they aren't supported by an ultracrisp framework.

MY DOUGH IS STICKING TO THE SCISSORS. Try spraying down the scissors with nonstick spray or rubbing them trepidatiously with oil.

MY BATTER IS LUMPY. Sometimes it takes a second for choux to come together, just keep mixing.

STILL LUMPY—MORE LIKE CHUNKY. That's scrambled eggs, time to start over.

MAKES 12 TO 18

4 tablespoons unsalted butter

290 to 340 grams water, divided

3 tablespoons dark brown sugar

½ teaspoon kosher salt

1 cup all-purpose flour

1 large egg, beaten

Neutral oil (such as canola, vegetable, or grapeseed), for frying

1 cup sugar

1 tablespoon ground cinnamon

1 cup melted dark chocolate, for dipping

Your favorite icing, for dipping

Heavy cream, as needed

In a medium high-walled saucepan, combine the butter, 240 grams of water, brown sugar, and salt. Stir to combine. Bring the mixture to a simmer. Remove the saucepan from the heat and add the flour. Mix vigorously until a stiff ball of dough forms.

Return the saucepan to the stovetop and cook over medium heat, stirring constantly with a rubber spatula, until a thick fond covers the bottom of the saucepan. Remove from the heat, then slowly add the egg and mix slowly at first and then vigorously again until fully combined. Add enough water to form a thick paste. Transfer the dough to a pastry bag fitted with a large star tip.

Pipe the batter into 6- to 8-inch logs on a parchment-lined sheet tray. Freeze the churros for 30 minutes.

Meanwhile, add about 2 inches of oil to a large high-walled skillet and heat to 375°F. Line a large plate or sheet tray with a layer of paper towels.

Using your hands, gently lower the chilled churros into the oil. Fry, keeping the churros in motion to prevent them from sticking to one another, until all sides are evenly browned, about 2 minutes. Transfer to the prepared plate or sheet tray.

In a wide bowl, whisk together the sugar and cinnamon.

Add the still-warm churros to the cinnamon sugar and toss until fully coated.

Serve with melted dark chocolate or icing thinned with heavy cream.

PAIN AU CHOCOLAT

"Ohhh, someone thinks they're hot shit—you're gonna make croissants from scratch? You think you can do better than (or even come close to) a real pastry chef? Gonna take an awful lot of time, not to mention physical effort, all just to see your deflated little bread-turds drowning in a pool of their own leaky butter. Don't you have laundry to do, bills to pay, lawns to mow? It isn't just a waste of time, it's a borderline *irresponsible* use of your time—you could get one at the bakery and continue pretending to be an adult participating in a society. I mean, who do you think you are?"

—The Voice in your Head (right now)

Yeah, croissants are scary. Despite being made from nothing more than flour, butter, salt, and yeast, they present far more perils and potential pitfalls than your average baked good. But let's take another look at this interior monologue of yours. First, you just can't expect to make perfect croissants on your first try, it's borderline impossible—so try viewing this first round as a "practice run." Next, you seem concerned about the time—while it does indeed take a full twenty-four hours to yield a batch of dough, most of the time is spent waiting, and the vast majority of raw effort is expended early on (in making the butter square, for instance). Lastly, I wonder why you're being so hard on yourself—after all, aren't you just beating yourself up for being no good at a skill—one that you haven't even learned yet?

How I've Screwed This Up

The answer to this question depends on who you are: are you an absolute newcomer to baking (and cooking) in general? Then, while maybe I've made a couple funny-looking ones, I've had mostly successes in the world of fine French pastry. Are you a fine French pastry chef? Then I've never made anything even resembling a croissant, I'm doing it wrong, I'm saying it wrong, I'm wronging it wrong.

Troubleshooting

HOW DID YOU KNOW MY INNER VOICE IS A TOTAL DICK? Because everyone's is.

TRUE. ALSO, MY CROISSANTS BAKED UP IN A PUDDLE OF BUTTER. Unless you make the dough like, perfectly, you're gonna lose a little bit of butter. If it's really swimming in a puddle, however, two things might've happened: the dough (before proofing) may have become too warm at some point, smearing the layers during the rolling and folding process. Alternately, if the layers weren't formed evenly due to weird dough or butter distribution, it can cause massive leaks throughout your pastry.

MY CROISSANTS DIDN'T RISE. Your yeast might be dead—add a teaspoonful to a little bit of warm water and see if it starts to foam up—if not, toss it.

MY CROISSANTS STILL DIDN'T RISE. Might've been the cuts—cutting croissants is a delicate process for a reason, because smudged or pinched edges not only ruin the croissants aesthetic, they can impede its ability to rise. Make sure you're making single, clean cuts with a sharp blade!

MY CROISSANTS STILL DIDN'T RISE. Careful not to brush the cut sides of the pastry with egg wash, which can also impede rise.

MY CROISSANTS HAVE BIG GAPING HOLES IN THEIR CRUMB. The interior of a croissant should be a webby network of stretchy strands, and while the gaps between them should be sizable, they oughtn't be gaping. This usually indicates underproofed croissants.

I DON'T WANT TO PRONOUNCE "CROISSANT" LIKE THAT. Like with the "w" sound built in there?

YEAH. Well then at least we're both philistines.

MAKES 8

Dough
240 grams milk, warmed to 70° to 75°F

180 grams pastry flour

180 grams bread flour, plus more as needed

40 grams sugar

36 grams unsalted European-style butter, softened

1 tablespoon kosher salt

2 teaspoons instant dry yeast

Neutral oil (such as canola, vegetable, or grapeseed), for greasing

Butter Block
226 grams (2 sticks) unsalted European-style butter, cold

Bread flour, for dusting

Chocolate
32 chocolate batons (chocolate baking sticks)

Egg Wash
1 large egg yolk

1 tablespoon heavy cream

⅛ teaspoon kosher salt

½ teaspoon sugar

MAKE THE DOUGH: In a stand mixer fitted with the dough hook attachment, combine the milk, pastry and bread flours, the sugar, softened butter, salt, and yeast. Mix at medium speed until a shaggy dough forms, 30 seconds to 1 minute.

Transfer the dough to a lightly floured surface and knead until the dough is homogenous, 1 to 2 minutes. The dough will still be tacky but it shouldn't stick to the work surface; if it is too sticky, add more bread flour as necessary.

Transfer the dough to a lightly oiled bowl. Cover with plastic wrap and allow it to proof until about doubled in size, about 2 hours.

Turn the dough out onto a lightly floured work surface. Using a rolling pin, roll the dough out to a 8-inch-by-12-inch rectangle ½-inch thick. Wrap in plastic wrap and freeze until chilled and semifirm, 20 to 25 minutes.

MEANWHILE, MAKE THE BUTTER BLOCK: Place the sticks of butter on a lightly floured work surface. Using a French rolling pin, beat the butter until it is pliable. Fold the butter in half every time it becomes flat, adding flour as needed to prevent sticking. Repeat the beating and folding process until the butter doesn't crack when folded.

Once the butter is still cold but malleable, shape the butter block into a rectangle about half the size of the croissant dough and ½-inch thick.

Wrap the butter block in plastic wrap and refrigerate for at least 5 minutes, up to 20 minutes, then use immediately.

Place the butter block on one half of the dough. Fold the dough over the butter block and crimp the sides with your fingers to enclose the block. Wrap in plastic wrap and refrigerate for 20 minutes.

Place the dough on a lightly floured work surface with the folded edge on the left side. If you imagine the dough as a book, the spine should be on the left. Roll the dough out to a rectangle ½-inch thick, about 8- to 10-inches wide by 16- to 18-inches long.

Perform a 3-fold by folding the top section of the dough two-thirds over itself. Fold the bottom half completely over the top half. Wrap and refrigerate the dough for 20 to 30 minutes, then roll out the dough and perform two more 3-folds (refrigerating and rolling out in between each fold).

Wrap the dough tightly and refrigerate overnight.

The next day, transfer the dough to a lightly floured work surface, ensuring the folded edge (or spine) is on the left.

Roll the dough out to a rectangle ⅓-inch thick. Trim the edges of the dough to create a square that is 12-inches wide by 12-inches long.

Using a large sharp knife or a pizza cutter, slice the dough in half to create two rectangles 6-inches wide by 12-inches long. Slice each rectangle into four 3-inch by 6-inch pieces, resulting in a total of 8 dough rectangles.

Place two chocolate batons at the short end of each rectangle. Roll the croissant dough over the two batons, then place two more batons over top of the first roll. Finish by rolling the dough until a log to cover the chocolate batons and press down firmly to seal the croissant. Transfer the croissants to a parchment-lined baking sheet, making sure to place the croissants seam-side down.

Cover the baking sheet with plastic wrap and allow the croissants to proof at room temperature until puffed but not quite doubled in volume, about 2 hours. Toward the end of the proof time, preheat the oven to 400°F.

MEANWHILE, MAKE THE EGG WASH: Combine the egg yolk, heavy cream, salt, and sugar in a small bowl. Whisk to combine and reserve in the refrigerator until ready to use.

Once the croissants have proofed, brush only the tops with the egg wash. Take care not to get any egg wash on the cut sides of the croissants, which will inhibit proper rise.

Bake for 10 minutes, then reduce the oven temperature to 375°F and bake for an additional 10 to 15 minutes, until the internal temperature of the croissants reaches 210°F.

Remove the croissants from the oven, transfer to a wire rack and allow to cool for 15 to 20 minutes before enjoying!

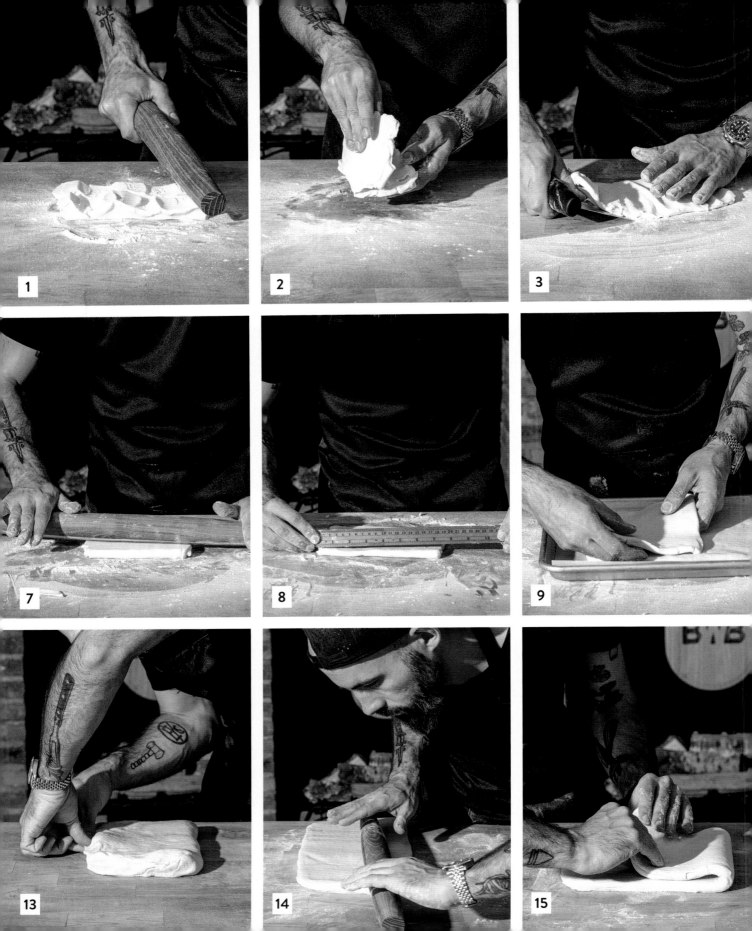

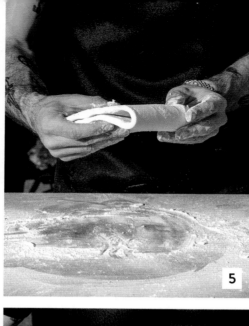

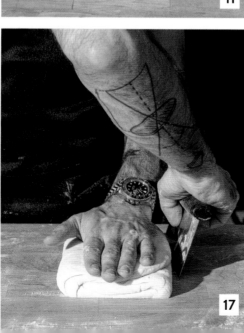

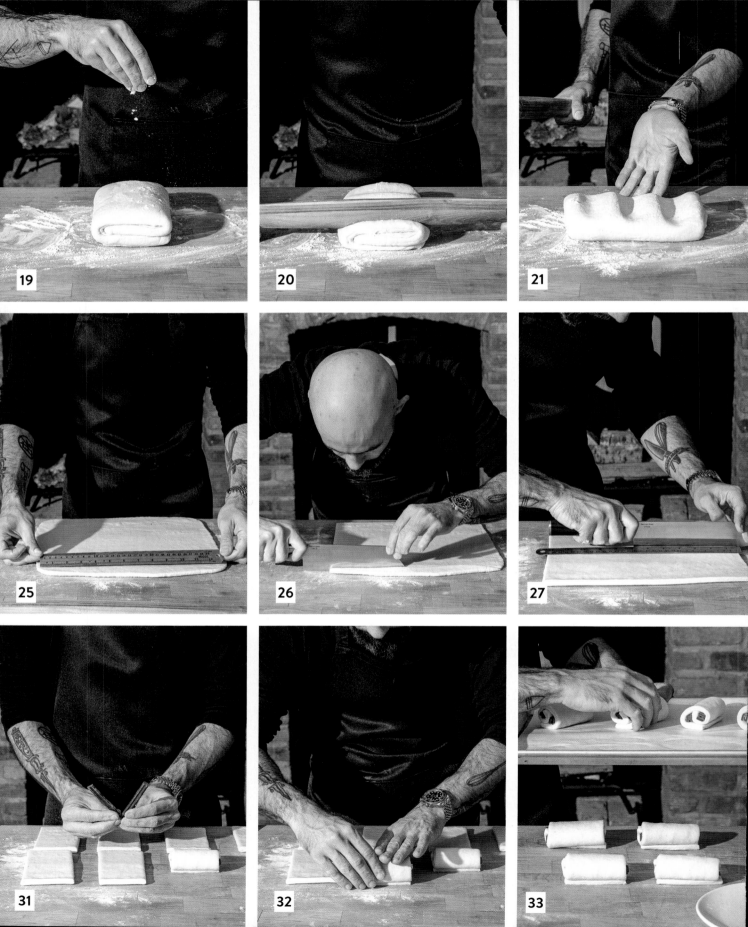

DOUGHNUTS

Doughnuts represent not only this book meeting its deep-fried dessert quota, but one of the few and proud examples of food so craved that it begs the question: shall I eat it for breakfast or dessert? While this Boston Cream doughnut, stuffed to its limit with pastry cream and crowned with chocolate glaze might suggest the latter, you wouldn't catch any sideways looks from across the breakfast bar were you to stuff one between your unbrushed teeth, still in slippers and a terry cloth robe. Then, ashing a cigarette into the air beside you, you'd growl that those ten thousand steps a day aren't for your health, after all.

Okay that got gritty. I'll save that material for my next book, likely a cooking murder mystery novel following the exploits of a loose cannon doughnut chef who doesn't play by the rules.

How I've Screwed This Up

According to some (very vocal) doughnut proponents (doughponents), the light blonde hula-hoop running around the outer rim of my 'hnuts is unacceptable in a perfect yeasted doughnut. Others, however, claim that this ring is an essential characteristic of a classic Boston Cream. I don't know who to believe, so I'll just assume that I'm wrong in some way.

Troubleshooting

LET'S GET THIS OUT OF THE WAY. IS IT DOUGHNUTS OR DONUTS? I doughn't know. As with virtually all of these arguments, I say do what you want, society is no worse off for either's existence.

MY DOUGHNUTS DOUGH IS TOO WET. This dough needs pretty solid gluten development, so if it looks significantly slack in its early stages, don't be afraid to add a little extra flour, 50 grams at a time. Once the dough starts clearing the sides of the bowl, let it knead to completion.

MY DOUGHNUTS ARE SHORT 'N' TOUGH. While you do need gluten development, this dough can certainly be overkneaded. After proofing, it should be light and springy, not dense and tight. Alternately, your oil may be too cold, which can prevent the doughnuts from springing fast enough before a crust forms.

MY DOUGHNUTS COLLAPSED. This is usually indicative of overproofing, so make sure to dry 'n' fry the doughnuts before they've had a chance to overferment.

MY DOUGHNUTS ARE GREASY. Oil is definitely too low—hot oil causes less absorption during the frying process, so you end up with fluffier, crispier doughnuts.

Yeasted Doughnuts

MAKES 6 TO 8 DOUGHNUTS

350 grams all-purpose flour, plus more for dusting

75 grams sugar, plus more for sprinkling (if making jelly doughnuts)

7 grams instant dry yeast

1 teaspoon kosher salt

225 grams whole milk, warmed to about 100°F

3 large egg yolks

Frying oil (such as peanut, grapeseed, or vegetable), plus more for greasing

1 to 1½ cups seedless jelly flavor of choice (optional)

Pastry Cream (recipe follows; optional)

Chocolate Glaze (recipe follows; optional)

In a large bowl, combine the flour, sugar, yeast, and salt. Whisk to combine thoroughly. Add the milk and egg yolks, then using a wooden spoon or by hand, mix until it forms a large shaggy dough, 2 to 3 minutes.

Turn out the dough onto a lightly floured surface and knead until smooth, about 8 minutes. Transfer to an oiled bowl, cover, and let rise until doubled in size, about 1 hour.

Turn out the dough onto a floured work surface, then roll out to about ½-inch thick. Using a 3½- or 4-inch biscuit cutter dusted with flour, cut the dough into rounds and transfer to a floured rimmed baking sheet. Optionally, reroll the dough scraps and cut out more rounds. Cover with a clean dish towel or plastic wrap, and let rise until visibly puffed, 45 minutes to 1 hour.

Heat 3 inches of frying oil in a large high-walled skillet over high heat to 350°F. Line a large rimmed baking sheet with a layer of paper towels.

Working in batches, add the doughnuts to the oil and cook until deeply golden brown, 45 seconds to 1 minute. Using tongs or a metal spider, carefully transfer to the prepared baking sheet. For jelly-filled doughnuts only, allow the doughnuts to cool for 1 minute, or until cool enough to handle, then sprinkle them with more granulated sugar.

Allow all of the doughnuts to cool completely before coating and/ or filling. Transfer the fillings into separate pastry bags each fitted with a small round pastry tip.

For filled doughnuts, use a paring knife to make an entry point about ½ inch in diameter into the side of each doughnut. Fill the sugar-coated doughnuts with jelly and the uncoated doughnuts with Pastry Cream filling.

For the cream-filled doughnuts, dip the top third of the doughnuts into the Chocolate Glaze, allowing the excess to drip off over the bowl.

PASTRY CREAM

Makes about 2 cups (enough to fill 8 doughnuts)

340 grams whole milk

100 grams sugar

1 teaspoons kosher salt

15 grams cornstarch

115 grams beaten eggs (from 2 to 3 large eggs)

10 grams unsalted butter, cubed

1 teaspoon vanilla paste

In a medium saucepan, combine 600 grams of the milk, 75 grams of the sugar, and the salt. Bring to a boil over medium heat, stirring occasionally to avoid scorching.

Meanwhile in a small bowl, combine the remaining milk with the cornstarch and the remaining 25 grams of sugar.

In a large bowl, combine the eggs with the remaining sugar.

Once the milk mixture is at a boil, remove from the heat and add a little bit at a time to the beaten eggs in a large bowl, whisking constantly. Transfer to the same saucepan and bring to a boil over low heat, stirring constantly. Add the cornstarch mixture and cook, whisking vigorously, until the pastry cream is thickened and no longer tastes of cornstarch, 1 to 2 minutes.

Remove from the heat and strain it through a fine-mesh sieve if you notice any graininess or small pieces of cooked egg. Add the butter and vanilla paste and stir to combine thoroughly.

Pour the pastry cream onto a rimmed baking sheet lined with plastic wrap. Cover the cream with more plastic wrap to prevent a skin from forming. Let it cool to room temperature, then refrigerate to cool completely, up to 3 days before using.

CHOCOLATE GLAZE

Makes about 1 cup (enough to glaze 8 doughnuts)

8 ounces chopped dark chocolate, finely chopped

½ cup whole milk

¼ teaspoon instant espresso powder

¼ cup light corn syrup

Add the chocolate to a medium heatproof bowl, ideally glass, to keep the glaze warm longer.

In a small saucepan, combine the milk, espresso powder, and corn syrup. Bring to a boil over medium heat, stirring occasionally to avoid scorching the milk. Pour over the chopped chocolate and allow the mixture to sit for 30 seconds. Stir to combine and keep warm until ready to use. If the glaze hardens, quickly reheat it over the stovetop for 5 seconds at a time, mixing constantly, until liquid again. Take care not to burn the chocolate by leaving it on the burner for too long.

CINNAMON ROLLS

Cinnamon Rolls are, without a doubt, the apex of dessert-for-breakfast technology—so it only makes sense that we'd utilize all the latest in cinnamon roll–making technology. A tangzhou, in a method developed by Yvonne Chen, uses a microwave to pregelatinize some of the flour's starches, allowing the buns to retain more moisture and slow staleness. Butter is added slowly as the dough is kneaded in a stand mixer, chunk by chunk, giving a briochelike texture to the resultant roll. Buttermilk adds a distinctive twang, not to mention added tenderness to the chewy-soft crumb of every towering spiral, while cream cheese frosting glaciers melt across the cinnamon-sugar topography. Pull 'em apart, eat 'em whole, cut 'em up with a fork and knife for all I care—just make 'em already!

How I've Screwed This Up

This episode is an old favorite for its two batches of cinnamon rolls, the second's improvements all a direct result of mistakes made with the first batch. I crowded the rolls in too small a pan, cut between them after baking for some reason, and frosted too late, resulting in oblong, pinched rolls with blocky frosting. For my second attempt, I put them in a proper 13-by-9 pan, kept the rolls together for pulling apart later, and frosted within that perfect ten-minute window where frosting drapes rather than melts. Each mistake informed the technique and yielded better results next time, which is just about as ideal an outcome as I can imagine in the kitchen.

Troubleshooting

MY ROLLS ARE WEIRD SHAPES. Make sure they're not too crowded in the pan—when all that yeast activates and the roll has nowhere to rise, it spurts out where it can, often in oblong directions.

MY ROLLS ARE SHORT AND TOUGH. Gluten may have been overdeveloped, or the yeast may have been DOA.

MY ROLLS COLLAPSED. Usually that means overproofed (overproved?)—little less time on the rise next batch!

MY FROSTING MELTED/DIDN'T DRAPE. You've gotta frost these at a pretty specific temperature window to get that "cinnamon roll in the bakery window" look, which we've found to be after ten minutes of cooling in the pan.

MY FILLING LEAKED OUT AND TURNED HARD ON THE BOTTOM. Sounds like there wasn't enough fat in the filling (or too much sugar), make sure you evenly apply soft butter to every square inch of the dough.

MY ROLLS STARTED BURNING ON TOP BEFORE THEY FINISHED COOKING THROUGH. Try baking in the bottom half of the oven, as the rising tops can sometimes come too close to the oven's edge, singeing their tips.

MAKES 12 ROLLS

Dough

150 grams water

470 grams all-purpose flour, plus more as needed

165 grams buttermilk, cold

2 large eggs, at room temperature

2 teaspoons kosher salt,

50 grams granulated sugar

1 packet (2¼ teaspoons) dry instant yeast

70 grams unsalted butter, cubed and at room temperature

Neutral oil (such as vegetable oil, canola oil, or grapeseed oil), for greasing

Cinnamon Sugar

80 grams granulated sugar

50 grams light brown sugar

1½ tablespoons ground cinnamon

¼ teaspoon kosher salt

60 grams unsalted butter, at room temperature

35 grams unsalted butter, melted

Cream Cheese Frosting (recipe follows)

MAKE THE DOUGH: Combine the water and 30 grams of the flour in a small saucepan. Whisk to thoroughly combine. Cook over medium-low heat until very thick, bubbling, and the temperature reaches 175°F, 4 to 5 minutes. Make sure to whisk the paste constantly to avoid clumping and burning.

Transfer the flour paste to a stand mixer fitted with the whisk attachment. Add the buttermilk and mix on low speed until a homogenous paste forms, 1 to 2 minutes. Add the eggs and salt to the now lukewarm paste and mix until combined, about 30 seconds. Add the remaining 440 grams flour, the granulated sugar, and yeast to the bowl. Switch to the dough hook attachment and mix on medium-low speed until combined, 1 to 2 minutes. Knead on medium speed until the dough is smooth but very sticky, 2 to 3 minutes.

Scrape down the sides of the bowl and the dough hook, then add the butter a few chunks at a time and mix on medium-high speed until all of the butter is well incorporated and the dough is no longer sticking to the sides of the bowl, 5 to 7 minutes. If the dough is still very sticky, add more flour as needed to achieve a smooth dough which clears the sides of the mixing bowl.

Generously oil a large bowl, then with lightly oiled hands, shape the dough into a taut ball; place in the bowl, cover with a clean damp kitchen towel or plastic wrap, and let rise until doubled in size, 60 to 90 minutes.

MEANWHILE, MAKE THE CINNAMON SUGAR: In a small bowl, combine the granulated sugar, brown sugar, cinnamon, and salt. Whisk to combine, then set aside.

Lightly oil the bottom and sides of a 9-by-13-inch baking dish. Line with parchment paper, leaving 2 inches overhang on the longer sides. The parchment paper will make it easier to remove the rolls after baking.

Lightly oil your work surface and rolling pin, then turn out the dough. Knead for 15 seconds to de-gas the dough then roll out to a 12-by-20-inch rectangle about ⅓- to ½-inch thick.

Spread the room temperature butter onto the dough, then generously sprinkle with the cinnamon sugar. Roll the dough into a log, starting with the 20-inch side closer to you. Place the dough seam-side down and trim off about ¾ inch from each end, then slice the rest into 12 equal slices using a large knife.

Add the cinnamon rolls, cut-sides up, to the prepared baking dish, spacing about ½ inch apart. Cover the dish with a damp clean kitchen towel or plastic wrap. Let the rolls proof until visibly puffed and just starting to touch each other, 45 minutes to 1 hour.

Toward the end of the proofing time, preheat the oven to 375°F.

Uncover the dish and brush the tops of the rolls with the melted butter. Bake for 25 to 30 minutes, until golden brown and the internal temperature reaches 195° to 200°F.

Remove the rolls from the oven and let cool in the baking dish for 10 minutes.

Using the parchment paper overhangs, remove the rolls as a whole from the baking dish. Frost the cinnamon rolls immediately with the Cream Cheese Frosting.

Pull apart, serve, and enjoy!

CREAM CHEESE FROSTING

Makes about 2 cups

115 grams cream cheese, at room temperature

80 grams unsalted butter, at room temperature

½ teaspoon kosher salt

200 grams powdered sugar, sifted

1 to 2 tablespoons heavy cream (or as needed)

In a stand mixer fitted with the whisk attachment, combine the cream cheese, butter, and salt. Mix until well combined, 1 to 2 minutes. Add the powdered sugar and mix on medium-low speed until well combined, 1 to 2 minutes. If the frosting becomes too thick, thin it out with the heavy cream.

Set aside at room temperature for up to 4 hours until ready to use.

STEP-BY-STEP IMAGES, PAGE 448-449

ICE CREAM BASE (CRÈME ANGLAISE)

Ice cream base, as you may have guessed, makes a handy base for homemade ice cream. Called by its other name, crème anglaise, the pre-churn custard becomes a dessert condiment worth twice its weight in hot fudge. Any dry or drab cake, bread pudding, brownie, or cookie gets an instant facelift from a generous drizzling of this flavorful sauce, particularly Bourbon Apple Pie (page 414). If you insist on agitating the mixture in a refrigerated vessel, however, it will involuntarily turn into ice cream.

How I've Screwed This Up

As a child, I was the proud owner of a freezable plastic bucket with a flimsy plastic fin assembly which, when operated correctly, could in fact make ice cream. Having little discipline, patience, or life experience, my ice cream often ended up icy.

Troubleshooting

MY EGGS CURDLED. Time to toss it and start again—unfortunately there's no saving overtempered eggs. Put the hot custard in a spouted container from which you can pour it very slowly, and wrap your bowl in a moist kitchen towel to secure it in place while whisking constantly. Keep that whisking going during the second cook!

BUT THEY ONLY CURDLED A LITTLE TINY BIT . . . It's actually very difficult to prevent curds of any kind, so if you've just got little ones forming around the outside of the pan toward the end of cooking, that's normal and they can/should be strained out prior to churning.

MY ICE CREAM IS ICY. This is due to large ice crystals forming in the custard, which happens when the ice cream is frozen too slowly or isn't churned well enough. Alcohol, having a much lower freezing point than water, can help keep things creamy: add a shot to your batch before churning.

MY ICE CREAM IS STILL ICY. Icy ice cream can sometimes be saved by effectively re-churning it, this time in the blender. Break up your ice cream into manageable pieces and blitz it in the blender until it resembles soft serve, refreeze, and enjoy.

MAKES ENOUGH FOR ABOUT 1 QUART OF ICE CREAM

425 grams whole milk

340 grams heavy cream

1 vanilla bean, seeds and pod or 2 teaspoons pure vanilla extract (or extract/flavoring of choice)

1 ounce non-diastatic malt powder (optional)

190 grams sugar

6 large egg yolks

1 teaspoon kosher salt

Chocolate chips, crushed cookies, cereal, or other inclusions of choice (optional)

Prepare a large bowl of ice water and set aside.

In a medium saucepan, combine the milk, cream, vanilla, and, if desired, the malt powder and about half of the sugar over medium-high heat. Bring to a boil, stirring occasionally, to avoid scorching. Remove from the heat.

In a medium bowl, whisk the egg yolks with the remaining sugar. Add the hot milk mixture a little at a time, whisking well after each addition.

Transfer the custard to the medium saucepan and cook over medium-low heat, stirring constantly to avoid curdling the eggs, until thickened and reaches 180°F.

Strain the custard through a fine-mesh sieve into a sealable container. Stir in the salt, then cool the ice cream base over the prepared ice bath until it reaches room temperature (72°F). Refrigerate overnight to 3 days.

When ready to churn, line a small (9-by-13-inch) baking sheet with an even layer of plastic wrap.

Churn the ice cream base in an ice cream machine, according to the manufacturer's instructions, until it reaches the consistency of soft-serve ice cream. Transfer to a large sealable container. If adding inclusions, fold them into the ice cream with a rubber spatula now.

Freeze the ice cream for at least 4 hours to completely harden.

ICE CREAM SANDWICHES

Ice cream sandwiches typically manifest themselves in one of two ways: a slab of frozen dairy-style product excreted between two rations of imitation chocolate byproduct, or a well-meaning attempt to class up the joint by sandwiching ice cream between two cookies. While the former would be considered boring even by a small child's standards, the latter is undone by the freezer, wherein cookies become rocks filled with smaller, harder rocks. After peeling some of the sticky-soggy brown matter from a factory-made version off my fingertips, the answer hit me like a ton of brick-shaped sandwiches: cake. Specifically, our cakey brownie, which is basically just cake: cake remains firm but tender in the freezer, making it an ideal vehicle for both your hands and teeth. Ice cream sandwiches also seemed a fitting way to close out this book: it's a recipe that's every bit as simple or complex as you want it to be. As you can see, the "ingredients" are simply recipes found elsewhere in the book, easily substituted with a box of chocolate cake mix and/or store bought ice cream. If Saint Nicholas recently smiled upon you and saw that a new ice cream churner be tucked away underneath the Holiday Tree, here's an excellent opportunity to experiment with inventive custards or dairy alternatives. If baking's more your bag, your favorite cake batter will work wonders as a vehicle for ice cream (my favorite is carrot cake). Or just buy both and have a whole tray of these ready in time for tomorrow—because at no matter what level, you still made something, and it came out better for your making it. That's *The Basics* in a nutshell.

How I've Screwed This Up

Ice cream sandwiches, like quite literally everything else, are subject to freezer burn—and with their shiny onyx exteriors, start to look like moldy ice cream sandwiches real fast. Wrap these up tight in plastic wrap to prevent freezer burn, and when some inevitably builds up, give it a bristling with a BBQ brush to shake off the snow!

Troubleshooting

ARE YOU SURE YOU DIDN'T END THE BOOK ON THIS RECIPE SO YOU DIDN'T HAVE TO WRITE ANY TROUBLESHOOTING? I like to think of myself as an effective storyteller—and effective storytellers, no matter the subject, choose their words judiciously. My stories are exactly as long as they ought to be, and that includes troubleshooting.

BULLLLLLLLSHIT. Yep.

STILL, THIS IS OUR LAST CONVERSATION, ISN'T IT? Yeah, this is the final chapter, figuratively and literally. I've been wondering what would happen when we ran out of headnotes to write about. All things must come to an end, I suppose.

WILL I DREAM? Shut up, you're just me, don't try to *AI* me.

WELL, HOW DO YOU PROPOSE WE WRAP THINGS UP? I guess with an expression of gratitude, something that dessert itself very often is. Learning to cook with you has brought more meaning and depth to my life than I ever could've imagined—I'll never stop being grateful for the absurd adventures we've shared and have yet to share, in and out of the kitchen. Cooking, like any act of love, isn't perfect: sometimes we make a mess, sometimes we get burned, but even when it breaks our heart, it proves to be worth the effort. So keep cooking, okay?

I WILL IF YOU WILL. Deal.

MAKES: 12 (3-INCH SQUARE) ICE CREAM SANDWICHES

Nonstick cooking spray

Cakey Brownies batter (see page 425)

1 quart homemade ice cream (see page 450)

Preheat the oven to 350°F. Line a large (13-by-18-inch) rimmed baking sheet with parchment paper and coat with nonstick spray.

Pour the Cakey Brownies batter into the prepared baking sheet and, using a large offset spatula, evenly disperse the batter. Bake 12 to 14 minutes, until the center of the cake bounces back. Invert the cake onto a wire rack then again onto another wire rack so it can cool on top of the parchment paper.

Allow the cake to cool completely then cut in half to create two roughly 9-by-13-inch pieces. Wrap each in plastic wrap and freeze until completely firm, at least 4 hours.

ASSEMBLE THE ICE CREAM SANDWICHES: On the first layer of cake, spread the ice cream then top with the second layer of cake. If the ice cream is too hard to spread, allow it to sit at room temperature for 5 to 10 minutes, then try again.

Wrap the ice cream sandwich slab tightly in plastic wrap and freeze until the ice cream is completely firm, 3 to 4 hours.

Slice the slab into 12 (3-inch square) ice cream sandwiches. Serve immediately or wrap each sandwich individually and freeze for up to 3 months.

ACKNOWLEDGMENTS

There are few things in this book I can truly take responsibility for apart from the alliteration, crude humor, and run-on sentences, like this one, which I'm overextending for the sake of the bit, to which, you will find, I am committed. I am little more than an amalgamation of everything I've learned from others, and my only accomplishment is managing to remember some of it, making my creative contribution to it (read: dick jokes), and distilling it here to you.

Outside of my pedantic headnotes and half-remembered stories, the biggest contributor to these pages has been Kendall Beach, an extraordinary talent that joined us during the height of the pandemic as a kitchen producer. It didn't take long for her to find her way in front of the camera, where she could showcase what she is: an immutable force of positivity, knowledge, and curiosity. Outside the kitchen, Babish is no longer just a pseudonym; it's a thriving business, one that wouldn't exist without my best friend and business partner, Sawyer Jacobs. Even before we were old enough to drive, when we'd spend our sleepovers scheming our fantastical futures, I wouldn't have dared to dream as big as our lives have turned out to be. Brad Cash, ever since first arriving at my fourth-floor Harlem walk-up to film the very first episode of *Basics*, has been an unremitting and essential collaborator in the realization of The Babish Culinary Universe. Eve Attermann, my intrepid literary agent, has worked alongside Ben Davis, Miles Gidaly, and the entire team at WME to make my fairytale career a reality. Kevin Grosch and Keith Johnson of Made in Network have tended to and bolstered our seedling venture into a creative powerhouse, catering to even my wildest ideas with care and enthusiasm. Without the daily help of their intrepid producer, Emilija Saxe, the BCU would likely have burnt to the ground several times over by now. While only having joined us in the past year-ish, Steve Clark and Nico Borbolla have already begun to feel like family, and they excite me on a daily basis with their new ideas and perspectives. Alvin Zhou inspires me every day with his unflappable work ethic, creativity, and positivity when exploring nigh on impossible dishes. Tim Duggan, Ross Woodruff, Jessica Opon, Sohla El-Waylly, Rick Martinez, Laura Cardona, Rachel Dolfi, Abby Glackin, Jeff Meyer, and so many others are all owed a debt of gratitude for the ways in which they've helped to build the channel into what it is today.

While the BCU wouldn't exist without the people above, this book would be little more than a digital pile of syntax errors were it not for the dedicated and passionate team who saw to its completion. Justin Schwartz, apart from demonstrating Christ-like forgiveness for my perpetually pushed deadlines, is the kind of editor that every author hopes to find: one that makes you believe in yourself as a storyteller. If you can understand the sentences on these pages, it's by virtue of Susan Choung, the tireless and eagle-eyed copy editor with whom I've worked on my last two books (did that sentence make sense, Susan? Seemed iffy to me). World-renowned photographer Evan Sung, who also captured the photos for *Binging with Babish*, is as generous with his talent as he is with his time, patience, and creativity—I can't imagine making a book without him. Food-styling dynamic duo Spencer Richards and Dana Seman, eschewing food photography hacks (like motor oil "maple syrup" or mashed potato "ice cream"), beautifully and accurately recreated every recipe, so that each could be both photographed *and* taste-tested. Even after a marathon eleven-day photo shoot, most of it spent scurrying between three sweltering kitchens on three separate floors, I found myself wishing we could've had more time together. Until the next book, I suppose! I also owe a great debt of gratitude to Roy Choi—for being a friend, a mentor, and the author of this very book's touching foreword.

My mother, in the short time we had together before she passed away, managed to instill in me a love of cooking, of life, and of others. I often say I have my mother's heart and my father's eyes—for storytelling, for aesthetic, for car maintenance—but he's given me so much more than that. He dedicated his life to his two sons, making sure that they grew up with full bellies, college educations, and strong moral compasses. My brother, David, now raising two boys of his own, still manages to find time to be a big brother whenever I need it. When I had a mental breakdown in the spring of 2022, he and my father were waiting to pick me up outside the hospital—I hadn't told them that anything was wrong, nor had I asked them to drive the seven hours south to New York City—they simply knew I needed them. Barb, Kelly, Donna, Lauren, Josh, Christopher, Everett, and the rest of my kin have supported and loved me into who I am today.

Lastly, thank you. Yeah, you, the one with whom I've been having a conversation throughout these pages. I'd never have imagined such a beautiful life for myself in my wildest dreams, and more than virtually anyone else, I have you to thank for it. Every time you've watched, shared, or liked, you've added a brick to the foundation of the BCU. This now-dizzyingly high platform is growing as a tool for both viewers and creators, and while it may take many forms in the future, its purpose will always remain the same: to tell kind, informative, and entertaining stories. Thank you, not only from me, but from the bevy of people that have come to call this channel home. I hope that you're having as much fun as we are.

INDEX

Note: Page numbers in *italic* indicate photos.

A

Ahi Tuna, Seared, Tostadas, 246–247
Aioli
    Faux Lemon, Grilled Artichokes with, 213, *214*, 215
    Le Grand, 216–217
Ajitsuke Tamago, 175
Allspice, 34
Anchovy Broth, Korean (Dashima), 253
Apple Pie, Bourbon, 414, *415*, 416–417, *417*
Artichokes, Grilled, with Lemon Faux-Aioli, 213, *214*, 215
Attenborough, Sir David, 232

B

Babka, *78–79*, 79–80, *81–83*, 84–85
    Chocolate Filling, 84
    Cinnamon Sugar Filling, 84
    Everything Filling, 84
    Simple Syrup, 85
    Streusel, 85
Bacon
    B.L.E.C.T., 312–313, *313*
    Candied, 313
    Classic Seasoning, 311
    Guanciale Seasoning, 311
    Homemade, 308, *309*, 310–311
    Pastrami Seasoning, 311
    -Roasted Brussels Sprouts, 203–204
    Spring Vegetable Quiche with Lots of Cheese and, 182–185, *183*

Bagels, 72, *73*, 74
Baguettes, 86, *87–88*, 89–90, *90–91*
Baked Eggs, Pastrami Hash with, 179, *180*, 181
Baked Mac and Cheese, 132
Baking, 404–405
Balsamic reductions, 29
Barbecue Sauce, 333
Bare simmer, 23
Basics with Babish, 14, 15, 17, 34
Basil, 34
Basil Oil, 157
    Sweet Corn Caramelle with Beurre Blanc and, 157
Bay leaves, 34
Béchamel, 29, 336
Béchamel Lasagna, Sausage and, 334, *335*, 336
Beef, 344–345
    Bone Broth, 347
    Cheesesteak Pinwheels, 361, *362*, 363, *364–365*
    Corned, Beer-Braised, with Herby Horseradish Cream, 380, *381*, 382–383
    Demi-Glace, 346–347
    frozen, 25
    Meatloaf, 348, *349*, 350–351
    Oxtail Birria Tacos, 352, *353*, 354–355, *355–357*
    Porterhouse, Reverse-Seared (and Forward-Seared), with Compound Butter, 394–395, *395*, *396*, 397
    Pot Roast, Dad's, 358, *359*, 360
    Ribeye, Butter-Basted, 398–399
    Rib Roast with Yorkshire Pudding, 390, *391*, 392–393
    Shepherd's Pie, 370, *371*, 372–373

    Short Ribs, Braised, with Potatoes Aligot, 366, *367*, 368–369
    Steak Tartare with Tarragon Vinaigrette and Quail Egg, 384, *385*, 386
    Tenderloin with Sauces, 400–401
    World Famous* Chili (con Carne), 387, *388*, 389
Beef Jus, 393
Beer-Braised Corned Beef with Herby Horseradish Cream, 380, *381*, 382–383
Binging with Babish, 13, 17
B.L.E.C.T., 312–313, *313*
    Homemade Mayonnaise, 312
Blender Mac and Cheese, 130, *131*, 132
Blonde roux, 29
Boiling points, 23
Bone Broth, 347
Bourbon
    Apple Pie, 414, *415*, 416–417, *417*
    -Mustard Pan Sauce, Roasted Pork Tenderloin with, 314, *315*, 316
Braised Short Ribs with Potatoes Aligot, 366, *367*, 368–369
Bread, 42–43. *See also* Pizza
    Babka, *78–79*, 79–80, *81–83*, 84–85
    Bagels, 72, *73*, 74
    Baguettes, 86, *87–88*, 89–90, *90–91*
    Brioche Dough, 62, *63*, 64–65
    English Muffins, 75, *76*, 77
    Hamburger Buns, 64
    Marble Rye, 66, *66–67*, 68, *69–71*
    Monkey, Herb-Garlic, 65
    Pan Cubano, 51–52, *51–55*
    Rosemary Focaccia, 44, *44–47*, 46

Roti, 58–59, *59–61*
Sandwich Loaf, 56–57
Southern-Style Cornbread, *48*, 49–50
Bread and Butter Pickles
Nashville Hot Chicken with, 294, *295*, 296–297
Quick, 297
Brioche Dough, 62, *63*, 64–65
Broccoli Rabe Pesto, Sausage Tortelloni with, *146*, 146–147
Broth, 31
Beef Jus, 393
Bone, 347
Korean Anchovy (Dashima), 253
Tonkotsu, 329, *329*
Tortellini en Brodo, 158, *159*, 160
Brown Butter, Butternut Squash Ravioli in, 140–141, *142–145*, 144
Browned Butternut Squash Soup, 200, *201*, 202
Brownies, 423, *424*, 425–427
Cakey, 425
Fudgy, 426
Melty, 427
Brown roux, 29
Brussels Sprouts, Bacon-Roasted, 203–204
Buerre Blanc, 157
Sweet Corn Caramelle with Basil Oil and, 154, *155*, 156–157
Buffalo Gochujang, Fried Wings with, 298, *299*, 300
Buns, Hamburger, 64
Burgers
Pimento Smash, 377, *378*, 379
Steakhouse, 374, *375*, 376
Butter
-Basted Ribeye, 398–399
Brown, Butternut Squash Ravioli in, 140–141, *142–145*, 144
Buerre Blanc, 157
Compound, 287

Compound, Reverse-Seared (and Forward-Seared) Porterhouse with, 394–395, *395*, *396*, 397
Compound, Whole Spatchcocked Chicken with, 285, *286*, 287
Tarragon, Flounder en Papillote with, 244–245, *245*
Butternut Squash
Browned, Soup, 200, *201*, 202
Ravioli, in Brown Butter, 140–141, *142–145*, 144

C

Cacio e Pepe, 133–134, *135*
Caesar Salad, Real Deal, 211–212
Cake, Tres Leches, 410, *411*, 412–413, *413*
Cakey Brownies, 425
Chocolate Frosting, 425
Candied Bacon, 313
Cannoli, 418–419
Capers, Fried, Lemon-Butter Tilapia with, 248, *249*, 250
Caponata, 224–225
Caramelized Onions, 376
Carbonara, 136, *137–138*, 139
Carbon-steel cookware, 23
Cast-iron cookware, 23–24
Cayenne, 34, 36
Ceviche, Red Snapper, with Mango and Jalapeño, 258, *259*
Ceylon cinnamon, 36
Charcoal grills, 25
Charred Winter Vegetables with Roasted Garlic Vinaigrette, 198–199
Chashu Pork, 328
Cheesecake, 420, *421*, 422
Cheese Grits, 239
Cheesesteak Pinwheels, 361, *362*, 363, *364–365*
Cheesy Mashed Potatoes, 373
Chicago-Style Pizza, *102*, 102–103, *104–105*

Chicken, 266–267
Braised, One-Pan Crispy, and Fennel Pasta, 282, *283*, 284
Breasts, "Airline," with Herb Pan Sauce, 275, *276*, 277
Cornish Hens with Fig-Port Sauce, 290–293
Filling, Green Chile, 341
Nashville Hot, with Bread and Butter Pickles, 294, *295*, 296–297
Orange, Really Orangey, 301–303, *303*
Parmesan, 278, *279*, 280–281, *281*
Piccata, 270–271
Quesadillas, 272, *273*, 274
Stock, 268–269
Whole Spatchcocked, with Compound Butter, 285, *286*, 287
Wings, Fried, with Buffalo Gochujang, 298, *299*, 300
Chicken Noodle Soup, 288–289
Chili (con Carne), World Famous*, 387, *388*, 389
Chili powder, 36
Chimichurri, 401
Chips, 237
Fried Haddock with, 234, *235*, 236–237
Chocolate
Babka Filling, 84
Cookie Dough, 409
Frosting, 425
Glaze, 443
Churros, 428, *429*, 430, *431*
Cinnamon, 36
Cinnamon Rolls, 444, *445*, 446–447, *447–449*
Cinnamon Sugar Babka Filling, 84
Classic Cookie Dough, 408
Classic Seasoning, 311
Cloves, 36
Cold Lobster Rolls, 256
Compound Butter, 287

Reverse-Seared (and Forward-Seared) Porterhouse with, 394–395, *395*, *396*, 397

Whole Spatchcocked Chicken with, 285, *286*, 287

Confit Garlic, 293

Convection, 25–26

Cookie Dough

Chocolate, 409

Classic, 408

Master, 406–407, *407*

Cooking Do's and Don'ts, 18–21

Cooking terms, 23–32

Cooking times, 32

Cookware

carbon-steel, 23

cast-iron, 23–24

nonstick, 24

sauté pan, 29, 31

stainless steel, 24

Corn, Sweet, Caramelle with Beurre Blanc and Basil Oil, 154, *155*, 156–157

Cornbread, Southern-Style, *48*, 49–50

Corned Beef, Beer-Braised, with Herby Horseradish Cream, 380, *381*, 382–383

Cornish Hens with Fig-Port Sauce, 290–293

Confit Garlic, 293

Parsnip Puree, 293

Cream

Crème Anglaise (Ice Cream Base), 450–451

Herby Horseradish, 383

Herby Horseradish, Beer-Braised Corned Beef with, 380, *381*, 382–383

Pastry, 443

Cream Cheese Frosting, 447

Crème Anglaise (Ice Cream Base), 450–451

Crispy Gnocchi with Gorgonzola Dolce, 148, *149*, 150–151, *151–153*

Cumin, 36

Curry powder, 36

D

Dad's Pot Roast, 358, *359*, 360

Dark brown roux, 29

Dashima (Korean Anchovy Broth), 253

Demi-Glace, 346–347

Bone Broth, 347

Desserts, 404–405

Bourbon Apple Pie, 414, *415*, 416–417, *417*

Brownies, 423, *424*, 425–427

Cannoli, 418–419

Cheesecake, 420, *421*, 422

Churros, 428, *429*, 430, *431*

Cinnamon Rolls, 444, *445*, 446–447, *447–449*

Doughnuts, 440, *441*, 442–443

Ice Cream Base (Crème Anglaise), 450–451

Ice Cream Sandwiches, 452, *453*, 454

Master Cookie Dough, 406–407, *407*

Pain au Chocolat, 432, *433*, 434–435, *436–439*

Tres Leches Cake, 410, *411*, 412–413, *413*

Deviled Eggs, 189–190

Dillweed, 37

Dinner parties, cooking for, 18

Dipping Sauce, 323

Do's and Don'ts, 18–21

Dough

Brioche, 62, *63*, 64–65

Cookie, 406–409, *407*

Fresh Pasta, 116–118, *117–119*

kneading, 43

Pie, 417

sourdough, 42–43

windowpane test for, 32, 43

Doughnuts, 440, *441*, 442–443

Chocolate Glaze, 443

Pastry Cream, 443

Yeasted, 442

Dried ingredients

herbs, 28, 34–39

pasta, 28

spices, 34–39

Dry aged beef, 346

Dry Rub, 333

E

Eggnog French Toast, 172, *173*, 174

Egg(s), 166–167

Ajitsuke Tamago, 175

Baked, Pastrami Hash with, 179, *180*, 181

Deviled, 189–190

French Scrambled, with Roasted Mushrooms on Toast, 168, *169*, 170, *171*

Jammy Scotch, 191, *192*, 193

Quail, Steak Tartare with Tarragon Vinaigrette and, 384, *385*, 386

Spenedict (Eggs Benedict with Speck), 186, *187*, 188

Spicy Honey Shakshuka, 176, *177*, 178

Spring Vegetable Quiche (with Lots of Bacon and Cheese), 182–185, *183*

Electric stovetops, 31–32

Emulsifiers, 24

Emulsion, 24

English Muffins, 75, *76*, 77

Equipment, 20

Everything Babka Filling, 84

F

Falafel with Lemon Tahini, 218, *219*, 220–221, *221*

Farmers' markets, 197

Fat, 24, 24–25

Fennel Pasta, One-Pan Crispy Braised Chicken Thighs and, 282, *283*, 284

Fig-Port Sauce, Cornish Hens with, 290–293

Finishing salt, 29

Fish, 232–233. *See also* Seafood Flounder en Papillote with Tarragon Butter, 244–245, *245*

Fried Haddock with Chips, 234, *235*, 236–237

Lemon-Butter Tilapia with Fried Capers, 248, *249*, 250

Poke Bowls, 240, *241*, 242–243

Red Snapper Ceviche with Mango and Jalapeño, 258, *259*

Seared Ahi Tuna Tostadas, 246–247

Whole Branzino with Grilled Lemons, 260–261, *262–263*

Flatbreads
Rosemary Focaccia, 44, 44–47, 46
Roti, 58–59, *59–61*

Flounder en Papillote with Tarragon Butter, 244–245, *245*

Focaccia, Rosemary, 44, 44–47, 46

French Scrambled Eggs with Roasted Mushrooms on Toast, 168, *169*, 170, *171*

French Toast, Eggnog, 172, *173*, 174

Fresh ingredients
herbs, 28, 34, 37, 39
pasta, 28

Fresh Pasta Dough, 116–118, *117–119*

Fried Capers, Lemon-Butter Tilapia with, 248, *249*, 250

Fried Haddock with Chips, 234, *235*, 236–237
Chips, 237
Tartar Sauce, 237

Fried Rice, Vegetable, 226, *227–228*, 229

Fried Wings with Buffalo Gochujang, 298, *299*, 300

Frosting
Chocolate, 425
Cream Cheese, 447

Frozen foods, 25, 196

Fudgy Brownies, 426

G

Gaffigan, Jim, 28

Garlic
Confit, 293
Roasted, Vinaigrette, Charred Winter Vegetables with, 198–199

Gas grills, 25

Gas Grill–Smoked Ribs, 330, *331*, 332–333

Gas stovetops, 31, 32

Ginger, ground, 37

Glaze
Balsamic reductions, 29
Chocolate, 443

Glossary of cooking terms, 23–32

Gnocchi, Crispy, with Gorgonzola Dolce, 148, *149*, 150–151, *151–153*

Gochujang Buffalo Sauce, 300
Fried Wings with, 300

Gorgonzola Dolce Sauce, 151
Crispy Gnocchi with, 148, *149*, 150–151, *151–153*

Green Chile Chicken Filling, 341

Grilled Artichokes with Lemon Faux-Aioli, 213, *214*, 215

Grilled Lemons, Whole Branzino with, 260–261, *262–263*

Grills, 25

Grill–Smoked, Gas, Ribs, 330, *331*, 332–333

Grits
Cheese, 239
Shrimp and, 238–239

Ground ingredients
ginger, 37
pepper, 28
spices, 31, 34, 36, 37

Guanciale Seasoning, 311

H

Haddock, Fried, with Chips, 234, *235*, 236–237

Hamburger Buns, 64

Hash, Pastrami, with Baked Eggs, 179, *180*, 181

Heat
convection, 25–26
indirect, 26
and Maillard reaction, 26, 28
stovetop, 26, 28
and types of stovetops, 31–32

Herb-Garlic Monkey Bread, 65

Herb(s), 34–39
dried vs. fresh, 26, 34, 37, 39
Pan Sauce, "Airline" Chicken Breasts with, 275, *276*, 277
Tarragon, Steak Tartare with Quail Egg and, 384, *385*, 386

Herby Horseradish Cream, 383
Beer-Braised Corned Beef with, 380, *381*, 382–383

Homemade Bacon, 308, *309*, 310–311
Classic Seasoning, 311
Guanciale Seasoning, 311
Pastrami Seasoning, 311

Homemade Mayonnaise, 312

Horseradish Cream, Herby, 383
Beer-Braised Corned Beef with, 380, *381*, 382–383

Hot Lobster Rolls, 257

Hot peppers, cutting, 20

I

Ice Cream Base (Crème Anglaise), 450–451

Ice Cream Sandwiches, 452, *453*, 454

Indirect heat, 26

Induction stovetops, 31, 32

Iodized salt, 29

J

Jalapeño, Red Snapper Ceviche with Mango and, 258, *259*

Jammy Scotch Eggs, 191, *192*, 193

Jus, Beef, 393

K

Kneading dough, 43
The Knickerbocker, 266
Korean Anchovy Broth
    (Dashima), 253
Kosher salt, 29, 404

L

Lasagna, Sausage and
    Béchamel, 334, *335*, 336
Latkes, 205, *206*, 207
Lecithin, 24
Le Grand Aioli, 216–217
Lemon-Butter Tilapia with Fried
    Capers, 248, *249*, 250
Lemon(s)
    Faux-Aioli, Grilled Artichokes
        with, 213, *214*, 215
    Grilled, Whole Branzino with,
        260–261, *262–263*
    Tahini, Falafel with, 218, *219*,
        220–221, *221*
    Tahini Sauce, 221, *221*
Leonardo da Vinci, 18
Lobster Rolls, 254, *255*, 256–257
    Cold, 256
    Hot, 257

M

Mac and Cheese
    Baked, 132
    Blender, 130, *131*, 132
Mace, 37
Maillard reaction, 26, 28
Mango, Red Snapper Ceviche with
    Jalapeño and, 258, *259*
Marble Rye, 66, *66–67*, 68, *69–71*
Mashed Potatoes, Cheesy, 373
Master Cookie Dough, 406–407,
    407
Mayo(nnaise)
    Homemade, 312
    Sauce, Spicy, 243
Meatloaf, 348, *349*, 350–351
Melty Brownies, 427
Mise en place, 18
Mistakes, 13–15
    Do's and Don'ts to avoid, 18–21

Monkey Bread, Herb-Garlic, 65
Mother sauces, 29
Muffins, English, 75, *76*, 77
Mushrooms, Roasted, French
    Scrambled Eggs on Toast
    with, 168, *169*, 170, *171*

N

Nashville Hot Chicken with Bread
    and Butter Pickles, 294,
    295, 296–297
Neapolitan-Style Pizza, 106–107,
    108–111
New things, trying, 20
New York–Style Pizza, 99–101
Nonstick cookware, 24
Noodle
    Soup, Chicken, 288–289
    Tonkotsu Ramen, 326, *327*,
        328–329, *329*
North (East) Carolina–Style
    Pulled Pork, 317, *318*, 319
Nutmeg, 37

O

Oil(s), 28
    Basil, 157
    olive, 28
Oleo-Saccharum, 303
Olive oil, 28
One-Pan Crispy Braised Chicken
    Thighs and Fennel Pasta,
    282, *283*, 284
Onion powder, 37
Onion(s)
    Caramelized, 376
    Red, Pickled, 190
Orange
    Chicken, Really Orangey, 301–
        303, *303*
    Sauce, 302
Oregano, 37
Oregon Trail video games, 266
Organic vegetables, 197
Oxtail Birria Tacos, 352, *353*,
    354–355, *355–357*

P

Pain au Chocolat, 432, *433*,
    434–435, *436–439*
Pan Cubano, 51–52, *51–55*
Pan-Fried Tteokbokki, 253
    Korean Anchovy Broth
        (Dashima), 253
Pan Pizza, 96, *97*, 98
Pan Sauce
    Bourbon-Mustard, Roasted
        Pork Tenderloin with, 314,
        315, 316
    Herb, "Airline" Chicken Breasts
        with, 275, *276*, 277
Panzanella, 208, *209*, 210
Pappardelle Bolognese, 161, *162*,
    163
Paprika, 37
Parsley, 37
Parsnip Puree, 293
Pasta, 114–115
    Baked Mac and Cheese,
        132
    Blender Mac and Cheese, 130,
        131, 132
    Butternut Squash Ravioli in
        Brown Butter, 140–141,
        142–145, 144
    Cacio e Pepe, 133–134, *135*
    Carbonara, 136, *137–138*, 139
    Crispy Gnocchi with
        Gorgonzola Dolce, 148, *149*,
        150–151, *151–153*
    dried vs. fresh, 28
    Fennel, One-Pan Crispy
        Braised Chicken Thighs
        and, 282, *283*, 284
    Lasagna, Sausage and
        Béchamel, 334, *335*, 336
    Pappardelle Bolognese, 161,
        162, 163
    Sausage Tortelloni with
        Broccoli Rabe Pesto, *146*,
        146–147
    Sweet Corn Caramelle, with
        Beurre Blanc and Basil Oil,
        154, *155*, 156–157
    Tarragon Shrimp Scampi, 126,
        127–128, 129

Tortellini en Brodo, 158, *159*, 160

Trenette al Pesto, 120, *121*, 122

Pasta Dough, Fresh, 116–118, *117–119*

Pastaroni Salad, 222–223

Pastrami

    Hash, with Baked Eggs, 179, *180*, 181

    Seasoning, 311

Pastry Cream, 443

Pepper (freshly ground), 28

Peppercorns, 39

Pesto

    Broccoli Rabe, Sausage Tortelloni with, *146*, 146–147

    Pesto Formula, 123–124, *124–125*

    Trenette al, 120, *121*, 122

Pesto Formula, 123–124, *124–125*

Pickled Red Onion, 190

Pickles

    Bread and Butter, Nashville Hot Chicken with, 294, *295*, 296–297

    Quick Bread and Butter, 297

Pie

    Bourbon Apple, 414, *415*, 416–417, *417*

    Shepherd's, 370, *371*, 372–373

Pie Dough, 417

Pie weights, 405

Pimento Cheese Topping, 379

Pimento Smash Burgers, 377, *378*, 379

Pinwheels, Cheesesteak, 361, *362*, 363, *364–365*

Pizza, 94–95

    cheese for, 95

    Chicago-Style, *102*, 102–103, *104–105*

    Neapolitan-Style, 106–107, *108–111*

    New York–Style, 99–101

    Pan, 96, *97*, 98

Pizza Sauce, 101

Poaching, 23

Poke Bowls, 240, *241*, 242–243

Spicy Mayo Sauce, 243

Sushi Rice, 242

Tenkasu, 243

Pollan, Michael, 42

Pork, 306–307. *See also* Bacon

    Chashu, 328

    Potstickers, 320, *321*, 322–323, *323–325*

    Pulled, North (East) Carolina–Style, 317, *318*, 319

    Ribs, Gas Grill–Smoked, 330, *331*, 332–333

    smoking, 307

    Stewed, Filling, 340

    Tamales, 337, *338*, 339–341

    Tenderloin, Roasted, with Bourbon-Mustard Pan Sauce, 314, *315*, 316

    Tonkotsu Ramen, 326, *327*, 328–329, *329*

Potatoes

    Aligot, Braised Short Ribs with, 366, *367*, 368–369

    Cheesy Mashed, 373

    Chips, Fried Haddock with, 234, *235*, 236–237

    Latkes, 205, *206*, 207

    Pastrami Hash with Baked Eggs, 179, *180*, 181

    Shepherd's Pie, 370, *371*, 372–373

Pot Roast, Dad's, 358, *359*, 360

Potstickers, 320, *321*, 322–323, *323–325*

Poultry, 266–267. *See also* Chicken

Processed sugar, 404

Pulled Pork, North (East) Carolina–Style, 317, *318*, 319

Puree, Parsnip, 293

Q

Quesadillas, Chicken, 272, *273*, 274

Quiche Shell, 185

Quick Bread and Butter Pickles, 297

R

Ramen, Tonkotsu, 326, *327*, 328–329, *329*

Ramsay, Gordon, 20

Ravioli, Butternut Squash, in Brown Butter, 140–141, *142–145*, 144

Real Deal Caesar Salad, 211–212

Really Orangey Orange Chicken, 301–303, *303*

    Oleo-Saccharum, 303

    Orange Sauce, 302

Recipes, following, 20–21

Red Onion, Pickled, 190

Red pepper flakes, 39

Red Snapper Ceviche with Mango and Jalapeño, 258, *259*

Reductions, 28–29

    Demi-Glace, 346–347

Red wine reductions, 29

Reverse-Seared (and Forward-Seared) Porterhouse with Compound Butter, 394–395, *395*, *396*, 397

Ribeye, Butter-Basted, 398–399

Rib Roast with Yorkshire Pudding, 390, *391*, 392–393

    Beef Jus, 393

    Yorkshire Pudding, 393

Ribs

    Braised Short Ribs with Potatoes Aligot, 366, *367*, 368–369

    Gas Grill–Smoked, 330, *331*, 332–333

Rice

    Pan-Fried Tteokbokki, 253

    Sushi, 242

    Tteokbokki, 251, *252*, 253

    Vegetable Fried, 226, *227–228*, 229

Roasted Garlic Vinaigrette, Charred Winter Vegetables with, 198–199

Roasted Mushrooms, French Scrambled Eggs with, on Toast, 168, *169*, 170, *171*

Roasted Pork Tenderloin with Bourbon-Mustard Pan Sauce, 314, *315*, 316
Rolling boil, 23
Rolls
    Cinnamon, 444, *445*, 446–447, *447–449*
    Lobster, 254, *255*, 256–257
Rosemary, 39
Rosemary Focaccia, 44, *44–47*, 46
Roti, 58–59, *59–61*
Roux, 29
Rye, Marble, 66, *66–67*, 68, *69–71*

S

Saffron, 39
Sage, 39
Salad
    Caponata, 224–225
    Panzanella, 208, *209*, 210
    Pastaroni, 222–223
    Real Deal Caesar, 211–212
Salsa Roja, 341
Salt, 29, 404
Sandwiches
    B.L.E.C.T., 312–313, *313*
    Lobster Rolls, 254, *255*, 256–257
    Pimento Smash Burgers, 377, *378*, 379
    Steakhouse Burgers, 374, *375*, 376
Sandwich Loaf, 56–57
Sauce(s)
    Barbecue, 333
    Béchamel, 29, 336
    Béchamel, Lasagna, Sausage and, 334, *335*, 336
    Beef Tenderloin with, 400–401
    Bourbon-Mustard Pan, Roasted Pork Tenderloin with, 314, *315*, 316
    Chimichurri, 401
    Demi-Glace, 346–347
    Dipping, 323

Falafel with Lemon Tahini, 218, *219*, 220–221, *221*
Fig-Port, Cornish Hens with, 290–293
Gochujang Buffalo, 300
Gochujang Buffalo, Fried Wings with, 300
Gorgonzola Dolce, 151
Gorgonzola Dolce, Crispy Gnocchi with, 148, *149*, 150–151, *151–153*
Herb Pan, "Airline" Chicken Breasts with, 275, *276*, 277
Herby Horseradish Cream, 383
Herby Horseradish Cream, Beer-Braised Corned Beef with, 380, *381*, 382–383
Lemon Tahini, 221, *221*
Lemon Tahini, Falafel with, 218, *219*, 220–221, *221*
mother, 29
Orange, 302
Pizza, 101
Simple Tomato, 281
Spicy Mayo, 243
Tartar, 237
Sausage
    Lasagna, Béchamel and, 334, *335*, 336
    Tortelloni, with Broccoli Rabe Pesto, *146*, 146–147
Sauté pan, 29, 31
Scales, 21, 404
Scherer, Josh, 21
Scotch Eggs, Jammy, 191, *192*, 193
Scrambled Eggs, French, with Roasted Mushrooms on Toast, 168, *169*, 170, *171*
Seafood, 232–233. *See also* Fish
    frozen shrimp, 25
    Lobster Rolls, 254, *255*, 256–257
    Pan-Fried Tteokbokki, 253
    Poke Bowls, 240, *241*, 242–243
    Shrimp and Grits, 238–239
    Tteokbokki, 251, *252*, 253
Seared Ahi Tuna Tostadas, 246–247

Seasoning. *See also* Herb(s)
    Classic, 311
    Dry Rub, 333
    Guanciale, 311
    Pastrami, 311
    spices, 31, 34–39
    vanilla, 39
Shakshuka, Spicy Honey, 176, *177*, 178
Shell, Quiche, 185
Shepherd's Pie, 370, *371*, 372–373
    Cheesy Mashed Potatoes, 373
Shrimp
    frozen, 25
    and Grits, 238–239
    Scampi, Tarragon, 126, *127–128*, 129
Simmer, 23
Simple Syrup, 85
Simple Tomato Sauce, 281
Smoked Ribs, Gas Grill, 330, *331*, 332–333
Soup
    Browned Butternut Squash, 200, *201*, 202
    Chicken Noodle, 288–289
Sourdough, 42–43
Sous vide, 31
Southern-Style Cornbread, *48*, 49–50
Speck, Eggs Benedict with (Eggs Spenedict), 186, *187*, 188
Spices, 31, 34–39. *See also* Seasoning
Spicy Honey Shakshuka, 176, *177*, 178
Spicy Mayo Sauce, 243
Spring Vegetable Quiche (with Lots of Bacon and Cheese), 182–185, *183*
Stainless steel cookware, 24
Star anise, 39
Steakhouse Burgers, 374, *375*, 376
    Caramelized Onions, 376
Steak Tartare with Tarragon Vinaigrette and Quail Egg, 384, *385*, 386

Stewed Pork Filling, 340
Stock, 31
    Chicken, 268–269
Stovetops
    heat when cooking on, 26, 28
    types of, 31–32
Streusel, 85
Sugar, 404
Sushi Rice, 242
Sweet Corn Caramelle with
        Beurre Blanc and Basil Oil,
        154, *155*, 156–157

T

Table salt, 29
Tacos, Oxtail Birria, 352, *353*,
        354–355, *355–357*
Tahini, Lemon, Falafel with, 218,
        219, 220–221, *221*
Tamales, 337, *338*, 339–341
Tarragon, 39
    Butter, Flounder en Papillote
        with, 244–245, *245*
    Shrimp Scampi, 126, *127–128*,
        129
Tartar Sauce, 237
Tenkasu, 243
Thyme, 39
Tilapia, Lemon-Butter, with Fried
        Capers, 248, *249*, 250
Time, in cooking, 32
Toast
    Eggnog French, 172, *173*, 174
    French Scrambled Eggs with
        Roasted Mushrooms on,
        168, *169*, 170, *171*
Tomato Sauce, Simple, 281
Tonkotsu Broth, 329, *329*
Tonkotsu Ramen, 326, *327*, 328–
        329, *329*
Tools, kitchen, 20
Tortellini en Brodo, 158, *159*,
        160
Tortelloni, Sausage, with Broccoli
        Rabe Pesto, *146*, 146–147
Tostadas, Seared Ahi Tuna,
        246–247
Trenette al Pesto, 120, *121*, 122

Tres Leches Cake, 410, *411*, 412–
        413, *413*
Tteokbokki, 251, *252*, 253
Tuna, Seared Ahi, Tostadas,
        246–247

U

USDA Beef Grading System, 346

V

Vanilla, 39
Vegetable(s), 196–197. *See also
        specific vegetables*
    Charred Winter, with Roasted
        Garlic Vinaigrette, 198–199
    Fried Rice, 226, *227–228*, 229
    frozen, 25, 196
    organic, 197
    Spring, Quiche (with Lots of
        Bacon and Cheese), 182–
        185, *183*
Vinaigrette
    Roasted Garlic, Charred
        Winter Vegetables with,
        198–199
    Tarragon, Steak Tartare with
        Quail Egg and, 384, *385*,
        386

W

White roux, 29
Whole Branzino with Grilled
        Lemons, 260–261, *262–
        263*
Whole Spatchcocked Chicken
        with Compound Butter,
        285, *286*, 287
Windowpane test, 32, 43
World Famous* Chili (con Carne),
        387, *388*, 389

Y

Yeasted Doughnuts, 442
Yorkshire Pudding, 393
    Rib Roast with, 390, *391*,
        392–393

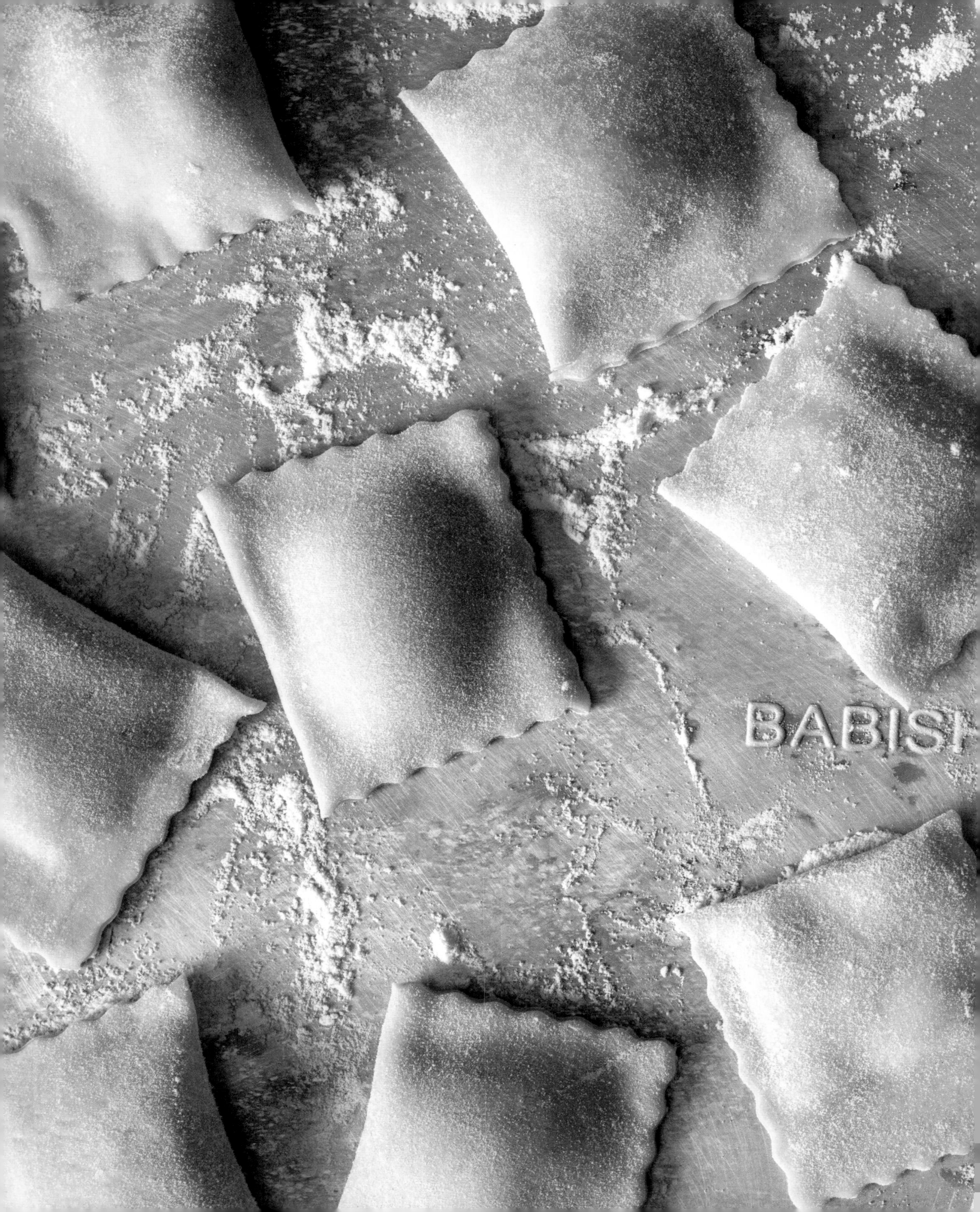
BABISH